Great

Lives

KEATS
by B. Ifor Evans

MARLBOROUGH
by Maurice Ashley

QUEEN ELIZABETH
by Charles Williams

WREN
by Geoffrey Webb

London 1941

READERS UNION LIMITED

by arrangement with

DUCKWORTH

THIS EDITION FIRST PUBLISHED 1941

Made 1941 *in Great Britain*
PRINTED AT THE TEMPLE PRESS, LETCHWORTH
AND PUBLISHED BY READERS UNION LIMITED
CHANDOS PLACE, CHARING CROSS, LONDON
Administrative Address:
DUNHAMS LANE, LETCHWORTH, HERTFORDSHIRE

Contents

*

Keats

BY B. IFOR EVANS

Chronology

1795 John Keats born

1817 *Poems* published

1818 *Endymion* published

1820 *Lamia, Isabella, The Eve of St Agnes and Other Poems* published

1821 Keats dies

Chapter I —1795-1817

ON 9th October 1794, at that church of fashion, St George's,
Hanover Square, Thomas Keats, head-stableman at the 'Swan
and Hoop,' Finsbury Pavement, married Frances Jennings, the
daughter of the owner of the inn. In October 1795 John Keats
was born. Of the parents but little is known; rumour spoke well
of the father and ill of the mother. He had come out of the
west country leaving no trace of his origins behind him, and John
Jennings of Finsbury Pavement had employed him as an ostler.
He won his way to the control of the stable and to the hand of his
master's daughter. All friendly testimony emphasized his in-
dustry and uprightness; gossip said that he coveted the social rung
above his own, but when in 1804 he died of a fall from his horse it
was malice alone that ascribed the accident to inebriety. Of his
wife more has been reported, but usually from prejudiced voices.
They complained that she was uneducated, indolently charming,
too generously affectionate, and sufficiently sexed to find mono-
gamy cramping. In 1805, a year after her husband's death, she
married a William Rawlings, 'a stable-keeper,' but from him she
was soon separated. In 1810 she died. Those who desire it will
find a facile formula in describing Keats as a sublimation of his
mother worked out in the terms of genius. Her children thought
well of her, and she lavished an impetuous, untidy affection upon
them.

George (1797–1842), the second son, and Tom (1799–1818)
shared with John Keats a deep intimacy for one another which
arose in part from their attachment to her. 'Fanny' (1803–89),
the only daughter and the one long-lived member of the family,
was still a child when her mother died. She grew into a 'fat,
blonde, lymphatic' woman, married to a Spanish man of letters,
Valentin Llanos, and sharing apparently but little of the temperament of her brothers.

From his mother Keats inherited his consumptive tendencies,
and from both his parents he learnt a consciousness of social caste.
Some ride horses and some groom them. Keats and his brothers

9

were to rise to the former class, and to have the education of
gentlemen, at Harrow even, if funds permitted.   Funds did not
permit, but they allowed John Keats to be sent to John Clarke,
who housed at Enfield a private school in a fine Georgian mansion,
the façade of which can now be seen in the Victoria and Albert
Museum at South Kensington.   Later, George and Tom followed
him there.   Those who remembered him in his schooldays recalled a high-spirited, undersized boy, pugnacious, generous, with
fits of melancholy which he did his best to conceal.   No one suspected precocity; rather they remembered a battling spirit without adequate supporting strength.   So when the usher struck his
brother Tom, he rushed up and smote the usher, 'who could, so to
say, have put him into his pocket.'   In those early years he was a
noisy, untidy, sprawling animal of a schoolboy, with moods, mere
moments, of rare and unaccountable sensibility.

The change when it came was sudden.   Adolescence syn-
chronized with his mother's death, and together they awakened
in him a deeper consciousness of the world.   He was lucky at that
moment to find a sensitive guide, Charles Cowden Clarke (1787–
1877), the son of the headmaster and a tutor in the school.
Clarke was to live to be ninety and to write garrulous reminiscences of more than he had ever known, but as a young man,
Keats's senior by eight years, he had all the gifts that seemed
most desirable: an enthusiasm for books, an excited interest in
poetry, and a political radicalism that included the reading of
Leigh Hunt's *Examiner*.   Books were no longer dead things once
Cowden Clarke was your friend.   The past became full of ex-
plorers, lovers, deities, and you could charge down on them
through the pages of a book, take what you would, and feel that
you too were an adventurer.   Cowden Clarke converted the
school library into a pirate ship with the world's treasures at
command for any one who had the courage to make the assault.
Keats devoured books one after the other, 'Mavor's collection, also
his *Universal History*; Robertson's histories of Scotland, America,
and Charles the Fifth; all Miss Edgeworth's productions . . .
Tooke's *Pantheon*, Lemprière's *Classical Dictionary*, which he
appeared to *learn*, and Spence's *Polymetis* . . . the *Aeneid* . . .
Burnet's *History of his Own Time*,' and, of course, Leigh Hunt's
Examiner.   Here was an education fitting for a poet!   Give him
another six years and ask him at twenty-one if he can write.

At this moment, however, there enters one Mr Richard Abbey,
a tea-merchant.   For, on the death of their mother, Keats and
the other children had been placed under his guardianship under

a trust deed of their grandmother, Mrs Jennings. Abbey held
the family funds, and though he has been represented as Keats's
evil genius, he was little more than an unimaginative, stern, and
rather muddle-headed man of commerce. He wished the boys
to follow some regular profession, and throughout he was more
favourable to George, the business man, than to Keats who
associated with poets, radicals, and other reprobates. At times
he seemed to hold back funds which Keats sorely needed, but his
hands were tied. Certain sums he paid to Keats; others he had
to retain in trust until Fanny came of age, and by then Keats
was dead: the rest of the family resources, blocked by an interminable Chancery suit, were not available for distribution. In
1811, Abbey determined that Keats must leave school and enter
some regular occupation.

So in the summer of 1811, still under sixteen, John Keats was
bound apprentice to Mr Thomas Hammond, a surgeon and
apothecary at Edmonton. The richest years of his youth, 1811–
1815, were spent amid the bottles and drugs in Hammond's
surgery, in following the doctor on his rounds, or holding the
horse while patients were visited, and, incidentally, in learning as
much of medicine as his master had the time or inclination to
impart. In the summer of 1815 he left Hammond to go to
London as a student in Guy's and St Thomas's Hospitals, and
nine months later he qualified for his apothecary's certificate.
Then suddenly, in the spring of 1817, he abandoned medicine for
poetry. Of what Keats thought of these years of his medical
training no distinct record remains. On his apprenticeship he
entered apparently without protest; he saw the thing through,
and then, despite Abbey's opposition, he turned his back on his
training. Seldom does he refer to these years, though in 1819 he
writes somewhat mysteriously: 'Seven years ago it was not this
hand that clench'd itself against Hammond.' If he disliked the
apothecary's routine, he valued the study of medicine as a
science. In May 1818, he suggested that every department of
knowledge is 'excellent and calculated towards a great whole,' and
added that he was glad that he had not given away his medical
books. Medicine never came into his poetry; the realism that
enters from close contact with the physical world, with the body,
its flesh and putrefactions, and the bright, clean hardness of bones,
is all removed from his iridescent verse. His poetical life came
into being in these years of medical study, but it was a thing
apart, stolen pleasure. It was as if, seated before a skull whose
every lineament had to be contemplated, he became aware of a

butterfly struggling to free itself from the mesh of bones, and, like his own Endymion, following the bright insect he forgot the skull which he had to study. Poetry took her natural possession over him, and it was his doggedness and his gifts of application that alone allowed him to see his medical course through to a conclusion. Thus it is within this period (1811–1816), and especially in the crucial months when he is a student at Guy's and St Thomas's, that his initiation into poetry must be sought.

For the artist in verse there are no regular schools, no appointed masters. The young painter may follow a programme of studies with exercises prescribed and encouragement given, but for the poet all is left to chance. True, if he is lucky, he may find friendly advice, and the assistance of an atmosphere where the arts are discussed, and where writing seems as natural as any other human activity. For Keats, in these early years, such aids were missing. He still had Cowden Clarke, who could lead him to Spenser, through whom he went, 'as a young horse would through a spring meadow—ramping.' But he had to forgo the company of other young men with interests similar to his own. He had his brothers, but they gave admiration rather than the fertilizing contact of mind with mind. His other associates during these early years, mostly George's friends, were worse than useless. George knew the simpering Mathew girls, and their egregious cousin, George Felton Mathew. Nothing is more pathetic than that Keats, in this formative period, had to rely on this amateur of the arts who thirty years later, in setting down his reminiscences, wrote more of himself than of the genius he had once known. George had also introduced him to Georgiana Wylie, charming and sensible by all accounts, and later to become George's wife. There were medical friends too, including Henry Stephens, who abandoned medicine for the more profitable occupation of manufacturing ink. But there was no one except Clarke who could nourish his spirit.

Was it strange that verse came haltingly? Hammond's surgery, pill-boxes, stable-duties, suburban sitting-rooms, the Mathew girls, coy and gamesome, such was the round of his daily life. How could these be transfigured into verse, to the forests of Spenser's timeless romance, with fair nymphs on white horses, and caparisoned knights and dreams of beauty unending? For they were there marching through his mind, these legions of the imagination, marching incessantly from now almost to his death, an unending procession, with Endymion and Psyche and Apollo, and all the hierarchy of Greek mythology, mingling with the troops of chivalry, and nature in her gentle emblazonry of flowers as a background. He strove to bring these fantasies into verse: he failed, and he knew that he had failed. He seemed as one whose dreams were crowded with riches, but in the waking hours the rhymes came clumsily; the lines stumbled; the phrases fell awkwardly into the wrong shapes. And when he was awake and looking steadily at Edmonton, or London, there was not so much to write about after all. He persisted, as he had persisted in his medical course, and the day came—it was not so far distant—when the black symbols of the letters on the page before him actually corresponded to the texture of his dreams.

Meanwhile, unless these earliest poems are seen as the product of this struggle, they will appear not only ineffective but dull, and at times nauseating. The occasions are trivial; the Mathew girls send him a shell, and he steals the trip-trip-tumble of Tom Moore's anapaests to thank them. He attempts an *Imitation of Spenser*, cluttering the verses with 'poetic diction,' and only saving the poem with a description of a swan, adapted from Milton. In Spenser he finds a vocabulary for the description of 'dainty nakedness,' which, though innocuous enough in the ideal world of the *Faerie Queene*, falls into flat vulgarity in the associations of these early poems. Spenser had described the two 'damzelles,' who bathed before Sir Guyon, exposing their 'snowy limbs' for his temptation: the glory has departed when Keats, in the notorious poem in which 'Thalia' rhymes with 'higher,' complains that the 'beauties' of Miss Wylie are 'scarce discern'd,'

> Saving when, with freshening lave,
> Thou dipp'st them in the taintless wave.

In describing women he had developed the habit of making an inventory of desirable qualities, as if he were a horse-dealer parading a thoroughbred—'soft-dimpled hands, white neck and creamy breast.' All this occurs in his poetry before Leigh Hunt can be charged with responsibility, and it can recur in an alarming way in his most mature verses. He had models, more respectable than Leigh Hunt, though lamentably misused, both in Spenser's frank, ingenuous stare at the nude, and in the suppressed and frustrated sensuality of Milton. To these Keats contrived in his innocence to add a half-jocular, half-wanton vulgarity. Neither of his models could have led him to lines such as:

> So fondly I 'll breathe, and so softly I 'll sigh,
> Thou wilt think that some amorous Zephyr is nigh:
> Yet no—as I breathe I will press thy fair knee,
> And then thou wilt know that the sigh comes from me.

Also he seizes the form of epistolary couplets, the style of poetic
dishabille, to write chatting verses to G. F. Mathew.   He had
models in Drayton, and, for the verse form, in Browne's *Britannia's
Pastorals*, but in his hands the verse degenerated into a medley of
thoughts, aspirations, and descriptions.   Later he employed the
same form more firmly in addresses to his brother George and
Charles Cowden Clarke.   In watching Keats's development in
these earliest stages it is interesting to see him failing to find himself, but when one ceases to think of Keats, and considers the
poems as poems, their weakness offends, and memories of them
recur to trouble the contemplation of his later work.   It is as if
in an art gallery some daubed banality found in close proximity
to a great picture had offended by its very existence, and grown
into a nuisance, even a desecration.

Among these early poems there are a number which show
Keats's attachment to political radicalism, nurtured by his reading of Leigh Hunt's *Examiner*, and enhanced by the knowledge
that Cowden Clarke knew Leigh Hunt.   One day, in the spring
of 1816, Cowden Clarke, when visiting Leigh Hunt at Hampstead,
took with him a few of Keats's compositions.   His selection
probably included Keats's sonnet *Written on the day that Mr
Leigh Hunt left Prison*, an early ineffective outpouring; and
possibly *Calidore*, a pastiche of Spenser and Hunt's own *Story
of Rimini*.   Hunt detected amid the frou-frou of Keats's early
verses the presence of 'exuberant specimens of genuine though
young poetry.'   He had the wisdom to select the best of Keats's
early poems and the generosity to print it.   It can be found
tucked away in the right-hand bottom corner of a page of *The
Examiner* for 5th May 1816, and it reads:

> O Solitude! if I must with thee dwell,
>   Let it not be among the jumbled heap
>   Of murky buildings; climb with me the steep,—
> Nature's observatory—whence the dell,
> Its flowery slopes, its river's crystal swell,
>   May seem a span; let me thy vigils keep
>   'Mongst boughs pavillion'd, where the deer's swift leap
> Startles the wild bee from the fox-glove bell.
> But though I 'll gladly trace these scenes with thee,
>   Yet the sweet converse of an innocent mind,
>   Whose words are images of thoughts refin'd,
> Is my soul's pleasure; and it sure must be
>   Almost the highest bliss of human-kind,
> When, to thy haunts two kindred spirits flee.

Nothing in Keats's life has been more unjustly represented
than Leigh Hunt's influence upon him.   When Keats met him

in 1816, Leigh Hunt was thirty-two years old, and the hero of all the radical and advanced groups in the country. He had just undergone a two years' imprisonment in Surrey gaol for a most deliberate and bludgeoning libel on the Prince Regent. He had converted his prison room into a fantastic bower with designs of roses beneath a cerulean blue, and the wit of the town, even Byron, then in the height of his London elegance, had paid court to him. Nor did the foulness of the epithets of his libel, nor his quixotic attitude in captivity, disguise the boldness of his attack and its importance in the development of liberty of comment. Not only had Hunt the reputation of intrepid freebooting in journalism—'I write what I will and you, Mr Attorney, may sue when you wish'—but in his prison retirement he had established his reputation as a poet. Extracting the moving episode of Paolo and Francesca from Dante's *Inferno* he had retold it as *The Story of Rimini*. Later the poem was to be severely condemned, and its honeyed epithets, mingling with a knowing and frivolous vulgarity, deserved punishment. Leigh Hunt had taken the loveliest of romantic legends, where all the finer shades of pathos and sentiment meet, and reduced it to common flirtation, culminating in the couplet:

> The two divinest things this world has got,
> A lovely woman in a rural spot.

But many of Hunt's contemporaries saw the poem with different eyes. They caught, beneath the flippancy, a spirited exuberance and they realized, as did Keats, that here was the couplet, free, rapid, and, despite licence and wantonness, endowed with new possibilities as a narrative medium. Byron, to whom it was inscribed, found it 'quaint here and there' but 'devilish good.'

Such was the Leigh Hunt to whom Keats was introduced, and all the penalties of that friendship have been emphasized by Keats's biographers. Penalties, it is true, there were in plenty. Hunt, with his *Story of Rimini*, encouraged Keats in his artful dalliance in the description of love, where all could be reduced to the values of an apprentice in a street-corner encounter. Further, Hunt was the target of all Tory criticism; over him the slime of *Blackwood's* and the *Quarterly* was to be poured, and Keats was to be swept in as an associate. But there was another side to the reckoning. Hunt was the first real man of letters that Keats had known, and one whose generous affection and even uncritical enthusiasm encouraged him to overleap his tentative approaches to verse. For Hunt, whatever were the limitations of his own work, had, in his recognition of Shelley and Keats, a prophetic power: he judged them not as their contemporaries did, but with the eyes of posterity. In *The Examiner*, Hunt was Keats's first publisher, and, later, in an article on *Young Poets*, in December 1816, he was to couple the names of Shelley and Keats as poets of brilliant promise. Fundamentally Keats and Leigh Hunt were opposed in temperament. Leigh Hunt had a resilience, a superficiality that gave him the comfort of a florid gaiety. His was a nature for whom tragedy was impossible, and he passed through crises that had the potentiality of tragedy with his nature unwounded. Keats had the sensibility which led his nature to suffer. Between these two, intimacy would inevitably lead to friction, and for Keats that realization came quickly. But even after the rupture had been made, Hunt welcomed him back in the most difficult months of his life, and comforted him. Meanwhile, Keats's excitement in knowing this man, whom of all others he wished to know, brought a quickening of his own development.

Friendship with Leigh Hunt gave him a new realization of himself, and a rare excitation infused his whole being. Already he knew, within himself, that he was to be a poet, and one in an age when verse was to have a special glory. No longer the tepid approaches to creation, the verses to the Misses Mathew, or even to Georgiana Wylie, and not for long these time-destroying studies in anatomy, physiology, chemistry, and *materia medica*. He would break through and join the company of those who refashioned earth's loveliness with words. Fortunately, in the summer of 1816, he caught this first exuberance into a poem, *I stood tip-toe upon a little hill*:[1] later it was to have pride of place as the opening poem in the volume of 1817, with a motto from Leigh Hunt's *Story of Rimini* set proudly at its head. Critics of Keats's poetry have noted the poem's technical deficiencies, the headlong tumble of the couplets, with rhymes caught breathlessly in passing, the epithets poured lavishly from a Huntian cornucopia, and the half-shy, half-feverish dalliance at the approach of

> the soft rustle of a maiden's gown
> Fanning away the dandelion's down.

All this can be said, and justly, but of major importance is the fact that Keats is discovering himself. For months he had known the wards and dissecting rooms of a London hospital, and now, in Hampstead, he looked on Nature in her gentlest mood, watched

[1] The poem was completed later in 1816, possibly in 1817.

the colours and shapes of flowers, and more successfully than ever before found words and images to describe his sensations:

> Here are sweet peas, on tip-toe for a flight:
> With wings of gentle flush o'er delicate white,
> And taper fingers catching at all things,
> To bind them all about with tiny rings.

Nor is contemplation, even at this earliest stage, far away from sensuous delight. 'In the calm grandeur of a sober line' the poet holds captive the moments in Nature that have impressed him, and from them he arises out of the pettiness of habitual self, and minor cares and discomfitures. Such must be the mood for the poet's interpretation of legends. For Nature is not an emptiness: the fauns and dryads are moving through the trees; Psyche and Cupid are there, and Diana and Endymion. The figures of the myths which he had first met in Lemprière's dictionary were moving now in the countryside near London, and to them he would soon return. For the moment it is enough that he has discovered himself. At the conclusion of the poem he asks, 'Was there a Poet born?' He at least knew the answer.

Even if the poet was born, the apothecary had still to pass his examinations. In the spring of 1816 his mind had turned so rapidly away from medicine to poetry that it was a rare tribute to his endurance that on 25th July 1816, he sat and passed his test for an apothecary's certificate. A month before his examination the recollection of Milton's simile, in *Paradise Lost*, on Satan watching Eve ('As one who long in populous city pent') led him to write a sonnet which outstrides anything of the days before he met Leigh Hunt:

> To one who has been long in city pent,
> 'Tis very sweet to look into the fair
> And open face of heaven,—to breathe a prayer
> Full in the smile of the blue firmament.
> Who is more happy, when, with heart's content,
> Fatigued he sinks into some pleasant lair
> Of wavy grass, and reads a debonair
> And gentle tale of love and languishment?
> Returning home at evening, with an ear
> Catching the notes of Philomel,—an eye
> Watching the sailing cloudlet's bright career,
> He mourns that day so soon has glided by:
> E'en like the passage of an angel's tear
> That falls through the clear ether silently.

Once July's exacting business was over, he turned, in August 1816, to write epistles to his brother George and to Cowden Clarke, telling them of his 'mad ambition,' and of what this new

revelation of life meant to him.   He recounts his hesitations now
transmuted by a sudden glow, in which everywhere, 'in water,
earth, or air,' he sees poetry.   With all his agitated delight he still
feels hesitant, knowing that the phantasms that were beating
at the door of his imagination had yet to be released.   So, in his
epistle to Cowden Clarke, he writes the modest lines:

> With shatter'd boat, oar snapt, and canvas rent,
>   I slowly sail, scarce knowing my intent;
>   Still scooping up the water with my fingers,
>   In which a trembling diamond never lingers.

Then suddenly, only two months later, a diamond, unmistakable,
was left in his hand.

The development of a creative artist is not necessarily regular
or methodical.   After repeated failures, and perplexed and self-
torturing efforts, even after stretches of barrenness, a sudden
moment of intense experience allied to sustaining powers of
creation will arise.   True, that part of an artist which is intellectual, the substratum of ideas and values to which his creation
is attached, will show some rational coherence.   But power to
achieve appears with unexpected suddenness.   Such an annuncia-
tion of the poetic spirit, if its coming can be traced, ranks with the
most important facts in a poet's biography.   With Keats the
hour is marked, and the conditions so circumstantially known
that they can be described in some detail.

In the autumn of 1816, Mr Alsager, a financial correspondent of
The Times, lent Charles Cowden Clarke a beautiful copy of the
folio edition of Chapman's translation of Homer, and Clarke at
once summoned Keats to share the delight of exploring the
volume.   Keats, still a medical student and lodging with his
brothers in the Poultry, seized the opportunity of seeing a book
which he had long wished to possess, and, on an evening in October 1816, he walked over to Clerkenwell, where Cowden Clarke
was staying.   On through the night until dawn they read,
plunging here and there, and picking out the 'famousest passages.'
Then Keats walked home.   Cowden Clarke did not rise early the
next morning, but when he came down he found on the break-
fast-table an envelope in Keats's handwriting.   Its sole content
was a sonnet, of which the later published version reads:

ON FIRST LOOKING INTO CHAPMAN'S HOMER

> Much have I travell'd in the realms of gold,
>   And many goodly states and kingdoms seen;
>   Round many western islands have I been
> Which bards in fealty to Apollo hold.

> Oft of one wide expanse had I been told
>   That deep-brow'd Homer ruled as his demesne;
>   Yet did I never breathe its pure serene
> Till I heard Chapman speak out loud and bold:
>   Then felt I like some watcher of the skies
>   When a new planet swims into his ken;
> Or like stout Cortez when with eagle eyes
>   He stared at the Pacific—and all his men
> Look'd at each other with a wild surmise—
>   Silent, upon a peak in Darien.

Of the significance of this poem Leigh Hunt wrote twelve years later: 'That noble sonnet . . . which terminates with so energetic a calmness and which completely announced the new poet taking possession.'

On that dawn walk to the Poultry, Keats fought and overcame the phantasms of his imagination with which he had grappled before with only dubious success. When he said 'Good night' to Cowden Clarke, his mind was filled, as far as any mind can be, with one thought alone—of Homer as revealed by Chapman. But in the early morning hours that *idée génératrice* called back into his consciousness memories that, beginning with the immediate recollections of the evening, passed out over the years until they reached back to the school at Enfield, and to Keats's first traffickings with the poets. They came, these thronged memories, one calling to the other, and crowding and jostling each other as they came—the handsome folio of Chapman—the fifth book of the *Odyssey*—the shipwreck of Ulysses—the memory of Bonnycastle's *Astronomy*, a school prize—Bonnycastle and the poets—Bonnycastle's extract from Pope's Homer, the fifth book—Bonnycastle and the new planets—Herschel's planet—the old red-brick school-house at Enfield—the West India merchant who built it—the school library—Robertson's *America*—Darien—the Pacific—the Titian picture and Cortez——Apollo, patron of poets, and so back to Homer again. And out of this welter of enthusiasm and recollection, like a water-lily out of the mud, arose a moment of creative power, and so the far-reaching resources of stored suggestion concentrated into a single imaginative experience and the sonnet was produced.

The months of the late autumn of 1816 must have been some of the happiest in Keats's life: his medical courses were over and his examinations passed; he had dominated, if only momentarily, the restless shapes that went coursing through his mind; above all, Leigh Hunt was his friend. Further, the thought had already crept in that medicine as a career might not be necessary after all.

It was rumoured that Scott was paid handsomely for his verse romances, while the guineas fell in a golden shower whenever Tom Moore gave his poems to the printer. Keats had enough money to struggle on for a year, perhaps two, and then might not his work bring in a sufficient reward for him to be a poet and nothing but a poet? Leigh Hunt encouraged him in this view during the frequent visits that he paid to the cottage in 'the Vale of Health' in Hampstead.

The determination to make poetry a career led to the longest poem of this period, *Sleep and Poetry*. The conception came to him one night at Leigh Hunt's, as he lay on a couch that had been converted into a bed. He pictures himself lying on the couch in the quietness that follows an evening of unrelenting sociability. Here he is in Hunt's own study, crowded with busts of poets, and of Alfred and Kosciusko, and with prints of scenes such as are found in Poussin's full-bodied treatment of the antique, or views combining classical architecture with romantic scenery in the manner which Claude practised so fluently. An over-garnitured room, and yet possessing the very atmosphere to lead Keats at this moment to come to terms with his own mind. *Sleep and Poetry* is his *Prelude*, his first attempt to fathom for himself his approach to life as a poet. Leigh Hunt's influence upon the poem is obvious, and from him Keats derived the easy flow of the couplets, but in the thought he is already looking beyond Leigh Hunt to Wordsworth. Encouraged by Leigh Hunt he found himself directing a petulant attack against the regular eighteenth-century couplet, and in particular against Pope:

> They sway'd about upon a rocking horse,
> And thought it Pegasus.

Keats's approach to Pope is obviously uncritical, and his condemnation led to the just anger of Byron. The cool tessellated couplets of Pope have a studied control which Keats failed to admire. The only passages in Keats's letters which seem conceited are his comparisons of his own powers with those of Pope. Six months later, he wrote: 'When Tom who meets with some of Pope's Homer in Plutarch's Lives reads some of those to me they seem like Mice to mine.' As literary criticism his comments on Pope are deplorable; but a creative writer will often develop strength out of the very excess of an antagonism or an enthusiasm towards other writers. Hatred of Pope had already led to his exultant discovery of Chapman, and now again he was fostering his strength by looking on Pope rather as a personal enemy than as a predecessor.   Nor did he fail to realize that Pope's Augustan classicism symbolized an approach to poetry fundamentally different from his own.   For Pope, the intellect sat supreme over the imagination, fashioning its activity into a hard, brittle perfection, rigidly censuring all that offended against good sense. For Keats, poetry 'should be great and unobtrusive, a thing which enters into one's soul, and does not startle it or amaze it with itself, but with its subject.'   Already, in *Sleep and Poetry*, he knew that Pope's way was not his way, but he was not equally clear as to the road down which he would travel.   He was conscious of immaturity:

> O for ten years, that I may overwhelm
> Myself in poesy.

Despite this sense of his inadequacy he hurried forwards to the publication of his first volume of verse, and in March 1817 his *Poems* appeared.   The volume aroused no recognition from the public; the great reviews ignored it; a few of the minor ones patronized it; Leigh Hunt gave a discriminating critique in *The Examiner*, but that had no followers.   The publishers, in a letter to George Keats, even suggested that the public thought themselves abused by the issue of such a volume.   If Keats lacked general success, he had the minor consolation of knowing that a large and distinguished circle of friends was interested in him.   Almost at once his friend Benjamin Bailey, an Oxford undergraduate, discovered a new publisher in John Taylor, of Taylor & Hessey, and to the end of Keats's life Taylor continued one of his most loyal supporters.   Through Leigh Hunt he could claim the acquaintance of Haydon the sculptor, of Hazlitt, and of Lamb.   He could have had Shelley's friendship had he wished it, but a terrible self-consciousness smote him whenever he met Shelley.   He seemed almost afraid that Shelley would snub him, or interfere with his methods of work.   So they seldom met, and, when they did, Keats was possessed of a disastrous feeling of inferiority.   When Keats was dying, Shelley invited him out to Italy, but Keats held himself away.   Similarly, to the end, in criticizing one another they substituted for enthusiasm a cold, precise, half-antagonistic comment.   Shelley felt that *Endymion* had treasures, 'though treasures poured forth with indistinct profusion.'   Keats replied: 'You, I am sure, will forgive me for sincerely remarking that you might curb your magnanimity, and be more of an artist, and load every rift of your subject with ore.' If he was awkward with Shelley, he was at home with other men of his own age. To John Hamilton Reynolds, a minor poet whom he met through Leigh Hunt, he wrote some of his best letters, and Reynolds introduced him to Charles Wentworth Dilke and Charles Brown, who were to be his closest friends. With a sense that he was valued by an increasing number of friends he turned away from the volume of 1817 and engaged his mind elsewhere.

Chapter 2

March 1817–November 1817: *Endymion*.

IN March 1817, Keats's brothers persuaded him to rest for a time in the country, and in April 1817 he went to Carisbrooke, in the Isle of Wight, where the view from his window seemed like a Claude picture—'delightful wood-alleys, and copses, and quick freshes'—with Carisbrooke Castle in the background. He had determined to execute a poetical work far more ambitious than the pieces of the volume of 1817, and already on 17th April 1817, he was able to write that he would begin *Endymion* forthwith. By the end of November 1817 the poem of over four thousand lines was finished. In the record of outward events, these months of intense composition seem restless. Carisbrooke proved too lonely, so, by May, Keats had fled to 'treeless' Margate, where he was joined by his brother Tom. By 16th May, tired of Margate— 'I was not in my right mind when I came'—he set off for Canterbury, with the hope that memories of Chaucer would set him 'forward like a Billiard Ball.' June found him back in Hampstead, but in September he accepted an invitation from Benjamin Bailey to go to Oxford. Bailey, who was reading for orders, watched Keats as he worked at the third book of *Endymion*, and had some influence on its development. By 8th October, Keats was back once again in Hampstead. In November he went to Surrey, to the Burford Bridge Inn, where, on 28th November 1817, he finished his longest and most criticized poem.

How came he to venture upon such an ambitious task? The motives were numerous, but chief among them lies the substitution in the spring of 1817 of Benjamin Robert Haydon for Leigh Hunt as a dominant influence over his mind. Haydon, whose *Autobiography and Memoirs* give his pathetic story, was genius demoniac but ill-fated. Solemn, humourless, unpractical, he had a torrential energy, a passionate conviction of a mission,

a lust for large activity, with a belief that God presided over whatever he did.   Unfortunately, he believed himself to be a painter,
an art for which he possessed only a crude and mediocre talent
that resulted in the vast acreage of his historical canvases:
'Dentatus,' 'The Raising of Lazarus,' and 'Christ's Entry into
Jerusalem.' As a propagandist, or a rhetorician, even as a
writer, he might have succeeded.   As it is, from his life of intense and frustrated effort, with suicide at its close, there remain
only his successful effort in bullying the nation to realize the
value of the Elgin Marbles, and the spur which he gave to Keats's
ambition in 1817.

  For Keats had come to realize the gulf that separated him from
Leigh Hunt, 'who elegantly chats and talks.' He had no desire
to quarrel with Leigh Hunt, nor to enter into the bickerings of
Hunt and Haydon. He believed in tolerance in friendship:
'Men should bear with each other—there lives not the Man who
may not be cut up, aye hashed to pieces on his weakest side.'
But despite tolerance he wished to free himself from the excessive sociability of the Hampstead circle, and its petty complications. There was Mrs Hunt borrowing silver from Haydon and
squabbling over its return, and chatter, and music, and im-
provisations—all preventing a man from having his talk out
without fatuous interruptions. Further, he wanted his 'own
unfettered scope,' without the danger of being called 'Hunt's
élève.' Keats's attitude has its ungenerous side, but he realized
that it was essential for his development. In Haydon he found
a different world, one of intense endeavour, with a high dedication
of purpose. Haydon could be 'hashed to pieces on his weakest
side,' and he would rush like a bull into squabbles with the Hunts,
but when he and Keats were alone, and when they wrote to each
other, a large ambition was awakened in Keats to achieve in
poetry the same vastness of conception as governed Haydon's
historical pictures. Keats tried for a time to meet each man at
his own level. He confesses once in his letters that he adapts his
'scribblings,' to answer each correspondent, in his mood. So
in the spring of 1817 he treats Hunt with gentle badinage, but to
Haydon he opens out his heart on poetry. Thus when Haydon
urged that he should avoid Hunt for a time, and when his brothers
suggested rest in the country, it seemed that all counsels were
working in the same direction, and he set out on the journey that
led him first to Carisbrooke and ultimately to the composition
of *Endymion*.

  Throughout his work on *Endymion* two contrary moods fight

for the possession of his mind. He is either feverishly anxious
to master his ambitious subject, or he is humbling himself in the
consciousness of his own immaturity. Later, when the reviews
tore his poem to pieces and flung the scraps on the offal-heap he
was not seriously moved. He had been criticizing the poem to
himself all through its composition: 'My own domestic criticism
has given me pain without comparison beyond what *Blackwood*
or the *Quarterly* could possibly inflict.' The first preface which
he wrote to *Endymion* and then rejected on Reynolds's advice
shows clearly his attitude:

> This poem must rather be considered as an endeavour than a thing
> accomplished; a poor prologue to what, if I live, I humbly hope to do.
> In duty to the Public I should have kept it back for a year or two,
> knowing it to be so faulty; but I really cannot do so,—by repetition
> my favourite passages sound vapid in my ears, and I would rather
> redeem myself with a new poem should this one be found of any
> interest.

It is the same judgment that he expresses to Haydon in May
1817: 'Truth is I have been in such a state of mind as to read
my Lines and to hate them. I am one "that gathers Samphire,
dreadful trade"—the Cliff of Poesy towers above me!' At the
same time, the legend of Endymion possessed him:

> The very music of the name has gone
> Into my being.

He knew that he had to conquer somehow, and overcome in
some way, however imperfectly, this theme that dominated him,
and a persistent restlessness pursued him until he had finished the
work. To read or even to criticize *Endymion* in a cold, calculating spirit is to miss the whole mood of its composition. To seek,
as some have done since Mrs F. M. Owen's ingenious study in
1880, a set and formal allegory is to impose an intellectual conciseness on the most baroque of English romantic poems.

The legend had attracted him ever since, in *Sleep and Poetry*,
he imagined the poet who in 'fine wrath' told the story of 'meek
Cynthia' and her Endymion. He had now tracked the legend
into many places, from Lemprière's dictionary to Fletcher's
Faithful Shepherdess and to Drayton's *Man in the Moone* and his
Endimion and Phoebe.[1] Fed from these sources on the origin
of the theme, and entangling them with his refashioning of other
legends, he had dipped the whole into the flush beauty of the
English countryside and added his own cloudy symbol of the
relation of poetry to life.

Everywhere in the poem there is profusion. In the verse

[1] Lowell, i, 320.

itself the unstopped couplets sway into melodies that Keats attempted to regulate only by 'the adroit management of open and close vowels.' Regularity of movement, except in a few isolated passages, he abandoned to experiment with harmonies that grew reckless as they obeyed the fantastic movement of the theme. Equally, he worked into the story a lavishness of fancy until the central design was obscured in the exuberance of detail. From all classical standards the poem is formless, but a baroque cathedral with its profuse ornamentation would be similarly condemned if judged from a standard equally remote. The restlessness of the months in 1817 when the poem was composed is reflected in the work itself, but in compensation there is added a sense of speed, the daring of youth, a plunge into the ocean of verse. The very excesses of the poem are reminiscent of that quickened delight in words which led the Elizabethan to pursue them as ardently as if a conceit had been a 'fatal Cleopatra.' Over all incidental sources this Elizabethan, or, more precisely, Shakespearian spirit dwells. After he had worked at the poem for a month, he asked Haydon if it was too daring to think that Shakespeare presided over his work. His letters in April 1817, when he began the poem, are full of references to Shakespeare, and as he flings himself into the story of the love of Endymion and the Moon Goddess his mind goes back to *A Midsummer Night's Dream*, a play over which the image of the moon presides.

Despite all charges of incoherence, the outline of the poem, though not suggestive of its quality, can be easily extracted. Book I opens with the Festival of Pan, and around the altar gather troops of children, youths and maidens, and 'a venerable priest.' On Endymion's entry the priest performs the rites, while a chorus sings the Hymn to Pan, the lyric which Wordsworth thought to be 'a pretty piece of paganism.' The crowd breaks up, and Endymion stays to speak with the priest and the older men. He has striven to control himself through the festival, but now troubled recollections carry him into a swoon. On awaking, he finds that Peona, his sister, is comforting him with great tenderness, and Endymion tells her of his vision, half dream, half reality. He has seen

emerge
The loveliest moon that ever silver'd o'er
A shell for Neptune's goblet.

With the moon came the vision of the moon goddess, Diana, though Endymion did not know, until the end, of her identity. With this sight, all ordinary life became dreariness.

Book II, the most fantastic part of the poem, describes Endymion's search for this vision. It reads like a dream into which memories of classical legends and of *Arabian Nights'* adventures have been mingled in a wild and interminable profusion: Endymion's chase of the butterfly that flew from a bud dipped in water—the fountain at which the butterfly is lost and a nymph appears—the journey through a cavern to an underworld—the prayer in loneliness to Diana—the sight of the sleeping Adonis—the encounter with Venus—the brief glimpse of Cybele conveyed effectively in the lines:

> Came mother Cybele! alone—alone—
> In sombre chariot; dark foldings thrown
> About her majesty, and front death-pale,
> With turrets crown'd.   Four maned lions hale
> The sluggish wheels; solemn their toothed maws,
> Their surly eyes brow-hidden, heavy paws,
> Uplifted drowsily, and nervy tails
> Cowering their tawny brushes.   Silent sails
> This shadowy queen athwart, and faints away
> In another gloomy arch.

There follows the exit from the cavern into the 'middle air'—the journey on the back of an eagle, down, down to earth—the dream meeting with his love—the loneliness of waking—the quest again—and this time down to the sea.

If Book II is the least controlled section of the poem, Book III is, in compensation, calm and ordered. Written mainly in Oxford under the influence of Benjamin Bailey, it has a simple, narrative outline. Yet the conciseness lacks something of the courageous boldness of Book II. Endymion in the sea meets Glaucus, and the adventures of Glaucus and Scylla, modified out of Ovid, and given a romantic conclusion, are elaborately interlaced with Endymion's own adventures.

Book IV makes a sudden and unexpected opening with the lament of an Indian maiden, a human with whom Endymion falls in love. Throughout this final book, Enydmion goes through a series of adventures in which he is either in love with the Indian maiden or is ashamed that he can abandon his visionary lover. Gradually it is borne in upon the reader that Diana and the Indian maiden are one. Endymion is not aware of this, nor does he realize that he is to undergo an apotheosis. This last Book has an intricacy of detail: the love of Endymion for the Indian maiden—the steeds which Mercury calls out of the earth—the ride through the sky—the sleep of Endymion and the Indian maiden while the horses slumber on the mists—the journey back to earth—the desire to abandon the quest—the return to Peona—the desire for solitude and for human activity. In all this multitude of adventures, Keats holds fast to the theme that the human love of the Indian maiden and the visionary desire for the goddess are one. Only one episodic passage enters, when the Indian maiden sings to Endymion the exquisite lyric, *O Sorrow*, with its effective double movement. All else leads to the conclusion where Endymion realizes that he is immortal, and that in his human love he has reached his ideal quest.

Such is the bare outline of the theme, decked out and adorned in the poem by labyrinthine devices of fancy. To search for an allegorical interpretation is to lose the impetuous mood of Keats's composition as he skimmed one shape after another from the cauldron of his imagination. Yet the poem is not mere narrative; in the personality of Endymion Keats had in mind his own personality, and through the general form of the legend he worked out his own conception of poetry. In the poem itself he only partially solved his problem, but its composition led him to more settled conceptions, as appears from his letters during these months. Even the letters are not completely consistent, but he can be seen ferreting his way through towards a definite conclusion. Thus the passages on poetry in the letters of 1817 and 1818 are the most important section of his prose, and they serve, incidentally, in the elucidation of *Endymion*.

He saw clearly that a poet might follow the way of Shakespeare or the way of Dante and Milton: he might fashion into poetry all that experience had brought within the range of his sensibility, or he might interpret experience in the values of a prescribed philosophy. Keats's own inclination lay towards Shakespeare. In February 1818 he wrote: 'We hate poetry that has a palpable design upon us.' A few months earlier—December 1817—he had defined the Shakespearian quality as '*Negative Capability*, that is, when a man is capable of being in uncertainties, mysteries, doubts, without any irritable reaching after fact and reason.' He further defined the poetic character in October 1818 as: 'No character—it enjoys light and shade; it lives in gusto, be it foul or fair, high or low, rich or poor, mean or elevated. It has as much delight in conceiving an Iago as an Imogen. What shocks the virtuous philosopher, delights the camelion Poet.' His temperament urged him to follow this method, but his satisfaction in pursuing it is blocked by Wordsworth, whom he admires, and who is a 'virtuous philosopher.' He attempts at times to blot Wordsworth out of his mind with some disparaging

comment, but he is instinctively conscious of his own debt to
Wordsworth. This forces him in the famous 'Mansions of
Thought' letter of May 1818, the most sustained of all his critical
pronouncements, to adjust his own approach to poetry to Wordsworth's. He describes human life as, first, 'the infant or thought-
less Chamber,' secondly, as 'the Chamber of Maiden-Thought,'
where adolescence awakens to a sensuous delight in life and its
'pleasant wonders.' Finally, the realization that 'the world is
full of Misery and Heartbreak, Pain, Sickness, and oppression'
darkens the Chamber of Maiden-Thought. The greatness of
Wordsworth lay in his exploration of this final stage of experience, but that greatness disappeared to the degree that Wordsworth had subdued that experience, as Milton had done, to the
values of a dogmatic philosophy.

In this 'Mansions of Thought' letter, he has come closer than
was his custom to Wordsworth, but in a letter to Bailey of 22nd
November 1817, he set out most precisely his individual attitude.
Phrases from this letter have been quoted and misapplied in the
criticism of Keats, but once the sequence of thought is set out
it can be seen to contain the central principle of his poetry, the
link between *Endymion* and the odes. The crucial passage in
this letter reads:

> I am certain of nothing but of the holiness of the Heart's affections
> and the truth of Imagination—What the imagination seizes as
> Beauty must be truth—whether it existed before or not—for I have
> the same Idea of all our Passions as of Love they are all in their
> sublime, creative of essential Beauty. . . . The Imagination may
> be compared to Adam's dream [1]—he awoke and found it truth. I
> am the more zealous in this affair, because I have never yet been
> able to perceive how anything can be known for truth by conse-
> quitive reasoning—and yet it must be. Can it be that even the
> greatest Philosopher ever arrived at his goal without putting aside
> numerous objections? However it may be, O for a Life of Sensations
> rather than of Thoughts!

Keats then comments on another 'favourite Speculation':

> That we shall enjoy ourselves hereafter by having what we called
> happiness on Earth repeated in a finer tone. . . . Adam's dream
> will do here, and seems to be a conviction that Imagination and its
> empyreal reflection is the same as human Life and its Spiritual
> repetition.

In this last letter, written in the week that *Endymion* was
completed, he came to express in prose the suggestion that underlies the poem. The way to true knowledge lay not with reason-
ing but with sensation. Thus sensation was to be sought not as

[1] *Paradise Lost*, viii, 470–82.

an end in itself but as a way to knowledge. Such sensation accepted with 'Negative Capability' was truth as far as it was known, the earthly prototype of the heavenly essence of truth. So Endymion had found the end of his quest now in the mortal Indian maiden and now in the goddess Diana, only to discover at the close that they were the same.

So had Keats sought in *Endymion* to fashion an ideal world which is the poem itself. All this, which he works out minutely in his letters, he had expressed in the opening passage in lines that have become hackneyed by repetition. Once they are read in relation to the letters they are seen to contain the governing elements of his approach to experience and to poetry:

> A thing of beauty is a joy for ever:
> Its loveliness increases; it will never
> Pass into nothingness; but still will keep
> A bower quiet for us, and a sleep
> Full of sweet dreams, and health, and quiet breathing.
> Therefore, on every morrow, are we wreathing
> A flowery band to bind us to the earth,
> Spite of despondence, of the inhuman dearth
> Of noble natures, of the gloomy days,
> Of all the unhealthy and o'er-darkened ways
> Made for our searching: yes, in spite of all,
> Some shape of beauty moves away the pall
> From our dark spirits. Such the sun, the moon,
> Trees old, and young, sprouting a shady boon
> For simple sheep; and such are daffodils
> With the green world they live in; and clear rills
> That for themselves a cooling covert make
> 'Gainst the hot season; the mid forest brake,
> Rich with a sprinkling of fair musk-rose blooms:
> And such too is the grandeur of the dooms
> We have imagined for the mighty dead:
> All lovely tales that we have heard or read.

Later in the odes he was to refashion the same thoughts with greater poetic certainty.

Chapter 3—1818

London—Devonshire—*Isabella or The Pot of Basil*—The northern tour—
Tom's death—*Blackwood's* and the *Quarterly* attack *Endymion*.

THE year that follows the composition of *Endymion* is the most crowded and momentous in Keats's life. In 1817, late in November, he had completed the poem at Burford Bridge Inn, and he had stayed on there for a few days to begin his work of revision. Then he came to London, and his nominal task was

B

still the revision of the poem. This he commenced, and, as has
already been seen, his letters show that as he corrected the poem
he also reconsidered its dominant ideas. But he did not work
consistently. Now that he was back in Town after these eight
months of strenuous, often lonely, labour, he felt the delight of
being packed in with his fellow men again: he dined out; he went
to dances; he talked late into the night; he even joined in the
entertainments of the 'fashionables,' who have a mannerism in
'their very eating and drinking, in their mere handling a de-
canter.' For Keats was no longer an unknown surgeon's apprentice from Edmonton. True, the great world had not heard of
him, but he had a wide acquaintance in the literary Bohemia of
the 'coming young men,' and he could meet the literary notables
whenever he wished. In London he associated particularly with
Charles Wentworth Dilke and Charles Brown, who shared a
double house at Wentworth Place, Hampstead. Dilke's interest
in literature was sufficient to quell any timidity Keats may have
felt on account of his aristocratic origins. Charles Brown, the
son of a Scottish stockbroker, had proved himself woefully unsuccessful in commerce, but he had been left with a competence
by a brother who had served the East India Company. He was
deeply attached to Keats, and Keats admired his animal spirits
and his delight in verses. From Hunt, Keats kept his distance;
for apart from temperamental differences, he felt that Hunt had
treated *Endymion* unsympathetically. Hunt had found Book I
unnatural, and the conversation too 'high-flown.' 'He must first
prove,' Keats writes, 'that Caliban's conversation is unnatural.'

Wordsworth was in Town, and the peak of these months was
Haydon's party for Wordsworth, to which Keats was invited. Haydon, who was proud of his party, describes it with naïve pleasure:

It was indeed an immortal evening. Wordsworth's fine intonation
as he quoted Milton and Virgil, Keats's eager, inspired look, Lamb's
quaint sparkle of lambent humour, so speeded the stream of conversation, that in my life I never passed a more delightful time. All our
fun was within bounds. Not a word passed that an apostle might
not have listened to. It was a night worthy of the Elizabethan age,
and my solemn Jerusalem flashing up by the flame of the fire, with
Christ hanging over us like a vision!

Keats, however much he enjoyed the evening, found Wordsworth
less pleasant at close quarters than he had been as a name: the
knee-breeches, the egoism, the anxiety to please official gentlemen
in the Stamp Department, above all, the gentle and insidious
condescension, helped to turn Keats away from a man to whom
he was deeply indebted.

But he enjoyed these London days and nights! He took his fill of society, entertainments, and late carousings. He galloped through his physical resources, and for the first time the mention of ill health comes creeping into the letters—'I have been racketing too much, and do not feel over well'—casual comments, but ominous when one knows what they prelude. At times he was restless and overtired, and depression would fall on him and he would fret over the uncertainty of his future. The contrast of the two moods can be seen in a letter to Reynolds for January 1818. He copies out some light-hearted verse trifles, such as he wrote frequently in these months:

> Hence Burgundy, Claret and Port,
> Away with old Hock and Madeira.

But a moment later in the same letter he writes out the sonnet which opens:

> When I have fears that I may cease to be
> Before my pen has glean'd my teeming brain,
> Before high piled Books in charactery
> Hold like full garners the full ripen'd grain—
> When I behold upon the night's starr'd face
> Huge cloudy symbols of a high romance,
> And feel that I may never live to trace
> Their shadows, with the magic hand of chance . . .

The London months were too riotous for steady composition, and, besides, there was *Endymion* to revise; but in another letter to Reynolds he copied out as a postscript to an attack on Wordsworth two poems which have the wistful memory of the 'uncontaminated and unobtrusive beauty of the earlier ways in poetry.' One was the *Robin Hood* poem:

> Gone, the merry morris din,
> Gone, the song of Gamelyn,
> Gone, the tough-belted outlaw
> Idling in the 'grenè shawe.'

The other was his tribute to the Elizabethans:

> Souls of poets dead and gone,
> What Elysium have ye known,
> Happy field, or mossy cavern,
> Fairer than the Mermaid Tavern?

They both recall the sonnet with which he had introduced his volume of 1817:

> Glory and loveliness have passed away;
> For if we wander out in early morn,
> No wreathèd incense do we see upborne
> Into the east, to meet the smiling day.

London had provided three happy if exhausting months.

Suddenly they ended, and the first crisis of 1818 was announced.
Tom Keats was ill with what proved ultimately to be consumption. He was in Devonshire, at Teignmouth, and George,
who was without employment, was looking after him. But
George was now of age, and determined to marry the sixteen-
year-old Georgiana Wylie, to set out for America, and acquire
fourteen hundred acres of Government land. The plan was
pantisocratic without the Pantisocrasy. George had to come to
London to settle his affairs, and Keats was summoned to Devonshire to look after Tom. The change was drastic—from London,
with its unending entertainments, to the solitary company of
Tom, whom Keats loved, but who was ill and dispirited, and
whom Keats, with his medical knowledge, must have known to
be seriously affected. Nor did the countryside provide any consolation, for the weather was wet and cold and Devonshire seemed
'a splashy, rainy, misty, snowy, foggy, haily, floody, slipshod
County.' He was driven in on himself, on his own mind, and on
poetry, and by the end of April 1818 he had completed the first
of his narrative poems, *Isabella or The Pot of Basil*.

Isabella is one of the few poems by Keats that resulted from
an entirely external prompting. With his friend John Hamilton
Reynolds he had determined to execute a series of poems based on
Boccaccio's *Decamerone*. Reynolds, whose attempts were issued
in 1821 in *The Garden of Florence and Other Poems*, admired
Keats's poem, and thought that it deserved separate publication.
For *Isabella* Keats chose the story of the fifth novel of the fourth
day. Boccaccio's simple and brief narrative tells of how Lisa-
betta's brothers put her lover to death; he appears to her in a
dream, and shows her where he is buried. She privately brings
away his head; and, putting it into a pot of basil, laments over it
a considerable time every day. At length her brothers take it
away from her, and she dies for grief. Keats effected a few minor
changes in detail: he moved the setting from Messina to Florence,
and reduced the number of the brothers from three to two.
Such modifications were trifles, but along with them he introduced for the murder of the lover, Lorenzo, a fresh motive which
is suggestive of his own mind. In Boccaccio, the brothers contrived the crime simply to punish an illicit lover whose conduct
had troubled them. Keats, seizing upon the fact that they were
rich merchants and Lorenzo only a poor employee, invents for
Isabella a wealthy suitor favoured by the brothers, and throws
an atmosphere of class-prejudice and malice over their deed.
Though politics do not enter persistently into Keats's poetry,

his letters show that he was still, even when away from Hunt's influence, a Radical, and that hatred of privilege was a flaming passion in his mind. George's failure to obtain employment in England had aroused this motive with fresh vigour, and a month after *Isabella* was finished he wrote to Bailey that George 'is too independent and liberal a Mind to get on in trade in this Country. . . . I would sooner he should till the ground than bow to a Customer.' Thus across the pathos of Boccaccio's story, and in contrast with its sentimentality, there flashes, like an angry streak of lightning, an abuse of vested interests so violent in its intensity that it might have come from a Marxian pamphleteer:

> With her two brothers this fair lady dwelt,
>   Enriched from ancestral merchandize,
> And for them many a weary hand did swelt
>   In torched mines and noisy factories,
> And many once proud-quiver'd loins did melt
>   In blood from stinging whip;—with hollow eyes
> Many all day in dazzling river stood,
> To take the rich-ored driftings of the flood.
>
> For them the Ceylon diver held his breath,
>   And went all naked to the hungry shark;
> For them his ear gush'd blood; for them in death
>   The seal on the cold ice with piteous bark
> Lay full of darts; for them alone did seethe
>   A thousand men in troubles wide and dark:
> Half-ignorant, they turn'd an easy wheel,
> That set sharp racks at work, to pinch and peel.
>
> Why were they proud?   Because their marble founts
>   Gush'd with more pride than do a wretch's tears?—
> Why were they proud?   Because fair orange-mounts
>   Were of more soft ascent than lazar stairs?—
> Why were they proud?   Because red-lin'd accounts
>   Were richer than the songs of Grecian years?—
> Why were they proud? again we ask aloud,
> Why in the name of Glory were they proud?

Keats apologized to Boccaccio as soon as he had completed this episode of wrath, and, a hundred years later, Mr G. B. Shaw commented that these were some of the sanest stanzas in Keats's work.

Boccaccio's story, with its mixture of sentimentality and the macabre, has a centre of weakness in it which nothing can eradicate, and Keats, influenced by memories of Chaucer's treatment of the pathetic, tended to over-emphasize the sentimentality. Salome bearing the head of John the Baptist on a charger can well be a thing of terror, but Isabella feeding with her 'thin tears' the head of Lorenzo in a 'garden-pot' may well arouse the

Spirits Ironical and Cynical. Keats himself was uneasy later about the poem, and in September 1819 he wrote:

It is too smokeable. . . . There is too much inexperience of life, and simplicity of knowledge in it—which might do very well after one's death—but not while one is alive. There are very few would look to the reality. I intend to use more finesse with the Public. It is possible to write fine things which cannot be laugh'd at in any way. Isabella is what I should call were I a reviewer, 'A weak-sided Poem' with an amusing sober-sadness about it.

Individual moments in the poem call for little but admiration and Lamb and others have noted the realistic power with which Keats, despite one unfortunate phrase, describes Isabella's discovery of Lorenzo's body:

> She gaz'd into the fresh-thrown mould, as though
>   One glance did fully all its secrets tell;
> Clearly she saw, as other eyes would know
>   Pale limbs at bottom of a crystal well;
> Upon the murderous spot she seem'd to grow,
>   Like to a native lily of the dell:
> Then with her knife, all sudden, she began
> To dig more fervently than misers can.
>
> Soon she turn'd up a soiled glove, whereon
>   Her silk had play'd in purple phantasies,
> She kiss'd it with a lip more chill than stone,
>   And put it in her bosom, where it dries
> And freezes utterly unto the bone
>   Those dainties made to still an infant's cries:
> Then 'gan she work again: nor stay'd her care,
> But to throw back at times her veiling hair.

Some of Keats's critics have given *Isabella* a high place in estimating his whole achievement as a poet. His advance in many directions must be allowed: his epithets are illuminating and the diction controlled. The *ottava rima*, with its oft-recurring rhyme, moves smoothly, and frequently with power. All these improvements are in technique, the reward of breaking himself in on the four thousand lines of *Endymion*. Yet he knew that in *Isabella* he had attempted, at Reynolds's promptings, a less difficult task than in *Endymion*, but he had learnt that narrative in verse was within his power, and he was to attempt it again in *The Eve of St Agnes* and in *Lamia*.

In May 1818, Keats returned to Hampstead: Tom seemed well enough to travel, and, as George was to be married before the end of the month, the brothers were anxious to be in London. Further, Keats's mind was set on a walking tour in Scotland which he and Charles Brown had planned to undertake together.

For Keats, the expedition was not merely a holiday, but a part of his poetical education. As he told Bailey, he was anxious to put his knapsack on his back and 'make a pedestrian tour through the north of England and part of Scotland—to make a sort of Prologue to the Life I intend to pursue—that is to write, to study, and to see all Europe at the lowest possible expense. I will clamber through the Clouds and exist.' He had been anxious to set out as early as May, but Tom's ill health and George's plans for marriage and emigration had intervened. George had determined to sail for America at the end of June 1818, and it was arranged that Keats and Brown should accompany them as far as Liverpool.

On 22nd June the four of them mounted the coach at the 'Swan and Two Necks,' in Lad Lane, and commenced their thirty-two-hour journey. Keats had determined to say his farewell to George without the harrowing delay of awaiting the actual sailing of the American boat. So he and Brown took the coach that went from Liverpool to Lancaster, and, arriving there in the crowded and inhospitable atmosphere of an election, they took to the road in the rain on Thursday, 24th June 1818, and set out northwards.

The northern tour, which was to have been the prelude to his life as a poet, proved in reality his undoing. He came to this expedition with his health already weakened by the exhausting months in London, followed by the damp, chilly exile to Devonshire, where he had worked strenuously at *Isabella* and the revision of *Endymion*. Mental distress at Tom's illness and the departure of George had aggravated his physical condition. The consumptive tendency, inherited from his mother, had always lain latent within him, and now, when his resistance was lowered, he gave it a chance to take possession. Brown had a stronger constitution; he could be careless of his health with impunity, and it was not in his nature to observe that his over-eager companion was undertaking risks that would finally lead to fatal consequences. Neither he nor Brown took the least precautions: they travelled without a change of clothes, slept in ill-provided inns, rose at four, and walked a dozen miles without breakfast. They were often wet, underfed, and tired, but the one thing of which they seemed incapable was rest. Some demon urged them on to tramp, to climb, continuously, exhaustingly, until, after less than two months, Brown writes that they have covered on foot six hundred and forty-two miles, and this often over difficult country. Soon after Keats's return to London he was to face the

attacks of *Blackwood's* and the *Quarterly*, and, in the view of
Shelley and Byron and of many others, their cruel ferocity drove
him to death. He was undoubtedly wounded by attacks which
he knew would injure him, but a dignified and manly pride
protected him from giving way. The root of his ultimate distress
may be found in the quiet, unobtrusive comments on his health
which intrude into his letters before the summer tour had drawn
to a close.

The consequences proved disastrous, but the tour itself was a
joyous and high-spirited adventure. From Lancaster they
pushed on to Bolton-le-Sands and then to Burton, which was so
crowded with soldiers that dinners, let alone beds, were difficult
to obtain. They went on to sleep at End Moor, and from there
next morning they passed through Kendal to Bowness, on Lake
Windermere. They spent the night at Ambleside, and in the
morning called at Grasmere to see Wordsworth, who was away
electioneering in the Tory interests at Lowther Castle. Their
route lay through Wythburn, where they slept a night, to Kes-
wick; they circled Derwentwater, visited the falls of Lodore, and
one morning, starting at four, began to climb Skiddaw. After
Skiddaw they moved north from the Lakes, through Ireby and
Wigton, to Carlisle. From there they got the coach to Dumfries,
where they visited the tomb of Burns. They then worked their
way through Dalbeattie to Kirkcudbright. Brown, discovering
that they were in Guy Mannering's country, stirred Keats out of
his normal chilliness towards Scott by accounts of Meg Merrilies,
and Keats almost straightway caught something of the spirit
of this wild creature who existed in a novel which he had not read:

> Old Meg she was a Gipsy,
>   And liv'd upon the Moors:
> Her bed it was the brown heath turf,
>   And her house was out of doors.

The Kirkcudbright coast pleased Keats, and he and Brown
moved on by way of Glenluce and Stranraer to Port Patrick.
Then, as if Scotland were not enough, they took a flying trip to
Ireland, hoping to visit the Giant's Causeway, but, discovering
the distances to be too great, they tramped to Belfast and back
and returned by the packet from Donaghadee to Port Patrick,
and so back to Stranraer. Still following the coast, they walked
through Ballantrae to Girvan, and then by way of Maybole to
Ayr. Keats had two outstanding moments on the journey, both
of which he tried to convey in verse; one was his view of the
Ailsa Craig—'Ailsa struck me very suddenly, really I was alarmed'

—and the other, more disappointing in its results, was an attempt
to allow his own sensations to conquer the garrulity of the custodian in Burns's cottage at Alloway. From Burns's country
they went to Glasgow, and then to Dumbarton and Loch Lomond
and Loch Fyne, and to Inveraray and so down to the coast at
Oban. From Oban they undertook a journey which remained for
Keats the most memorable of the whole tour, but one which over-
taxed his strength more than anything had done. By ferry they
crossed to Kerrara, and from there to Mull. They crossed the
whole island—nearly forty miles of difficult going in bad weather
—until they were opposite Iona. They crossed to Iona, which
could not fail to impress them; they hired another boat to take
them to Staffa and back to Mull by Loch na Keal. It is in the
letters describing these island expeditions that Keats mentions
his colds and sore throats, and he was sufficiently ill to have to
delay at Oban on his return. Once Keats imagined that he had
recovered, he and Brown set off with their usual zest and made
their way by Ballachulish and Loch Linnhe to Fort William,
where they delayed to climb Ben Nevis. The last spurt weakened
Keats still further, and when he reached Inverness on 6th August
1818, he felt compelled to consult a doctor, who at once forbade
him to continue the tour. Even had not this warning prevented
him, a letter from Dilke announcing a relapse in Tom's condition
would have driven him back to London, without completing the
projected journey south through Edinburgh.

Keats returned to London by a smack sailing from Cromarty,
and arrived in the middle of August 'as brown and as shabby as
you can imagine, scarcely any shoes left, his jacket all torn at the
back, a fur cap, a great plaid and his knapsack.' The sea voyage
had improved his throat, and tanned him such a deep brown that
to his friends he presented a deceptive appearance of good health.
The months that followed were to exercise a crushing strain upon
him. For three months he was to be Tom's constant companion in a noisy lodging, to watch him growing weaker, and
finally to be present by his side on the night in December when
he died. During this period he struggled with *Hyperion*, and,
despite all his affection for Tom, he seemed to feel at times an
uneasiness that amounted to irritability at the position in which
he was placed. Tom's illness stood between him and what he
had within him to do:

I wish I could say Tom was any better. His identity presses upon
me so all day that I am obliged to go out—and although I intended
to have given some time to study alone, I am obliged to write, and

*B

plunge into abstract images to ease myself of his countenance, his voice, and feebleness—so that I live now in a continual fever—it must be poisonous to life, although I feel well.

Keats seemed to see his own life being consumed as well as Tom's, and more than once he turned away from the composition of *Hyperion* feeling that he had no power within himself to continue. It may have been the recollection of these months that led him to write, in July 1819: 'I confess I cannot bear a sick person in a House especially alone—it weighs upon me day and night—and more so perhaps when the case is irretrievable.'

Into the middle of this period of depression came the onslaughts of the reviews against *Endymion*. The first attack appeared at the beginning of September 1818 from *Blackwood's Edinburgh Magazine*, then conducted as a bludgeoning Tory journal by John Wilson and J. G. Lockhart. *Blackwood's* devoted four articles in all to the Cockney School, and Leigh Hunt had already endured vituperation which implied that his verse possessed no merit and his life not a shred of decency. The articles were signed 'Z' and were the work of Lockhart, then twenty-three years old, and later to be Scott's son-in-law and biographer. The fourth article was reserved for Keats. In part, as Andrew Lang was to suggest later, the criticism could be justified as merely heartless, hard-hitting condemnation of defects which any sober criticism, particularly one of classical allegiances, might have detected in Keats's work. Certain passages, however, went beyond this and were intended to inflict a personal wound. Such was the famous advice to Keats to abandon poetry:

> It is a better and wiser thing to be a starved apothecary than a starved poet; so back to the shop, Mr John, back to 'plasters, pills and ointment boxes,' etc. But, for Heaven's sake, young Sangrado, be a little more sparing of extenuatives and soporifics in your practice than you have been in your poetry.

Even more wounding to Keats than these personal passages was the wholesale and unqualified condemnation of 'the calm, settled, imperturbable, drivelling idiocy of *Endymion*'! This was followed at the end of September by an article in the *Quarterly* by John Wilson Croker: less personal and violent than Lockhart's reckless attack, it had an equal power of affecting Keats, by its cold, unrelenting annihilation of his poem.

Keats was sufficiently human to be hurt, but he was not sufficiently weak to be crushed. The articles had caught him in a month when he was already harassed by Tom's weakness and by the difficulty that he was encountering with *Hyperion*. One effect was undoubtedly to lead him into cautious, almost calculating methods of composition in that poem. He realized, too, that these criticisms would shut him off from a public that might remunerate him for his work, and, if he affects a pose at all, it lies in his declaration that he does not care for the public, and that he will write for himself and his friends alone. Within his own heart he felt deeply that no one had seen sympathetically into the meaning of *Endymion*. He knew the weakness of the poem, but part of his very life was in it. In the month after the reviews appeared he wrote:

I will write independently—I have written independently *without Judgment*. I may write independently and *with Judgment* hereafter. The Genius of Poetry must work out its own salvation in a man: It cannot be matured by law and precept, but by sensation and watchfulness in itself. That which is creative must create itself. In *Endymion*, I leaped headlong into the Sea, and thereby have become better acquainted with the Soundings, the quicksands, and the rocks, than if I had stayed upon the green shore and piped a silly pipe and took tea and comfortable advice.

Meanwhile, if the reviews attacked him he had the minor consolation of seeing his friends gathering around in his defence.

Chapter 4—*November 1818: Fanny Brawne*

Tom's death and the review criticisms and difficulties with *Hyperion* were not the sole agitations in Keats's mind at the end of 1818. In November he had met Fanny Brawne. By December, the very month of Tom's death, he had probably confessed his love to her. Ever since H. Buxton Forman, in 1878, published Keats's letters to Fanny Brawne, criticism has sat in solemn judgment over this crisis in his life. He has been condemned for his cloying and unrestrained outpourings, and his morbid jealousy, while Fanny Brawne has been judged with equal severity because she failed to recognize his genius or even to discover the depth of his distress. Matthew Arnold, the chief of the prosecuting side, shows in his essay of 1880 the quality of the attack. After quoting one of Keats's letters, he writes:

A man who writes love-letters in this strain is probably predestined one may observe to misfortune in his love-affairs; but that is nothing. The complete enervation of the writer is the real point for remark. We have the tone, or rather the entire want of tone, the abandonment of all reticence and all dignity, of the merely sensuous man, of the man 'who is passion's slave.' Nay we have them in such wise that one is tempted to speak even as *Blackwood* or the *Quarterly* were

in the old days wont to speak; one is tempted to say that Keats's
love-letter is the love-letter of a surgeon's apprentice. It has in its
relaxed self-abandonment something unbred and ignoble, as of a
youth ill-brought-up, without the training which teaches us that we
must put some constraint upon our feelings and upon the expression
of them. It is the sort of love-letter of a surgeon's apprentice which
one might hear read out in a breach of promise case in the Divorce
Court.

Such is Arnold's attack, but not by such ways can this crucial
phase in Keats's life be understood, or its influence on his work
estimated.

The data for exploring the erotic side of any personality must
obviously be incomplete, and with Keats, despite the letters, we
are left in a tantalizing condition of half-knowledge. It appears
that despite all his early verses of love dalliance he retained an
innocence in experience which only increased his mental excit-
ability. Up to 1818, he seemed happier in the company of men:
with them he was at his ease, his mind alert, and his liveliness of
nature genially developed. With women he felt at once shy and
coy, nervous and excited, with an odd belief that some sort of
amorous approach was probably desirable. He treated women
very much as he treated Shelley, with a morbid sense of ill ease,
and a disastrous self-consciousness. Throughout his life he had
no intellectual companionship with women; even when he sent
his journal letters across the Atlantic to George and Georgiana
Keats he was alert and sincere with his brother, but always in
danger of becoming hoity-toityish for the benefit of his sister-in-
law. Further, in 1818 a number of motives led him to consider
more precisely what his relations with women would be: Tom was
dead; George was married and in America; and though he had
numerous friends he was more bereft than ever before of intimate
companionship. Also, his companion in the northern tour of
1818 had been Charles Brown, and from what we know of him
he would have led the talk frequently to sexual relationships,
and his views were probably pungent and peculiar. For over in
Ireland, in 1819, Brown was to wed an Abigail Donohue and
become the father of a son whom at the age of two he was to
remove to England without taking any further notice of the
mother whose biological usefulness was then at an end.

Before he met Fanny Brawne, Keats's mind had thus been
driven towards this problem of love and its more practical and
sexual aspects. His letters show him aroused by more than one
contact and yet anxious not to be aroused, but to be free, to husband his little stock of guineas, to travel, to educate himself, and

so to write verse. His dread was that he might wake up and find himself married, and with routine cares killing the spark of life that he knew to be within him. He tried to convince himself that no woman could dominate him. His friendships shall be with men: with women he will have encounters inevitably, but he will remain free:

I hope I shall never marry. Though the most beautiful Creature were waiting for me at the end of a Journey or a Walk; though the carpet were of Silk, the Curtains of the morning Clouds; the chairs and Sofa stuffed with Cygnet's down; the food Manna, the Wine beyond Claret, the Window opening on Winander mere, I should not feel, or rather my Happiness would not be so fine, as my Solitude is sublime. Then instead of what I have described, there is a Sublimity to welcome me home. The roaring of the wind is my wife and the Stars through the window pane are my Children. The mighty abstract Idea I have of Beauty in all things stifles the more divided and minute domestic happiness—an amiable wife and sweet Children I contemplate as part of that Beauty, but I must have a thousand of those beautiful particles to fill up my heart.

Already, before Fanny Brawne came, he had met two women who attracted him sufficiently for him to feel that he was testing his resolution. On both occasions he found himself secure. One of these was the mysterious lady whom he met first at Hastings, and whose name he never knew. If we are to believe the letters, the briefest and mildest *passade* followed. Suddenly, in October 1818, he met her again, in London, talked with her, walked with her, finally went home with her. He gives his own account of what took place:

We went upstairs into her sitting room, a very tasty sort of place with Books, Pictures, a bronze statue of Buonaparte, Music, aeolian Harp; a Parrot; a Linnet, a Case of choice Liqueurs &c. &c. &c. She behaved in the kindest manner—made me take home a Grouse for Tom's dinner. Asked for my address for the purpose of sending more game. As I had warmed with her before and kissed her, I thought it would be living backwards not to do so again—she had a better taste: she perceived how much a thing of course it was and shrunk from it, not in a prudish way but in as I say a good taste.

Keats met her again; she made more presents of game, but, whatever else passed between them, she left him as untroubled as he was before she had passed his way.

Along with this elusive and unnamed Hastings lady there had appeared at the same time in the Reynolds' household a Miss Jane Cox, who had proved more formidably attractive. In September 1818, Keats writes: 'I never was in love—yet the voice and shape of a Woman has haunted me these two days.'

He saw her again in October, and he writes to George and Georgiana in America to confess how he is fascinated by her:

> She is not a Cleopatra, but she is at least a Charmian. She has a rich eastern look: she has fine eyes and manners. . . . You will by this time think I am in love with her; so before I go any further I will tell you I am not—she kept me awake one Night as a tune of Mozart's might do.

He was interested, aroused, and curious, but he found that he could hold himself aloof. 'Do not think,' he writes to his brother, 'that my Passions are headlong or likely to be ever of any pain to you.' And then Fanny Brawne came, and he knew that he was beaten. He had made a pattern in life for himself, to study, to write, and to keep himself apart, and suddenly the pattern had broken.

To Wentworth Place in Hampstead there had come a Mrs Brawne, a widow of independent means, with her two daughters, Fanny and Margaret, and her son, Samuel. A tolerant and kindly person, she welcomed acquaintance, and soon she was on social terms with Brown and Dilke, who lived in the next house, and so John Keats came to know her and her family. Fanny, the eldest of the children, was then eighteen, lively, vivacious, with a fondness for society and dancing, a little indulged by a well-to-do mother, but not without intelligence or even kindliness. Above all, she was a *petite*, and Keats could meet her without the self-consciousness about his own stature interfering with the frankness of their first encounter. From the very first she seems to have awakened in him a passion that was like a distemper in the blood. There is no suggestion that she encouraged his submission: it came instinctively, powerfully. Indeed, she had nothing to gain by the devotion of this penniless young poet of twenty-four: he could not dance; he was awkward in company; he had no idea of the round of entertainments which a young lady of her position had the right to expect from those who favoured her. That she was attracted to him may be admitted, but her nature was not awakened to passion, and she had no profound interest in the arts, nor any outstanding vigour of intellect. She was only eighteen, and, though fond enough of Keats, she did not realize, except towards the end, the torment that she had awakened. At her age, and with her experience, she could have read the most distraught of his letters merely as an impetuous expression of love, though an expression more apt to frighten than to strengthen the affection of her gently sensuous nature. But nothing has been more unjust than the condemnation under which she has suffered. The worst that can be brought against her was that she flirted with Brown, and that ten years after Keats's death she married.

Nor was Keats a satisfactory lover. She had aroused in him a fever that could not be appeased, and left him distraught in her presence, and towards the end morbidly, even petulantly, jealous whenever she was absent. Had he lived, he would have come through this unrest, and seen her with the eyes of common day, 'quite himself again,' but with some indefinable increase of experience such as Shakespeare would have understood. To stand over him in solemn tribunal as Arnold does, is only to acknowledge that one aspect of life is shut off from one's understanding. In human experience one can only judge by what one knows, and Arnold, who speaks of 'relaxed self-abandonment,' is obviously among the untouched. He misses the quality of Keats's love for Fanny Brawne just as he missed the quality of the legend of *Tristram and Iseult*, or even as he must have failed to appreciate Shakespeare's *Troilus and Cressida*. For this was not mere sensuality with its implication of an experience sought out consciously, found pleasurable for a time at least, and so exploited. Keats knew no happiness in this passion for Fanny Brawne; he tried more than once to shake it off; but it possessed him with unescapable virulence.

The critics of Keats have often followed Arnold in describing Keats's passion for Fanny Brawne as if it were an episode all of one quality and as if its effect upon his creative sensibilities was wholly disastrous. Such a view misrepresents the whole relationship. He had met her late in 1818, and for months afterwards he lived in the house next to her in Hampstead. The history of lovers is always most fully recorded in their periods of separation, for then they write to each other: when they are together, as Keats and Fanny Brawne were from February to July 1819, no record of their relations is likely to exist. Yet these months are the one triumphal passage in their association, for during this spring and summer Keats's love contrived to increase his creative powers. It was not that he attempted to transfer his passion directly into verse—it was too tumultuous and chaotic for that— but in this early agitation he turned to verse as a catharsis for his malady, and the resultant pieces crowd in on one another with astounding rapidity. The first result therefore of his love for Fanny Brawne is that he sustains the most consistent period of poetic creation ever endured by a poet of his years, and with verses as calm and mature as he ever produced. Not only was he

working at *Hyperion*, but from February to July 1819 he completed *The Eve of St Agnes*; he wrote the opening of *The Eve of
St Mark* and the main series of the odes, and on 28th April he
composed *La Belle Dame sans Merci*.

In the middle of July he withdrew from Hampstead to Shanklin, and from then until December he did not see Fanny Brawne.
His first letters to her date from this period.   He had felt his life
at Hampstead, so close to a love that could not be consummated,
growing intolerable, and conscious of his own poverty, his own
ill health, and the impossibility of marriage, he had withdrawn
to apply himself to work, and to await some more hopeful turn in
his affairs.   Fanny Brawne was obviously a little mystified by his
departure, and sometimes, when dissatisfied with his letters, she
pleaded that he should return.   His own alleged account of this
flight does not seem to cover all his motives.   One part of his
nature was seeking release from this passion and hoping that
loneliness might bring it.   He even writes to Fanny Brawne a
passage disclosing some such intention:

I have never known any unalloy'd Happiness for many days
together: the death or sickness of some one has always spoilt my
hours—and now when none such troubles oppress me, it is you must
confess very hard that another sort of pain should haunt me.   Ask
yourself my love whether you are not very cruel to have so en-
trammelled me, so destroyed my freedom.

But deeper than this there dwelt within him the belief expressed
so clearly in the odes that physical experience once it is over
leaves an aftermath of melancholy and disillusionment.   The
whole thought of the odes, as will appear later, is the exploration
of whether the temporary joy of physical fulfilment compensates
for the sequel of the destruction of a beauty that had previously
been ideal.   Even had all practical circumstances favoured this
union there was a side of Keats's nature that would have held
itself apart in an agony of self-torment.

In August he went from Shanklin to Winchester, still holding
himself away, and his mind was strenuously engaged with creative
work, with *Lamia*, and the ode, *To Autumn*, and the revision of
Hyperion.   In Winchester his determination to keep away from
Fanny Brawne seemed to be growing successful.   He wrote a
'flint-worded letter,' without 'silken Phrases or silver sentences':
he even had to excuse himself for delay because his hours had been
full of business and his mind of poetry.   For a moment it would
seem that the fever was passing, and that he had discovered the
road back to habitual self: 'I see you through a mist: as I dare say

you do me by this time.   Believe in the first Letters I wrote you:
I assure you I felt as I wrote—I could not write so now.'   His
mind was sufficiently occupied with practical difficulties: his own
finances were low, and George required help, but he had reached
that point of calm where he could urge such considerations as
excuses for neglecting a passion that once would not have borne
to be neglected.

Yet it was not over.   In September 1819 he came for a few days
to London, but kept away from Hampstead, as if afraid of the
effect of such a visit: 'I love you too much to venture to Hampstead, I feel it is not paying a visit but venturing into fire.'   He
returned to Winchester, still in possession of himself, and remained there until October.   Then he came to London, to find a
permanent lodging from which he could start a journeyman's
work in letters, and earn money to help George and find a way of
living for himself.   He returned to London with the determination not again to venture himself near Fanny Brawne; but Hampstead seemed so close, and his College Street lodgings so lonely,
and perhaps now after all these months he would be strong even
in her presence.   He went and was completely annihilated; every
project that he had made turned to dust around him.   Then it was
that he wrote the letter of abject surrender which Arnold has
chosen to quote as if it were typical of the whole correspondence:

You have absorb'd me.   I have a sensation at the present moment
as though I was dissolving—I should be exquisitely miserable without
the hope of soon seeing you.   I should be afraid to separate myself
far from you.   My sweet Fanny, will your heart never change?
My love, will it?   I have no limit now to my love. . . .   Your note
came in just here.   I cannot be happier away from you.   'Tis richer
than an Argosy of Pearles.   Do not threat me even in jest.   I have
been astonished that Men could die Martyrs for religion—I have
shudder'd at it.   I shudder no more—I could be martyr'd for my
Religion—Love is my religion—I could die for that.   I could die for
you.   My Creed is Love and you are its only tenet.   You have
ravish'd me away by a Power I cannot resist; and yet I could resist
till I saw you; and even since I have seen you I have endeavoured
often 'to reason against the reasons of my love.'   I can do that no
more—the pain would be too great.   My love is selfish.   I cannot
breathe without you.   ⸎

His passion became a torment, and no longer, as in its earlier
phases, did it stimulate his creative power.   He could only go up
to Wentworth Place and live close to her, seeing her when he
could, and send her little notes to the house next door.   It must
be remembered that he was already within a few months of the
crisis of 3rd February 1820, when a severe haemorrhage showed

that he had not long to live. From the day that he went to Wentworth Place to visit her in December 1819 to his departure from England in September 1820 he was dominated by her and his own disease. Nothing comes through from these months but a record of a sick mind, fevered and distressed, petulant at times, and morbidly jealous, but with lucid intervals, when, seeing himself as he was, he begged those around him to forgive his excesses. For Fanny Brawne herself this last phase of their love must have been the most difficult. Keats was no longer even fair to her by any common standard of conduct, but she seems to have understood, to have tolerated his accusations of ill faith, and at one crisis to have helped her mother to nurse him in their own home. Even in her comments after his death, though at times she seems barely appreciative of his genius, she speaks with quiet understanding of this final period in England. When he went to Italy, at the request of his friends, he wrote to her no more, but his mind remained with her, and had he had his own way he would have stayed in England and died in Hampstead, very near to this presence that unwittingly had helped to destroy him.

Arnold and those who have condemned this love have failed to see that this last phase was only one aspect of Keats's relation to Fanny Brawne. In all, it has three movements, first there is recognition, then withdrawal, and finally total, even abject, surrender; and while this last may produce only pathos and even humiliation the early stages served to arouse Keats to his outstanding period of poetic creation.

Chapter 5—1819

The Eve of St Agnes—The Eve of St Mark—The odes—Lamia—La Belle Dame sans Merci.

THE work of the last eighteen months of Keats's poetical activity has such variety of theme and form that some categorizing Polonius might comment that of ode, sonnet, lyric, ballad-lyric, romance, narrative, epic narrative, he had them all! Yet within the diversity one can discover two major and dividing motives. On the one hand there are poems that look back to his previous work, to *Isabella*, to *Endymion*, and even to the moods of his earliest verses. He has gained in poetic mastery, and he is using that additional craft to express more adequately something which he has already said. Such are *The Eve of St Agnes, The Eve of*

St Mark, and, to some extent, the odes.   On the other hand, in
Hyperion, and *The Fall of Hyperion*, he seems to be working away
from his earlier work to a new stage in his creative development.
Lamia remains uneasily between the old world and the new.

Keats's letters, especially the 'Mansions of Thought' letter of
May 1818, show that he expected some change of sympathy with
increased experience.   He had sooner or later to pass from the
place where 'we become intoxicated with the light and the atmosphere,' and where 'we see nothing but pleasant wonders.'   In
Hyperion he attempts to effect that change.   The trouble that
Hyperion gave him, the delays, the excuses for delay, the fresh
attempts, indicate that he was working at a poem that had a
different conception of poetry behind it.   The presence of Fanny
Brawne made this change in orientation more difficult: he found
himself unable to think his way through *Hyperion*, and he turned
aside more than once to poems in which his passion gained
sublimation and release.

Thus, in January and February 1819, he wrote *The Eve of
St Agnes*.   After some exhausting months at Hampstead, and a
Christmas during which he had probably gained from Fanny
Brawne a promise of her attachment, he had gone to Chichester.
He had taken with him some sheets of thin paper, intending
probably to use them for one of his journal letters to George and
Georgiana; instead, he employed them for the poem.   He was
going back to the mood in which eight months previously he had
written *Isabella*, and once again the ultimate source of the fable
was Boccaccio, whose version of the story occurs in the early
Il Filocolo.   No English rendering of this existed in 1819, and so
Keats must have found it either in conversation with Leigh Hunt
or from a French source.

The human action of the poem is simple, a Romeo and Juliet
theme without its tragic conclusion, worked out in a medieval
setting and on the background of an old superstition.   Madeline
had deserted the guests on the feast of St Agnes's·Eve, believing
that if she retired to her chamber a vision of her lover might
appear to her.   Instead of the vision, there appeared the lover
himself, Porphyro, who had hidden himself to wait for her.   So
they became lovers, and escaped together out into the night.
Keats, choosing the Spenserian stanza, has wrought this theme
sumptuously with decorative detail.   Not that the passion of the
lovers is obscured—that was a theme too close to him in these
months to be forgotten—but it is surrounded with luxurious
description, ensuring that the whole shall be seen in a glamorous

atmosphere. It comes through in the opening description of Madeline's home:

> Soon, up aloft,
> The silver, snarling trumpets 'gan to chide:
> The level chambers, ready with their pride,
> Were glowing to receive a thousand guests:
> The carved angels, ever eager-eyed,
> Star'd, where upon their heads the cornice rests,
> With hair blown back, and wings put cross-wise on their breasts.

The visitor to the Victoria and Albert Museum at South Kensington can find in the relief of the façade of Keats's old school those very angels, their wings 'cross-wise,'[1] testifying to that perpetual recapturing of memories, whether from life or from books, that contributed so largely to the picturesque side of Keats's work.

Yet Keats, as his letters show, was not fully satisfied with the charmed Christabel atmosphere of the poem. He complained to his publisher of its deficiencies of 'character and sentiment': 'I wish to diffuse the colouring of St Agnes Eve throughout a Poem in which Character and Sentiment would be the figures to such drapery.' He is half conscious of the fact that romantic narrative, exploited in *Isabella* and *The Eve of St Agnes*, is not enough: 'I am more at home amongst men and women. I would rather read Chaucer than Ariosto.' At the time he imagined that he might ascend to dramatic poetry, which, with Shakespeare in mind, he regarded as the height of poetry. This belief led him, in the summer of 1819, to the profitless task of a collaboration with Charles Brown in the tragedy of *Otho the Great*.

Before abandoning romantic narrative he attempted one more poem left as a memorable fragment, *The Eve of St Mark*. A product of the same mood as *The Eve of St Agnes*, based alike on a superstition with a medieval background, it was to tell of how on one evening in the year watchers at the church porch could see the vision of those who were to die of disease. The theme was one peculiarly attractive to the Pre-Raphaelites, and D. G. Rossetti was led to describe this and *La Belle Dame sans Merci* as 'in manner the choicest and chastest of Keats's work.' In the fragment that remains, Keats has caught into his octosyllabic couplets the atmosphere of the cathedral town in the evening:

> The silent streets were crowded well
> With staid and pious companies,
> Warm from their fire-side orat'ries;
> And moving, with demurest air,
> To even-song, and vesper prayer.

---

[1] Noted by Professor V. de S. Pinto.

> Each arched porch, and entry low,
> Was fill'd with patient folk and slow,
> With whispers hush, and shuffling feet,
> While play'd the organ loud and sweet.

In vivid contrast with this placid movement of normal life is his description of the room of Bertha, who was to watch for the apparitions on the fated night:

> Down she sat, poor cheated soul!
> And struck a lamp from the dismal coal;
> Lean'd forward, with bright drooping hair
> And slant book, full against the glare.
> Her shadow, in uneasy guise,
> Hover'd about, a giant size,
> On ceiling-beam and old oak chair,
> The parrot's cage, and panel square;
> And the warm angled winter-screen,
> On which were many monsters seen,
> Call'd doves of Siam, Lima mice,
> And legless birds of Paradise,
> Macaw, and tender Avadavat,
> And silken-furr'd Angora cat.

Here was the elaborately worked detail, ready, as it were, in poetical invoice, for insertion into the background of one of Rossetti's pictures. Such passages were to influence the romanticism of the nineteenth century, and to join with other influences to affect poetical descriptions from Rossetti to *The Sphinx* of Oscar Wilde.

If in these poems he worked out one side of his genius he contrived at the same time to find a fresh and final expression in the odes for that conception of the relation of Truth and Beauty which had governed *Endymion* and which recurred so frequently in the letters. The main group of odes is possibly the most satisfactory and complete element in the poetry of his maturity, the culmination of intuitions, experiences, and contemplations present in his mind even before *Endymion*. Here his imagination is magical and yet disciplined by a certain rigidity of form that adds to the enchantment. The order of the odes remains uncertain, yet probably the *Ode to Psyche*, which Keats wrote out in a journal letter to George and Georgiana Keats in April 1819, is the first. For he seems conscious in transcribing this poem that his genius has broken through and taken possession of new territory, just as earlier he realized that in the Chapman sonnet he had discovered something unknown to him before. He writes:

The following poem—the last I have written—is the first and the only one with which I have taken even moderate pains. I have for the most part dash'd off my lines in a hurry. This I have done

leisurely—I think it reads the more richly for it, and will I hope
encourage me to write other things in even a more peaceable and
healthy spirit.

There lies an incongruity between the importance which Keats
attached to the poem and the attention which it has received
from his critics.   Both Sir Sidney Colvin and Dr Robert Bridges
place it among the least successful of Keats's attempts in strophic
form.   Colvin sees in it nothing more than Keats's realization
'of the meaning of Greek nature religion and his delight in
imagining the beauty of its shrines and ritual.'   Miss Amy Lowell,
in her uneven but too much abused volumes, is in her most unhappy mood in describing this poem.   She seems to regard it
as a piece with a regular stanzaic pattern, while the 'two unrhymed lines in the published version' are 'a slight blemish.'
A cursory examination of the poem shows that it has no regular
stanzaic pattern: the number of unrhymed lines is at least three.
The unrhymed lines are part of the beauty of the poem; they
occur in the earlier stanzas.   The last stanza is fuller, and completely rhymed, gathering into itself the melody and the meaning
of the poem.

In the *Ode to Psyche*, Keats suggested his own thought through
a memory of a legend which had already attracted him in *I stood
tip-toe*, and one which has appealed to poets down to Robert
Bridges, who used two lines from Keats's ode as a motto in his
Eros and Psyche.   Keats could have found the story in a number
of places.   Probably he was aware of William Adlington's sixteenth-century translation of the *Metamorphoses* or *Golden Ass* of
Apuleius.   The setting of the story in Apuleius's narrative would
have fascinated him, the lovely idyll set into a record of boisterous
adventure.   Walter Pater, who incorporated a prose translation
of the Cupid and Psyche story into *Marius the Epicurean*, has
commented on the significance of this setting:

One of the episodes in the main narrative, a true gem amid its
mockeries, its coarse though genuine humanity, its burlesque
horrors, came the tale of Cupid and Psyche, full of brilliant, life-like
situations—*speciosa locis*—and abounding in lovely visible imagery
(one seemed to see and handle the golden hair, the fresh flowers, the
precious works of art in it!) yet full also of a gentle idealism, so that
you might take it, if you chose, for an allegory.

Yet while Keats probably knew Apuleius, one other recollection was more immediately in his mind as he came to write the
poem.   In 1811 there was published a poem, *Psyche*, by Mrs
Mary Tighe, which had already been privately issued in 1805.

Mrs Tighe was a 'blue-stocking' poet, born in Ireland, a consumptive like Keats, and, like him, fretful and unhappy in love. She sought consolation in literature, and, as was still a fashion in the early nineteenth century, she chose to write in imitation of Spenser. Her *Psyche* is Spenserian both in form and sentiment, a poem which Dr Samuel Johnson would have been delighted to annihilate. It is an interesting museum piece of the method of a mild and minor Spenserian. For her poem she accepted the general outline of Apuleius's story and then revalued it in the terms of chivalry. She found Cupid a most unsatisfactory young god: to lie sick on one's bed while one's mistress is attempting dangerous adventures is no role for a Spenserian champion. So, in *Psyche*, Cupid disguises himself and follows the young girl through all her difficulties. Only in the last moment of triumph does he disclose his Olympian identity. The myth had become an allegorical romance in Mrs Tighe's hands, and the Spenserian stanza, allowed to ripple on line by line, had completed the effect of mild sweetness. Such was the poem uppermost in Keats's mind when he came to his ode, yet strangely enough it belonged to his earlier enthusiasms of 1816 and 1817, which he had long outgrown. Already in December 1818 he had written: 'Mrs Tighe and Beattie once delighted me—now I see through them and can find nothing in them or weakness, and yet how many they still delight.' Yet something remained from that earlier uncritical enthusiasm to be transfigured in this poem.

The ode detaches itself from the obligations of narrative poetry to recount the story: it is removed even farther than the Ovidian idyll from direct dependence on a fable. This allusiveness allows Keats to concentrate upon one element, the personality of Psyche, and through her he releases into expression a group of abstract ideas which lie behind *I stood tip-toe* and *Endymion*, and which recur with such frequency in the letters. Nor has the poem the obscurity in argument which has sometimes been ascribed to it. He imagines that he sees two lovers together, and he recognizes them. Cupid, 'the winged boy,' can claim no particular attention: he is already a god, and adequately attended to by the Muses. But Psyche—surely Psyche should be a goddess! She appeared a little too late in the history of things for the Greeks to deify her. Yet he will do so—in his mind she shall be a goddess; and so suddenly in the last stanza he builds up a thickly wreathed complication of images for the mental apotheosis of Psyche:

Yes, I will be thy priest, and build a fane
  In some untrodden region of my mind,
Where branched thoughts, new grown with pleasant pain,
  Instead of pines shall murmur in the wind:
Far, far around shall those dark-cluster'd trees
  Fledge the wild-ridged mountains steep by steep;
And there by zephyrs, streams, and birds, and bees,
  The moss-lain Dryads shall be lull'd to sleep;
And in the midst of this wide quietness
  A rosy sanctuary will I dress
With the wreath'd trellis of a working brain,
  With buds, and bells, and stars without a name,
With all the gardener Fancy e'er could feign,
  Who breeding flowers, will never breed the same:
And there shall be for thee all soft delight
  That shadowy thought can win,
A bright torch, and a casement ope at night,
  To let the warm Love in!

Keats has been criticized for over-elaboration in this last stanza; yet I believe that the emphasis was deliberate and came from his realization that he had grappled successfully with a different element in his thought. He pleads in the poem: I cannot see you, Psyche, as a goddess; I cannot behold the beauty of you as you were, but I can recreate you in poetry. The shrine of the mind dressed by the working brain is as important as the actual contact with experience in the physical world. Instead of being worshipped, as you might have been, as a physical form, you shall be worshipped as the memory in the mind of all things that are beautiful. So he had come back to render more subtly the thought which lies behind the opening lines of *Endymion*: 'A thing of beauty is a joy for ever.'

Equally it is the thought which underlies the other odes. They each elaborate one aspect of the position outlined in the Psyche poem, and their close unity is shown by Keats's employment in them all, of the same regular stanza, of ten lines, the quatrain of a Shakespearian sonnet with the sestet added. The actual form of the sestet varies but the main pattern of the stanza is the same, and gives support to the suggestion that Keats came to his own conception of a poetical form for the ode through his study and employment of the Shakespearian sonnet.

The *Ode to a Nightingale* was written in May 1819, while he was living with Charles Brown in Wentworth Place, Hampstead, and Sir Sidney Colvin [1] has reproduced a facsimile of the original manuscript which serves to show how happy Keats was here in

[1] *Monthly Review*, March 1903.

his revisions.   The two lines, so much admired that they have
become hackneyed,

> magic casements, opening on the foam
> Of perilous seas, in faery lands forlorn,

appeared in Keats's draft first as:

> the wide casements opening on the foam
> Of keelless seas in faery lands forlorn.

Some have been misled into seeking an origin for the poem in a
simple recollection of Tom's death.   Keats's life was so emotionally crowded in the spring of 1819 that the past had little room in
which to rise and torment him.   Fanny Brawne had entered his
life just as Tom was leaving it, and it is his own agitation and his
own attempt to find a way through that dominates the Nightingale ode.   Once the ode is seen as an experience apart from the
crisis of Tom's death, its relation to the other odes becomes more
apparent.   Even Robert Bridges, who wrote that he 'could not
name any English poem of the same length which contains so
much beauty,' does not allow the full development of Keats's
thought within the poem.

The *Ode to a Nightingale* opens with the same recognition of
the impermanence of beauty in the physical world which dominates the Psyche ode.   Keats is led here to melancholy in seeing
that beauty inevitably perishes and asks that he may

> Fade far away, dissolve, and quite forget
>   What thou among the leaves hast never known,
> The weariness, the fever, and the fret
>   Here, where men sit and hear each other groan;
> Where palsy shakes a few, sad, last gray hairs,
>   Where youth grows pale, and spectre-thin, and dies;
>   Where but to think is to be full of sorrow
> And leaden-eyed despairs,
>   Where Beauty cannot keep her lustrous eyes,
>   Or new Love pine at them beyond to-morrow.

So, forgetting the nightingale, he is led to seek methods of escape
from this dilemma, present so frequently in romantic poetry.
He asks first that he may become inebriated and so forget the
world.   But he rejects the solution of Bacchus, the way of the
opiate, and substitutes poetry, or the life of the imagination, as a
triumph over the impermanence of beauty:

> I will fly to thee,
> Not charioted by Bacchus and his pards,   ·
> But on the viewless wings of Poesy.

Later he toys with the idea of suicide with 'easeful Death' as a

relief from life, but this solution too must be rejected for with
death all beauty would disappear:

> Still wouldst thou sing, and I have ears in vain—
> To thy high requiem become a sod.

In poetry alone is there the possibility of maintaining beauty lost
as a physical experience by the recreating power of the imagination: thus the nightingale's song is not one song but a song unending, into which memories of every individual song have been
gathered:

> Thou wast not born for death, immortal Bird!
> No hungry generations tread thee down;
> The voice I hear this passing night was heard
> In ancient days by emperor and clown:
> Perhaps the self-same song that found a path
> Through the sad heart of Ruth, when, sick for home,
> She stood in tears amid the alien corn;
> The same that oft-times hath
> Charm'd magic casements, opening on the foam
> Of perilous seas, in faery lands forlorn.

The shrine of Psyche in the mind is the only protection against
the death and defilement of things beautiful in the physical and
material world. While this is the main argument, the whole of
Keats's poem is not held within it. He postulates this per-
manence of an ideal beauty, but not wholly with satisfaction:

> the fancy cannot cheat so well
> As she is fam'd to do.

Whatever may happen to the permanent, idealized recollections,
the physical song does die:

> thy plaintive anthem fades
> Past the near meadows, over the still stream,
> Up the hill-side; and now 'tis buried deep
> In the next valley-glades.

And half spoken there rests the thought that there is some ecstasy
in physical contact with Beauty that cannot be found by the life
of the imagination.

This last aspect of his thought gains fuller emphasis in the
Ode on Melancholy: it renders this ode less general in its suggestion than the Psyche poem, less placid than the *Grecian Urn*, but
it yields at the same time a powerful concentration, absent in the
Nightingale. Melancholy, the aftermath of Delight, is inseparable
from Beauty and Joy. If Joy be embraced to the full, then
Melancholy must be the sequel. The solution of the shrine of
Psyche was one of suspense from this crisis of Joy; the temper
was contemplative, platonic rather than hedonistic. Here the

emphasis lies rather with the exultant glory of the moment of
delight, seized out of experience, and found in itself sufficiently
compensating for the melancholy that must inevitably follow.
The second stanza, where Keats shows how Nature can restore
the mind thus obsessed by Melancholy, has intimate recollections
of *I stood tip-toe* and of *Endymion*, while the last stanza, where his
thought is compactly expressed, is perhaps the most keenly
individualized in all the odes:

> She dwells with Beauty—Beauty that must die;
>   And Joy, whose hand is ever at his lips
> Bidding adieu; and aching Pleasure nigh,
>   Turning to poison while the bee-mouth sips:
> Ay, in the very temple of Delight
>   Veil'd Melancholy has her sovran shrine,
>   Though seen of none save him whose strenuous tongue
>   Can burst Joy's grape against his palate fine;
> His soul shall taste the sadness of her might,
>   And be among her cloudy trophies hung.

The *Grecian Urn*, the most philosophical statement of the
position that underlies the odes, has been treated somewhat
harshly by some of Keats's critics, possibly because it has run
away with the praises of his more injudicious admirers. Robert
Bridges, in many ways the most sensitive of the minds that have
appraised Keats's verse, speaks coldly of the poem.

The thought [he writes] as enounced in the first stanza, is the
supremacy of ideal art over Nature, because of its unchanging
expression of perfection; and this is true and beautiful; but its ampli-
fication in the poem is unprogressive, monotonous, and scattered,
the attention being called to fresh details without result—which
gives an effect of poverty in spite of the beauty.

Undoubtedly the poem has weaknesses in detail, particularly in
the cacophony of the opening line of the last stanza, yet in this
ode Keats reworked with greater certainty the idea which underlies the Psyche ode. The suggestion for the poem arose, as is
frequent with Keats, from a number of sources; memories of the
Elgin Marbles, the Parthenon frieze, the reproduction of the
Sosibios vase in the Musée Napoléon, of which Keats had made a
tracing, and, more generally, of classical paintings by Claude and
Poussin. These recollections are so rich that the poem has a
stronger basis of concrete detail than any of the other odes, and
this may have given rise to Bridges's criticism, but the main
theme is not obscured in the illustrations. Keats suggests that
the figures on the vase are the permanent representations in art
of deeds which if enacted in life would be consummated and so

disappear.   If instead of those shapes we had the living counter-
parts of which they are the image, the music would pass, the loves
die, the joy be made bitter by regret: but, on the urn, they are
'unravish'd' perpetual figures.   Thus they are symbols of that
beauty of the imagination, which, once defined, remains permanent.   Further, this life of the imagination, which endows
moments of beauty wherever perceived with an eternal life, is
as real as the life of fact.   Indeed more real, for, while the life of
the material world passes, the imaginative life endures.   This
life of the imagination Keats had already symbolized in the shrine
of Psyche and in the unending song of the Nightingale.   He had
long contemplated it, and it was as early as November 1817, in
a letter to Benjamin Bailey, that he had set out an opinion
which reads almost as if it were a paraphrase of the conclusion of
the ode:[1]

> O Attic Shape!   Fair attitude! with brede
>   Of marble men and maidens overwrought,
> With forest branches and the trodden weed;
>   Thou, silent form, dost tease us out of thought
> As doth eternity: Cold Pastoral!
>   When old age shall this generation waste,
>   Thou shalt remain, in midst of other woe
>   Than ours, a friend to man, to whom thou say'st,
> 'Beauty is truth, truth beauty,'—that is all
>   Ye know on earth, and all ye need to know.

No stanza in Keats's work has been more misunderstood.   To
equate 'truth' in these lines to the sum of what is known of the
world is to reach a position which is absurd and almost the contrary of what Keats wished to express.   For him 'truth' means
here the continuous existence in the imagination of what the
power of man to perceive as beautiful has seized out of the world.

It can be seen thus that in the odes he does not reach an
absolute conclusion; rather he reworks from different approaches
the same body of thought.   Nor were the odes unallied to his
personal experience.   Underlying his passion for Fanny Brawne
there lay the fact that he distrusted the fulfilment of his love as
much as he desired it.   In the odes he sublimates that dilemma
by dealing with it symbolically and not directly, and by enlarging
it with a more general conception of the relation of experience to
an ideal life.   But the impelling power behind the odes lay in
the self-tormenting tragedy of his own temperament.

Keats's other odes stand a little apart from this main group.
He had made earlier experiments in strophic verse of which the

---

[1] See p. 28.

Ode to Pan in *Endymion*, Book I, and the Song to Sorrow in Book IV are the most memorable. In the immediate period of the great odes there are others, allied sometimes in form but varied in theme. Of these the *Ode on Indolence* has the closest parallel with the main group; it is a product of the same months, written in the same stanza, and frequently reminiscent of them in phrasing. While the main odes show Keats grappling successfully with a difficult element in his thought, *Indolence* shows him luxuriating in a mood. A passage in his journal letter to George and Georgiana Keats for March 1819 describes the temper in which the poem arose:

This morning I am in a sort of temper indolent and supremely careless: I long after a stanza or two of Thomson's Castle of Indolence. My passions are all asleep from my having slumbered till nearly eleven and weakened the animal fibre all over me to a delightful sensation about three degrees on this side of faintness—if I had teeth of pearl and the breath of lilies I should call it languor—but as I am, I must call it laziness. In this state of effeminacy the fibres of the brain are relaxed in common with the rest of the body, and to such a happy degree that pleasure has no show of enticement and pain no unbearable frown. Neither Poetry, nor Ambition, nor Love have any alertness of countenance as they pass by me: they seem rather like three figures on a Greek vase—a man and two women whom no one but myself could distinguish in their disguisement. This is the only happiness, and is a rare instance of advantage in the body overpowering the mind.

Keats is not wholly serious in this description, as one can see from the prefatory passage on the black eye which he had received in playing cricket: 'I am glad it was not a clout.' Equally the poem has not the seriousness of the other odes: it is a successful piece of poetic day-dreaming, the neutral point between *Melancholy* and the *Grecian Urn*. Keats, as we know from his letters, enjoyed writing it, but he excluded it from the volume of 1820.

The lines *To Autumn*, of September 1819, deservedly popular among Keats's simpler nature poems, are not described as an ode in the volume of 1820, nor do they possess that organic unity of structure which distinguishes the main odes from discursive or narrative poetry. *To Autumn* is ultimately descriptive though saturated with a single atmosphere, and given a suggestion of pattern by its personification of the season. The occasion which aroused its composition is recounted in the letter to Reynolds for September 1819:

How beautiful the season is now—How fine the air. A temperate sharpness about it. Really, without joking, chaste weather—Dian skies—I never lik'd stubble-fields so much as now—Aye better than the chilly green of the Spring. Somehow a stubble-plain looks warm —in the same way that some pictures look warm. This struck me so much in my Sunday's walk that I composed upon it.

And in another letter of the same date, amid a passage of banter and persiflage, he breaks off suddenly—'You like poetry better' —and transcribes the lines *To Autumn*.

The poem *To Fanny*, often described as an ode, was written in the spring of 1819, but was not published until Lord Houghton issued it in 1848. Lord Crewe found in his collection an autograph manuscript version with both the first and the fourth stanzas missing. As Lord Houghton's version has disunity in theme and form it is possible that the so-called *Ode to Fanny* is an unfinished draft of a poem, possibly of two poems. It cannot certainly be judged in the same way as the greater odes. Considered biographically it has poignant and human interest, but as a poem it appears too rhetorical and strident. It combines taking phrases with lines that cry out pathetically to be understood, but their reception is marred by some oddity or weakness of expression. The unevenness, the continual sense that one will fall back into the less happy moments of the earliest Keats, combined with moments that are secure, can be found in the final stanzas:

> I know it—and to know it is despair
> To one who loves you as I love, sweet Fanny!
> Whose heart goes flutt'ring for you everywhere,
>   Nor, when away you roam,
>   Dare deep its wretched home.
> Love, Love alone, has pains severe and many:
>   Then loneliest! keep me free,
>   From torturing jealousy.
>
> Ah! if you prize my subdued soul above
> The poor, the fading, brief pride of an hour;
> Let none profane my Holy See of love,
>   Or with a rude hand break
>   The sacramental cake:
> Let none else touch the just new-budded flower;
>   If not—may my eyes close,
>   Love! on their last repose.

The poem would seem to have preceded immediately the composition of the *Ode to Psyche* and the beginning of the great odes. Somehow, in these spring months of 1819, Keats gained such power over himself as to realize that verses such as these *To Fanny* were 'smokeable.' The letter of April 1819 in which he speaks of writing in a 'more peaceable and healthy spirit' gains an additional significance if we are to see him turning at that

time from the feverish stanzas of the *Fanny* poem to the odes,
where the storm of passion has found its centre of calm.

Half-way between the odes and *Hyperion* there lies *Lamia*,
Keats's most notable narrative poem. It differs from *Isabella*
and *St Agnes* in that it is more than a romance. Behind its fable
there lurks the shadow of a symbolic meaning, and one closely
related to the thought of the odes. Further, Keats has abandoned
both the *ottava rima* and the Spenserian stanza, and coming back
to the couplet, with Dryden now as his master, he has set aside
the experimental wildness of *Endymion* for a more regular and
disciplined movement. The story he had found in Robert
Burton's *Anatomy of Melancholy*, a volume which engaged him
continually during the spring of this year. There Burton transcribes from Philostratus a story of how Lycius, a youth of
Corinth, met a phantasm in the form of a 'fair gentle woman,'
and found much pleasure in her company and would at length
marry her. To the feast came his master, the philosopher
Apollonius, who saw immediately through the 'fair and lovely'
semblance and beheld the phantasm as it was, a serpent-witch,
a lamia. 'When she saw herself descried, she wept, and desired
Apollonius to be silent, but he would not be moved, and thereupon
she, plate, house, and all that was in it, vanished in an instant.'
Keats further concludes his poem with the death of Lycius.

Out of the simple brevity of Burton's story Keats created a
well-organized narrative. A swiftly-moving prologue portraying
Hermes and Lamia, reveals the bewitched serpent and by giving
a clue to its transformation suggests the action which is to follow,
and carries us naturally into Corinth. Once the theme is initiated
the emphasis is maintained forcefully, except for the few notori-
ously weak passages. The narrative is conducted with a quick,
certain movement fresh to Keats's poetry, while every incident
that gives possibility of colour is fully exploited. He lavishes
detail in the description of the serpent, and, more successfully,
in the account of her transformation into a woman:

> Left to herself, the serpent now began
> To change; her elfin blood in madness ran,
> Her mouth foam'd, and the grass, therewith besprent,
> Wither'd at dew so sweet and virulent;
> Her eyes in torture fix'd, and anguish drear,
> Hot, glaz'd, and wide, with lid-lashes all sear,
> Flash'd phosphor and sharp sparks, without one cooling tear.
> The colours all inflam'd throughout her train,
> She writh'd about, convuls'd with scarlet pain:
> A deep volcanian yellow took the place
> Of all her milder-mooned body's grace;

> And, as the lava ravishes the mead,
> Spoilt all her silver mail, and golden brede;
> Made gloom of all her frecklings, streaks and bars,
> Eclips'd her crescents, and lick'd up her stars:
> So that, in moments few, she was undrest
> Of all her sapphires, greens, and amethyst,
> And rubious-argent: of all these bereft,
> Nothing but pain and ugliness were left.
> Still shone her crown; that vanish'd, also she
> Melted and disappear'd as suddenly;
> And in the air, her new voice luting soft,
> Cried, 'Lycius! gentle Lycius!'

He had shown his power of throwing a single atmosphere over *The Eve of St Agnes* and *The Eve of St Mark*, and he contrives here to give firmly the background of a Corinth, Elizabethan and romantic rather than Greek and classical in effect. He erects more pictures of normal life than the earlier narratives had allowed:

> Men, women, rich and poor, in the cool hours,
> Shuffled their sandals o'er the pavement white,
> Companion'd or alone; while many a light
> Flared here and there, from wealthy festivals,
> And threw their moving shadows on the walls,
> Or found them cluster'd in the corniced shade
> Of some arch'd temple door, or dusky colonnade.

While in contrast stand out in lavish splendour the descriptions of the banqueting hall in Part II:

> Of wealthy lustre was the banquet-room,
> Fill'd with pervading brilliance and perfume:
> Before each lucid pannel fuming stood
> A censer fed with myrrh and spiced wood,
> Each by a sacred tripod held aloft,
> Whose slender feet wide-swerv'd upon the soft
> Wool-woofed carpets: fifty wreaths of smoke
> From fifty censers their light voyage took
> To the high roof, still mimick'd as they rose
> Along the mirror'd walls by twin-clouds odorous.
> Twelve sphered tables, by silk seats insphered,
> High as the level of a man's breast rear'd
> On libbard's paws, upheld the heavy gold
> Of cups and goblets, and the store thrice told
> Of Ceres' horn, and, in huge vessels, wine
> Come from the gloomy tun with merry shine.

Keats himself thought well of the poem, for, writing to George and Georgiana Keats in September 1819, he comments: 'I have been reading a part of a short poem I have composed lately call'd *Lamia*—and I am certain there is that sort of fire in it which must take hold of people in some way—give them either pleasant or unpleasant sensation.' It had this very quality which Keats notes, a liveliness, and a firmness in outline, which distinguish it from *Isabella* and *The Eve of St Agnes*. Yet strangely enough, here where his work seems to have been purged of some of the unfortunate phrasing of the earliest poems, he falls back more than once into the unabashed vulgarity of some of the pre-*Endymion* pieces. Suddenly, towards the end of Book I, he allows himself to write:

> There is not such a treat among them all,
> Haunters of cavern, lake, and waterfall,
> As a real woman.

It is as if a friend whose habits and speech one had admired suddenly gave way to a strain of mawkishness, which offended so much more because its presence had never been suspected. Yet in justice it must be allowed that these passages are few, and they occur only on the rare occasions when Keats seems momentarily to have lost touch with his theme.

Underlying the narrative lies a general suggestion akin to a moral, which some of Keats's critics have found distressing. Lamia, Keats has suggested, gathers within herself all that is beautiful, and is yet a serpent. To Lycius she is all beautiful: to the philosopher Apollonius, who sees with the cold eye of reason, she is all serpent. Once he speaks, beauty vanishes; Lamia disappears, and Lycius dies. How should the blame be proportioned? Keats does not leave the reader to draw his own conclusion, but sets it out himself, even before he has recounted the final action:

> What wreath for Lamia? What for Lycius?
> What for the sage, old Apollonius?
> Upon her aching forehead be there hung
> The leaves of willow and of adder's tongue;
> And for the youth, quick, let us strip for him
> The thyrsus, that his watching eyes may swim
> Into forgetfulness; and, for the sage,
> Let spear-grass and the spiteful thistle wage
> War on his temples. Do not all charms fly.
> At the mere touch of cold philosophy?
> There was an awful rainbow once in heaven:
> We know her woof, her texture; she is given
> In the dull catalogue of common things.
> Philosophy will clip an Angel's wings,
> Conquer all mysteries by rule and line,
> Empty the haunted air, and gnomed mine—
> Unweave a rainbow, as it erewhile made
> The tender-person'd Lamia melt into a shade.

What doubt can there be of Keats's intention once it is remembered that *Lamia* is the narrative companion of the odes?

C

Beauty, as met and encountered in the physical and material world, has its deceits, for all beauty has impermanence; its sequel is melancholy, and it is at times near to evil. The perception of beauty in the human form is surrounded by still greater treacheries. Even were he ignorant of this from his own experience, Keats could not have escaped the knowledge from his close reading of Shakespeare, particularly of *Troilus and Cressida*. But, as in the *Ode on Melancholy*, he would not maintain that for this motive should the experience be avoided. To live with reason alone would be, as it were, to see the truth of fact without the truth of the imagination, 'the dull catalogue of common things,' and not the rainbow.

One may not approve of the conclusion, and it is not all that Keats has to say on the matter, but that is clearly what he suggests in the poem. Further, there seems to haunt him in these months a vision of a certain fatality in passion, an element in physical beauty and its power of enthralment which is akin to evil but inevitable. Already, in *The Eve of St Agnes*, he had written the lines:

> He play'd an ancient ditty, long since mute,
> In Provence call'd, 'La belle dame sans mercy.'

And in April 1819, five months before he began *Lamia*, he composed on this title the most memorable of all his short poems: *La Belle Dame sans Merci*. This lyric, written with a subtle variation of the ballad metre contrived by shortening the fourth line, was published by Leigh Hunt in *The Indicator* for May 1820. The published version varies from the copy which Keats wrote out in his journal letter to George and Georgiana Keats under the date of April 1819. This original version, more finished in some of its details than the published version, opens with the following stanzas:

> O what can ail thee Knight at arms
>   Alone and palely loitering?
> The sedge has withered from the Lake
>   And no birds sing!
>
> O what can ail thee Knight at arms
>   So haggard, and so woe begone?
> The Squirrel's granary is full
>   And the harvest 's done.
>
> I see a lily on thy brow
>   With anguish moist and fever dew,
> And on thy cheeks a fading rose
>   Fast withereth too—

I met a Lady in the Meads
    Full beautiful, a faery's child
Her hair was long, her foot was light
    And her eyes were wild—

I made a Garland for her head,
    And bracelets too, and fragrant Zone
She look'd at me as she did love
    And made sweet moan.

This lyric is the most miraculous piece in all Keats's work. All the elements which at times disfigure his other poems are eliminated, while suggestions of the medieval world, its chivalry, and mystery, are captured with indefinite variety. He, who knew little of the Middle Ages, had entered into the world of imaginative suggestion which they yielded for romantic poetry. This he had achieved without a guide: Coleridge had indicated the general direction, but not the definite path, nor was there much assistance from the precise source from which he had gained the title to the poem. Leigh Hunt, in a prefatory note in *The Indicator*, states that the poem was suggested by the title *La Belle Dame sans Mercie* of a poem once believed to have been Chaucer's translation of verses by Alain Chartier, a poet of the Court of Charles II of France. If so, it was the title alone that helped him, for the poem, which he had probably read in Chalmers's *English Poets*, among the pieces 'imputed to Chaucer,' could yield nothing profitable. His mind may have been set working by a note in Chalmers that 'M. Aleyn, secretary to the King of France, framed this dialogue between a gentleman and gentlewoman, who finding no mercy at her hand, dieth of sorrow.' Such a phrase would attract him, for already, in the odes and in *Lamia*, he had come to see that Love was not the unending joy of his own early verses, but a pleasure wrought around with pain. More directly than in the odes he symbolized his own unappeased passion for Fanny Brawne, and if Fanny stands at one side of his imagination the Venus of Tannhäuser watches over the other. Did he know the great legend that lay behind his theme, or had he stumbled on it by some happy combination of intuition and personal experience? He had come, half unconsciously one suspects, to image forth not only the world of medieval Romanticism, but, more precisely, the theme of love's fatality so frequently explored by English and French decadent poets in the nineteenth century. Here with less acridity is the situation of *Laus Veneris*, nor could Keats's poem have been absent from Swinburne's mind.

As Dr Mario Praz has indicated in *The Romantic Agony*, Keats implies in this lyric, as in *Lamia* and in the *Ode on Melancholy*, some of the themes which are defined later with conscious satanic power by Baudelaire and Swinburne.

Chapter 6

Hyperion and *The Fall of Hyperion*—The sonnets—Keats's imagery.

THE theme of *Hyperion* seems to have been present in Keats's mind before the completion of *Endymion*, when under Haydon's influence he was still seeking a large subject for a narrative poem. Already, in January 1818, in writing to Haydon on a project for illustrating the poem, he speaks of its design:

'In *Endymion* I think you may have many bits of the deep and sentimental cast—the nature of *Hyperion* will lead me to treat it in a more naked Grecian Manner.' The poem had not then reached the stage of composition, but it was present in his mind. To the end of 1819, as long as he could work at making verses at all, the theme was with him, and months later when, in August 1820, he wrote to Fanny Brawne that, 'the last two years taste like brass upon my Palate,' it was with a phrase adapted out of *Hyperion* that he was describing his condition. From this long occupation with the theme two pieces remain: *Hyperion, A Fragment* and *The Fall of Hyperion, A Vision*. *Hyperion, A Fragment* was published in the volume of 1920, with the prefatory note, that it was 'an unfinished poem,' printed at the publisher's request and 'contrary to the wishes of the author.' The publisher's advertisement stated: 'The poem was intended to have been of equal length with *Endymion*, but the reception given to that work discouraged the author from proceeding.' Whatever may be truth about *Hyperion*, this publisher's statement is obviously false. Keats himself scrawled through the note in one copy and wrote: 'I had no part in this: I was ill at the time,' and more particularly against the comment on *Endymion* he wrote: 'This is a lie.' In a letter to Reynolds of 22nd September 1819, he states his own reason for abandoning the poem: 'I have given up Hyperion—there were too many Miltonic inversions in it—Miltonic verse cannot be written but in an artful or rather artist's humour.' He states the same opinion more forcibly in his journal letter of the same month: 'Life to him would be death to me. I wish to devote myself to another sensation.' But, while dissatisfied with *Hyperion, A Fragment*, he did not abandon the theme, nor even blank verse as a medium, and during the summer and early autumn of 1819 he worked at an attempt to rewrite the poem in the form of a vision, and this second version was published by Lord Houghton in 1856. Lord Houghton thought that *The Fall of Hyperion, A Vision* was the first draft of the poem, but Colvin showed, to the satisfaction of all except Miss Amy Lowell, that it must be Keats's attempt to recast the poem.

Hyperion, A Fragment and *The Fall of Hyperion, A Vision* have caused more critical disturbance than any of Keats's other poems. Any approach to them must allow that they are crucial in the study of his work. Here I express my own view, which, I hope, is not discordant with the facts, and has as little superstructure of theory as the circumstances will allow. The published poem *Hyperion, A Fragment* seems to me a complete poem. Nothing could be added to it, and, if it had been continued, any addition could only have weakened the effect already made. True, in the edition of 1820 the poem ends in the middle of a line:

> Apollo shriek'd;—and lo! from all his limbs
> Celestial * * * * * * * * * * * * *

But, if the Woodhouse transcript has any authority, the poem ended:

> Apollo shriek'd;—and lo! from all his limbs
> Celestial Glory dawn'd, he was a god.

When the theme first came to him he may well have conceived an epic companion to *Endymion*, but on coming to work at the material he found that it would not bear such treatment. This contrast between the conception he had of the poem and the poem which the material actually allowed accounts in part for his delays and hesitations in its composition. Nor was this all, for *Hyperion* was not to be mere narrative, but, as with *Endymion*, the shadow of an allegorical meaning was to lie over it. While *Endymion* was to reveal the progress of Keats's own mind, *Hyperion* more ambitiously was to figure forth the progress of the world itself. One may not now (1934) be enamoured of this idea of progress, but Keats, like Shelley, obviously was. 'The old order changeth, yielding place to new'—such was Keats's underlying thought, with the suggestion that the new order was inevitably better than the old. Yet a great creative work can transcend the body of political or philosophical thought to which it owes its original impetus. Shelley's *Prometheus Unbound* is Godwinian perfectibility and Platonic idealism if judged by the intellect alone. Similarly, *Hyperion* reduced in the same way has nothing fresh to add to the treacherous belief in the inevitable 'march of progress.' To judge thus is of course to see *Hyperion* and *Prometheus Unbound* merely as contributions to thought, irrespective of their form, and it is in their form that their power lies. For *Hyperion*, like *Prometheus Unbound*, transmutes theory into a poetical reality, a piece of experience. It departs from the radical commonplaces from which it arose, and so transforms them by the power of poetry that they can affect as an imaginative experience minds which would have remained unmoved or antagonized by the theory as set down in simple prose.

The speech of Oceanus in Book II gives the clue to Keats's whole intention. The Titans are in council: Saturn is with them, soon to be joined by Hyperion. They dispute whether they shall arouse themselves to oppose the new order of gods, or realize that their fall is inevitable. Oceanus realizes that the new must overcome the old, and Keats, without attempting to disguise his sympathies, pours his own mind into the speech with which Oceanus addresses Saturn:

> . . . it cannot be:
> Thou art not the beginning nor the end.
> From chaos and parental darkness came
> Light, the first fruits of that intestine broil,
> That sullen ferment, which for wondrous ends
> Was ripening in itself. The ripe hour came,
> And with it light, and light, engendering
> Upon its own producer, forthwith touch'd
> The whole enormous matter into life.
> Upon that very hour, our parentage,
> The Heavens and the Earth, were manifest:
> Then thou first-born, and we the giant-race,
> Found ourselves ruling new and beauteous realms.
> Now comes the pain of truth, to whom 'tis pain;
> O folly! for to bear all naked truths,
> And to envisage circumstance, all calm,
> That is the top of sovereignty. Mark well!
> As Heaven and Earth are fairer, fairer far
> Than Chaos and blank Darkness, though once chiefs;
> And as we show beyond that Heaven and Earth
> In form and shape compact and beautiful,
> In will, in action free, companionship,
> And thousand other signs of purer life;
> So on our heels a fresh perfection treads,
> A power more strong in beauty, born of us
> And fated to excel us, as we pass
> In glory that old Darkness: nor are we
> Thereby more conquer'd, than by us the rule
> Of shapeless Chaos.

And there follows the idyllic speech of Clymene in which the irresistible glory and beauty of Apollo, the new god, are described.

Keats's relationship to the theme of *Hyperion* has been aptly summarized by W. P. Ker in a note which has been unduly neglected.

Might it not be said that the story was left as it is because it is complete? It is the story of Progress; of an Idea with which the mind of Keats was possessed. He is one of the believers in 'the march of intellect.' The earliest quotation in the *New English Dictionary* for that phrase is 1827. Keats, in the wonderful letter of 3rd May 1818, speaks of 'the general and gregarious advance of intellect,' and says, 'there is really a grand march of intellect'— some years before the Idea became hackneyed into a motto for mechanics' institutes and Macaulay on Bacon. Keats was quite clear in prose about the successive periods in the quest for truth and beauty; this is the argument of *Hyperion*. The argument is such that it cannot be continued, epically, beyond the place where Keats leaves it. How was he to declare the beauty of the Olympians? He had declared it already in the speech of Oceanus; but to represent Apollo in his glory meant nothing less than a miracle; an increase of radiance, such as Dante describes in the *Paradiso*, something brighter than the visible sun itself. When Keats had given his best, and he had given no less, to Saturn and the older dynasty, what more could he give to Apollo?

Keats felt that he could give no more, and he set aside the poem that had troubled him so long, but the attempt to find a new direction in verse, and to find it through the story of Hyperion, still pursued him. Recalling memories of Dante, whom he had read during the Scottish tour, he attempted to retell Hyperion's story as a vision in *The Fall of Hyperion*, emphasizing the allegory, and employing Moneta, a sole survivor of the race of Titans, as his guide. The fragment of *The Fall of Hyperion* that remains has two distinct parts. In the first he attempts to state his attitude to verse; in the second he begins to rework the earlier Hyperion poem into the visionary form. Of these the former is by far the more significant. Some critics have found in it the deepest expression of Keats's genius. He seeks to set aside the unreal world in which he felt much of his own poetry had dwelt:

> The poet and the dreamer are distinct,
> Diverse, sheer opposite, antipodes.
> The one pours out a balm upon the world,
> The other vexes it.

He sees that the poet must break away from the isolated contemplation of his own personality to identify himself with the world:

> Thou art a dreaming thing,
> A fever of thyself; think of the earth.

Out of that identity with the world the poet must develop a
universal sympathy, and employ his art in relation to it:

> None can usurp this height, returned that shade,
> But those to whom the miseries of the world
> Are misery, and will not let them rest.
> All else who find a haven in the world,
> Where they may thoughtless sleep away their days,
> If by a chance into this fane they come,
> Rot on the pavement where thou rotted'st half.

Keats, it is true, had never expressed in verse form this aspect of
his belief of what the function of poetry should be, though there
are suggestions of it in *I stood tip-toe*, but in his letters the whole
content of these passages can be found set out, in the letter of
Reynolds of 3rd May 1818, and in other letters of that period.
There he had already realized the way down which he wished to
travel—towards the long poem, epical in range, philosophical in
intention, and imbued with the generous humanitarian side of the
radicalism of Leigh Hunt. But an artist cannot go where his
intellect wishes him to go unless his intellect is in harmony with
his intuitions. Keats's critics, in admiring *The Fall of Hyperion,
A Vision*, have frequently confused what Keats wanted to do
and what he actually achieved. He has proceeded in this fragment no further than in the letters, and, while admiring his
tenacity, it would be unwise to extract grounds for believing
that we are watching the birth-throes of a philosophical poet.
It may be, but, on the other hand, the evidence of *The Eve of
St Agnes, Lamia*, and the odes shows how he could be called away
from the task presented by his intellect to the creations that his
whole capacity as a poet cried out for him to perform. As it is,
The Fall of Hyperion announces an intention which he might or
might not have fulfilled. The evidence that he might have succeeded can be found rather in *Hyperion, A Fragment*. For here,
more than anywhere else in English poetry, even more securely
than in *Prometheus Unbound*, which deals largely with the same
subject, the revolutionary idea of progress gains its fullest poetic
expression. Nor is the pattern of that idea so far removed,
though other values must be added, from the evolutionary conceptions which occupied the nineteenth century. Had Keats
lived, he might have been the epic poet of the nineteenth-century
world, and that world needed such a poet. But he did not live;
the poetry remained unwritten, and from what he had achieved
he gave leadership in the nineteenth century to the Romantic
poets, and even ultimately to the Decadents.

In considering Keats's work chronologically, the sonnets are apt to be neglected, yet, apart from Wordsworth, he is the major sonnet-writer of the Romantic period. Twenty-one sonnets appeared in the volume of 1817, and he had written twice that number more before his death. He had begun early with the sonnet, using the Petrarchian pattern studied in Milton and Wordsworth, but later he came to abandon this for the Shakespearian form. In both forms he had success; to recall some of the titles alone will show that: *Keen fitful gusts*; *To one who has been long in city pent*; the Chapman sonnet; *On a Picture of Leander*; *When I have fears that I may cease to be*. To these must be added the poem known for a long time as Keats's 'Last Sonnet.' It was believed that Keats had written the poem on his way to Italy in September 1820. The discovery of an earlier draft of 1819 has shown that the poem belongs rather to the period of the odes. Keats recopied the lines off Lulworth Cove because their mood seemed appropriate to that moment of his departure from England:

> Bright star! would I were steadfast as thou art—
>   Not in lone splendour hung aloft the night,
> And watching, with eternal lids apart,
>   Like Nature's patient, sleepless Eremite,
> The moving waters at their priestlike task
>   Of pure ablution round earth's human shores,
> Or gazing on the new soft fallen mask
>   Of snow upon the mountains and the moors—
> No—yet still steadfast, still unchangeable,
>   Pillow'd upon my fair love's ripening breast,
> To feel for ever its soft fall and swell,
>   Awake for ever in a sweet unrest,
> Still, still to hear her tender-taken breath,
> And so live ever—or else swoon to death.

His sonnets have an easy and unpretentious movement; he has avoided, on the one hand, the preciousness of conceit, and, on the other, the pedantic vacuity which marks so much mere sonneteering. He studied the form, adapted it to his purposes, and possibly allowed its verse pattern to help in the structure of his ode stanza.

The study of Keats's mind in his poetry tends to obscure his power over imagery and epithet which gave him his closest affinity to Shakespeare. Robert Bridges, in a passage so excellent that it cannot well be surpassed, analysed the nature of this gift which Keats so eminently possessed.

I mean [he writes] the power of concentrating all the far-reaching resources of language on one point, so that a single and apparently effortless expression rejoices the aesthetic imagination at the moment

* C

when it is most expectant and exacting, and at the same time
astonishes the intellect with a new aspect of truth.

This mastery of phrase and imagery can be seen everywhere over
his poetry.   Sometimes it comes through in a single phrase:

> , to envisage circumstance, all calm
> That is the top of sovereignty.

Or in brief description:

> Mid hush'd, cool-rooted flowers;

or set in a fuller background:

> As in mid-day the sickening east-wind
> Shifts sudden to the south, the small warm rain
> Melts out the frozen incense from all flowers,
> And fills the air with so much pleasant health
> That even the dying man forgets his shroud.

Sometimes it is not imagery precisely considered, but a vast
picture, a Haydon landscape compressed into a few lines, as in
the close of the Chapman sonnet; or, equally, a picture of quiet
and silence, as in the lines at the opening of *Hyperion*, with their
unconscious recall of Donne:

> No stir of air was there,
> Not so much life as on a summer's day
> Robs not one light seed from the feather'd grass,
> But where the dead leaf fell, there did it rest.

Chapter 7—1820-1

The last months in England—The Italian journey—Rome—Death—and
after death.

THE record of Keats's verse for 1819 shows that he endured as
much in those months as any creative writer of his age has ever
done.   Behind this activity of the imagination there limped the
laggard steps of the routine of daily life.   He had spent the
spring and the early summer of 1819 at Hampstead.   At the end
of June he had gone to Shanklin to stay with James Rice, an
invalid and one of his kindliest friends.   He and Rice were
sufficiently ill and dispirited to depress each other; but the arrival
of Charles Brown, with his buoyant good-humour, stirred Keats's
mind, and the collaboration with Brown on *Otho the Great* was
begun.   From Shanklin he writes the earliest of his letters to
Fanny Brawne, which have already been considered.   In August,
still with Brown as his companion, he had moved to Winchester,

and there he had stayed until October. Wherever he was, and
however deeply his imagination was moved, three demons per-
petually pursued him: the knowledge of his own ill health; the
devilment of financial embarrassment; and, strengthened by
these, the distress of his passion for Fanny Brawne. To his own
money difficulties he had to add Haydon's requests for loans,
urged with all the effrontery of one who has lived on borrowing.
In Kentucky, George was in difficulties. A certain Mr Audubon
had persuaded him to take shares in a Mississippi river-boat; it
might have proved a profitable venture had not the boat been
already at the bottom of the Mississippi River when George paid
for his shares. George, as is the nature of relations abroad,
looked towards home for help. He hoped that Keats could raise
funds either from his own slender supply or by negotiating with
Mr Abbey for money from the family trust. In 1819, alone in
Winchester after Brown's departure, Keats tried to see a way
through his difficulties, and he wrote to George a long, admirable
letter describing his own lack of funds, estimating what help he
could give, and suggesting ever so gently that perhaps George was
not quite astute enough to deal with the business men of Kentucky: 'In truth I do not believe you fit to deal with the world or
at least the American world. But good God—who can avoid
these chances? You have done your best. Take matters as
coolly as you can and confidently expecting help from England
act as if no help was nigh.' To help George some money-making
activity was essential, and in October 1819 he came up to London,
to College Street, Westminster, where from two 'cheap and quiet'
rooms he 'hoped to work his way with the rest.' His intentions
are not completely clear, but it is obvious that he was prepared
to undertake routine work in the reviews, essays, dramatic
criticism, and journalism. He probably came to London with
the fixed resolution that he would not see Fanny Brawne, but he
saw her and was completely overcome: 'I shall be able to do
nothing. I should like to cast the die for Love or death. I have
no patience with anything else.' With a certain sense of fatality,
as if pained that it was thus that things should be, he made his
act of surrender and went to live with Brown at Wentworth
Place, next door to Fanny Brawne.

Of what happened during the next months but few records
exist: he struggled still with the revision of *Hyperion*, and spent
mornings on that strange production *Cap and Bells*; also the 1820
volume of verses had to be prepared for the press. But in the
main this was the period so dominated by Fanny Brawne that

consistent work was impossible. In January 1820, George Keats was in England, attempting to improve his financial situation. There seems some absence of the earlier intimacies in this encounter of the two brothers. George was busy going here and there as his affairs called him, and Keats himself had formed deep attachments that loosened the earlier close union of the brothers. Further, Keats may have felt half consciously that his brother was calling too easily on his slender resources to cover his errors in American speculation. The outstanding result of the encounter is Keats's charming journal-letter of January 1820 to his sister-in-law in Kentucky, the last of his letters to show those qualities of sympathy, good humour, and adroitness, which mark all the best of his correspondence. On 28th January, George began his return journey by the Liverpool coach, and six days later came the first crisis of Keats's malady, and he knew that he had not long to live.

On the night of 3rd February 1820 he had travelled from London to Hampstead, and Brown's narrative may be accepted as an account of what happened:

At eleven o'clock, he came into the house in a state that looked like fierce intoxication. Such a state in him, I knew, was impossible; it therefore was the more fearful. I asked hurriedly, 'What is the matter? You are fevered?' 'Yes, yes,' he answered, 'I was on the outside of the stage this bitter day till I was severely chilled,—but now I don't feel it. Fevered—of course a little.' He mildly and instantly yielded, a property in his nature towards any friend, to my request that he should go to bed. I entered his chamber as he leapt into bed. On entering the cold sheets, before his head was on the pillow, he slightly coughed, and I heard him say,—'That is blood from my mouth.' I went towards him; he was examining a single drop of blood upon the sheet. 'Bring me the candle, Brown, and let me see this blood.' After regarding it steadfastly he looked up in my face with a calmness of countenance that I can never forget, and said—'I know the colour of that blood;—it is arterial blood;—I cannot be deceived in that colour;—that drop of blood is my death-warrant. I must die.'

And the next morning he wrote a pathetic little note to Fanny Brawne, to be delivered to the house next door, begging her to come and see him.

At the end of March he was allowed to move about again, but the improvement did not last. His situation was made more difficult since Brown was letting Wentworth Place, and a lodging had to be sought elsewhere. He found rooms in Kentish Town, only to discover that he was too ill to be alone. At this moment Leigh Hunt re-entered Keats's life, and, with that warm kindliness which was his most genial characteristic, he took him to his home in Mortimer Terrace, and there he remained until the middle of August 1820.

In July 1820 his poems *Lamia, Isabella and Other Poems* were published, and, when Keats was too ill any longer to care, his verse gained some recognition from the critics: a generous notice from Lamb, adulation with some adroit criticism from Leigh Hunt in *The Indicator*, and encouragement from some of the more powerful magazines, including *The British Critic*, which had joined in the onslaught on *Endymion*. *Blackwood's* remained silent, but later, in an article on Shelley's *Prometheus Unbound*, Keats is mentioned with an air of tolerant condescension, while the suggestion was let loose that his ill health was largely due 'to the critical castigation his *Endymion* drew down on him.' Most significant of all in this growing acceptance of Keats was Jeffrey's article in the *Edinburgh Review*. Jeffrey had chosen to be silent on the publication of *Endymion*, but now, with the *Lamia* volume before him, he had the courage to speak out for the earlier poem, and, while condemning its excesses, he is prepared to make an appreciation of its 'beauties' a criterion of critical sensibility. If only this had come sooner. As it was, Keats refers to the volume only once or twice in his letters, and then almost casually: 'My book has had good success among the literary people and I believe has a moderate sale.' He could extract no pleasure from literary success, for, with his medical knowledge, he knew that he was to die soon, and even when the doctors thought that there was little the matter with him, and that he would recover, he wrote that he could not believe them 'until the weight and tightness of my chest is mitigated.'

In the summer of 1820 his mind became dominated by his disease, and with the realization that he would lose Fanny Brawne. His letters turn from the outpourings of passion to pathetic confessions of ill health and despair, mingled with recriminations, withdrawn no sooner than made. The Fanny Brawne letters for these months are the most distressing that Keats wrote: disease was increasing his agitation and driving him to a petulance that was not previously apparent. In July he accused Fanny Brawne of 'flirting with Brown,' and, in a passage which 'begets a storm of passion,' he writes:

Brown is a good sort of Man—he did not know he was doing me to death by inches. I feel the effect of every one of those hours in my side now; and for that cause, though he has done me many services, though I know his love and friendship for me, though at this moment I should be without pence were it not for his assistance, I will never see, or speak to him until we are both old men if we are to be.'

A month later he is writing to Brown a friendly letter, and adding: 'You must think of my faults as lightly as you can.' Later, in the middle of August, he flung himself out of Leigh Hunt's house, because a discharged servant had kept back one of Fanny Brawne's letters. Yet in this last phase Hunt had treated Keats with great kindness, even if the care his household supplied was only a combination of muddle with geniality. Once again, in a calmer moment, Keats recognized that he was wrong, and he wrote that Hunt had behaved very kindly to him.

From Leigh Hunt he went back to Hampstead to the house of Mrs Brawne, and there, worn out, he allowed both the mother and the daughter to care for him. It had become obvious that another winter in England would prove fatal, and an Italian journey was suggested. Keats obviously detested the scheme. He was leaving Fanny Brawne with a premonition that he would not return. He knew that he was going away to die as 'a soldier marches up to a battery.' Further, he knew that he had not the funds necessary for the journey, though this difficulty his friends soon overcame. John Taylor, his publisher, who always treated him with extraordinary kindness, gave generous help, and a fund was started which provided all the money that was immediately necessary. Unfortunately, Charles Brown was away in the Highlands during these months, for, had he been in London, he would have been Keats's natural companion for the voyage. As it was, Joseph Severn, the painter, accompanied him, and in September they set sail in the *Maria Crowther* for Naples.

The last phase of Keats's life has to be seen through Severn's accounts, and no source could be more deceptive. Severn was a painter, ambitious, not over-sensitive, and sufficiently young to regard his own personality as the universe's centre. The journey to Italy marked for him a fresh opportunity in his career. He was leaving a difficult home-life for an experience that promised novelty, adventure, coloured and quickly changing scenes, and all manner of minor excitements. He was kindly to Keats, and before the end, in Rome, he was to have a difficult time, but he had a centre of complacency, a belief that his view of the world must be that of everybody else. He mistook Keats's pathetic semblance of good spirits, paraded with difficulty, for genuine enjoyment. Yet even Severn could not suggest that the voyage could be less than a torment to a man in Keats's condition. Thirty-four days were occupied in the journey to Naples: the food was wretched, the cabins fœtid, and there was another consumptive on board: in the Channel there had been storms and endless delays, followed by a gale for three days in the Bay of Biscay. Small wonder that Keats was ill and worn out when they landed.

For Severn the discomfitures of the voyage were soon forgotten in the pageant of delights which Naples presented; the

scores of Neapolitan boats with gorgeous heaps of autumnal fruits —grapes, peaches, figs, melons, and many other kinds I had never before seen, all in such abundance that it seemed as though we had arrived at the Enchanted Island—an illusion heightened by the endless array of picturesque skiffs and shallops, with sweet stirring music coming from many of them, the tinkling of the guitars mingling with happy laughter and innumerable shouts, cries and exclamations of all kinds. Perhaps the novelty alone was an irresistible charm and made our haven seem, to me at least, as though it were the shore of Paradise.

In other circumstances Keats would have shared Severn's delight, just as once he had shared the luck of the road with Brown. But now he could no longer share anything. In pathetic contrast to Severn's enthusiasm there stands Keats's brief comment: 'I cannot say a word of Naples, I do not feel at all concerned in the thousand novelties around me.' It was not ill health alone that affected him, but the feeling that he would never see Fanny Brawne again. From Naples he writes to Charles Brown:

I can bear to die—I cannot bear to leave her. O God! God! God! Everything I have in my trunks that reminds me of her goes through me like a spear. The silk lining she put in my travelling cap scalds my head. My imagination is horribly vivid about her—I see her—I hear her.'

He had longed to be left in England to die, but instead there was this living death of the Italian journey, and with no purpose but to keep himself posthumously alive for a little while longer. He had come because all friendly voices had urged him to come, but he knew now after all he had suffered that they were wrong.

For one moment in a Neapolitan theatre his old radical ardour flared up. The sight of armed sentries on the stage of the San Carlo Theatre led him so to despise 'the debasement of the Neapolitan character' that he determined to make without delay for Rome. They travelled in a small carriage over bad roads, and rested in uncomfortable inns, and even the beauty of the country which stirred Severn left Keats listless and unmoved. In the middle of November 1820 they entered Rome by the Lateran Gate, and went to a lodging, by the Piazza di Spagna, found for them by Dr Clark, to whom Keats had had a letter of

introduction. Once he was settled and comparatively independent, Keats urged Severn to go out and seek introductions that
would help his profession and generally to occupy himself more
as a painter than a nurse. He seemed better than he had been
since he left England; he could walk and even ride a little. But
in a letter from Rome to Charles Brown one sees half expressed
the wish that he might have been left to die in England: 'I have
an habitual feeling of my real life having passed, and that I am
leading a posthumous existence.' For five weeks the routine
of his life remained normal, but he had the persistent sense that
he was waiting the coming of some crisis. On 10th December
1820, it came, a haemorrhage, and then another, until he begged
Severn for laudanum. The weeks that followed were the worst
of all; and Severn, even if he had been self-centred earlier, became
now ungrudgingly devoted. The situation was difficult: Severn
had no knowledge of Italian, and the authorities had informed
him that if a death occurred the furniture and all his possessions
would be burnt. What could be done he did. Through January
and February he watched over Keats, day by day, without assistance, and, apart from nursing, he had to dust, and sweep, and
prepare the dry toast and water, which the medical authorities
of the time prescribed for consumptives. Also he found time to
write to friends at home, and his story, set down both then and
later, remains on record. Of the sick man's account of his suffer-
ing no record remains. Severn suggests that he did not complain,
but all that he endured comes through in his final words to Severn,
spoken on 23rd February 1821, when he knew that he was dying:
'Severn—I—lift me up—I am dying—I shall die easy;—don't be
frightened—be firm, and thank God it has come.' Severn lifted
him up in his arms. 'The phlegm seemed boiling in his throat,'
and so he lived on for seven hours more, and then gradually he
sank into death so quietly that Severn thought he slept.

Three days later he was buried in the Protestant cemetery in
Rome.

His reputation has had the strangest vicissitudes. As often
happens with the death of a man of genius who has been the centre
of his circle, there were numerous differences among his friends
after his death, and so no memoir was written. But, if his friends
held back, Shelley, who had been deeply moved by Keats's death,
stepped in, and at Pisa in July 1821 he issued *Adonais*. Despite
its magnificence as a threnody based on the model of Moschus, it
incorporates, quite innocently, an insidiously false impression
of Keats's personality. According to Shelley, this premature

death was to be ascribed to the savage attacks of the reviews
on a nature 'not less delicate and fragile than it was beautiful.'
Even after a century, with the whole evidence of Keats's life
and letters to weigh against it, this impression remains, and to
many he lingers in the imagination as

> A pale flower by some sad maiden cherished.

Byron, who had fumed and ranted against Keats as a 'tadpole
of the Lakes,' had been deeply impressed by *Hyperion*, and under
Shelley's influence he was moved to accept Keats's death as the
pathetic defeat of a sensitive and weak nature by hostile criticism.
Into Canto XI of *Don Juan* he flung a stanza half contemptuous
and yet with an under-current of pity:

> John Keats, who was killed off by one critique,
>   Just as he really promised something great,
> If not intelligible, without Greek
>   Contrived to talk about the gods of late,
> Much as they might have been supposed to speak.
>   Poor fellow! His was an untoward fate;
> 'Tis strange the mind, that very fiery particle,
> Should let itself be snuffed out by an article.

Byron thus helped Shelley to fix upon the early nineteenth
century an image of Keats as false as the image of Coleridge
which was prevalent in the same decades. After the reviews of
the 1820 volume there was little detailed criticism of his work.
Hazlitt in an article on Shelley's posthumous poems, in *The
Edinburgh Review* for July 1824, worked in a reference to Keats,
and once again continued the suggestion that he had been
hounded to death by criticism: 'The shaft was sped—venal,
vulgar, venomous, that drove him from his country with sickness
and penury for companions and followed him to the grave. And
yet there are those who could trample on the faded flower.'
Hazlitt is returning to the very language of Shelley's poem in
building up this same treacherous image of a beauty that is
pampered, effeminate, too weak for the work of the world, and
kept alive only with caresses. Each of these men had intended
to do Keats some service, and yet more effectively than the
bludgeoning reviews they had attached to him a reputation which
his whole life cries out to deny. The old hostility lingered on in
some places, and in the reviews, even to the middle of the century,
there can flare up an attack on 'apothecary' poetry and the
vulgarity of 'cockney' Romanticism.

Gradually in the universities there were found groups of young
men who read Keats's verses with enthusiasm. In Cambridge,

among his admirers were Arthur Hallam, Tennyson, and Monckton Milnes.   Tennyson studied Keats's use of colour and imagery, and for a time he fidgeted with Keats's ideas on the relation of experience to life, though in *The Lotus Eaters* and *The Vision of Sin* he was inclined to reduce them to moral didacticism set out on a romantic setting.   Richard Monckton Milnes (afterwards Lord Houghton) was from a social point of view the most distinguished member of the Cambridge group.   He became a figure in the political world, his contacts with men of letters varied from Swinburne to David Gray, and, as the most travelled and sociable of Victorians, he was equally at his ease in London, in Paris, or Rome, as in his own estate at Fryston.   Swinburne's biographers have discovered that Monckton Milnes's interests in literature were wider than was previously imagined, and that his library at Fryston contained one of the most notable collections of erotica in Europe.   Whatever were Monckton Milnes's sophistications, he had a genuine interest in letters, and after meeting Joseph Severn in Rome, and Charles Brown in Florence, he conceived, as early as 1834, the project of writing Keats's life.   A popular personality, on whom politics, society, and the arts can make equal claims, will complete an arduous literary task only with difficulty.   It is a tribute to Monckton Milnes that he saw the work through, though for Keats's reputation it is regrettable that its publication should have been delayed until 1848.   With this biography the life of Keats was for the first time disentangled from the rumour and misrepresentation that surrounded it, and set into something that approached a true perspective.   Further, Monckton Milnes's own reputation helped to carry Keats's name into quarters where previously it had been but little known, and he supplemented his biography with a selection of poems and a memoir in 1854.

In these same years, Keats's verses were fascinating the Pre-Raphaelite poets, who were to find in him a predecessor who seemed to them to have enunciated their own principles on art. D. G. Rossetti, as his letters to Buxton Forman show, had studied Keats's work in detail; *The Eve of St Mark* and *La Belle Dame sans Merci* in their use of coloured detail seemed to image that visionary medieval dream-world out of which much of Rossetti's poetry arose.   All Rossetti's associates admired Keats, and most of them were indebted to him; Holman Hunt and Millais used his poems as themes for pictures; William Morris confessed whole-hearted allegiance; on Swinburne his influence was profound, as can be seen now that M. Lafourcade has issued Swinburne's unpublished poem on the *Hyperion* theme. The Pre-Raphaelites, without any conscious intention of misrepresentation, were employing Keats as a symbol of their own theories of art, and out of his contemplation of Beauty they were developing a narrower image of their own.

Meanwhile, in the sixties, Matthew Arnold was bringing a new vitality in criticism into the reviews, and in his earlier essays he extended a generous tribute to Keats's work. In 1865 he used Keats as a basis of comparison with Maurice de Guérin, and in his *Study of Celtic Literature* he allows that Keats has a 'natural magic' in poetry, and finds in the *Ode on a Grecian Urn* both Greek and Celtic elements: 'it is composed with the eye on the object, a radiancy and light clearness being added.'

Then in 1878 came the publication by H. Buxton Forman of *The Letters of John Keats to Fanny Brawne.* Nothing proved a greater setback to Keats's developing reputation. The public was offended that the letters should have been published, and Keats's admirers were still more outraged that he should have written them. Matthew Arnold in his essay on Keats in 1880 is less appreciative than in his earlier references, and it is the Fanny Brawne letters that have led him to return to the formula of unmanliness and cockneyism in explaining Keats's nature, though he is prepared to concede a Shakespearian quality in the phrasing of the poems. Swinburne followed Arnold's example, and retracted his earlier admiration to complain that any one should 'snivel' in this way: the poet of *Laus Veneris* found himself distressed by Keats's expression of his passion, while his allegiance to Gautier and Baudelaire led him to find Keats's aestheticism too naïve, and an attachment to Mazzini drove him finally to find it too narrow. Yet Keats remained, an inspirer of this later Romanticism, and ultimately in Oscar Wilde one can see an admiration that does not stop short of plagiarism. Wilde in compensation composed one of his best sonnets on the theme of the sale by auction of Keats's love-letters.

Meanwhile, the sober study of his life and his work was developing. In 1880 Mrs Frances M. Owen had published a study of *Endymion* which while it emphasizes the allegorical element did at least assert the intelligibility of the poem. Seven years later, in 1887, Sir Sidney Colvin published his first life of Keats, and later, in 1917, after a life devoted to the study of the theme, he issued his standard biography. Of all Keats's critics, Sir Sidney Colvin has had the freshest mind, free from too zealous advocacy and, above all, without any preconceived view to enforce. With his work, the portrait of Keats's life is disabused of the falsities which supporters and enemies had both attached to it, while its detailed search for sources leaves little for later workers to recover. While Sir Sidney Colvin was preparing his biography, Dr Robert Bridges constructed the most notable study in English (1895) of Keats's poetry: he comes with the sensitiveness of a poet of classical allegiance to distinguish all the coloured and daring delights of a romantic verse. Above all, he emphasizes the poet in Keats, without, as some recent criticism would appear to do, making excessive claims for Keats, the philosopher. This trend, apparent in the studies of J. Middleton Murry and Clarence D. Thorpe, has produced illuminating critical work, but there lies the danger that in its pursuit the image of Keats may once again be falsified. For he of all writers is one whom it is difficult to consider dispassionately; the excesses of his verse, the untutored elements in his mind, the 'brave translunary' phrases, the drop into bathos, the wisdom of the letters, the outpourings to Fanny Brawne, the pathos of his disease, from one side to the other these sway us until we are of one party or the other. So it has ever been; he is over-idolized by Hunt, befouled by the reviews; he is turned into a beautiful weakling by Shelley, into a Pre-Raphaelite by Rossetti, and he appears as a decadent, a sort of English Baudelaire, to the later Romanticists, and now as a philosophical poet. Perhaps even beyond the tragedy of his brief existence, and almost apart from his verses, he comes for those who watch him to symbolize an attitude towards life, and one that changes even as the watchers change.

A NOTE ON BOOKS

THE standard life is Sir Sidney Colvin's *John Keats* (1920), and all other critical and biographical studies are indebted to his work. Miss Amy Lowell's gargantuan two-volume biography (1925) has been too much abused in this country: it has fresh material, and, despite verbiage, is frequently discerning. The standard edition of Keats's poems is E. de Selincourt's, which should be consulted in the fifth edition (1926). The letters have been collected by M. B. Forman in two volumes (1931). Considerable interest is still attached to *Life, Letters, and Literary Remains of John Keats* (1848), by Richard Monckton Milnes (Lord Houghton), for this was the first attempt at a biographical record.

Of critical work the following, quoted in chronological order, would seem to be the most significant: Frances Owen's *John Keats* (1880), with its attempt to explain *Endymion*; Robert Bridges's *John Keats* (1895), a most discriminating study of the poems; J. Middleton Murry's *Keats and Shakespeare* (1925), an imaginative attempt to trace Keats's development as a poet; Clarence D. Thorpe's *The Mind of J. Keats* (1926), which emphasizes the philosophical aspects of Keats's work; H. W. Garrod's *Keats* (1926), of particular interest for its study of Keats's sonnets; and J. Middleton Murry's *Studies in Keats* (1930).

Marlborough

BY MAURICE ASHLEY

Chronology

1650	26th May	Born
1667	14th September	Commission as Ensign
1672	March–May	At sea
1674		Fighting under Turenne in Flanders
1678		Marriage
1679–81		With James, Duke of York, in Brussels and Edinburgh
1685	5th July	Battle of Sedgemoor
1688	November	Glorious Revolution. Churchill at Salisbury
1689		Marlborough in Flanders under Waldeck
1690	September	Campaign in Ireland
1692	January	Dismissed from Army
1696	Summer	Fenwick case
1698	April	Marlborough restored to favour
1701	August	Conclusion of Grand Alliance
1702	February	Accession of Queen Anne
1704	2nd July	Battle of the Schellenberg
	13th August	Battle of Blenheim
1706	23rd May	Battle of Ramillies
1708	11th July	Battle of Oudenarde
1709	May	The Allied 'preliminaries'
	11th September	Battle of Malplaquet
1711	31st December	Marlborough dismissed
1712	November	Marlborough leaves England
1714	1st August	Death of Queen Anne. Marlborough returns
1722	5th June	Death of Marlborough

Dates of events in England are given in Old Style, of events in Europe in New Style; the difference between Old Style and New was ten days in the seventeenth century and eleven days in the eighteenth century.

Chapter I—*The Path to Fame : 1650-88*

Birth—Education—The Court of Charles II—Marriage—James's Servant —Battle of Sedgmoor—The Glorious Revolution.

JOHN CHURCHILL, first Duke of Marlborough, was the ablest soldier who ever commanded the British Army and the most talented general who ever served the British Crown. He was the least jealous and best beloved of commanders-in-chief. The strongest rebuke said to have been administered by him was a message through his secretary, 'my Lord Duke is surprised.' He never chided a servant or spoke harshly to an N.C.O. The soul of charm, grace, and courtesy, there were few who knew him intimately who did not yield to his spell. Yet there was dross among the gold. A first-rate soldier, he was a second-rate statesman. As a politician he was in the main simply an ambitious opportunist who could not bear to be out of office. Excelling chiefly in those diplomatic manœuvres which would advance himself or his army, he seldom, if ever, exerted his influence for the causes of peace or justice in which he was not directly concerned. His avarice and meanness made him a laughing-stock. He clung zealously to the trappings and emoluments that went with military power, even writing on occasion abject letters to his political opponents so as to ensure that he should in no circumstances lose his estates. In Lord Morley's phrase, he was an instance of that 'strange dualism in men which makes them . . . sometimes strong and sometimes weak.'

John Churchill was born at Ash House near the village of Musbury in Devonshire in the early hours of 26th May 1650. He barely survived the dangers of seventeenth-century childbirth. Out of twelve brothers and sisters only five lived beyond childhood. John himself was born a weakling and not expected to live, as is shown by his immediate baptism at Ash House on the day of his birth. His father, Winston Churchill, was a small landowner who fought on the Cavalier side in the Civil War. Twice fined for his royalism, he reared his family in decent obscurity during the Cromwellian era. But John Churchill's mother (a Drake distantly connected with Sir Francis's family) came of a Roundhead family, and it was in the security of his maternal grandmother's house that he was born.

The education which Winston Churchill provided for his eldest surviving son was brief but varied and useful. Winston himself instilled those principles of veneration for the institution of monarchy and the Protestant religion which his son never entirely forgot. Soon after the Restoration of King Charles II Winston was given a small appointment at Dublin. Thus John went for a time to the Dublin City Free School, but was afterwards transferred to St Paul's School in the City of London. He learned to write and spell well enough for practical purposes and acquired a smattering of Latin. But his wider education was to be obtained in service at the court of Charles II, where he picked up French, dabbled in astronomy, saw the plays of Shakespeare, and acquired all the graces of society life.

Meanwhile, his sister Arabella, who was two years his senior, had been making steady worldly progress. A plainish girl with nice legs, she had caught the roving eye of the king's only brother, James, Duke of York, afterwards King James II, and she combined the duties of Maid of Honour to the first Duchess of York with those of mistress to the duchess's husband. To her, clearly, John owed his appointment as page to James, Duke of York, which he obtained at about the age of sixteen, although Winston (now knighted) held the view that 'it is no great preferment to be a page.' However, there was the adolescent John Churchill, handsome, well-mannered, with an influential sister, ensconced in the highest circles of English society, and he used all his opportunities.

Three very different women played their parts in the life of John Churchill. First, Arabella. Then his distant kinswoman, the exotic Barbara Villiers, Duchess of Cleveland, first mistress *en titre* to King Charles II, whose lover Churchill was to become. Finally, Sarah Jennings, a haughty and respectable but lovely Maid of Honour, who was to be Churchill's wife. For ten years, from the age of seventeen to twenty-seven, he mixed his sexual and military experiences in well-chosen proportions. In September 1667, he secured a commission as ensign and served at Tangier, then an English possession, and also aboard the fleet against the Mediterranean pirates. On his return to England, this graceful, engaging ensign with fair hair and blue eyes, now twenty-two years old, became the father to one of the Duchess of Cleveland's many offspring. By that time Charles II had tired of the lady and when he caught Churchill in her room he said—

at least so court scandal had it—'Go! You are a rascal, but I forgive you because you do it to get your bread.' Barbara was generous to her lovers and, with that monetary carefulness which Churchill was always to show, he invested £4,500 of the money that she bestowed on him in a form of life insurance.

Another interlude of soldiering now occurred. England was engaged in her third war against her trade and naval rivals, the Dutch, and Churchill's First Company of the Guards was aboard the fleet when it took part in the drawn naval battle of Sole Bay. For his share in the fighting, his patron, James, Duke of York, had him made a captain. In the following year (1673) Captain Churchill went as a volunteer with the Duke of Monmouth, Charles's favourite bastard, to the siege of the Dutch fortress of Maastricht, where he was wounded, saved Monmouth's life, met Louis XIV, the King of France, and generally distinguished himself. So considerable a mark did he make that, although England now withdrew from the war, he was summoned to Paris and appointed colonel in command of one of the English infantry regiments in French pay against the Dutch and their allies of the Holy Roman Empire, and fought under the famous French general, Turenne. The English Government was informed towards the end of the campaign that 'no one in the world could possibly have done better than Mr Churchill has done and M. de Turenne is very well pleased with all our nation.'

On his return to court, Churchill's amours became so notorious that they seemed likely to submerge his newly acquired military reputation. The reports of the French ambassador in England which reached Versailles in November 1676 told of how he had left Barbara Cleveland, 'after pillaging her of 100,000 livres,' and was seeking marriage with the pretty but quarrelsome sixteen-year-old Sarah Jennings. In spite of Turenne's tribute and Louis XIV's direct knowledge, the story was circulated that he was winning his way exclusively through feminine influence, and the French War Minister said nastily that his master did not want 'dishonourable and dishonoured carpet knights in his armies.' But John Churchill was indifferent now to offers of regiments. He fell in love as most men fall in love once only in their lives. If he did not at first seek marriage—as some of Sarah's notes to him suggest—he was soon impelled to do so. The girl's off-handedness and harsh treatment of her suitor and his parents' opposition heightened his desire. Somewhere and at some time about 1678 (exactly where or when is not known) Captain John Churchill and Sarah Jennings were married. The 'good fairy' at their marriage, in Mr Churchill's words, was Sarah's mistress, Mary of Modena, second wife of James, Duke of York. Ten years later—such are the exigencies of political life—we shall see John and Sarah egging on Mary of Modena's step-daughter to blackguard the character and morals of this 'good fairy' of their wedding day.

The married life of the Churchills opened in what was for persons of their class and ambitions a condition of comparative poverty. John had to manage on the rather variable perquisites of a Colonel of Foot, a commission which he was allowed to purchase in February 1678, and on his salary as Gentleman of the Bedchamber, and later Master of the Wardrobe to James, Duke of York. To maintain their place in high society without private means demanded the most rigid economy. At first the ambitious young couple could afford no home of their own, and Sarah was packed off to live with her parents-in-law in the country. Sarah promptly quarrelled with her mother-in-law, as she had previously quarrelled with her own mother, and ultimately John took a house in Jermyn Street, London, where he had had his bachelor lodgings.

There is no doubt that it was in these years of scraping and straitened circumstances that Churchill acquired those habits of 'meanness' and 'avarice' for which he was famous throughout his life. The need to earn an adequate income bound him to his master, the increasingly unpopular Duke of York. At first he had hopes of an active army career at a time when Charles II's foreign policy required France to be threatened with an Anglo-Dutch alliance. Churchill was sent over to concert arrangements with the Dutch prince, William of Orange, who had just married James's elder daughter, Mary. But the French and Dutch made peace, and for the next five years, at the height of James's unpopularity, Churchill had to act as glorified messenger boy and valet to one of the most hated men in England.

It had been known for some years that the heir presumptive to the English throne was an enthusiastic Roman Catholic, and his brother Charles II's efforts to decree toleration for members of that Church had roused the fears and jealousies of the Anglican Parliament. In 1678 a shady informer named Titus Oates had come forward with the story of a Popish plot which shook England from top to bottom. The House of Commons tried to secure the enactment of an Exclusion Bill, which would have prevented the Catholic James from succeeding to the throne, and Charles, though determined by hook or crook to save James's hereditary rights, thought it best that he should leave the country. In March 1679 Churchill had therefore to accompany him to his exile in Brussels.

During the years of exile Churchill made himself indispensable to James, but at the same time was clever enough neither to offend his master's opponents nor to cause his master to suspect his own loyalty. His earliest biographer states that Churchill was against Exclusion, 'and told me he thought it the highest act of injustice for any one to be set aside from his inheritance upon bare suppositions of intended evils.' Those who opposed Exclusion came to be known as Tories, and thus for the next twenty-five years Churchill ranked as a leading Tory. He went on missions to Charles II and to Louis XIV, asking them to exert their influence on James's behalf; but he also allowed himself to be pressed by his friends at court to keep James away from Whitehall. In 1680 and 1681 James's place of exile was shifted from Brussels to Edinburgh, where he was appointed Royal Commissioner and behaved with harshness and stupidity. Churchill was careful to let it be known that he did not approve of this conduct or of any idea of James acting independently of Whitehall, and even went so far as to write to a friend at court, after a vain attempt had been made to reconvert James to Protestantism, that, without this, 'sooner or later we must be all undone.' But, by tact or dissimulation, he retained the duke's confidence, and when in 1682 Charles finally outmanœuvred the Exclusionists or Whigs, as they were now called, James could return to London and Churchill could claim his rewards, a barony in the peerage of Scotland and the combined emoluments of two regiments.

For the last three years of King Charles II's reign no Parliament met, no war came, and James virtually governed the country. This was a period of profit and ease for the new Lord Churchill, who basked in favour at court. Dr Gilbert Burnet, afterwards Bishop of Salisbury, who was later to know the two Churchills intimately, wrote of him about this time:

He knew the arts of living in a Court beyond any man in it. He caressed all people with a soft and obliging deportment, and was always ready to do good offices. He had no fortune to set up on: this put him on all the methods of acquiring one. And that went so far into him, that he did not shake it off when he was in a much higher elevation: nor was his expense suited enough to his posts.

In 1683 a new accession of money, office, and influence came to the Churchill fortunes. His wife sought and obtained an appointment as Lady of the Bedchamber to Princess Anne, James's second daughter, when her marriage to Prince George of Denmark required her to set up a separate establishment, and later Sarah was promoted First Lady, with her salary doubled. Anne, like all the Stuarts, was passionately attached to favourites. She once wrote to Sarah warning her against another woman, and reminding her of 'what the song says—to be jealous is the fault of every tender lover.' Sarah retained Anne's affection for about twenty years, while Churchill came to share her valuable favour. During this period the Churchills enjoyed the blessing of healthy children, although their first child had died in infancy. John was always a devoted paterfamilias who delighted in sunning himself in his family mansions. But from domestic joys and sinecure duties he was compelled to turn when in February 1685 the opportunist Charles II died, and a Roman Catholic king ruled a Protestant realm.

As during the last seven years of Charles's reign, Churchill continued to be a foremost and trusted servant of King James II and to acquire offices and honours, which included an English peerage and the governorship of the Hudson's Bay Company; but at the same time he tactfully expressed his disagreement with the king's policy. James's intention was to stretch his prerogatives to the utmost to acquire equality, if not predominance, for his fellow religionists and to attain a position not dissimilar from that of the neighbouring autocrat, Louis XIV of France. But at first he half-hid his intentions. When he sent Lord Churchill to inform Louis of his accession to the throne, he cancelled his original orders to ask for a subsidy such as Louis had been accustomed to dole out to Charles II. At the outset of his reign James had a loyal Parliament and he promised to respect the rights of the Church of England .

Thus it was that when James's half-brother, the Duke of Monmouth, invaded England in the Protestant cause in June 1685 he chose a most unpropitious moment and few wealthy or influential men joined him. This western invasion afforded Churchill an opportunity for an independent display of his military gifts. In spite of his meagre experience, he was entrusted by James with the command of the troops sent to repel Monmouth's brave but poorly armed volunteer force in Somerset. Once Churchill came into contact with Monmouth, though with only a small body of cavalry, he never let go. He clung on to him, cutting off the stragglers, until Monmouth ventured on the desperate but not ill-considered course of a night attack on the

royal army as it lay encamped on the field of Sedgmoor (5th July).
As soon as Churchill heard of the surprise, he came hastily on the
scene, reinforced the Royalist flank where it was weakest, and at
dawn organized a successful attack which captured the enemy's
artillery. To him was due the main credit for the victory; but
before the battle he had been superseded in the nominal command by a naturalized Frenchman, Lord Feversham. Churchill
was resentful. This personal factor further alienated him from
James II.

The easy suppression of the rebellion encouraged the obstinate
James on the most autocratic courses. But he first had the
rebels viciously punished, to the open displeasure of Churchill.
James used the rebellion as an excuse to build a large standing
army, which he filled with Roman Catholic officers and encamped
on Hounslow Heath to overawe London. He introduced a new
ecclesiastical court to act as a curb on the Church of England.
He forced Roman Catholics into office everywhere, even into
positions from which they had been specifically excluded by
Act of Parliament. A secret Protestant opposition was gradually
created in which Whigs joined with Tories and entered into
treasonable correspondence with James's son-in-law, William of
Orange. Churchill, a sincere Protestant, resisted the pressure
brought upon all court dignitaries to enter the Roman Catholic
Church and seems to have told James that he disapproved of
what he was doing. But he did not resign his offices, and instead
successfully used his wife's and his own growing influence with
James's fervently Anglican daughter Anne to carry her over to
the opposition camp. Churchill himself assured William that he
was resolved, 'although I cannot live the life of a saint, if there
ever be occasion for it, to show the resolution of a martyr.' In
the summer of 1688 an unexpected blow fell upon this secret
opposition: Mary of Modena bore James a male heir. Hitherto
the hope had prevailed that James's early death and the accession of the Protestant Mary of Orange would put a speedy end
to the Catholicizing policy; now its infinite continuance was
promised. Sarah, Anne, and the rest hastened to spread the
false story that the birth was an imposture, and under the
Churchills' influence Anne wrote a series of nauseating letters to
her sister to that effect. The conspirators then invited William
to cross the sea and save England and her Church from James
and his infant. Churchill, a little later, wrote independently,
putting his honour in William's hands and again asserting that
he was ready to die for his religion.

In November William landed in Tor Bay with a large army and Churchill prepared to go over to him. He first arranged for Sarah and Anne to join William at an appropriate moment, while his brother George, who was in the Navy, was to help carry over the fleet. His own job was to neutralize and, if possible, enlist the army in the cause of revolution. James, betrayed on all sides, still trusted this man who had been his page and servant and appointed him lieutenant-general, taking him to Salisbury to confront William's motley Protestant horde. Churchill first tried to kidnap the king and take him to William. This move, which might have prevented war, is vouched for not only by contemporary Royalist authorities, but also by the French ambassador who was with James and Churchill at Salisbury. Churchill must have realized that if it came to a clash between James at the head of the English Army and a foreign army officered by Dutchmen—who had been England's enemies for a generation—the rebellion would be defeated. There was a significant pointer to the army's attitude, when another traitor officer, Lord Cornbury, tried to lead some troops across the lines and they refused to follow him. It is all the more surprising therefore that at this critical moment, at a council of war, Churchill should have urged James to fight. This advice—which could only have been given because Churchill knew that it would not be followed—was the very depth of double dealing. But James refused to advance and thereby sealed his fate. Princess Anne joined William safely, and, thanks in part to the plotting of the Churchills, a bloodless revolution was effected.

Churchill's part in the revolution was deliberately unscrupulous. As a Protestant he disliked James's measures; as a man of unsatisfied ambitions he had his grievances. But he would not burn his boats until he must. It was against his nature to resign his commissions or to commit himself irretrievably by joining the exiles in Holland, for then he could not have righted himself with the king if things went wrong. He did make an attempt to compromise between personal interest and abhorrence of James's policy by seeking command of an English regiment abroad, but what he would never do was to exclude himself from the thick of events.

Chapter 2—Rewards and Punishments: 1689-1702

Command in Flanders and Ireland—Opposition to William III—The Fenwick Affair—Reconciliation and Promotion—The Grand Alliance.

CHURCHILL tactfully refrained from voting for the establishment of a regency when the throne was declared 'vacant,' and this Tory project, to which William was adamantly opposed, was defeated by two votes in the House of Lords. The Churchills' influence was exerted to persuade Anne to waive her hereditary right to the immediate succession in order that William might remain king even should his wife, Anne's elder sister, predecease him. Churchill was rewarded by being created an earl with the title of Marlborough, by being made a member of the Privy Council and one of the nine Lords Justices who governed England in William's absence, and by being confirmed in his lieutenant-generalship. But he did not regard these honours as sufficient; he hankered after the lucrative post of Master-General of the Ordnance and a supreme command. He resented the fact that William gave the command of his army in Flanders to a man of sixty-nine and of his army in Ireland to one of eighty. The truth was that, largely because of Marlborough's power over Princess Anne, the new monarchs never had full confidence in him; William thought him 'very assuming' and Mary told her husband: 'I can never either trust or esteem him.' In due course Marlborough was to reciprocate by stirring up opposition to William in the Army. But first he showed his military worth in Flanders and Ireland.

William had come to England, not out of any altruistic regard for English liberties, but to make certain of her participation in the coming war against Louis XIV. He laboured to build a Grand Alliance against the French King, who had declared war on Holland as the Dutch ruler was on his way to England. Thus, immediately after the Revolution of 1688, England and Holland went to war with France. In the summer of 1689 Marlborough distinguished himself at the battle of Walcourt in Flanders, where he headed the Household Cavalry in a counter-attack on the French. Meanwhile, James II, with French and Irish troops, had been defeated at the battle of the Boyne in Ireland, and Marlborough, on his own initiative, volunteered to cap this success by capturing the towns of Cork and Kinsale in the six

D

weeks which remained of the campaigning season of 1690. Co-operating closely with the fleet, he accomplished in twenty-three days what William's Dutch commanders had failed to do in a year. But he was found no further independent employment, and his indignation knew no bounds. Overpowering and unscrupulous ambition henceforward guided his conduct. When in the next year William offered to take him to Flanders as lieutenant-general, Marlborough refused to go except as commander of the English troops, and preferred to stay in London to raise opposition and foment discontent against the monarch whom he had helped to establish on the throne.

Marlborough's campaign against William—the least successful of his campaigns—was based on a mixed crew of allies. First he took steps to secure his line of retreat by opening a correspondence with the Court of St Germains in France, to which the defeated and betrayed James II had now retired. He induced Princess Anne to write a contrite letter to the father she had abandoned. James himself seems to have been fool enough to believe Marlborough's message of penitence, and to credit his promises of help. William had speedily made himself so unpopular with his English subjects that the possibility of a Jacobite restoration, especially if he were defeated in the French war, was serious. So Marlborough was not the only eminent Englishman to enter into these intrigues to safeguard himself. But in Princess Anne there was another and a Protestant candidate for the reversion of the throne. Marlborough won her gratitude by compelling William to raise her allowance from £30,000 to £50,000, and his wife encouraged her to speak of William as 'Mr Caliban' and the 'Dutch abortion.' It was no wonder that a personal quarrel broke out between Mary and her sister over Sarah's position and influence. William was warned that Marlborough's parliamentary attacks and army cabals were a move in the interests of Anne. With these impulses to action William hit back swiftly, and Marlborough was dismissed from all his offices, while Mary, less wisely, had him thrown into the Tower on what proved to be a false charge of conspiracy.

On his release on bail in 1692 Marlborough redoubled his intrigues against William and entered into a closer correspondence with St Germains. In the House of Lords he was the most enthusiastic exponent of an amendment to a new Treason Bill to the effect that an English peer must henceforward be tried by the entire House of Lords, even if Parliament were not sitting, instead of, as previously, by a special commission chosen by the king.

William was, of course, reluctant to facilitate the defence of peers at a time when treason was rife. That Marlborough was guilty of treason there was no doubt. He sent a number of encouraging messages to James II and, although the famous letter which Macaulay and other historians supposed him to have written betraying an English naval attack on Brest in 1694 is in all probability a forgery, it may be that he made some casual remark to one of the Jacobite emissaries in England after he had ascertained that this information had already reached Louis XIV from other sources. His cold wrath against William could easily have overcome his loyalty to that extent. He certainly did not betray to the exiled king any naval or military information of value, if only for the simple reason that, being out of office, he had no secrets to betray. Nor was this kind of treason what William suspected. William knew, and did not care, that not only Marlborough, but some of his ministers, to safeguard their skins and estates, were at this time writing friendly letters to St Germains. William's real grudge against Marlborough was that he was trying to turn the English Parliament and English Army against the Crown when in the midst of the war with France.

At the end of 1694 Queen Mary died childless and Princess Anne was brought a step nearer the succession. Marlborough now felt it to be in his own interest to patch up his differences with William. He made an indirect offer of his services, and when William achieved his one personal success of the war, he induced Princess Anne to write a congratulatory letter to the king. William gradually responded to these overtures. In the following year, when a certain Jacobite, Sir John Fenwick, was arrested for plotting a rising in England and in his confession charged Marlborough among others with a treasonable correspondence with King James, William took not the slightest notice. Marlborough, in evident confidence that Fenwick had no letters of his to back the accusations, put a bold face on the business. He pressed on an Act of Attainder to ensure Fenwick's conviction, while his brother George exclaimed: 'Thrust a bullet down his throat. Dead men tell no tales!' But at the same time Marlborough took the precaution of frightening out of the country Lord Ailesbury, another Jacobite who had been on that side of the divided Jacobite camp with which he had in fact been in communication. And therefore, when the French war was over, but not before, William could restore Marlborough's offices and as a further mark of reconciliation appoint him governor to Anne's nine-year-old son, the Duke of Gloucester.

The Treaty of Ryswick (1697), by which the long conflict between William III and Louis XIV was brought to an end, was a compromise. For nine years Louis had fought against England, Holland, Spain, Savoy, Austria, and many German princes and had held his own. In the treaty he kept the conquests won in earlier wars and gained the important town of Strasbourg, although he surrendered in exchange three German towns which he had taken. To secure their frontier, the Dutch were permitted to maintain garrisons in the Spanish Netherlands (Belgium) and William was recognized as King of England. But the treaty did not look like a permanent settlement, for it was known that one reason which induced Louis to sign an instrument which left him in a weaker position than when Charles II ruled England was the approaching extinction of the Spanish Habsburg line. With the death of Charles the Sufferer, the last Spanish Habsburg, the break-up of the vast Spanish Empire seemed certain. Louis, whose wife was the half-sister of Charles the Sufferer, hoped to profit extensively and was anxious to concentrate his superb diplomatic resources on preparing for the delightful eventuality.

William was, of course, well aware of all this and knew that the possession of Spanish Flanders by the French Crown would be the greatest menace imaginable to the strategic security of England and Holland. He set himself to prevent the danger. He had reason to know that, although he was of the same age as Marlborough, he had not much longer to live. If his life's work of preserving the Dutch Republic against the ambitions of France was to be continued, he had to find a successor who would maintain the Anglo-Dutch alliance. After toying with the idea of remarriage, he chose instead to adopt a chance which would take into full account the feelings of the English ruling classes. Princess Anne, the Protestant heir to the throne, who had an apparently healthy son in the Duke of Gloucester, was a popular figure. Her friend and adviser, Marlborough, was the best English general. Whilst his intrigues were but the spite born of thwarted ambition, his military genius was enduring. His wife's intimacy with Anne also made it certain that on William's death he would be promoted to the highest offices in the State. Moreover, Marlborough was classed as a Tory and, with the ending of the war and after the general election of 1698, the Tories formed the majority in the House of Commons. Therefore, for calculable political reasons, King William chose Marlborough as his successor in the struggle against France.

Marlborough, for his part, was careful to neglect none of his contacts; he kept up an increasingly perfunctory correspondence with the exiled Jacobites; he supported the Tory Party on all party questions; and he again drew a draft on Princess Anne's gratitude by pushing her husband's claim to a large sum of money which William had been reluctant to concede to him. Nevertheless, he welcomed the king's favour.

The half-lunatic King of Spain slowly passed away (November, 1700), but before he did so he bequeathed his throne to Philip of Anjou, grandson of Louis XIV, in order to preserve the unity of his empire. Although Louis had entered into negotiations with William to divide the Spanish possessions with the Habsburg Austrian Emperor, and had signed two partition treaties to this effect, he could not resist this glorious opportunity of family aggrandizement, and decided to accept the will. William was shocked to the core. 'I am perfectly persuaded,' he said, 'that if this will be executed England and the Dutch Republic are in the utmost danger of being totally lost and ruined.' He therefore urged the Dutch 'to oppose so great an evil,' and promised 'to engage people here, by prudent conduct, by degrees and without perceiving it.' Both England and Holland at first recognized the will, so reluctant were they to embark on another war. But Louis XIV's immediate expulsion of the Dutch garrisons from Belgium, and his replacing of them by French troops, powerfully affected public opinion in both countries. By the middle of 1701 the Opposition parties in London and Amsterdam were begging William to prepare for war. At this crisis William turned to Marlborough; he appointed him Commander-in-Chief of the English forces and Ambassador Extraordinary with the task of framing another Grand Alliance to compel the French king to withdraw his troops from Belgium, of preventing the union of France and Spain, and of obtaining satisfaction for the Austrian Emperor's claims on the Spanish inheritance.

In his negotiations for the Grand Alliance of 1701, Marlborough disclosed his strength as a diplomatist. He was careful not to offend the constitutional susceptibilities of the English Parliament; he helped to reconcile the sharply opposed claims of the Dutch and the Imperialists; and he saw that the English demands for colonial and trade compensations were met. The terms of the second Grand Alliance were:

(1) That there should be no union between the Crowns of France and Spain.

(2) That the Austrian Emperor Leopold's second son, the Archduke Charles, should be awarded the Spanish possessions in Belgium and Italy.

(3) That the Dutch should have a string of fortresses in Belgium to protect them permanently from France; and

(4) That England and Holland should keep their overseas conquests.

The treaty was signed on 7th September 1701; on 16th September James II died and Louis unwisely recognized his son James Edward, known to history as the Old Pretender, as the rightful King of England. This insult rallied the country to the new war. William hastily dissolved Parliament and secured a Whig victory, and the Whigs were rabid for a grand-scale attack on the French. William also had taken the clever precaution of associating Marlborough, the 'Tory general,' with him in the signature of the Treaty. He had acted just in time. For in February 1702 he died. Scarcely concealing their pleasure, the Marlboroughs and Anne entered upon their heritage of joy and trouble.

Chapter 3—The Grand Vizier : 1702-3

Queen Anne and her first Cabinet—War of the Spanish Succession—Campaigns of 1702 and 1703—'No Peace without Spain'—Obstructions of Dutch and High Tories.

HISTORIANS have recently attempted to revalue the character of Queen Anne, and have even compared her to her predecessor, Queen Elizabeth. But there is some difficulty in fashioning a heroic figure out of this stout, gouty, gluttonous little woman with her dull husband and frequent miscarriages. Her perpetual card-playing, her gambling, her love of tittle-tattle, her school-girlish 'crushes,' and her fancy for drinking spirits out of a tea-cup—Anne's 'cold tea' was a contemporary joke—were harmless habits enough. The essential fact about her was that she was every inch a Stuart, with most of the Stuart faults. She inherited her grandfather Charles I's propensity for court favourites and also his ingratitude to loyal servants. She possessed all the Stuart obstinacy, but she was lucky in that her obstinacy fitted the mood of the day and her bigotry happened to lie in the direction of the Church of England and not the Church of Rome.

At first all went as William planned. Anne confirmed Marlborough in his post as Commander-in-Chief, awarded him the long-coveted office of Master-General of the Ordnance, and made him in effect her First Minister, the 'Grand Vizier,' as an undersecretary called him. He seized every chance. War, he knew, was the sphere of action in which he could employ his innate genius. He helped to prepare the queen's first speeches, in which she promised to carry on the war against France, and he hurried across to The Hague to assure the Dutch that, in spite of the death of their Captain-General, they could count on the military co-operation of England, and reject any offers of a compromise from France. Then Marlborough returned to London to assist in the construction of Anne's first Cabinet.

The new Government was mainly Tory in complexion, with an admixture of moderate Whigs. Marlborough asked that his conscientious and modest friend, Sidney Godolphin, should be Lord Treasurer to manage the national finances, and advised that another old friend, the Whig *magnifico*, the Duke of Shrewsbury, should be offered a Cabinet post. Broadly, he and Queen Anne were agreed that a coalition rather than a party Government was necessary to carry on the war successfully. Anne inclined to the Tories because they were, above all, the Church of England party, and she was a devoted daughter of the Church. Marlborough was then classed as a Tory; but his views were substantially modified, not only by the needs of the day, but by the fact that his assertive wife, now promoted to be Keeper of the Privy Purse, Royal Mistress of the Robes and Groom of the Stole, was an outspoken Whig. Marlborough was not immune from his wife's effort to make herself a political figure in the world. There lay a cause of future discord. But meanwhile this somewhat incongruous quartet—Anne, determined, small-minded, and hopeful; Marlborough, at length at the summit of power; Godolphin, an immaculate but nervous civil servant, with betting as his moral outlet; and Sarah, domineering and ambitious—formed the personal basis of the new English Government. Anne wrote in blind affection to Sarah in the following year: 'We four must never part till death mows us down with his impartial hand.

War was jointly declared on France by England, Holland, and the Emperor on 15th May, and a week later Marlborough sailed for the second time to Holland. He was detained for some weeks behind the lines over the troublesome question of who was to

succeed William III as Captain-General of the Dutch forces.
Marlborough's serene confidence had already made a deep impression at The Hague. Although various princes competed for
the honour, the Dutch of their own accord preferred William's
implied choice and ultimately Marlborough was appointed to the
post at £10,000 a year, which raised his income from his various
offices to over £60,000. He concealed his pleasure from the
queen, who had instructed him to procure the post for her stodgy
husband, Prince George. Although the post gave Marlborough
command over the English and Dutch forces, and the numerous
mercenaries in their pay, the Dutch Government sent with him
on the campaign two deputies whose advice he was bound to seek
on questions of high strategy. William had been able to select
his own field deputies and consequently had not been hampered
by them, but the new deputies had every intention of seeing that
the English commander did not jeopardize Dutch security or
take undue risks with the Dutch army.

It thus happened that half the campaigning season was over
before Marlborough assumed his command. The French held
at the beginning of the war all the fortresses in Belgium, on the
Rhine and on the Meuse, except Maastricht. They had overrun
the territories of the Elector of Cologne and the Bishop of Liège,
and the Prussian territory of Cleves which adjoined the Dutch
Republic. The Dutch, on Marlborough's advice, had laid siege
to Kaiserwerth on the Lower Rhine, while the French army
looked on helpless from the left bank. Marlborough's supreme
confidence in warfare always contrasted with his hesitations in
politics. As soon as he took command, he assured the Dutch
that he would 'rid them of their troublesome neighbours' and,
rapidly crossing the Meuse, he compelled the French to retreat for
fear of their lines in Belgium being threatened. The manœuvre
caused the two armies to converge on each other at right angles
and a splendid chance of attacking the exposed flank of the
French was offered. But the Dutch deputies refused to fight
and risk the army that stood between their territory and the
French. Four times altogether the Dutch deputies rejected
opportunities of fighting in a favourable situation which Marlborough presented to them. However, the French were outmanœuvred and were forced impotently to watch four important
fortresses on the Meuse—Venloo, Stevenswert, Ruremonde, and
Liège—fall with relatively little resistance. The line of the
Meuse as well as of the Lower Rhine was cleared and Holland
was freed from invaders. The Dutch General Athlone was com-

pelled to admit that 'the success of this campaign is solely due to
this incomparable chief, since I confess that I, serving as second
in command, opposed in all circumstances his opinions and proposals.'   Judged by William's standards in the previous war, the
achievement was brilliant and Marlborough himself was alone
disappointed, for he had wanted to bring the French to battle
and not merely to take a few fortresses.

After an adventurous journey down the Meuse, in which he
was nearly captured by a French raiding party, Marlborough
returned via The Hague to England.   He was enthusiastically
received in Holland, but it was nothing to his reception in England, where his success was contrasted with the Austrian General
Eugene's failure in Italy and the inability of Admiral Rooke to
take Cadiz as Marlborough had wished.   Queen Anne rapturously
offered Marlborough a dukedom and £5,000 a year during her
lifetime to support the dignity.   She also asked the House of
Commons to grant an income to go with the title for all time.
But although the Tory majority voted with a back kick at
William III that Marlborough had 'retrieved the honour of
England,' they jibbed at what they regarded as an unconstitu-
tional request.   Marlborough, who had been urged by his wife
not to accept the title unless handsome provision were made, was
chagrined at the refusal, and this marked the first step in his
alienation from the Tory Party.

For other reasons too he grew angry with the right-wing
Tories, who were led by the queen's uncle, Lord Rochester.   He
thought that Rochester was pushing too hard for purely party
advantages, and endangering the national effort to win the war.
A wholesale attack which had been launched during the summer
by the High Tories in the Cabinet on Whig J.P.s and place-
holders conflicted with the 'non-party' views of Marlborough and
Godolphin, while the High Tory argument that the war should
be waged mainly by sea and on the Spanish colonies was in contradiction to Marlborough's strategical scheme of winning the
war by beating the French army and invading France.   The
crying-up by this section of the Tories of Sir George Rooke's
lucky feat in capturing a Spanish treasure fleet at Vigo Bay after
the fiasco of Cadiz was regarded by Marlborough as a direct insult,
and he was now driven to assert his influence; when Rochester
refused to go to Dublin to assume his office as viceroy, Marlborough drove him from the Cabinet.

On top of the Tory manœuvres, the Dutch obstructions, and
the Whig intrigues of his wife came the most personal blow of all

*D

to Marlborough when in February 1703 his only surviving son
John, a youth of sixteen at Cambridge, died of smallpox. Marlborough returned to Holland in the early spring of 1703 with a
heavy heart. The dynast in him was sorely disappointed.
Power, money, and glory had been accumulated, but for what?
'I 've lost what is so dear to me,' he murmured in one of his
spells of depression. 'It is fit for me to retire and not toil and
labour for I know not who.' But he was soon to smell the joy
of battle again.

The war was now spreading to the farthest corners of Europe
and over every quarter the English commander cast his per-
spicacious eye. In spite of Rooke's failure at Cadiz, Marlborough
continued to urge the allied navies to seek a base in the Mediterranean so that France might be distracted in the south. At the
same time he pressed for money and assistance to be sent to the
French Protestants, who had risen against Louis XIV in the west
of France. This move was a natural counter to Louis's own
successful efforts at stirring up insurrection among the Magyar
subjects of the Emperor, who were disturbing Vienna from the
rear. Louis also now effected another diplomatic coup when with
lavish promises he persuaded the Elector of Bavaria, one of the
most powerful princes in Germany, to join his side. On account
of the Elector's defection the French decided to make their
principal effort in the 1703 campaign on the Upper Rhine, and
Hector de Villars, the ablest French general, was dispatched to
join forces with the Bavarians. Before the normal winter suspension of operations was ended, he began his campaign by
taking the town of Kehl. Marshal Villeroi, in command in
Flanders, was also inspired to retake Liège, if he could, early in
the campaigning season, but otherwise to act on the defensive
and hold the allied forces so as to prevent them from assisting
the harassed Emperor.

Marlborough, however, was also early in the field, and at first
hoped that he might be allowed to draw off pressure from the
emperor by invading Belgium, even at the risk of a battle with
Villeroi. But the Dutch maintained their veto on battles, and
asked the duke instead to take Bonn on the Rhine, in order to
clear their communications with the empire. Under Marlborough's personal supervision that town was bombarded into
surrender so quickly that Villeroi had no time to make a counter
move. Marlborough, ever fruitful in expedient, now proposed
to the Dutch what he termed his 'Grand Design,' a remarkable

strategical scheme which marks the heights of his military genius. His plan was that he himself would hold Villeroi's main army immobile whilst one Dutch general, Cohorn, attacked Ostend, another menaced Antwerp from the west, and a third approached from the north-east. If the Governor of Antwerp divided his forces to save Ostend, Antwerp would fall, and, if not, Ostend would. But Marlborough reckoned without his collaborators. Cohorn calmly obtained permission from the Dutch Government to alter his orders so as to turn his part into a mere plundering expedition. Opdam, one of the other Dutch generals, began his move before any diversion of forces from Antwerp had taken place and then omitted to fortify his line. Consequently his army was caught by the French in superior numbers and Opdam ran away thinking it would be crushed. His second in command retrieved the error (Battle of Eckeren, 2nd July) and Marlborough unjustly got the blame even from the Dutch. Ten days later Marlborough again created an opportunity by manœuvring Villeroi out of his lines, but the Dutch were now far too frightened to consent easily to a battle, and while they debated the chance was lost. So for the remainder of a disappointing campaign Marlborough had to be content with the capture of two petty fortresses, Huy, below Liège on the Meuse (25th August), and Limburg, which was then Spanish territory (27th September). Under the terms of the Grand Alliance, both the Dutch and the emperor's representative claimed the right to administer Limburg, and Marlborough had to arrange a clever but temporary compromise. After the fall of Limburg he sourly observed that he was 'not fond of staying with an army that does nothing but eat forage,' and returned to England as soon as he could.

Marlborough's claims to be a great statesman and diplomatist would stand higher if he had exerted himself as actively over far-reaching decisions of national policy as he did over matters in which the strength of the army or the working unity of his military alliance was directly concerned. His attitude to the treaty with Portugal, which had been concluded in May 1703, is a case in point. He had long pressed for an alliance with Portugal so as to secure Lisbon as a base for the English Navy, but seems to have been indifferent to the terms of the treaty. Yet one of its terms was of fundamental importance for the future of the war. In order to obtain the assistance of the allied forces in an attack on his country's traditional enemy, Spain, the King of Portugal had managed to induce the English Government to extend its war aims to include not merely compensation for the emperor, as laid down by the Treaty of the Grand Alliance, but also an astonishing clause that 'no peace shall be made till the House of Austria be in possession of the whole monarchy of Spain.' The Dutch naturally hated this clause being forced upon them; it meant an indefinite prolongation of the war, it tilted the balance of power decisively in favour of the Habsburgs; and the Emperor, for whose presumed benefit the clause was added, showed himself most reluctant to send his son to Spain. Yet there is no indication in his letters that Marlborough protested or even inquired about a clause which was entirely contrary to the original aims of the Grand Alliance, and was, indeed, to contribute in the end to his downfall. All he objected to then was that he had to part with some of his troops and send them to the Peninsula.

The High Tories joined hands with the extremist Whigs in censoring Marlborough for his ill success in the campaign of 1703. Godolphin grumbled that, though he was indifferent to 'the hot men of either party,' the obstructionism of the Dutch 'gives too just a handle for clamour against our great expense of carrying on this war in their country.' Dutch non-co-operation, Villars's deep penetration into Germany, which even menaced Vienna, and the continued incompetence of the English Navy had combined to make the war situation so unfavourable that Godolphin expected the Government would be torn to pieces. Further fuel was added to the flames of Marlborough's ire because the Dutch failed to give effect to their promise to cease trade with France, and, while the Whigs sniffed at his operations, his wife continued to advocate their wider representation in the Cabinet. In all the circumstances it was not so surprising that he spoke of 'retiring from these uneasy and troublesome broils' as that he was persuaded to retain his command without any reconstruction of the Cabinet. But his patience proved wise, for the High Tories provoked Anne personally, and in the course of the following year she dismissed their representatives in the Cabinet, although as yet no more Whigs entered the Government.

Chapter 4—The Conquering Hero: 1704

The March to the Danube—Battle of the Schellenberg—Devastation of
  Bavaria—Relations with Eugene—Battle of Blenheim—Rewards
  and Consequences—Return to the Moselle.

AT the end of the second campaign of the war the position of the
Grand Alliance was critical. True, thanks to Marlborough, the
Dutch Republic was safe, but England's third ally, the Emperor,
was in desperate danger. Magyar rebels were within twenty miles
of Vienna on the east, whilst, owing to the defection of the Elector
of Bavaria, the French were on the line of the Danube stretching
from Ulm to Linz, within a few days' march of Vienna, with an
army twice the size of the Austrians. Thus at the very moment
when the English Government was promising to put the Archduke Charles on the throne of Madrid, his father, the Emperor
Leopold, was tottering on his throne at Vienna. In the centre
of the vast war front the French had also advanced and, by the
capture of Landau and other fortresses, held a strong position on
the Upper Rhine. Here their troops were faced by Imperialists
under the Margrave Louis of Baden, whose methods of warfare
were slow and antiquated and who was thought in Vienna to be
capable of following the Elector of Bavaria into the French camp.
In Italy, though, owing to the success of the sea powers, a new
ally had been gained in the Duke of Savoy-Piedmont, the Imperialists were in no way able to resist the French. The immense
French front therefore stretched (outside Italy) in the form of a
ladder inclined to the left of the European map, with its top
resting near Antwerp and its foot on the Danube.

Marlborough was filled with gloom at this outlook. In the
course of the winter he reached the conclusion that the only way
in which the Alliance could be saved was for him to make a
personal effort to rescue the Emperor. Direct appeals had
reached him from Vienna, and they well accorded with his mood
of resentment against the Dutch. In January he told the
imperial ambassador extraordinary, Wratislaw, that he intended to induce the Dutch to agree to a move on the Upper
Rhine or the Moselle whereby he might assist the overthrow of
the Elector of Bavaria; but he added that he could not hope to
employ more troops than the number which were actually
English or in English pay. His daring decision to separate the
Dutch and English armies and to carry the latter away from the
northern theatre of war was the first stage in the courageous

scheme which he finally evolved for a march as far as the Danube. As spring approached, it gradually became plain to him that a threat to invade France by way of Lorraine from the Moselle might not save Vienna, and that more far-reaching remedies were needed. In April he obtained authorization in general terms from the queen to separate the two armies and to use the English troops to aid the empire. He asked that Prince Eugene, the best Imperialist general, should be sent to the Upper Rhine, and he sowed in Dutch minds the idea of a campaign on the Moselle so as to induce them to lend him at least a portion of their troops to act away from their frontiers. But although all the necessary preparations were made for a march south, it was not until the spring was well advanced that he finally decided on the bold hazard of a six-hundred-mile flank march down to the Danube to knock out the Elector of Bavaria and save Vienna.

At the beginning of May he disclosed his intentions to Godolphin. He told Wratislaw that 'the issue in this matter is victory or death,' but he also said in more cheerful mood, 'the more I think of the expedition the better I am pleased with it.' On 19th May, after he had reviewed what he called his 'little army' of some 50,000 men (of whom 16,000 were English), the extraordinary enterprise began. For its success he had to create a fog of war to deceive the French, lest they barred his path or cut his supplies. He managed to persuade them first that he intended to invade Lorraine and then, as he moved farther up the Rhine, that he was going to attack Alsace. Not until he left the line of the Rhine for a sharp turn east below the Neckar valley by way of Heidelberg was his real intention revealed to the enemy, and not till then were the Dutch authorities and German princes officially informed of his destination. He deceived not only the French but many of his own allies, and yet he did this without in any way hustling or weakening his troops on the march. They plodded methodically on. Marlborough and the cavalry went ahead, his brother, General Charles Churchill, with the infantry behind. They went forward at a steady rate of ten miles a day, setting out at sunrise and encamping about midday. 'Surely,' wrote an English captain, 'never was such a march carried on with more order and regularity and with less fatigue both to man and horse.' The soldiers enjoyed the expedition. The interfering Dutch field deputies were left behind and, although the States General at first appealed to the Duke in terror to return, they soon realized that he was carrying the war with him, for Villeroi, the French general in Holland, was compelled to follow him, and the Dutch then of their own accord sent reinforcements after him.   At length, on 10th June at Gross-Heppach on the road to the Danube, the Duke, Prince Eugene, and the Margrave of Baden forgathered to concert operations.   After a magnificent banquet, it was arranged that Eugene with 30,000 men should station himself on the Rhine to watch the French generals Villeroi and Tallard, who commanded the army there, while Marlborough and the Margrave should move together into Bavaria.   On 22nd June Marlborough and the Margrave joined forces on the edge of the Swabian Jura Mountains north-west of Ulm.   The command over this joint force of 80,000 had been delicately settled beforehand.   Baden as a prince was of higher rank than Marlborough, but the Emperor promised that Marlborough's views on strategy should be decisive, although the two generals were to enjoy the honour of giving the actual orders and issuing the password on alternate days.   It would indeed have been ludicrous for Marlborough to have come all this tedious way unless he had first obtained a guarantee that his wishes would be respected. Moreover, he had the address to work smoothly with the touchy Margrave.   On 1st July, as they approached the Danube, he proposed to him that they should storm the fortress of the Schellenberg which lay beside the town of Donauwörth in order that they might cross the Danube into the heart of Bavaria and threaten its capital, Munich; the Margrave agreed.   This plan meant that the attack could not be launched until late on the morrow, after the troops had marched fifteen miles, and also that a frontal onslaught would have to be made on a well-fortified position guarded by veteran Bavarian troops.   But there were three advantages in the hurried move.   First, that of a surprise, since the Bavarian commander, Count D'Arco, would not expect an attack so soon; secondly, the fortifications to the west were incomplete and could not be completed by that time; thirdly, if there were delay, Marsin, the French general on the Danube, and the Elector of Bavaria, whose army was only some twenty miles away, would be able to send reinforcements.   Marlborough asked his troops for this tremendously unorthodox exertion since delay would mean, he asserted, 'either the enemy will escape or will have time to finish their works.'   It was these factors and not the half-legendary story of the alternation of the command which caused the battle of the Schellenberg to be fought on 2nd July 1704.

As the fortress was situated between the Danube and an impenetrable wood, only two main lines of attack were open, from

the north-west and the west. Although, or because, the fortifications to the west were the weakest, Marlborough took command
of the English troops who were to deliver a storm on the 'death
angle' near the wood from the north-west. After a forced march
along bad roads, picked battalions began the attack at six in the
evening. At first the Bavarians threw them back with ease
and inflicted heavy losses; General Goor, the Dutchman on whom
Marlborough greatly depended, was shot dead in the first charge.
But the fierce pummelling which his forces received at this point
obliged D'Arco to divert men from the west, while the commander at Donauwörth disgracefully neglected to man his pali-
sades. In consequence, the Margrave of Baden, although met by
an enfilading fire, found less difficulty. While Marlborough was
hammering at the north-west, he 'walked into' the fortress on
the west; it was an obvious case of cause and effect, although
Marlborough's detractors did not fail to allege that the 'experienced' Margrave had shown himself more astute than his
colleague.

The capture of the Schellenberg was an expensive victory for
those days. The Allies had 1,500 men killed and 4,500 wounded,
and over a quarter of the English engaged were casualties. The
Bavarians probably had about the same number of casualties, but
barely 5,000 of D'Arco's troops escaped to join the Elector. An
English officer who took part described it as 'a considerable
advantage purchased at a dear rate rather than a victory.'
Marlborough himself confessed that the action was 'a little expensive.' Was the conquest worth the price? The lie of the
country suggests that the Schellenberg could not have been
masked and that swift progress into Bavaria was barred unless
it were taken. The question is whether Marlborough was wise
to hurry. Alone among Marlborough's biographers, his latest is
a little hesitant in allotting praise:

It is arguable [writes Mr Winston Churchill], though by no means
provable, that if he had waited till the 3rd and brought the whole
army into play on both sides of the wood, the enemy even though
reinforced could not have held so extended a line and possibly life
might have been spared. But the fear of reinforcements was decisive
upon him.

The days which followed the victory of the Schellenberg were
in the nature of an anticlimax for Marlborough, as he was neither
able to besiege Munich nor to bring the Franco-Bavarian army
to battle. The Emperor, although lavish in his congratulations,
had been parsimonious in providing siege guns, while Marsin and

the Elector took up an impregnable position at Augsburg. Marlborough crossed the Danube, after occupying two small fortresses the better to clear his communications across the river, and encamped for ten days at Friedburg, where he faced his enemy. At this period there was a hope that the Elector of Bavaria might be induced to abandon the French alliance. By way of warning him of the consequences of refusal and in spite of the protests of his colleague, the Margrave of Baden, Marlborough ordered that Bavaria should be laid waste save so far as this affected the supplies of his own army. Hundreds of villages were set on fire, barns destroyed, stocks seized, and a plentiful harvest was prevented from being reaped. Various reasons were assigned by Marlborough for this terrible devastation. In a letter of 16th July, he wrote that it was 'in order to get the Elector to hearken to terms'; but on 29th July he said 'it was to deprive the enemy as well of his present subsistence as future support on this side'. Between the two dates, however, it had become obvious that the Elector had made up his mind to stick to the French, and probably the devastation begun for one reason was continued for another. Marlborough wrote twice to his wife deploring the burnings as 'contrary to my nature,' but, nevertheless, he ordered them to be continued and indeed extended.

One reason why the Elector of Bavaria had refused to negotiate with the Allies was the news that Marshal Tallard had left the Rhine, and was coming to his help. Prince Eugene, who had remained on the Rhine to keep watch against both Tallard and Villeroi, was unable to prevent Tallard's departure but, leaving two-thirds of his own army behind to watch Villeroi, followed him to the Danube. Much has been written about the close and spontaneous friendship between the fiery, French-hating Eugene and Marlborough when they met for the first time at Gross-Heppach and became 'two bodies with one soul.' In the long run, no doubt, a real friendship was attained through their comradeship in arms. But it would be a mistake to imagine that this first month of contact was a perfect honeymoon. Eugene was very critical of Marlborough's strategy after the fall of the Schellenberg. The credit for taking the fortress he believed was due to the Dutch General Goor, and Marlborough's failure to achieve anything substantial in these July days Eugene attributed to Goor's death on the battlefield. He argued that Marlborough should have forced the elector to battle at Augsburg by cutting his communications and that he ought at least to have prevented the junction with Tallard. Marlborough, for his part, at the same time thought that it was Eugene's business to prevent this junction. 'I depend very much on the vigilance of Prince Eugene,' he told Godolphin, 'for should Tallard join the elector it would draw the business to a greater length than is for the good of the country.' However, Tallard did join the elector south of the Danube on 7th August, and on 11th August Eugene joined Marlborough some miles farther down the river. Before this, and in spite of their desire to fight a battle, Marlborough and Eugene allowed the Margrave of Baden to take off 15,000 men to lay siege to Ingoldstadt. They preferred to dispense with an embarrassing colleague even at the cost of weakening their forces.

The united French forces, which numbered about 4,000 men more than the Allies without the Margrave (56,000 against 52,000) and were superior in artillery, did not expect to be attacked. On the night of 12th August they were entrenched in a strong position which stretched four miles from the Danube to the woods farther north. On the right of their line was the tiny village of Blenheim, in which Tallard posted nine battalions with eighteen battalions in support. The centre of the French line was protected by the deepish and muddy Nebel stream, and was less strongly held. Tallard, in fact, believed that the stream constituted so dangerous an obstacle to his enemy that the allied troops could be freely permitted to cross it and could then be driven back into it. On the left of the French line was concentrated the original army of Marsin and the elector, with the village of Ober Glauheim on their right. Such were the French dispositions which Marlborough and Eugene determined to assault on the morning of 13th August 1704. They achieved an important moral surprise by attacking at all, but the delay involved in the elaborate deployment of their army (about four and a half hours) gave the French ample time for their preparations. It was arranged that Eugene should command on the allied right facing Marsin and the elector, while Marlborough should take charge on the centre and left. On his left the Duke put Lord Cutts with sixteen battalions to deal with the twenty-seven French battalions in or around Blenheim. Eugene was likewise markedly inferior in numbers to his opponents on the French left. Thus Marlborough was left with a preponderance of force, which he could and did in fact use in the centre.

The battle opened with a fierce but unavailing onslaught on Blenheim by the English troops, similar to their assault on the 'death angle' at the Schellenberg. But after two hours Marlborough ordered Cutts to desist and be content with 'containing' (holding) the enemy. At the same time Eugene had been repulsed at the other end of the line, while Marsin, an able general, who evidently either did not know or care about Tallard's preconceived ideas, ordered a flank attack from Ober Glauheim on Marlborough's centre as it began to struggle across the Nebel stream. Eleven battalions, including the Irish in French service, executed a brilliant charge which, had it been followed up sufficiently quickly, might have reversed the result of the battle. Marlborough galloped to the threatened spot, threw in his reserves, and appealed to Eugene for cavalry. This was the crisis. Eugene, though hard pressed, responded promptly, a dangerous counter-move was repulsed and by 4.30 in the afternoon Marlborough's forces were all safely across the Nebel. As the result of the sustained efforts of Eugene and Cutts on the right and left, the French were incapacitated from concentrating any flanking movement such as Tallard had planned against the allied centre. At the crucial point Marlborough had eighty squadrons and twenty-three battalions against fifty squadrons and nine battalions in the French centre. Thus after seven hours' fighting Marlborough saw that he had won. The nine French battalions, consisting mainly of young soldiers, made one heroic countercharge, but numbers told, and at about 5.30 in the evening a final allied charge decided the battle. Tallard himself was captured trying to fetch assistance from Blenheim.

Marlborough hastened to scribble a note on the back of a tavern bill to carry the news of the 'glorious victory' to his wife. Marsin and the Elector, on hearing that the centre was broken, withdrew their troops in fairly good order, and even counter-charged as they withdrew, but on the right twenty-seven battalions, who through the stupidity of their commander had all been drawn into and cramped helplessly in Blenheim village, were bluffed into surrender. Thus the Allies captured some 15,000 prisoners besides inflicting about 23,000 casualties. The allied losses were over 12,000, and they were too exhausted to pursue the French left.

The battle of Blenheim was one of the most immediately decisive battles in European history. It was the first time that the French had suffered defeat for over two generations. It saved Vienna and conquered Bavaria. It assured the ultimate aggrandizement of the House of Austria and was a final check to the territorial ambitions of Louis XIV beyond the Rhine. It was also a blow to the House of Stuart and enabled Marlborough and

Godolphin's Coalition Ministry to stay in office for another four years.

Marlborough had his material rewards. Queen Anne allotted to him the royal manor of Woodstock, on the site of which Sir John Vanbrugh was to build Blenheim Palace at the nation's expense. He was also made a Prince of the Holy Roman Empire, although the economical Emperor was careful to give him only fifteen square miles of territory at Mindelheim to support the honour, and this territory, being filched from the conquered Elector of Bavaria, was certain to become the matter of dispute when peace negotiations were opened. It was typical of Marlborough that, just as he refused to accept his dukedom until he was given an income to support it, he would not take his title of prince until he was given a principality.

After the battle of Blenheim the Danubian city of Ulm was recaptured and the Margrave of Baden, a little disconsolate at being left out at Blenheim, returned to the Rhine to besiege and take Landau for the second time, a feat which he achieved with the maximum of incompetence. Marlborough grew weary of covering this drawn-out siege and carried his own forces back to the Moselle, where he surprised Trèves and arranged for the capture of Trarbach with a view to an invasion of France along this valley in the next campaigning season. But his own toils even then were not at an end. He reluctantly agreed to an 800-mile journey to Berlin and back in order to persuade the King of Prussia not to divert his troops from the Central European war to a war which was in progress in the north. Thus it was not until the middle of December that the fifty-four-year-old conquering hero, unutterably weary, could reach London to savour the gratitude of his queen and country.

Chapter 5—Military Genius

Marlborough as Tactician and Strategist—Views on Naval Power—The Blind Spot of Spain.

MARLBOROUGH'S first three campaigns as Commander-in-Chief of the English Army had shown him to possess ideas about the tactical and strategical problems of warfare very different from those of his predecessors. In the first place, it was his consistent view, as he wrote to Godolphin in 1703, that 'if we cannot bring the French to a battle, we shall not do anything worth

being commended.' This emphasis on the importance of seeking battle was something comparatively new in the military conceptions of his generation. From the closing years of the Thirty
Years War a preference for defensive warfare and big sieges
rather than a showdown between two armies had prevailed in
Europe. The French general, Turenne, was a rare exception to
a run of continental commanders (including William III and
Louis XIV) who liked to avoid pitched battles. It is to be remarked that Marlborough served as a young man under Turenne
and was commended by him for his exceptional qualities. That
Marlborough learned something from Turenne can hardly be
questioned.

But to seek battle was one thing; to attain it quite another.
In those days not only did it take two to make a fight, but the
evasion of battle did not necessarily mean headlong retreat.
The French were invariably able to retire, if they preferred to do
so, to a strong prepared position where they could not be assailed,
while the mobility of Marlborough's armies was not such as to
make simple the task of catching the French in an unfavourable
position, and the lengthy and tedious business of deploying in
battle formation afforded frequent opportunities for escape.
Marlborough therefore had to resort to methods of surprise to
force the French to fight as an alternative to a humiliating retreat,
and it was his employment of surprise rather than his consistent habit of seeking battle that is the supreme proof of his
genius.

To the actual tactical dispositions for battle Marlborough made
several novel contributions. He revived Cromwell's and Rupert's
use of the cavalry as a shock instead of a missile weapon. The
early seventeenth-century custom had been to allow the cavalry
after going into the fray to halt and deliver musket fire, thereby
throwing away the advantage of their superior speed. Marlborough had his cavalry move at a brisk trot, fight in a line three
deep as under Cromwell and Rupert, and use the sword as their
exclusive weapon. According to Colonel Kane, who fought in his
army, the duke 'would allow the horse [cavalrymen] but three
charges of powder and ball to each man for a campaign, and
that only for guarding their horses when at grass and not to be
made use of in action.' With his infantry, on the contrary, he
laid primary stress on the correct employment of firearms.
The invention of the ring bayonet, which was fully introduced
into the English Army in 1703, got rid of the distinction which
existed in Cromwell's army between musketeers and pikemen, for

the two were henceforward combined. Moreover, the supersession of clumsier methods of loading by the general use of the
flintlock enabled Marlborough to attain from musketry a concentration of fire power never before known. He insisted upon
the importance of fire discipline in the infantry and established
firing by platoons instead of by ranks so as to enable the platoon
commander to direct the volleys and to maintain a more regular
fire than the French. Likewise, Marlborough recognized the
value of artillery, although cannon were still in a comparatively
primitive state. He selected able artillery commanders, but
always retained for himself the personal direction of the artillery
in battle. He sent his orders to his brigadiers without any inter-
mediary; at Blenheim he took personal charge of placing his
cannon and at Ramillies he was to give it an unusually urgent
role on the left wing. Shock tactics with the cavalry, disciplined fire in the infantry, personal care of the artillery—
these were the three main factors in Marlborough's tactical
success.

In battle tactics Marlborough demonstrated his brilliant un-
orthodoxy at Blenheim (and later at Oudenarde). Here was
none of the traditional elaborate manœuvring in the face of the
enemy, but a deliberately worked-out original plan. His move
against the centre at Blenheim was one not recognized in any
contemporary text-book of war. For it was generally assumed in
seventeenth-century military circles that such an attack would
be overwhelmed by the enemy's wings. Marlborough, however,
first made certain that the French wings were well held and then
gave his decisive order to break through the centre. There was
nothing rash in this, no uncalculated risks, no brutal trifling with
his soldiers' lives here or ever. And so when he asked his men for
a special effort they gave it willingly.

Marlborough had a marked perception of the value of sea
power. Having served on board the fleet as a subaltern and held
a commission in the Marines, he knew the difficulties and limitations of naval warfare. His only notable mistake in regard to
sea power was that he expected too much of a projected naval
raid on the western coast of France in 1708, while neglecting to
give the naval commanders adequate information about the
situation of the French forces in the neighbourhood. On
the other hand, he was constantly and rightly urging upon the
admirals the need of obtaining a base where the fleet could
winter in the Mediterranean. 'I conjure you if possible to take
Port Mahon [Minorca],' he wrote to General Stanhope in 1708,

and it was not his fault that this valuable base was not conquered before that year.

Although nearly all Marlborough's fighting was done in Flanders, nothing is more striking than his power of seeing the vast coalition as a whole. In his dispatches, we see him following distant events and relating them to each other with a consummate grasp of synthesis. His march to the Danube in 1704 and his proposed march to Italy in 1705 were in their daring simplicity strokes of true strategic genius. Never in military matters did he allow his direct concern in the war close at hand to dominate his mind. 'I am sensible,' he told Godolphin in 1704, 'that if I did not consider the good of the whole before my private concern, I ought not to be here.' In constantly relating one campaign to another, he perceived the virtue of an economy of forces; how a defensive in the Netherlands meant an offensive elsewhere; alternatively, how if the enemy could be held with small numbers in Germany, he could do what he liked in the Netherlands. In a debate in which he took part in 1707, he defended his concentration of forces in Flanders on the ground that, if the pressure were relaxed there, large numbers of French troops would be released from garrison duty to fight in campaigns elsewhere, whereas since in Spain the French were able to garrison their strong places with only one battalion, to shift the main allied military effort to Spain would be to violate grossly the principle of economizing their own forces.

But strategically Marlborough did have one real weakness, and that was in regard to the war in Spain, although for opposite reasons from those urged against him by his political enemies. He had advocated and supported the extension of the allied war aims to the conquest of Spain for the benefit of the Habsburgs, and never seems to have understood the tremendous prolongation of the war which was involved in this expensive and difficult project. He once confessed that he did not have time to read all the letters and dispatches from Spain and Portugal. Perhaps in consequence he never appreciated the stubborn guerrilla qualities and ineradicable partisanship of the Spanish people or the vast geographical obstacles to military progress on the Peninsula. He always insisted that he himself must remain near Holland, partly because, if he left, the Dutch might be induced to conclude a separate peace. But while he refused to go to Spain himself, to meet the wishes of the Whig Party, who largely for economic reasons were rabid for the French overthrow in Spain, he allowed his forces to be divided, thereby weakening his chances of

invading France from the north-east and at the same time allowing
inferior troops in the charge of quarrelsome generals to be constantly defeated in Spain.   Moreover, he did not realize that the
Spanish people had made their choice, and that he was required
to subdue a people as well as an army.   On the issue of Spain he
allowed political considerations to cloud his clear military judgment; and it is possible that it was of Spain that he was thinking
in the last days of life when aged, paralysed, and in virtual retirement as Commander-in-Chief, he was asked for his advice and
could be induced to utter only four words: 'Don't divide the
army.'

Chapter 6—Gloom and Cheer : 1705-6

Cabinet Reconstruction and General Election—The 'Triumvirate'—Disappointing Campaign of 1705—Battle of Ramillies—Conquest of
   Belgium—Allied Differences—Offer of Governor-Generalship.

THE victories on the Danube excited the patriotic enthusiasm of
the English people, but the High Tories, now that their leaders
had left the Cabinet, were distinctly dissatisfied.   Rochester said
that the losses of the French armies at Blenheim were no more
than a bucketful of water to the French king, and the Tory
majority in the Commons insisted on coupling the name of Sir
George Rooke with that of Marlborough in the congratulatory
address, because Rooke, more by luck than judgment, had that
August conquered the Rock of Gibraltar and fought a drawn
battle with the French off Malaga.   When Marlborough offered
Rooke a free ticket for a dinner given to him by the City of London, Rooke pointedly refused and became so antagonistic to the
ministry that the queen was compelled to dismiss him.   In the
domestic field the extreme Tories again tried to force through an
Occasional Conformity Bill, aimed at excluding the Nonconformists from political life, which had twice been defeated in
earlier sessions.   But they were defeated by their own moderates
in the Commons, while the Bill was again rejected by the Lords,
and Marlborough, who had previously voted for it, now voted
against it.   With these straws to show how the political winds
blew, Marlborough now decided that the effective continuation of
the war, his one concern, required a reconstructed administration
based solely on moderate Whigs and moderate Tories.   He personally demanded the Privy Seal of another High Tory, the Duke

of Buckinghamshire, and handed it to an influential and wealthy Whig, the Duke of Newcastle (April 1705).

At the general election which followed, the Queen was induced to use her influence against the extreme Tories, and the result was to increase the number of Whigs and 'Queen's Servants,' or non-party men, in the House of Commons at the expense of the Tories. Sarah had pressed on her husband the advisability of capitulating entirely to the Whigs in their hungry search of office, but he told her frankly that he believed it to be best for 'the Queen's service,' i.e. for the war, that 'neither party should have a great majority, so that both might be influenced for her interest.'

The reconstructed Government was based firmly on what was called the 'Triumvirate' of Marlborough, Godolphin, and Robert Harley, the moderate Tory leader who had become principal Secretary of State in 1704. But after the election the 'Triumvirate' in fact became dependent on the support of the well-organized Whig party, and before the year was out they were forced to throw a sop to that party by appointing one of its five leaders, Lord Sunderland, who also happened to be Marlborough's son-in-law, ambassador extraordinary in Vienna. While the election was in progress, Marlborough had sailed for the front in a cheerful mood. In the course of the election he was attacked for betraying the Church of England, but he knew that his victories counted more with the electorate than his views on occasional conformity.

The disaster on the Danube compelled Louis XIV to act on the defensive in 1705. By tremendous exertions he assembled three large armies to stand guard against the expected invasion of French or Spanish territory from the east; one army was under Villeroi in Flanders, a second under Villars on the Moselle, and a third under Marsin in Alsace. Marlborough had made up his mind to try to invade Lorraine by way of the Moselle, as he regarded this as the 'real road' into France. His plan was to begin the advance with two armies, one of 60,000 men under his own command from Trèves, which he had taken at the end of the previous campaign, the other of 30,000 Germans under the Margrave of Baden operating from Landau on the Upper Rhine. But a fatal combination of Dutch fears, Austrian shortcomings, Prussian dilatoriness, and the Margrave's jealousy prevented the realization of what seems in any case to have been an over-ambitious project. Nevertheless, Marlborough refused wholly to abandon it. Ultimately he decided to confront Villars, who had taken up an impregnable position, with an inferior army in the hope of tempting him to give battle. But Villars was too clever to take an unnecessary risk. For fifteen days Marlborough encamped opposite him in a neighbourhood where the Allies had no adequate source of supplies. Every night there were hard frosts, men deserted, and there was no proper commissariat. The Duke was sick with disappointment and confessed that 'nothing would do good except a battle' and that he could not have. The would-be invaders of France were compelled to retreat of their own accord. So disgusted was Marlborough that he took the unusual step of sending a message to Marshal Villars, apologizing for giving him 'poor sport' and putting the blame on the Margrave's refusal to co-operate.

Villeroi, in the absence of Marlborough from Flanders, retook the fortress of Huy and attacked Liège. This gave Marlborough an admirable excuse for disentangling himself from a humiliating situation. But the Dutch were too delighted with his return to complain; he at once recaptured Huy, although he told his wife despondently that 'the Lord knows what we shall do next.' Meanwhile, the German commander at Trèves had pusillanimously abandoned the town and Villars had advanced and driven the Imperialists from their lines. No wonder that Marlborough wrote 'I am weary of life' and announced once again his intention of retiring at the close of the campaign.

To those who are accustomed to regard Marlborough as a serene Olympian figure his conduct during this disappointing campaign of 1705 should be especially revealing. For the plain truth is that he was no more philosophical than any other man and equally prone to fits of depression when defeated or thwarted. In 1704 he had set out in a state of complete depression because of what had happened in the previous year, and in 1705 he had been optimistic for the same reason. When his allies disappointed him, he threatened to resign, and he used strong language and stronger action against the men who obstructed his military schemes. He was as sensitive to criticism as any other public man, but he chose to redeem his character with his sword.

In midsummer, 1705, he decided that if he could not count on the assistance of his allies to carry through his plans of campaign he must repeat the tactics adopted in the march to the Danube and bluff the Dutch into victory. His feat in breaking through the carefully prepared lines erected in Brabant by Villeroi was the march to the Danube in miniature. He persuaded the Dutch generals and field deputies who now rejoined him that

he had only reconnaissance objects in view.   But by swift night
marches, carried out solely by the troops in English pay, he so
feinted at the French lines and so befogged the French general
that he broke through at the weak point of Tirlemont with the
loss of only 200 men (29th July).   He led the crucial charge himself and was nearly killed when a French cavalry officer tried to
sabre him but fell off his horse.   Marlborough reported to Godolphin, with a slight touch of malice, that the Dutch did not
reach the lines until the action was all over, and that he had been
forced to 'cheat' them into following him at all.

But afterwards caution overcame him.   He refused to pursue
the advantage for fear that the whole French army were coming
up to repair the breach in their lines.   Had he done so he would
almost certainly have inflicted a severe defeat on a section of the
French infantry and taken the vital town of Louvain.   But he,
who earlier in the campaign had been ready to fight Villars with
inferior numbers far from his base, now held his hand.   Such was
the effect of the depressed mood induced by his failure on the
Moselle.   And yet here is the astonishing thing—with this small,
if striking, success behind him the mood of caution was quickly
overcome.   A few days later he manœuvred Villeroi into such a
position that he was compelled to surrender Louvain if he were
to save Brussels, but, instead of racing for Brussels, Marlborough
tried to persuade the Dutch deputies to agree to a battle roughly
on the site of the later battlefield of Waterloo.   A majority of the
Dutch generals, led by the choleric Slangenberg, refused assent,
just as they had refused to fight on an earlier and less favourable
occasion twelve days after the passage of the lines.   Marlborough
was bitterly disappointed.   For his forces at Waterloo were
greater by one-third than those of his enemy and he assured
Godolphin that he would have had a bigger victory than Blenheim if he had possessed supreme powers.

Once again the Duke yielded momentarily to anger and disappointment.   When the English Government, for obvious
political reasons, suppressed a passage in the *Official Gazette* which
would have disclosed to the world how the Dutch had obstructed
a victory, he exclaimed: 'I am very sure I must be madder than
anybody in Bedlam if I should be desirous of serving when I
am sure that my enemies seek my destruction and my friends
sacrifice my honour to their wisdom.'   He protested violently to
the Dutch at the behaviour of their generals and obtained the
dismissal of Slangenberg.   But he allowed himself as usual to be
persuaded to continue in office, gratified by the assurances of

Queen Anne and the new Emperor Joseph (elder brother of the
Archduke Charles) and by the spontaneous burst of enthusiasm
in Holland itself. He exerted himself to prevent the Dutch
discussing with the French peace terms which might involve their
recognizing Louis XIV's grandson as King of Spain, and he
started for Vienna to clear up a quarrel with Berlin 'by a great
many good words,' and to concert with the new emperor plans
for the next campaign.

Marlborough passed the winter of 1705–6 in comparative peace.
The Whigs, who saw their chance had come, were content to
bide their time and demonstrate their indispensability to the
Government. In January Lord Halifax, one of the Whig chiefs,
invited Marlborough, Godolphin, Sunderland, and eight leading
city merchants to dinner and thereby successfully opened the
campaign to raise £250,000 as a loan to assist the Austrian invasion of Italy. Here, in contrast to Spain and Belgium, the
allies' position was desperate, and Marlborough not merely sub-
scribed, but contemplated marching in person to the help of
Prince Eugene and repeating the triumphs of his Danube campaign on the banks of the Po. He had the Queen's consent and
sent his quartermaster, Cadogan, to obtain permission to lead
the German and Scandinavian troops into Italy. This plan was
finally thwarted early in May 1706 by a successful French offensive in Germany, which forced Louis of Baden to retreat from
his lines and frightened the Dutch. Marlborough therefore had
to content himself with sending Eugene a reinforcement of
10,000 men and planning an English naval diversion on the coast
of France which might draw off troops from the Italian and German fronts. For he was confident that the main war effort of
the French would be in Germany and Italy and that they would
stand stiffly on the defensive in Flanders. He foresaw no glory
for himself if he remained there, as he must. Hence he returned
from London to the front once more in the grip of melancholy.
But he was mistaken. Villeroi, the French commander in
Flanders, was surprisingly given definite orders to fight.

Thus it came about that in May 1706 Flanders saw the unusual
spectacle of two armies advancing with intent to fight. Cadogan,
sent with an advance guard to mark out a camp, was astonished
to find the French army occupying the very position for which
he himself was headed. It was a plateau in an area covered by
three streams, and the left of the French was covered by bogs
and in particular by one of the streams, known as the Little

Geete. As at Blenheim, the French position was based on a number of hamlets, on the left Autréglise and Offus, in the centre Ramillies, and on the right Franquenée and Taviers. The French line spread for four miles in concave fashion, so that the allied line opposite formed the chord of an arc. Marlborough, although he believed that his forces were inferior to those of the French (actually he was slightly superior, especially in artillery), determined to assault the magnificent French array. The lie of the land gave him one considerable advantage. The fold of a hill enabled him quickly to transfer troops from his right to his centre or left without the French being able to perceive the manœuvre. On this fact he based his plan of battle.

The battle (23rd May 1706) opened on the wings. Lord Orkney, with the English troops on the right, managed to get across the Little Geete and attacked the French between Autréglise and Offus, where their finest troops were concentrated, while the Dutch, powerfully assisted by carefully placed cannon, at once took Fraquenée and Taviers at the other end of the line on the left and Ramillies was stormed by allied infantry. Marlborough's object was to hold the French left with inferior numbers and to force them back from the villages at the centre and right. By the afternoon he was ready to begin his attack, but the French first counter-attacked between Ramillies and their right and drove back part of the Dutch. This was the crisis of the battle. Marlborough was prepared. He had ordered Orkney on the right wing, much to his disgust, to draw back from his attack, and had taken from him eighteen cavalry squadrons. While the French at Ramillies and on the extreme right were held in and prevented from delivering an enfilading fire, Marlborough had obtained a cavalry superiority of eighty-one squadrons against sixty-seven of the enemy at the vital point on his left centre. He now ordered up a further reserve of twenty-one squadrons, brought over from his right (all these movements of troops being concealed by the hill from the enemy). This gave him a decisive advantage of five to three. In the mêlée into which Marlborough flung himself he was nearly killed. He fell from his horse, and an aide-de-camp who held the stirrup of a fresh charger had his head blown off. Now the French cavalry broke. Villeroi vainly tried to form a fresh line on his left, but after a short breathing space Marlborough gathered his infantry, victorious at Ramillies village, linked them with the English battalions under Orkney, and wheeled his whole line to the right. The French crumpled and fled, pursued remorselessly by the allied cavalry. In the battle and pursuit the French lost 5,000 men and dared not stop until they had put the River Scheldt between themselves and their implacable enemy.

The consequences of Ramillies were more striking than those of any of Marlborough's other victories. One by one the chief Belgian towns fell, almost without resistance. Brussels, Louvain, Malines, Antwerp, Bruges, and Oudenarde surrendered. Marlborough proudly reminded his wife that King William III had unsuccessfully besieged Oudenarde with 60,000 men. In vain Louis XIV stripped his other fronts in an attempt to stem the tide. In July Ostend was taken. By August Marlborough had reached the French frontier and laid siege to Menin in France, which surrendered on 22nd August. Later, the captures of Dendermonde and Ath put the whole of Belgium into the hands of the Allies.

Victory presents problems almost as complex, if not quite as severe, as those of defeat. Louis XIV's problem was at least straightforward—to repair as best he could the damage done and to defend his frontiers. But with the conquest of the Spanish Netherlands, full of valuable booty, the Allies at once fell out among themselves. Godolphin, aware of the feeling at home, began to press on Marlborough the need of doing something for English interests, such as taking Dunkirk, which was the port whence French privateers were effectively menacing English commerce. Marlborough felt that he must not only refuse to carry out this project immediately, but must insist that in order to hold the alliance together England should declare that she had no territorial ambitions in this area. The Dutch were less restrained. They saw before their eyes the objects for which they had mainly entered the war fully attained. In a flash of Marlborough's sword the towns which they coveted to form their barrier against French aggression had become available. But the Austrians, for their part, claimed the right to rule Belgium as part of the Spanish Empire, of which their Archduke Charles had been acknowledged by the Allies as sole heir. Marlborough cared little for the final settlement of the rival claims. His one aim was now to hold the alliance together so as to be able to invade France and inflict a final crushing defeat on her. He manoeuvred to this end. In June he went to The Hague and was able to arrange a compromise whereby there was to be temporarily a joint Anglo-Dutch rule over the conquered provinces but the Habsburg claims were fully guaranteed for the future. The

Austrians remained uneasy and attempted to bribe the English
general by offering him the governor-generalship of the Spanish
Netherlands, in the name of the Archdule Charles, with a salary
of £60,000. There is some evidence that Marlborough himself
had prompted this offer as a proper payment for his work, and at
first he did not expect that the Dutch would take it amiss. But a
storm arose in Holland and Marlborough was compelled to refuse
the tempting offer. He did this with some reluctance and never
entirely abandoned the hope that it might be repeated at least
when the war was over. The Austrians, however, were not grateful; merely selfish. The rewards held out to him were but empty
honours designed to enlist a powerful advocate. The affair was
to create a permanent cleavage between Marlborough and the
Dutch Government, just as the refusal of the £5,000 a year in
perpetuity had split him from the English Tories.

The offer of the governor-generalship was not the only awkward
consequence for Marlborough of the victory of Ramillies. The
Dutch reasonably and naturally began to talk of peace. To him
this seemed neither natural nor reasonable. This was *his* war, in
which he had made a big name in Europe. Why should he
abandon it before he had marched on Paris? 'I am afraid,' he
wrote gloomily to Godolphin, 'our best allies are very fond of a
peace,' and he instructed the Dutch generals emphatically that
France was not yet reduced to her 'just bounds,' although what
the just bounds were he omitted to tell them.

To add to his perplexities, Marlborough learned in the autumn
of 1706 of political upheavals in England. Secure in their
majority, the Whigs were demanding a more powerful representation in the Cabinet. They sought as the first and easiest
step to make Marlborough's Whig son-in-law, Sunderland, Secretary of State. Harley, the Tory secretary, was reluctant and
Godolphin talked of resigning. Marlborough was fearful not
only of losing his friend, the Treasurer, but that such dissensions
in London would encourage the Dutch to seek a separate peace
with France. He pleaded with Godolphin for one more year in
which to 'win the war.' Although at first he had assured his
wife (who was, of course, rabid for Sunderland) that 'a villainous
race of vipers was planning to make the Queen uneasy at home,'
and that Sunderland was unsuited to a secretaryship of State,
by the autumn he had changed his tune. He begged Godolphin
to stay in office, and to convert Harley to accepting the Whig
terms. In October he pleaded with the stubborn Queen to be
governed 'by the only party which will rally in support of her

measures'—a very different tone from his non-party professions
of 1702 and later. Eventually the Queen unwillingly gave way.
In December Sunderland became Secretary, and the Queen
attended the baptism of his second son, of whom Marlborough
was godfather. The standards of Ramillies were in the same
week carried in triumph to the Mansion House, and the Duke was
fêted as a national hero. But in this year of victory, when
Eugene had also won an important battle at Turin, and the
allied position was consolidated in Barcelona, were sown the
seeds of future mutual allied distrust. The Dutch were avid for
a vast barrier which Marlborough would not concede to them, or
else they demanded peace. The Austrians remained content
that Marlborough should organize their victories with a minimum
of inconvenience to themselves. The alienation of the Queen
from Godolphin had begun, and Marlborough openly left the
Tory party without ever becoming a Whig.

Chapter 7—The Whigs' Servant: 1707

A Picture of Marlborough—Visit to King of Sweden—Fiasco at Toulon—
Ten Weeks' Inactivity in Flanders—Whigs Enter Cabinet—Harley Resigns.

MARLBOROUGH was now at the peak of his military career. A
contemporary Dutchman has drawn his portrait for us as he then
was. At fifty-seven the 'handsome page' had become 'a man of
about middle height, with the best figure in the world; his features
without fault, fine sparkling eyes, good teeth, and his complexion
of pink and white, such as the fair sex might envy; in brief, except
for his legs, which are too thin, one of the handsomest men ever
seen.' He spoke agreeably in bad French, had perfect manners,
gentleness, grace, and courage. His faults—boundless ambition
and 'sordid avarice'—were judged 'light in the scale against the
rare gifts of this truly great man.'

When in the previous year Marlborough had pleaded with his
friend Godolphin for one more year in which to win the war, he
little thought that the year 1707 would prove entirely humiliating
to the allied cause. Although the striking victory of Oudenarde
was to follow in the next year, the end of 1706 in fact marked the
summit of the Allies' military success. Had peace been concluded then, Marlborough would unquestionably have been
deemed the foremost soldier and diplomatist of his time, possibly

of all time. As it was, the campaign of 1707 was based on a serious miscalculation, proved a waste of opportunities, and enabled the French to recover from the disasters of the previous year. From the broadest military point of view there was little wrong with Marlborough's plan, which amounted to a double invasion of France. The scheme was that Prince Eugene, with the assistance of the Duke of Savoy's Italians and the German mercenaries dispatched by Marlborough from the north and the British fleet co-operating from the sea, should lay siege to the important French naval base of Toulon in the Mediterranean. Marlborough calculated that Louis XIV would be compelled to weaken his army in Flanders to meet this danger, and then he himself would be able to push into France along the Moselle valley. In his view, this double invasion of France would at once clear the French out of Spain, and force Louis to sue for an abject peace. But the French had the advantage of inner lines and were bound to have warning of the attack on Toulon. The Austrians, blind as ever to their long-term interests, were sluggish in moving, and from the beginning the time element was against Marlborough. Thus his plan, admirable in theory, was doomed from the start.

Before he opened his own initially defensive campaign in Flanders, Marlborough started on one of those diplomatic missions with strictly limited objectives at which he excelled. He went to visit Charles XII, King of Sweden, who had won a series of resounding victories in northern Europe and then, by turning his arms against Saxony, had frightened the King of Prussia and the Emperor and distracted their attention from the war against France. While delivering a shower of compliments Marlborough perceived that the young Swedish king, who regarded himself as a Protestant champion, had a 'natural aversion' from France, and was primarily anxious to crush his particular enemy, Peter the Great, Tsar of Russia. He did not therefore think it necessary to make any precise proposals to divert Charles's eyes from Germany, but simply arranged for the customary bribing of the Swedish ministers. His judgment proved correct; by the end of the year Charles XII turned from Central Europe and in due course marched to his destruction at the hands of Peter the Great. After soothing the King of Prussia on his way back to Holland, Marlborough returned to be greeted by the news that two big disasters had already befallen the Allies in the other theatres of war.

On 25th April the Duke of Berwick, the bastard son of James II

E

by Marlborough's sister Arabella, inflicted a considerable defeat on the mixed allied army at Almanza in Spain, and less than a month later the best French general, Villars, broke through the carefully constructed German defensive lines of Stolhoffen on the Upper Rhine and overran the state of Württemberg. Yet those two defeats need not have upset Marlborough's plans and did not in fact do so. Their main importance was that they unnerved the Dutch, and induced them to order their field deputies not to allow Marlborough to attempt any early action in Flanders. And so, as his forces were in any case markedly inferior to the French, Marlborough sat down to await the result of his 'unique remedy,' the attack on Toulon. His ten weeks' inactivity which now followed was later harshly criticized. Marlborough himself asserted in the House of Lords that 'it was impossible to fight the enemy in Flanders till the detachment was made to cover Toulon.' The Dutch deputies hid their orders to prevent a battle, in the evident hope that Marlborough would carry through some manœuvre similar to the forcing of the lines in 1705 or the bloodless campaign of 1703 which would enable them to be 'victorious without slaughter.' He seems to have been convinced that he could do nothing without risking the battle to which he knew the Dutch were opposed, although, as it happened, the French General Vendôme, who confronted him, had also been given orders not to fight. It is also possible that Marlborough's resentment at the way in which he had been treated by the Dutch over the question of the governor-generalship of the Spanish Netherlands in the previous year decided him to show them that he would not produce rabbits out of a hat when his military tricks were so ill requited.

The Toulon project proved a fiasco. The Emperor was more concerned to acquire immediate dominions in Italy than to beat the French. He made a separate treaty whereby the French troops taken prisoner in Italy were allowed to return home in exchange for French recognition of the Emperor's claims in northern Italy, and sent a large detachment of his troops to Naples, although Marlborough had begged him not to do so because they were needed at Toulon. Eugene went to Toulon in a completely defeatist mood, and perhaps unavoidable delay enabled the French to bring up reinforcements in good time. After a month the attempt was abandoned. Yet the French voluntarily sank their Toulon fleet and Villars was obliged to retreat across the Rhine partly in consequence of the attempt on Toulon. There is thus good reason to suppose that if the Toulon siege had been persevered with by the Austrians it would have had the vast strategical consequence that Marlborough had foreseen. As it was, even the weakening of the French forces in Flanders, which duly took place as Marlborough had foretold, did not afford him the expected chance of invading France from the north-east. He won Dutch permission for an offensive march, but an aged Dutch cavalry general in charge of the advanced guard, to whom he had given late but written instructions on how to catch the French, lost his way, and afterwards the French withdrew behind the guns of Lille. Marlborough returned to England after this fruitless campaign in a thoroughly bad temper, which was aggravated by political difficulties at home, and the Tory Opposition proceeded to attack the management of the war.

Marlborough's presence was badly needed in England, as differences had arisen between his two partners in the ruling triumvirate, Godolphin and Harley. It had been with some reluctance that Marlborough had given his support before the campaign began to the movement to force his son-in-law, the Whig Sunderland, upon Queen Anne as her second Secretary of State. The other Secretary of State, Robert Harley, had seen from the beginning that this was a first step in the direction of a wholly Whig Administration. Marlborough himself, though he acquiesced in Sunderland's appointment, at heart had remained convinced that a coalition Ministry was the best instrument with which to win an overwhelming victory over the French. In August 1706 he had written to Godolphin: 'I hope the reasonable men of the other party [the Tories] will not oppose the enlarging of the bottom so that it may be able to support itself.' This not very elegant phrase represented his conception of the Whig infiltration as simply a strengthening of the Coalition. When in England in 1707 he still tried to put this scheme into effect. He went to his friend the Duke of Shrewsbury, the leading Whig moderate, at his house in Oxfordshire and complained to him of his own and the Queen's uneasiness at the tyranny of the Whig oligarchy or Junto, as it was called, and suggested as an alternative to a purely Whig Ministry a new centre combination which should include Shrewsbury. But nothing came of this plan. Consequently Marlborough and Godolphin were obliged to capitulate to the demands of the Whig Junto, which meant getting rid of Harley, who intended to stick to the Tories through thick and thin. But this was not easy, for the Queen now personally preferred Harley to Godolphin. It was therefore doubtful whether she would accept her Treasurer's advice to promote the

Whig leaders to office. Marlborough for a long time hesitated to measure swords with Harley and provoke the Queen. In the course of the summer he told Sarah that he resented his treatment at the hands of the Whigs and particularly their attacks on his brother George at the Admiralty. But he found that if he intended to abide by Godolphin, who managed the war finances so amiably, he had no choice save to yield to the Whigs. A threat was now made by the Whigs to overthrow Godolphin, at the very time that he was completing the Act of Union with Scotland, unless they became supreme in the Cabinet. Harley, seeing which way the wind blew, prepared on his side to offer the Queen an alternative centre government of the very kind that Marlborough had proposed to Shrewsbury. As to the complex manœuvres that followed, it is sufficient to say that Marlborough and Godolphin offered their resignations, which the stubborn Queen was actually willing to accept rather than lose Harley and stomach the Whigs. But Harley, openly opposed by the hitherto victorious Commander-in-Chief, was unable to win the support of the moderate Whigs, without whom he could have no majority in the House of Commons, and he, not the queen, finally gave way and resigned. For the next two years a Whig Cabinet, anxious, like Marlborough, for the completest possible victory over France and Spain, ruled England. Marlborough, the ex-Tory, became their servant, and the Queen nursed her imaginary grievances and bided her time until she could call Harley back to power.

Chapter 8—A Brimstone of a Wife

Sarah's Influence on Marlborough—Her Temper and His Patience—Parsimony and Meanness—A Political Wife—A Case of Jealousy.

ANNE'S unwillingness to part with Harley was to some extent influenced by the fact that he had an advocate at court in the Queen's unobtrusive friend and dresser, the red-nosed Abigail Masham, and that by this time Anne had taken Mrs Masham as her confidante, while her intimate friendship with Sarah Marlborough was a thing of the past. This, however, was a minor factor in the situation, for we have long learned to despise the simple explanation which attributes Marlborough's rise to power in 1702 solely to his wife's friendship with Queen Anne or his ultimate fall in 1711 to Sarah's loss of Anne's affection. Marlborough became the allied Commander-in-Chief by reason of his own abilities and he lost his position because he was opposed to making peace when the country wanted peace. Sarah's place in Marlborough's life was different, though equally important. She helped to mould his character as a domineering wife can. He was in fact the henpecked husband *par excellence*. He acquired his monumental patience in the hard school of his own home.

Marlborough had married out of passion inspired by the youth, beauty, and vitality of Sarah Jennings. But in deciding to marry her handsome professional soldier she seems to have been influenced by something more than good looks. One of her few friends, the third Mrs Burnet, wrote:

Nor was it any blind or unreasonable passion that inclined her to prefer the Duke of Marlborough to all others, though his fortune then was in its infancy, but the effect of judgment. . . . She then saw that good understanding and those excellent qualities that have since made him the wonder of the world.

Sarah's ability to pick out able men is unquestionable. But though her push and thrust may have spurred him on, Marlborough's success was not her work, and she damaged rather than sustained his career. For she had a pen steeped in gall and a caustic tongue which lost her more friends than they made. Her temper was fierce and notorious. When a lampoon had compared Marlborough to the Roman Count Belisarius and Sarah asked Bishop Burnet where the comparison lay, he blurted out, truly enough: 'He had a brimstone of a wife.' She had an infinite capacity for quarrelling which extended not merely to her mother and mother-in-law and to Queen Anne, but to her husband, children, grandchildren, and most of her circle of acquaintances. Most of her daughters acquired their mother's temper and the Duke had to pour oil on the troubled family waters. After her husband's death, Sarah used to say that she received obedience and affection only from her three dogs.

Not only was Marlborough's patience home-grown, but so too was his parsimony. A detailed study of the relations between Marlborough and his wife would probably show that the reputation which he won in his lifetime for avarice was largely owing to her. From the very beginning she took control of their family finances.

Soon after my marriage [wrote Sarah], when our affairs were so narrow that a good deal of frugality was necessary, Lord Marlborough, though his inclination lay enough that way, yet by reason of an indulgent gentleness that is natural to him he could not manage matters so as was convenient to our circumstances. This obliged me to enter into the management of my family.

Though frugal, the Duke was capable of charity and self-denial. Plenty of examples of his 'indulgent gentleness'—gifts to the poor and wounded, loans to St John and subsidies to the poet Prior, for instance—are to be found. His refusal of the Governor-Generalship of the Netherlands and of Louis XIV's bribes show that power meant more to him than mere money. But Sarah's exaggerated carefulness in money matters was remarkable. She constantly wrote to her husband at the front bothering him about small questions of household management and preferred to waste his time checking a servant's honesty or the contents of the wine cellar than to leave him in peace to fight the war.

Likewise, as we have seen, Sarah constantly pestered her husband about political questions. Marlborough must be unique in history in having a wife who was for a time virtually his political opponent, a convinced partisan whose views he had to contest by post. From the beginning of the reign Sarah tried to foist the Whig Party on her husband and on the Queen. She wrongly imagined that the Princess Anne would remain her devout political pupil when she became Queen. Inevitably this alienated a ruler who was fully conscious of the dignity of her office. Moreover, Sarah came to neglect Anne, stayed away from court for long spells, interrupted her conversation, interfered in her personal affairs. It was not surprising that Anne turned for comfort elsewhere; and when after a long and violent quarrel Sarah was indiscreet enough to make some rude remarks about Anne's husband, Prince George, Sarah's loss of office as well as influence could only be a question of time.

In 1704, at the age of forty-four, Sarah came to the conclusion that her husband was unfaithful. The loss of her only son and the knowledge that she could not expect another may excuse or explain the accusations which she then made, naming a specific person. Marlborough assured her that he 'never sent to this woman,' although he added, 'as I know your temper I am very sensible that what I say signifies nothing.' On the eve of his march to the Danube he pleaded with her:

> If the thought of the children that we have had, or aught else that has ever been dear between us, can oblige you to be so good natured as not to leave my bed for the remaining time, I shall take it kindly to my dying day, and do most faithfully promise you that I will take the first occasion of leaving England, and assure you that you may rest quiet that from that time you shall never more be troubled with my hated sight.

When she saw him off at Harwich she handed him a 'paper,'

evidently containing further recriminations. 'I do own to you,' he wrote in reply, 'I have had more melancholy thoughts and spleen at what you said in that paper than I am able to express.' But a little later she relented and forgave. She even offered to go with him on the march to the Danube, and he was able to take the Harwich 'paper' out of his strong box and burn it. Who shall say that this quarrel is the only example of Sarah's cruelty to her husband or that this was the only suspicion that he aroused? Six years later old Lady Wentworth went to church, and afterwards described how

in the next pew to me there sits a young lady very genteel and very fair, but I think far from a beauty, but it is said she is kept by the Duke of Marlborough. . . .

Perhaps it was but village scandal. But who would have blamed the Duke if patient, henpecked, troubled by a thousand personal and public cares, he had turned for a while from his abnormal termagant wife and sought comfort elsewhere?

Chapter 9—France Invaded : 1708

Queen Anne and the Whigs—General Election—Loss of Ghent and Bruges —Battle of Oudenarde—Siege of Lille.

AFTER the dismissal of Harley at the behest of the Whig oligarchy, Marlborough and Godolphin, formerly Tories and then non-party men, became the prisoners of the Whigs. Under the inexorable pressure of the parliamentary facts they had surrendered. Queen Anne was as stubborn as ever. She refused to be more than polite to her new Cabinet Ministers, and did not hide her distaste for some of the leading members of her Government—with one exception, her Commander-in-Chief. Sarah, seeing the Queen's antagonism to the Whigs, and notably to her son-in-law, Sunderland, wrote Anne abusive letters. Godolphin was aware that the Queen would dismiss him as soon as she dared. Both therefore appealed to Marlborough to pacify the Queen, and when he was in the midst of the 1708 campaign he had to employ his time writing soothingly to Anne, trying to keep the home Government in being while he won the war. But gone was the intimacy of the early days. Frequent threats of resignation were uttered both by him and by Godolphin, but Marlborough's threats were mostly bluffs. The tactless conduct of Sarah, the growing boredom of Godolphin, who declared his life was a burden, the high-handed blackmail of the Whigs, the intrigues of the dismissed Harley, the indifference of the Queen never turned him from his determination to see the war through. Time, he was convinced, was all he needed. Once more, he pleaded: 'Give me one more year.'

A general election was now due, and a not unexpected event played into the hands of the Whigs. Louis XIV gave permission for a small expedition to invade Scotland in the name of the Pretender, 'James III.' Scottish discontent with the immediate results of the Act of Union, passed in the previous year, offered an opportunity; the genius of Admiral Forbin, commander of the Dunkirk privateers, provided the means. But Forbin's half-hearted expedition, carrying a pack of sea-sick exiles, was defeated as much by the elements as by Marlborough's elaborate precautions, and not a soldier landed. Nevertheless panic was widespread. The Whigs, who dubbed all Tories Jacobites—that is, secret followers of the exiled Stuarts—were given an election cry against 'traitors,' and the Queen's hopes that the moderate Tories would still hold the balance in Parliament were disappointed. The Whigs duly gained their majority, and pressed for fuller representation in the Cabinet, demanding the Presidency of the Council for their chief, Lord Somers. The Queen resisted, and Marlborough was begged to come back from Flanders to use his influence in the Whig favour. He not unnaturally refused; he wrote her letters as he was asked to do, but he knew that they would be of no effect; and he plunged into his plans for the campaign, fearful lest the notorious political difficulties in London should induce the Dutch, now tiring of the war, to rupture the alliance.

Marlborough aimed at achieving success in the new campaign by the use of surprise. He arranged that three armies should take the field in the northern theatre. The Imperialist general, the Elector of Hanover, the future King George I of England, was to operate with 45,000 men on the Rhine; Prince Eugene was to have 40,000 men on the Moselle; and Marlborough himself was to have 80,000 men in Flanders. He did not expect the Elector to act other than defensively; but he secretly planned that Eugene's army should join his and crush the French, who had about 90,000 men under the lascivious but not incompetent Marshal Vendôme. After a visit to Hanover to persuade the Elector to co-operate, Marlborough took up his headquarters with the army and awaited Eugene's arrival. On 11th June he wrote to Eugene: 'I request you to hasten in all diligence, for we can only reckon on a surprise which will depend on the little time you may take for your march between the Moselle and the Meuse.' But the customary delays of the Austrian and other German troops prevented Eugene from setting out, and meanwhile the French had prepared their own surprise blow. The discontent of the Belgians with the Dutch administration in the conquered Spanish provinces was exploited. A bold march by Vendôme across Marlborough's flank enabled the French to retake Ghent and Bruges at the beginning of July and to threaten Marlborough's communications with Ostend. For once Marlborough appears to have been caught by surprise, since the French had feinted against Louvain while he had hesitated to uncover Brussels.

Thus when Eugene at last arrived, but without his troops, to join the Duke in his camp near Brussels, he found him sunk in despondency. Physical weakness was the consequence or the accompaniment of mental depression. He was laid low with fever and had to be bled. But the presence of Eugene invigorated him. He decided no longer to await Eugene's dilatory army to give him a decisive advantage in man power, but to make an immediate counter-stroke. Vendôme, after he had taken Bruges and Ghent, determined to lay siege to Oudenarde, a small town which commanded the Scheldt between Ghent and Tournai on the French frontier. Marlborough took advantage of this move to persuade the French into believing that he was now advancing on the Scheldt merely in order to prevent the siege of Oudenarde, but in reality he was coming at them with battle in mind. When Cadogan with the advanced guard occupied the village of Lessines to the right of the Scheldt the deception had worked, for the French had no expectation of an allied offensive, and decided to cross the Scheldt lower down with a view to marching on Menin, another key fortress in allied hands. At 1 a.m. on the morning of 11th July Cadogan crossed the Scheldt south of Oudenarde with sixteen battalions and eight squadrons and ran into the French advanced guard consisting of seven Swiss batallions and twelve squadrons. As soon as the heads of the main army began to cross the pontoons which he had placed across the river, Cadogan decided to attack; the Swiss battalions were thrust back and surrendered and the French cavalry were driven off. Vendôme could at first scarcely credit the arrival of the allied army, whose infantry had marched fifty miles in sixty hours, but he decided to crush Cadogan with all his force. Trusting to his left wing simultaneously to launch an attack, he

* E

himself took command on the right. The left, through a mis-understanding, failed him.

Whether Cadogan's original attack was made on Marlborough's orders is uncertain. But as soon as the Duke took command the clash of advanced guards was developed by him into an 'encounter battle,' each regiment falling into its place to broaden the firing line as it reached the field across the river. Cadogan's forces became part of the right of the battle line, and at six o'clock in the evening Eugene was put in command of the whole of the allied right. On the left an essentially infantry battle in ground enclosed by woods and rivulets developed and ultimately, by bringing up his Dutch troops on the extreme left of his line, Marlborough threatened to envelop the French right flank completely. Although Eugene with the British cavalry more than held his own in the open ground on the right, it was on the allied left that the battle was won. Indeed, the French left, because it did not take its full share in the fighting, escaped relatively unharmed. But the whole French army was saved from annihilation only by the dark. It lost some 15,000 men in casualties and prisoners against the Allies' 3,000.

At Oudenarde Marlborough showed his genius for a type of contest entirely different from Blenheim or Ramillies. He thrust his men into line at the crucial points and shifted his troops from left to right with consummate coolness of judgment. But he owed much to the enemy's mistakes. Contrary to all the canons of war, he had been able to cross a river in face of a superior enemy late in the afternoon after a long and tiring march and by means of surprise win an overwhelming victory.

When the battle of Oudenarde took place the two armies were facing the wrong way; the Allies looked towards Holland, the French towards France. Afterwards the Allies were at last over the French frontier, while the French, by withdrawing towards Ghent, threatened the communications between the allied camp and the sea. Marlborough now proposed a daring project to Eugene, whose own troops had just joined him to give them a united force of 100,000 men. Let them mask the French frontier fortresses and advance into the heart of France. If they did so, the French would be obliged to leave Ghent and follow them. But the plan was too bold for Eugene. So instead, Marlborough vainly tried to move Vendôme from Ghent by ravaging the French provinces of Artois and Picardy. The Allies then laid siege to Lille, the biggest of the French frontier fortresses and one of the largest towns in France. The French command of the Bruges-Ghent canal made the obtaining of supplies for the siege through Ostend a matter of great difficulty. However, convoys were brought through, and on 13th August, the anniversary of Blenheim, Lille was invested; Eugene took charge of the siege while Marlborough directed the covering army, much inferior in numbers to the French who had more than replaced their heavy losses at Oudenarde since the Duke of Berwick, previously stationed on the Meuse, had now joined Vendôme with 27,000 men. So confident was Marlborough once again in the moral superiority of his men that he would have been glad to fight another battle; but the French twice refused it. Meanwhile, the siege of Lille, which was defended by the gallant old Marshal Boufflers with 16,000 men, went badly for the Allies. When in September Eugene was wounded and Marlborough for a time took over the operations he found grave deficiencies in supplies and incompetence among the engineers responsible for the sapping. Supplies were further endangered by the French occupying the line of the Scheldt and cutting communications with Brussels and Holland. But the road to the sea remained open and seven days later the French effort to relieve the town, not by fighting a battle but by stopping the allied convoys, was finally defeated at the engagement of Wynendael, when General Webb with 6,000 men repulsed a much superior force—a feat for which Marlborough gave him full credit, in spite of Thackeray's story in *Esmond*. On 22nd October Lille surrendered after ten weeks' siege, and at the price of some 12,000 casualties to the besiegers, though the citadel still resisted. It was not Boufflers's fault, and it is to his honour that by his courageous defence he prevented an imminent threat of his country being overrun by invaders. For if Lille had fallen as quickly as Marlborough had hoped it had still been his intention to thrust into the heart of France during that campaign. Instead, the Duke perforce turned to recapture Ghent and Bruges. He first forced the Scheldt at four separate points. Vendôme's counter-move in laying siege to Brussels, which had long been exposed to attack, was a failure and by the beginning of 1709 Brussels was relieved and Ghent and Bruges fell to the Allies. Thus the campaign, which contrary to the accepted rules lasted into the depths of winter, concluded according to Marlborough's 'heart's desire.'

Chapter 10—The Third Marlborough

The Three Marlboroughs—Secret Correspondence with Berwick—Its
motives—Relations with Jacobites—Their Four Phases.

THERE were three Marlboroughs. First, there was the public
figure, the patient, courteous, inscrutable, ever victorious
'Milord.' Secondly, there was the harassed and henpecked
private man, subject to vast fits of depression and actual physical
illness when things did not go right—the man who appealed,
cajoled and threatened, and abused his enemies in his private
correspondence. Thirdly, there was the master intriguer who
held secret conclaves with French or Jacobite agents, penned
anonymous letters and spun meaningless phrases of good advice
merely in order to safeguard his own personal position and property in the event of counter-revolution.

Never in the whole of Marlborough's life are his three selves
more fully visible in the light of history than during the year
1708. This was one of the most glorious years in his military
career. Yet during the same season the duke not only had that
tremendous fit of depression at the beginning of the campaign,
but was reduced to a constant state of worry by the stream of
complaining letters which reached him from London. He knew
that since the Whig infiltration into the ministry Godolphin
had lost the confidence of the Queen, that she had resented being
forced to admit more Whigs into the Cabinet, and that the
Government was maintained in power almost solely by his own
victories. Finally, simply by way of precaution, without saying
a word to a soul, Marlborough, after Oudenarde, entered into a
secret and indirect correspondence with the ministers of Louis
XIV to discover the likelihood of peace negotiations.

This secret correspondence was carried on through Marlborough's nephew, the Duke of Berwick. Berwick had become
by dint of sheer skill one of the leading generals in the French
Army, but he remained loyal to the exiled Court of St Germains,
and did what he could to promote the claims of his half-brother,
the Old Pretender, 'James III,' to the throne of Great Britain.
Marlborough's correspondence with the exiled court was not, of
course, a new departure; but now it took a novel turn. As there
are gaps in the surviving letters, the details are a little obscure;
but it seems that Berwick wrote first to thank his uncle for
exerting his influence to obtain mercy for Lord Griffin, an aged

Jacobite who had been captured from a French ship during the abortive expedition of the early spring. At the same time Berwick suggested a personal meeting between them to discuss possible terms of peace; but Marlborough evaded so compromising a step. As the correspondence developed, Marlborough expressed his wish that the French should make some peace proposals publicly in Holland. He did not specify exactly what proposals might prove acceptable but said they must 'conform to the interests of my country.' Although the correspondence continued by fits and starts, nothing came of it, because the French said that it was against the dignity of Louis XIV to open negotiations in Holland and demanded an armistice first. Two points, however, emerge from this section of the Marlborough-Berwick secret correspondence. First, Marlborough was committing himself to nothing dishonourable. His motive was to ensure that if peace negotiations were opened he should be kept informed about them and not presented with an accomplished fact by the French and Dutch. Yet, secondly, it was typical of the man that Marlborough also hoped to get something for himself if by any unexpected chance peace negotiations should prove fruitful, for in one letter he took care to remind Berwick that three years earlier an agent of the French king had promised him 2,000,000 livres (about £300,000) if peace were concluded with his help.

Another section of this same correspondence well defines Marlborough's real attitude to the Pretender. He told Berwick that he was willing to serve the Pretender 'without prejudice to the interests of my country' and provided that in promoting the Pretender's interests he was not merely benefiting France. Moreover, he clearly stated that he could not help the Pretender unless he were 'recalled by the nation.' Since 'James III' was as firm a Roman Catholic as his father and a notorious pensioner of France, the likelihood of his recall was small. Thus all that Marlborough did was to inform the exiled court that if after the death of Queen Anne England expressed a unanimous wish to bring back the Stuarts (instead, according to the Act of Settlement, of bringing in the electoral family of Hanover), he personally would not stand in their way. By this pledge he hoped to safeguard his own position and ward off a justly merited revenge for the manner in which he had treated the unfortunate James II.

This policy of 'reinsuring' himself against the event of a Jacobite restoration was probably the dominant motive for Marlborough's prolonged secret contacts with the exiled Stuarts.

But there were other motives, and in his thirty-year maintenance
of these contacts it is possible to detect four distinct phases.
The first phase was during the reign of William III, when Marlborough headed a sort of inchoate opposition to William and his
Dutch favourites. He then thought that it would do no harm
to bring the English Jacobites into his hotch-potch coalition
against the unpopular Dutch ruler. But when in 1701 William
selected Marlborough to carry on his feud with France the
Jacobite connections were at once loosened. Although Marlborough continued to inform the Jacobite agents that 'in the
proper time and place he will pay his debt to King James,' there
was reported in St Germains to be 'a manifest cooling' on Marlborough's part, and it was even proposed that the Pretender
should marry one of his daughters in order presumably to warm
him up again. Berwick himself never seems to have seriously
believed that Marlborough meant much by his polite messages
to St Germains; but he kept on writing to his uncle in case one
day the correspondence might prove a useful channel of communication. By the middle of the war most of the other leading
Jacobites came to agree with Berwick that Marlborough's professions of friendship meant nothing.

Thus we come to 1708-9, and the third phase in Marlborough's
relations with the Jacobites, in which he made use of his special
position to open a window on to the diplomatic schemes of the
Court of Versailles. Ever since the Allies overran Belgium and
the frontier of Holland was made safe, Marlborough was gnawed
by the fear that the Dutch would desert the Grand Alliance, and
thereby put an end to the war. His oft-avowed desire for peace
was only for peace on the most stringent terms. Consequently
he hoped by his letters to Berwick to prevent any separate
negotiations which might cut the ground from under the British
Government's feet.

The fourth phase of Marlborough's relations with the Jacobites
followed his own fall from power in 1711. He then came to have
two objects in view. First, there was again, and slightly more
urgently, his policy of personal reinsurance. Marlborough hoped
and expected that when Queen Anne died the Hanoverians would
peacefully ascend the throne. But there was just an outside
chance that if the Pretender should change his religion the Stuarts
would be brought back instead. In the late autumn of 1713
Marlborough sent a messenger or spy to Paris to see how the land
lay. But he then had a second object. By this time the Treaty
of Utrecht had been signed, and the Tories were in full cry against

the Whig 'warmongers.' Marlborough was afraid that in this revengeful mood they might confiscate his estates, and he begged Louis XIV—his arch-enemy!—to intercede with Queen Anne—his former friend!—to see that Parliament did not beggar him. In all the fantasy of Marlborough's elaborate but hollow intrigues with the Court of St Germains nothing is more extraordinary than this episode. At that time too he, the notorious miser, even thought it worth while to send 'a small sum' to Queen Mary of Modena as an earnest of his good faith. At precisely that moment, however, the Duke was also assuring the Elector of Hanover by post that his friends in England were anxious to serve the Hanoverian cause, and that he would do everything in his power to prevent the Tory Government from bringing in the Pretender. Thus he put a small sum on both the competitors for the throne of England and, having insured himself both ways, was on the death of Queen Anne restored to his estates and offices without difficulty.

But still the comedy dragged on. As late as 1716 an eminent Jacobite reported that Marlborough had told a Jacobite agent, 'with tears in his eyes,' that he intended 'to serve James III.' But the Duke of Berwick summed up the true state of the matter when he wrote in this same year that 'Marlborough has for these many years been in correspondence with his nephew [himself], and has always given assurances of his zeal for King James, but to this hour he has never explained in what manner he intended it.'

Chapter 11—The Twice-Lost Peace : 1709-10

The Dutch Barrier Treaty—Peace Negotiations with France—The allied 'Preliminaries'—Battle of Malplaquet—Fall of Tournai and Mons—Request for Captain-Generalship for Life—Quarrel with Queen over Abigail Masham—Peace Negotiations at Gertruydenberg.

MARLBOROUGH'S successes in the campaign of 1708, combined with French and Spanish defeats in other war theatres and a terrible frost which ruined the French crops and threatened starvation, made Louis XIV extremely desirous of peace. Informal contacts had long been maintained between France and Holland with a view to seizing any favourable opportunity for negotiations. The Dutch were now offered territorial concessions by France. Simultaneously, the Whig Ministry in London became

anxious to obtain Dutch support for the Protestant succession
to Queen Anne, and for the continuance of the war until the
wealth of the Spanish Empire was at their disposal.   Thus the
Whig ministers now spontaneously renewed the proposal that in
return for a guarantee of the succession Great Britain should
secure for the Dutch their coveted barrier of fortresses in the
Spanish Netherlands.   Marlborough, however, strongly opposed
conceding the Dutch their barrier before a general peace was concluded.   His dominant idea was to keep the Grand Alliance
together.   If the Dutch were granted special conditions he
thought the Austrians would be alienated and that the Dutch,
secure in their treaty, would at once become less enthusiastic for
the continuation of the war.   But, as so often, a personal element
entered into his calculations.   He had not abandoned the hope
that he would one day, when the war was over, become Governor-
General of the Spanish Netherlands.   The Emperor had recently
renewed this offer.   If those Netherlands, however, were to be
partitioned with British agreement in order to give the Dutch
their barrier fortresses, the Emperor would certainly not be so
willing to confer their governorship on a British general.   Hence,
by deliberate procrastination and intrigue, he did his utmost to
rupture the Barrier negotiations.

Marlborough had no such secret motive for preventing the
success of the negotiations with France, but he naturally objected
to any separate Franco-Dutch discussions until the Allies had
agreed together on demands that could be jointly presented to
the French delegates.   He succeeded in shelving the Barrier
negotiations, and inducing the Dutch and Austrians to agree on
a joint ultimatum to France which was euphemistically called the
'preliminaries.'   By these France was to surrender the entire
Spanish Empire, consisting of the Netherlands, Spain itself, the
Indies, Naples, Sicily, and Milan, as well as Strasbourg and
Alsace, to the Habsburg emperor and to yield a group of fortresses
to the Dutch.   In the event of Louis XIV's grandson, Philip of
Anjou, refusing to evacuate Spain within two months, the Allies
were by Article XXXVII to keep their gains and renew the war.
Torcy, the French Foreign Minister, who came to Holland to
treat, gave way point by point on all these severe terms, but
finally refused to sign the treaty without reference to Versailles.
Confident that the French were beaten beyond recovery, Marlborough fully expected the French king would be compelled to
sign and looked forward cheerfully to peace.   But Louis could
not agree to the clauses which in effect obliged him to make

immediate war on his own grandson, and the Allies' ultimatum was rejected.

Marlborough was staggered by the news. 'Are there then no counter-proposals?' he inquired. He thought, however, that if the Dutch were firm the French would be compelled to comply. Negotiations continued for a time, the Allies suggesting as an alternative to the obnoxious Article XXXVII that Louis XIV should hand over to them three towns in Spain as well as three in Flanders as a guarantee for the evacuation of Spain. But to force the Spaniards to surrender three towns was as hard as making them drive their own choice as king from his throne, and thus the war had to go on.

There is no question that the British Government was mainly responsible for the failure of the peace negotiations at a time when Marlborough's victories had forced France so low that she would have conceded nearly anything. Although some play has recently been made with an isolated quotation from Torcy's *Mémoires*, there is no evidence to show that Marlborough had any serious doubts about Article XXXVII until after the 'preliminaries' were rejected. Then both he and Eugene laid the blame for the breakdown of negotiations on the Dutch, which was entirely unfair. For the Dutch were only acting as the mouthpieces of the Allies, and consented to the far-reaching character of the 'preliminaries' only out of deference to the British Whig Government, and in the hope of thereby obtaining a guarantee of their Barrier. Marlborough became equally critical of the demand for the three Spanish towns and thought that the better plan would be for the Allies to make a separate treaty with the French, which would prevent them 'playing tricks,' and then themselves concentrate their war efforts against Spain. He optimistically thought that they could drive Philip out of Spain in six months if his grandfather ceased to help him.

Marlborough's attitude to the diplomatic negotiations of 1709 therefore differed from that of the Government of which he was a leading member. He differed from the Whigs over their desire to conclude a Barrier Treaty with the Dutch, and neglected his instructions on this point; he differed from them in his belief that if the Dutch were once guaranteed their Barrier, they would immediately desert the Grand Alliance; and he differed from them as to the best method of driving Philip of Anjou from Spain. At the same time he had become so accustomed to deferring to other people that whatever confidential views he might express he never exerted himself to enforce his own point of view on his

own Government. Thus it was by sins of omission rather than
of commission that Marlborough helped to prolong the war in
1709. He was still hopeful that the French were so demoralized
that one more battle would bring them to their knees. This was
the mood in which at the beginning of June he entered upon the
campaign.

Not only the unsuccessful peace negotiations, but a combination of other circumstances, delayed the opening of the campaign
of 1709. The frosty winter had been followed by a cold spring
which restricted the forage. Heavy rains washed away the
roads. The previous campaign had continued unusually late,
and a respite of six months was needed to collect new mercenaries.
Had Marlborough been able to start sooner, there were no oppos-
ing forces to prevent a march deep into the heart of France. As
it was, in spite of the starvation which stalked his land, the
Great Monarch, his glory now tarnished, had been able to rally
the French people. Villars, the only French general whose
career is comparable with that of Marlborough or Eugene, had
been put in command and by dint of push and bluff had gathered
an army of a sort behind him. He was able to use it to man the
defences which he constructed to the west of the line of frontier
fortresses. Lille had fallen, but there still remained three powerfully fortified towns—Ypres, Tournai, and Mons. Marlborough
decided against the hazard of attacking the gaunt but grim and
determined French army which held these new lines of La
Bassée south-west of Lille. Instead, after feinting against Ypres,
he laid siege to the town of Tournai, which, after much deep
sapping to avoid the mines, was surrendered by the governor on
30th July.

After the fall of Tournai the allied army moved against Mons,
still farther away from the main road to Paris, and Villars, surprised by their decision, left his own lines with a view to inter-
rupting the siege. Between the two armies there ran a screen of
forest, but in the forest were two big gaps. The Allies reached
the northern gap first, but Villars was first at the southern gap—
known as the gap of Malplaquet. Both sides were prepared to
fight. According to one opinion Marlborough tempted Villars
by leaving the gaps open. Another opinion has it that Villars
surprised Marlborough by feinting at the northern gap before
occupying the southern. In any case there seems little doubt
that Villars was willing, and had permission from Versailles, to
try a defensive battle in order to strengthen the morale of the raw

French troops and that, on the other side, Marlborough and Eugene preferred an attempt to destroy the last French army rather than simply cover the siege of Mons. Villars occupied the woods on both sides of the Malplaquet gap with infantry, built redans (earthworks) in his centre, and drew up his troops in a concave V-shape so that if the enemy entered between the two receding wings they would be overwhelmed by a withering fire. But the experienced generals opposite were too wise to fall into so obvious a trap. Their plan, on the contrary, was to assault the two French wings so fiercely that Villars would be obliged to weaken his centre; then fifteen battalions of British infantry, kept in reserve, could break through.

The battle was delayed for a day while the Allies awaited the arrival of eighteen squadrons under General Withers that were coming from Tournai. Marlborough was willing to begin without them, but Eugene refused, and it seems that he was right. For, although the extra day enabled Villars to fortify further his formidable position, Withers's men were to play a decisive part.

The battle opened on 11th September, as planned, with a fierce attack on the French wings resting on or in the woods. The resistance was unexpectedly severe. On the left wing of the Allies the splendid Dutch Blue Guards were mown down. On the right, commanded by Prince Eugene, the Germans were at first successful, but then checked. Marlborough had personally to go up and call a halt to prevent the annihilation of the Dutch on the left. Some blamed the young Dutch prince who had bravely led the charge for going beyond his orders, and making a reality of an attack which was only intended as a feint. There was no basis for this. Both French wings had to be assaulted simultaneously. But the battle was decided on the right largely by the arrival of Withers's men, who entered the woods at the extreme north by an unguarded path, and threatened to outflank the whole French position. Villars denuded his centre to meet the threat, and a desperate and bloody struggle swayed to and fro on the western edge of the woods. The redans were left almost defenceless, and the British infantry was able to clear the way for a cavalry advance, and the French line split asunder. Villars was badly wounded just as he heard this news and was preparing a counter-stroke. Marshal Boufflers, who took over the command, organized six vain charges against the British infantry who had occupied the deserted earthworks in the centre. He then withdrew his men in good order from the battlefield, and the Allies were too exhausted to pursue.

Judged by the larger issues, Malplaquet was a French victory.
It is true that the French were forced to evacuate the field and
abandon Mons to its fate.   But with inferior troops both in
numbers and in quality (the French were about 80,000 and the
Allies 100,000) they had inflicted far larger casualties.   The
Allies lost nearly one-fifth of their men, the French about 11,000.
Marlborough himself had to confess it was 'a very murdering
battle.'   Moreover, by entrenching himself and awaiting the onslaught Villars could scarcely have hoped for a decisive victory.
What he had done was to restore the honour of the French Army,
to keep his forces together, and to stave off the invasion of France.
When Marlborough wrote home after the battle, 'God Almighty
be praised, it is now in our power to have what peace we please,'
he was deceiving himself.   Malplaquet raised the spirits of the
French.   Never again in the war was there to be so fine an
opportunity of a Carthaginian peace as was thrown away after
the Oudenarde campaign.

The citadel of Tournai had at length fallen on 3rd September,
and Mons fell on 23rd October.   But in Spain there were no
corresponding allied successes, even though Louis XIV had been
compelled to withdraw most of his troops from the Peninsula.
Philip of Anjou controlled most of Spain except Catalonia, and
thus the parrot cry of 'No peace without Spain,' which Marlborough and Godolphin had originated and which had now been
wholeheartedly adopted by the Whig Government, was nowhere
nearer realization.   But the nation, after eight weary and costly
years of war, was demanding peace.   Swimming with the current,
Queen Anne could prepare her revenge on the Whigs whom she
detested.

While Marlborough had been fighting Malplaquet, Lord
Townshend, the Whig statesman who had been sent from London
as his diplomatic colleague, continued to negotiate with the Dutch
about their Barrier Treaty.   His view and that of the Home
Government was that if the Dutch were once promised their
Barrier they would be bound to continue the war until the French
agreed to surrender the 'cautionary towns' in Spain and thereby
pave the way for expelling the French prince from Madrid.   Marlborough, who followed the negotiations closely, disagreed
utterly.   He still favoured a separate treaty between the Allies
and France and a war against Spain alone conducted by himself.
As to the Barrier Treaty, he adhered to his opinion that once it
was signed the Dutch would desert the alliance.   He also thought

the Dutch demands excessive (as he privately explained to his Austrian friends) and that the treaty should not be signed without a specific promise from the Dutch not to make peace until the entire Spanish Empire was surrendered by Philip of Anjou. He therefore washed his hands of both affairs and left Townshend to sign, in October 1709, a Barrier Treaty whereby the Dutch were promised a long line of fortresses in return simply for a guarantee of the Hanoverian succession to the British throne. But the subsequent conduct of the Dutch proved that Marlborough was entirely wrong in his forebodings.

His refusal to take part in these diplomatic negotiations was the first outward sign of his declining influence. The Whig Junto had taken over the real direction of foreign policy and domestic questions. Throughout the summer, for instance, they had insisted that Lord Orford, their last member without office, should be put at the head of the Admiralty. Marlborough and Godolphin grumbled and Queen Anne openly objected. But Marlborough gave way. The queen, every inch a Stuart, proved less willing to consent to the arrogant Whig dominance and she secretly consulted Harley, the Tory leader, who came up the back stairs to see her through the connivance of Abigail Masham.

Abigail's growing influence not only worried the Whigs, but excited the jealousy of Sarah Marlborough, who, though she had long ceased to be friendly with her sovereign, was still her first lady-in-waiting. Sarah's quarrels with the Queen and his friend Godolphin's subjection to the Whigs made Marlborough all the more conscious of his declining power. He tried to re-habilitate himself in the eyes of the foreign courts and generals by asking the Queen, in October 1709, to make him Captain-General for life, an unprecedented request which she unhesitatingly refused. On her refusal he wrote her a reproachful letter. The result of the transaction was to weaken his influence with the Queen and to give a handle to his Tory enemies, who accused him of aspiring to a Cromwellian dictatorship.

A further cause of dissension arose between Marlborough and Queen Anne after his return from the war in the following month. Anne proposed to appoint Abigail's brother, Colonel Hill, to a vacant regiment. Marlborough strongly objected and again threatened to resign. He proposed to his Cabinet colleagues that they should jointly demand Abigail's dismissal and that he should confront the Queen with the alternative of dismissing either Abigail or himself. The Queen realized that she had gone too far and agreed to withdraw the Hill appointment; but she clung to Abigail. Marlborough still wanted to fight, but was overborne by Godolphin and the more timorous members of the Cabinet. In their view it was a bad issue on which to attack the Queen. Marlborough therefore withdrew his resignation, stomached Abigail, and merely wrote pathetically to Anne complaining that his 'love, zeal, and duty' had 'not been able to protect me against the malice of a Bedchamber Woman.'

In March 1710, leaving all this distasteful intrigue behind him, Marlborough went back to The Hague to prepare for the next campaign. But first he had to keep a watchful eye upon some new peace negotiations in progress in Holland at what was known as the Congress of Gertruydenberg. Louis XIV had not been especially cheered by the battle of Malplaquet, and his delegates again offered the Allies good terms. He would give up Alsace to the emperor and pay a subsidy to the Allies to help them dethrone his grandson. But the Dutch, who acted as the allied spokesmen, stuck to the harsh demand that Louis himself should expel his grandson from Spain within two months. If he failed to do this, the Allies were to be free to renew the war and to keep the 'cautionary towns' which Louis was expected to yield in order to gain even two months' grace. In making these excessive demands the Dutch were, however, only the catspaws of the Whigs, to whom they were now bound hand and foot by the Barrier Treaty. From Marlborough's private letters to Godolphin we know that the Dutch would have been perfectly willing to let Philip of Anjou have the throne of Sicily, which belonged to the Spanish Empire, to induce him to leave Spain quietly. The Austrians for their part would not hear of Sicily, but would have been ready to waive the demand that Louis should drive his grandson from Spain if the 'cautionary towns' were surrendered. The British Whigs alone stood by the full rigour of the demands. Marlborough, who had decided to abandon diplomacy and to confine himself to military activity, played no effective part at all in this vital matter. Indeed, he had resigned himself to a philosophic contemplation of political events and described changing the views of the Dutch or of the Queen as 'painting a blackamoor white.' So he stood idly by and watched the last chance of a triumphant peace being dissipated.

Chapter 12—War Without End : 1710-11

Reaction in favour of Tories—Shrewsbury Enters Cabinet—Campaign of 1710—Godolphin Dismissed—Marlborough Humiliated—Sarah Dismissed—Death of Emperor Leopold—Ne Plus Ultra Lines Crossed—Siege of Bouchain—War Weariness.

AFTER Oudenarde Queen Anne exclaimed, 'Oh, Lord, when will all this dreadful bloodshed cease?' After Malplaquet she began to conclude that it was her duty to take positive steps to end the war. She reflected much articulate and inarticulate public opinion which was steadily veering against Godolphin and the Whig administration. In consequence of the apparently unending war, food prices were rising, taxation was heavy, and the methods of recruiting severe. The supporters of war to the finish and of peace at a moderate price had become divided on distinct class lines. On the one hand, the commercial classes, in search of the reputed riches of the Spanish Empire, were pretty solidly behind the Whigs, and the new Bank of England continued to put its money on 'no peace without Spain.' On the other hand, the landed proprietors were sickened by the large increases in the land tax. As Sir John Packington was to put it a year later, only an end to the war would 'prevent the beggaring of the nation and prevent the moneyed men becoming lords of us who have lands.'

On top of social and economic discontents came a political dispute. On 5th November, the day on which William III had landed at Tor Bay, a High Church parson, Dr Henry Sacheverell, preached a sermon in St Paul's Cathedral condemning the doctrines of the Glorious Revolution. This infuriated the Whig Government, while Godolphin, whose Whiggism was scarcely noticeable, was offended at what he thought to be a personal attack on himself in the sermon. So the decision was taken to impeach Sacheverell for high treason. He was condemned in the House of Lords by a few votes, but received a purely nominal punishment. The effect of impeaching a somewhat obscure clergyman for a sermon was disastrous for the Whigs. The Opposition Tories were able to raise their old battle-cry, 'The Church in danger!'—an alarm to which even Marlborough's own chaplain succumbed. Property owners were also concerned at the subversive republican ideas which they detected in the terms of the impeachment. From this time onwards it became obvious that a general election would mean the defeat of the Government, and Queen Anne, now out of sympathy with the Marlboroughs, discarded cronies of her younger days, joyfully awaited the Whigs' overthrow.

Taking advantage of the Government's demoralization, Harley, the Queen's secret Tory adviser, began to detach the weaker members of the Cabinet from their loyalty to the Whig Junto and to Godolphin. He held out to them promises of high office in a reconstructed Cabinet and first preference shares in the Queen's favour. Such was the atmosphere of intrigue and royal antagonism which Marlborough discovered in London in the winter of 1709 and was to be the background of his next campaign. On 15th April, after he had sailed, Queen Anne, without consulting Godolphin, nominally her chief minister, introduced the Duke of Shrewsbury into the Cabinet as Lord Chamberlain. This was the thin end of the wedge. Shrewsbury was a Whig by repute and he and Marlborough had been friends for many years, but Marlborough knew at once that he was brought in as Harley's Trojan horse. Thenceforward, throughout spring and summer, Marlborough saw gloomily but helplessly the doom opening for his friends and supporters in England. He faced the prospect with patient resignation. He hoped that a general election would be postponed for the time being, so that the Whig majority in the Commons, still eager for the war, would be preserved; and even for a time imagined that some lucky turn in the campaign would revive his personal credit with his sovereign. 'If we have a battle,' he wrote in May, 'it must be the last. . . . I hope God will bless me with another opportunity of giving a mark of my zeal for the Queen and my country, and then I shall be less concerned at the behaviour [sic] I have received of late.'

But there was to be no 'last battle.' Flanders had become the major theatre of war and the French had concentrated the bulk of their man-power under the now recovered Villars to resist the Allied penetration into France. Before Villars took up his command, however, Marlborough and Eugene made their first move early in the season by turning the French lines and laying siege to Douai, the capture of which would open the way for direct invasion of France. But this town, well fortified and defended, did not in fact fall until 26th June, two months later. In the course of the siege Marlborough had an opportunity to attack the French army which he refused. Why he refused is a mystery. On the one side it is said that the assault of the fortified French lines took on a new value after the costly 'victory' of

Malplaquet; on the other that Marlborough was 'oppressed by the hostility of the Queen and the growing power of his foes in England.' Yet had he not written that he was seeking a battle that would be his last? The truth is that once again the general was in a thoroughly defeatist mood. A fortnight later, on 14/25th June, Sunderland, his son-in-law and ever the Queen's *bête noire*, was dismissed from the Cabinet and replaced as Secretary of State by a 'moderate.' Marlborough had vainly appealed to Shrewsbury to save Sunderland. The divided Whig Government failed to make any exertion on Sunderland's behalf, and on the contrary wrote jointly to Marlborough asking him not to show his resentment and to retain his command. Marlborough agreed; but henceforward washed his hands even of foreign politics. After the fall of Douai, Villars again gave Marlborough the chance to fight another Malplaquet, but he refused and turned aside to besiege a number of minor fortresses. His mind seems to have been paralysed by the political disasters at home. Although he and Eugene commanded 120,000 men, they failed to achieve anything of substantial military importance and thereby abandoned the last chance of forcing Louis XIV to sue for peace on the abject terms of which they both approved.

While Marlborough was being reduced to stalemate in Flanders, Godolphin was being steadily outmanœuvred in London. Slowly but surely Queen Anne, acting on Harley's advice, undermined the Whigs. The proud Junto of 1708 crumpled before a series of oblique attacks and up went the cry of 'Sauve qui peut!' The Duke of Somerset and the Earl of Halifax were detached from their Cabinet colleagues; to the Duke of Newcastle, another 'moderate,' Harley held out the promise of a reconstructed coalition Ministry similar to that of 1702. On 7th August Queen Anne struck her boldest blow: she dismissed without a kind word her Lord Treasurer Godolphin who had served his country with single-minded devotion for eight years. But still the leading Whigs clung to their offices, incapable of perceiving the rising storm. Even Harley himself did not appreciate how strong the Tory reaction of the electorate would be. But Shrewsbury saw the one big issue when he told the Austrian ambassador that 'England is badly in need of peace.' When in the autumn the general election took place, Anne showed that she had correctly interpreted the trend of feeling in the country. The Whigs were beaten by a majority of three to one; there could thus be no question of a moderate or middle ministry. Harley came back as the head of a purely Tory administration pledged to make peace.

Marlborough deeply resented the treatment of Godolphin. But he found it impossible to give up his command in the middle of the campaign, and Godolphin himself begged him not to do so. But Godolphin's curt dismissal finally ensured that no striking military results would be obtained that year. On 31st July–11th August, just before Godolphin went, Marlborough wrote to him:

I am of opinion that after the siege of Aire I shall have it in my power to attack Calais . . . but I see so much malice levelled at me, that I am afraid it is not safe for me to make any proposition; fearing, if it should not succeed, my enemies might turn it to my disadvantage.

He had to suffer a series of humiliations at the hands of Harley's new ministry. Cardonnel, his former secretary, was deprived of his office of Secretary at War; Cadogan, his right-hand man, ceased to be envoy to the Dutch; a commission was set up in London to decide army promotions; and three of his subordinates were cashiered for having drunk the toast 'damnation and confusion to the new Ministry.' Fearful of the general's popularity, the new ministers hired pamphleteers to ridicule his avarice and condemn his ambition. But in spite of these insults and his inability to win a major military success, Marlborough remained abroad until the end of the year, seeing to the conquest of a group of fortresses on the north-eastern frontier of France—Béthune, Aire, and St Venant—which prepared the way for a good campaign in the following year. Whatever criticisms may be made of his retention of offices after his return to England, his patriotic conduct under the grossest provocation after Godolphin's dismissal cannot be questioned.

Marlborough delayed as long as possible his return to England and his interview with the 'new vipers'—as he called them—who now governed the country. But when he did come, early in January 1711, he was pleased and surprised at the warm welcome which he received from the public. Abroad the armies and the Allies had rallied to him on the defeat of his political friends. The Dutch had cried, 'Lord! what will become of us?' should he relinquish his command. He was, in fact, the symbol of the continuing unity of the Grand Alliance, and without him the new Tory ministers began to be afraid that they could not exact reasonable peace terms from the French. So Harley now decided to abandon his intention of forcing Marlborough from his offices, but Queen Anne, always bolder than Harley, insisted for her part that Sarah must be dismissed from court. Consequently, Marlborough's first task on his return was to try to induce the Queen not to affront him through his wife. Sarah had been trying to blackmail the Queen by threatening the publication of Anne's letters to her. Marlborough would have none of that. But he submitted to every indignity to try to save his wife's position. He grovelled before the Queen. He carried to her a humble letter from Sarah which asserted that he could not live six months if she were sacked. The Queen was unmoved, and demanded Sarah's gold key of office as Groom of the Stole within two days. Sarah returned the key at once, but before she went she exacted a cash payment of £18,000 which she claimed the Queen owed her, and took care to remove even the brass locks from the doors of her palace apartments. On other questions Anne was equally stiff with her general. Marlborough was told that there could be no question of reinstating his three favourite officers who had been cashiered and that he must not suffer any votes of thanks to him to be moved in Parliament. He was also advised that 'he must draw a line between all that has passed and all that is to come and that he must begin entirely upon a new foot.' A combination of threats and promises was used to prevent his resignation.

Marlborough has left one record of his own reasons for keeping his command under such humiliating conditions. He told a Hanoverian minister that he did not want to expose himself to the censure of those foreigners who were his friends for refusing to serve the Alliance and that he wished to remain in a position to ensure the Protestant succession to the British throne. But this, of course, is what he had to tell the Hanoverian court which held the Protestant successor. As usual, there was a mixture of patriotic and personal motives in his mind. Blenheim Palace, that 'monstrous pile' on which he had set his heart, was still but half completed and the Tory Treasury had stopped payments. A promise was given him that the payments would be resumed if he kept his command. Hence he went quickly back to the war in March, while unbeknown to him the British Ministry was setting on foot secret negotiations for a separate peace with France.

These secret negotiations were made easier by an unexpected event. In April the young Emperor Joseph I died and his brother, the Archduke Charles, the Allies' candidate for the Spanish throne and empire, succeeded to the vast Habsburg dominions. Charles was at the time in Catalonia, which was the only part of Spain retained by the Allies after ten years of war. His succession to the throne of Vienna enabled the Tory Government to argue that the balance of power in Europe would be upset if a Habsburg ruler held sway not only over the whole of Austria and Hungary, the bulk of Italy, and modern Belgium, but Spain and the Indies as well, and that therefore the Whig view that peace should not be made without Spain being torn from Philip of Anjou was no longer valid. The emperor's death also had a disastrous effect upon the military campaign in France. Eugene, who had joined Marlborough at Douai, had to return to Germany with most of his troops to ensure that Charles was elected Holy Roman Emperor in his brother's stead, and Villars, the French commander, by detaching a few of his troops to the Rhine, was able to draw off from France a higher proportion of the Allied troops.

The situation at the beginning of the 1711 campaign was that a breach had been blown in the last defences of France. In consequence of the previous campaign, Arras and Cambrai remained the last important fortresses of the French frontier barrier between Ypres on the north-east and Valenciennes, Maubeuge, and Le Quesnoy farther south. Villars had done his best to protect the most vulnerable area with field fortifications, nicknamed the Ne Plus Ultra lines, stretching through Arras to beyond Bouchain, a small but useful fortress south-west of Valenciennes. In spite of his temporary conciliation with Harley, Marlborough was ill and depressed after the departure of Eugene. But at length he pulled himself together and determined to penetrate the Ne Plus Ultra lines. These were covered to the east by a number of rivers and inundations and were naturally weakest at their western end. Villars therefore concentrated his forces to the west, where Marlborough sat opposite him in the plains of Lens. Marlborough now planned an ingenious stratagem. One of the causeways across the rivers to the east of the Ne Plus Ultra was guarded by a fort named Arleux. By taking this fort, strengthening its defences and then allowing Villars to recapture it, Marlborough induced Villars himself to demolish it. Then Marlborough circulated the story that he was going to attack Villars's whole army at the other end of the lines. But while feinting to the west he detached Cadogan to collect an advance guard from Douai and also sent his artillery to the east. At nightfall on 5th August, after feinting again to the French left,

Marlborough rapidly marched with the whole of his army to the right of the long French lines. He thus gained several hours on the French which they could not hope to overtake. He crossed the River Sensée at two points near the demolished fort of Arleux and was over the Ne Plus Ultra lines without firing a shot. The French were not far behind, however, and a day later were drawn up in a strong position to the south-west of the allied forces. Villars had his wings well covered, and it was out of the question for Marlborough to attack him so long as he dreaded a second Malplaquet. Marlborough was censured in Holland for not attacking the enemy and had to explain that

there is not one general or other officer that have the least judgment in these matters but must allow it was altogether impossible to attack the enemy with any probable hope of success.

Instead, he laid siege to Bouchain. This siege was unique in the annals of eighteenth-century warfare. Villars was compelled to watch Marlborough bombard the town into surrender, although he had an army larger by some 6,000 men than that of the Allies. Marlborough constructed an elaborate series of earthworks to protect his communications, while he had the usual lines of circumvallation to the south to cut off the garrison from the French army. While Marlborough bombarded Bouchain, Villars bombarded Marlborough's siege army. But by 12th September the siege was successful, at the cost of some 4,000 casualties, and the garrison obliged to surrender as prisoners of war.

This proved to be Marlborough's last military achievement. He tried to persuade the Home Government to support him in the siege of Le Quesnoy and to allow his men to winter in the field in preparation for an early start in 1712, instead of going into their usual winter quarters. But Harley and St John were now, virtually unknown to Marlborough, deeply committed in the peace negotiations. They withheld supplies and sent Marlborough a 'bamboozling' letter. On this minor key ended Marlborough's splendid military career. The Duke was personally proud of the 1711 campaign and had more tapestries (which now hang in Blenheim Palace) made in commemoration of it than of any other campaign. He had finally refuted the silly but popular story that he could do nothing without Prince Eugene and had penetrated the strong French defensive lines and taken an important fortress in the teeth of a superior French army commanded by the best French general.

Nevertheless, Marlborough's military record would have been

even finer if it had ended in 1708 and peace had been concluded
in 1709. For since 1708, although the French frontier was
crossed and the last raw French army in the field, the Allies,
with their veteran soldiers and victorious general, had achieved
comparatively little. It is hard to believe that even if he had
been in command in 1712 the French would ever again have been
reduced to the straits in which they were after the battle of
Oudenarde and the fall of Lille. But everywhere there was war
weariness. The limit of endurance had been reached. So long
as the French could be made to promise trading concessions in the
Spanish Empire and Belgium went to a weak naval power,
there was no convincing British case for continuing the war until
Spain, never an easy country to subdue, had been reconquered.
When Marlborough asserted that without the unheard-of step of
wintering in the field there was no guarantee of a successful
campaign in the next year, he was in effect confessing that the
war had reached stalemate. Queen Anne wrote bluntly that
'the Duke of Marlborough shows plainer than ever by this new
project his unwillingness for peace.' And it may be that she
was right; that the war waged for a now almost hopeless end
had become so much part and parcel of his life that he could not
conceive of life without it.

Chapter 13—Winter Sunshine: 1711-22

Tory Peace Negotiations—Marlborough's Opposition, and Dismissal—
    Charges of Peculation—Treaty of Utrecht, 1713—Marlborough in
    Exile—Return—Last Days.

WHILE Marlborough was waging his last campaign, the British
Government was secretly completing its peace negotiations with
France. In April 1711, a series of new proposals which were
particularly generous in regard to openings for British trade in
the Spanish Empire were forwarded to London from Versailles.
The Dutch were to be guaranteed a substantial fortress barrier
and were informed of these proposals. The inner British Cabinet
was convinced that they offered a sufficient basis for negotiations, and Queen Anne personally authorized Matthew Prior, the
poet, to go to Versailles and pursue the matter in secret there.
The Tories were ready for a partition of the Spanish inheritance,
as provided in William III's Partition Treaties and the Grand
Alliance signed by Marlborough in 1701 (see pp. 97-8). The

negotiations soon took a favourable turn. Prior's mission could
not be concealed, and Marlborough learned of it, but only indirectly. Indeed, it was not until September, after the discussions had been transferred back to London, that Harley, now
Earl of Oxford and Lord Treasurer, at last wrote and informed
the Duke, nominally his Cabinet colleague, that the French had
made an offer of a general peace 'by the canal of England' and
—this was the crux—that the Queen had said 'she would enter
into no separate treaty.' But in fact a separate treaty in the
form of three preliminary agreements was signed between
Britain and France on 27th September–8th October whereby the
British demands were fully met, but the allied claims were only
specified in general terms, no care being taken to fulfil the
promises of the Anglo-Dutch Barrier Treaty of 1709 or to secure
Spain for the Emperor. Marlborough was kept in the dark about
these transactions, but suspected and disliked their general
character. Sarah Marlborough, delightedly poking her finger
into the pie again, employed pamphleteers to attack the Government, while the Duke himself, whose relations with the Court of
Hanover were close and amicable, incited Anne's destined successor, the Dowager Electress of Hanover, to protest against
abandoning Spain to the French claimant. Marlborough significantly came home from the war accompanied by a Hanoverian
ambassador sent to protest formally against the Anglo-French
agreement.

The day after his return, 19th November, Marlborough saw the
Queen and spoke against the ministerial moves and showed himself, in Anne's own words, 'dejected and uneasy.' But, as
always, he was burning his boats slowly, willing upon an appropriate inducement to put out the fire. When Parliament opened
the Queen announced that a time and a place had been settled
for the peace conference (it was to meet at Utrecht in January).
A fierce debate followed in the House of Lords and Marlborough
had to define his position. Supported by the Whig majority in
that House, he spoke firmly if not vehemently against 'peace
without Spain,' and indignantly denied that he was trying to
prolong the war for his own personal ends.

The Government was defeated in the Lords by eight votes,
but was, of course, upheld by the Tory majority in the Commons.
In these circumstances the Queen had no alternative but to
dismiss Marlborough from her service. There was nothing
improper about her decision. Marlborough was a member of
the Cabinet and not merely a soldier under orders. Although the

doctrine of joint Cabinet responsibility was in its infancy, it was
impossible to keep in office so influential a statesman who was
openly opposed to the peace proposals on which the Queen's
Government had decided. But the method of Marlborough's
dismissal was shabby. A trumped-up charge of peculation in his
capacity of Commander-in-Chief was brought against him by a
partisan Parliamentary Committee. He was accused of wrong-
fully accepting a percentage on the Army bread contracts and on
the pay of foreign mercenaries. The charge was ridiculous.
He was fully authorized, both by the Queen and by the Government of 1702 and by the foreign princes concerned, to take the
percentage to spend on his excellent intelligence service; and the
deduction from the bread contracts was a recognized perquisite
which he employed for the same purpose. His immediate
successor as Commander-in-Chief was not only offered but took
both percentages. The Tory rulers merely tried to cover the
late general with mud in the hope that some of it would stick so
as to offset the force of his criticism of their peace plans. Queen
Anne dismissed him with a letter so brutally ungrateful that he
threw it in the fire. He was abruptly relieved of his offices on
the last day of 1711. The next day the Duke of Ormonde was
made Commander-in-Chief in his place and twelve peers were
created to break the hostile majority in the Lords.

Marlborough retained his friends amongst the Whigs and his
popularity, especially in the Army, and he remained a potentially
dangerous Opposition leader; but, on the whole, he held his hand.
His famous colleague, Prince Eugene, arrived in London—too
late, as usual—and vainly tried to stop the progress of the British
peace negotiations. But he associated himself publicly with
Marlborough and bestowed praise upon him sufficient to stop
the mouths of those who would have lauded his prowess at Marlborough's expense. When Eugene returned to the war he found
that Marlborough's successor, Ormonde, had been ordered by
St John not to fight a battle while the negotiations were in progress, to the bitter humiliation of Marlborough's veterans. Marlborough later took part in a debate on these notorious 'restraining orders' and inquired pertinently how Ormonde could
be expected to undertake a siege without running the risk of a
battle. Deserted entirely by the British troops, Eugene could
not prevent the Dutch being defeated at the battle of Denain
on 24th July 1712, and the French were thus assured of obtaining
better terms than they had offered at Gertruydenberg two years
earlier, a result which reflected not only on the 'restraining orders'

but on Marlborough's and his friends' inability to conclude
peace earlier.

Marlborough withdrew to his country house at Holywell, near
St Albans. He could not live at Blenheim Palace, which was
still only half built, for the Ministry, while threatening to sue
him for his 'illegal' perquisites, stopped paying the workmen.
The Duke and Duchess lived together quietly although not un-
disturbed by calumny. Marlborough used his influence to help
needy disabled officers, wrote to Vienna about his princedom
of Mindelheim and took care of his sick friend Godolphin. In
August a clergyman who dined at St Albans saw the Duke and
Duchess and 'heard his Grace reprimand the Duchess for sitting
at prayers, but she obeyed not.' After the death of Godolphin
in September, Marlborough, alarmed at growing threats of law-
suits and even prosecution, decided to go abroad. Queen Anne
was glad enough to grant him a passport; and there is even a
story that Harley blackmailed him into going abroad by threatening to publish one of his secret letters to the Jacobites which had
come into his hands. There was certainly a secret meeting between them. But, as Mr Churchill writes, if this story is true
Harley was 'forcing an open door with a battering ram.' On
24th November the Duke shook the dust of an ungrateful England
from his feet.

During Marlborough's absence the group of separate agree-
ments between France and the Allies (excluding the Emperor)
known collectively as the Treaty of Utrecht were at last signed
(11th April, 1713). Philip of Anjou was recognized as Philip V
of Spain and the Indies; but both France and Spain promised
that the two Bourbon crowns should never be united. Great
Britain obtained Hudson's Bay, Newfoundland, Nova Scotia,
Acadia, St Christopher, Minorca, and Gibraltar, as well as trading
privileges in South America, and a monopoly of the slave export
trade. The Dutch, for their part, gained a considerable barrier
of fortresses (but less than had been promised them), certain
forts guarding the mouth of the Scheldt, and shared the trade of
Belgium with Britain. The Duke of Savoy obtained Sicily;
the Elector of Bavaria was restored to his dominions conquered
by Marlborough in 1704. In consequence of the war and the
treaty, Holland was soon to cease to be an effective commercial
rival to Britain, who also became the supreme naval power, and
laid her empire on firm foundations. The Whig merchants and
financiers who had supported the war so vigorously did well out
of the Tory peace.

F

Marlborough criticized the general character of the treaty on two grounds. First, he said it was a betrayal of the Allies. (The Emperor was so disgusted that he went on with the war.) Secondly, Marlborough objected to Spain being ruled by a Bourbon prince in spite of his renunciation of his right of succession to the French Crown. To Marlborough it could be, and was, answered that the Dutch had contemplated a separate agreement with France and the emperor had actually concluded separate agreements with France in 1707, and that this was the only assured way of making peace. Moreover, both the Allies gained handsomely from the partition of the Spanish Empire. As to the question of Spain and the Bourbons, why had he changed his mind since 1701? In any case, he overestimated the ease with which that country could be conquered. As in other political questions, undoubtedly personal factors influenced his view of the treaty. For instance, he had long hoped that after the peace the emperor would fulfil his promise of making him Governor-General of the Spanish Netherlands, and that the Dutch would at last approve. If the Allies were alienated by the peace treaties they would not trouble to gratify the British general who had won the war for them. There was also the princedom of Mindelheim in conquered Bavaria to be considered. Some of the very few letters which the Duke wrote in exile concerned this principality, which he visited in June 1713; in the long run he lost this too, and although he complained to Eugene, was not compensated. However, Marlborough neither wrote nor uttered any criticisms of the treaty when in exile. Some say that the resumption of the payments on the building of Blenheim Palace was the price paid for his silence.

When he first went abroad, although welcomed by magistrates and common people in Belgium and Holland, the Duke was lonely. He even had no secretary and was forced to pen letters in his own hand throughout. But in due course he was joined by his wife and his friend Cadogan. For over six months he stayed in Frankfort, leading a not wholly lazy existence. Thence he entered into communication with the Courts of both Hanover and St Germains, where dwelt the rivals for the British succession. He begged the Old Pretender for a pardon; but whereas he sent kind words to 'James III,' he actually entered into elaborate arrangements with the Electress of Hanover and her son, the future George I, as to the military and constitutional steps to be taken on Anne's death. And although he sent Mary of Modena, mother of the Pretender, a small sum, he offered to

lend £10,000 to the future George I. Where his treasure lay,
there was his heart also. When they heard at the beginning of
1714 that the queen had been taken ill, the Marlboroughs, both
mightily homesick after a year of exile, prepared to return. But
the Queen recovered, so they waited until the Parliament, which
had been elected in 1713, rose in July. On 30th July 1714,
Marlborough was already waiting to embark, and while he was
on the high seas the Queen expired (1st August), just after she
had again dismissed a former favourite, the serpentine Harley,
and, half-unconscious, handed his white staff to the Whig
potentate, the Duke of Shrewsbury, in the interests of the Protestant succession.

The accession of the German-speaking George I of Hanover
to the throne of Great Britain was peacefully accomplished with
scarcely a groan from the impotent Jacobites. Marlborough,
enthusiastically welcomed in London, was at once restored to
the post of Commander-in-Chief and Master-General of the
Ordnance, and a Whig Government, including his son-in-law
Sunderland, replaced the divided and nerveless Tories. In due
course Marlborough had his revenge on the Tory ministers, St
John, Viscount Bolingbroke, and Harley, Earl of Oxford, who
had been responsible for his dismissal in 1711. He frightened St
John from the country with threats of an Act of Attainder, and
one of his last public appearances was to vote (in vain) for
Harley's impeachment in 1717. As Commander-in-Chief, the
Duke reinstated his old officers in the commands from which they
had been expelled by the Tories and championed the claims of
the foreign Protestant officers who had served him so well in
Flanders. He also exerted his influence with Eugene to find
positions for officers barred from the British service by religious
and other disabilities. So there was a little fitful sunshine in the
winter of his life.

But Marlborough had small influence with the new rulers of
his country. They were not ungrateful for his services. Yet
the Whigs never entirely trusted him; nor did the new king.
And though he carried on, out of habit maybe, his polite inter-
course with St Germains, he was past successful intrigue or
active warfare. He directed only from his arm-chair the operations which were to bring about the defeat of the Scottish Jacobite
rising of 1715—his last snub to the exiles he had bamboozled
so long.

The Duke, now sixty-four, dwelt quietly at Marlborough House,

built by the Duchess on Wren's designs in 1709–11, at Windsor
Lodge and at Holywell, St Albans. He did not live to see the
completion of Blenheim Palace (finished in 1727) by which he
set such passionate store. The mighty dynast had no son. Of
his four daughters, Elizabeth Bridgewater, the third, predeceased
him in March, 1714, and his favourite, Anne Sunderland, died in
April 1716. The second death was probably a cause of his first
paralytic seizure in May of that year. A second seizure followed
in August. He made a partial recovery and spent time taking
the waters at Tunbridge Wells and Bath. He used, so it was said,
to walk to the spa at Bath so as to save the sixpence on the
chairman. He was, as he knew, but the shadow of the handsome soldier who had won the battle of Oudenarde at the age
of fifty-eight. One day he gazed at his portrait by Kneller and
murmured: 'This was once a man.' His domestic peace was
constantly rent. Sarah, still in full possession of her explosive
faculties, 'prowled round his couch like a she-bear guarding her
slowly dying mate and tearing all, friend or foe, who approached'
(Churchill). She quarrelled alike with his friend and successor
as Commander-in-Chief, General Cadogan, with Sir John Vanbrugh, the architect of Blenheim, and with her two surviving
daughters, Henrietta Godolphin and Mary Montagu. Marlborough's last extant letter, written in 1721, says: 'I believe I
am the worse to see my children live so ill with a mother for whom
I must have the greatest tenderness and regard.' He died, rich
and admired, on 16th June 1722, at the age of seventy-two and
was buried in Westminster Abbey. His body was later removed
to Blenheim Palace. There is the monument to the greatest,
if not the noblest or most selfless, of British soldiers.

BIBLIOGRAPHY

APART from Mr Winston Churchill's *Marlborough : his Life and Times* (4 vols., 1933–8), the principal sources for Marlborough's own correspondence are Archdeacon W. Coxe, *Memoirs of the Duke of Marlborough* (3 vols., 1818–19), the letters in which are partly but not entirely reprinted by Churchill, and Sir George Murray, *Letters and Dispatches* (5 vols., 1845). Lord Wolseley (*The Life of John Churchill to the Accession of Queen Anne*, 2 vols., 1894) and Dr Stuart Reid (*John and Sarah, Duke and Duchess of Marlborough*, 1914), also had access to the Blenheim papers. Their works have been superseded, but still contain a little important material. A few valuable Marlborough letters are in Sarah's *Private Correspondence* (2 vols., carelessly edited, 1838) and the *Bath Papers* (Historical MSS. Commission, vol. i). Dr Roderick Geikie also had access to the Blenheim papers for his posthumously published researches on the Dutch Barrier Treaty (Geikie and Montgomery, *The Dutch Barrier*, 1705–19, 1930) which throw a flood of light on Marlborough as a diplomatist. Werner Reese, *Das Ringen um Frieden und Sicherheit 1708-9* (1933), contains some new materials and views.

Professor G. M. Trevelyan, *England under Queen Anne* (3 vols.), gives an admirable background for the heroic period, and Mr David Ogg, *England in the Reign of Charles II*, for the earlier period. Mr Keith Feiling's *History of the Tory Party, 1640-1714*, is essential for an understanding of party politics. Excellent books on Marlborough's military career are C. T. Atkinson, *Marlborough* (1921), and Frank Taylor, *Wars of Marlborough* (2 vols., 1921). Marlborough's attitude to sea power is described in J. H. Owen, *War at Sea under Queen Anne, 1702-8* (1938). The best of Sarah Marlborough's lives is by Kathleen Campbell (1932). There are detailed Marlborough bibliographies in Churchill.

Queen Elizabeth

BY CHARLES WILLIAMS

1533	Birth of Elizabeth
1537	Birth of Edward VI
1547	Death of Henry VIII. Seymour marries Queen Catherine Parr
1549	Arrest of Seymour; examination of Elizabeth
1553	Accession of Mary
1554	Elizabeth imprisoned in the Tower (18th March); removed to Woodstock (14th May); marriage of Mary
1558	Death of Mary; accession of Elizabeth
1559	Coronation of the queen. First Parliament; the English service again used; reformation of the finances; beginning of the courtships
1560	Treaty of Edinburgh; rise of Dudley; death of Amy Robsart
1561	Return of Mary Stuart to Scotland; English troops in France; Francis Bacon born
1562	Hawkins's first slave voyage
1564	Robert Dudley made Earl of Leicester; Marlowe and Shakespeare born.
1565	Marriage of Mary Stuart and Darnley
1567	Flight of Mary Stuart
1569	Norfolk conspiracy and Northern Rebellion
1570	The pope issues Bull of Deposition: *Regnans in Excelsis*
1571	Beginning of the Anjou courtship; first official persecution
1572	Ridolfi Plot; execution of Norfolk; beginning of the Alençon (Anjou) courtship
1580	Coming of the Jesuit missionaries; Raleigh knighted; Drake completes voyage round the world
1581	Edmund Campion executed.
1584	Death of Alençon; assassination of William of Orange; the Instrument of Association
1586	The Babington Plot; execution of Mary Stuart
1587	Essex becomes Master of the Horse; Sir C. Hatton Lord Chancellor
1588	Spanish Armada; death of the Earl of Leicester
1593	Death of Marlowe
1598	Deaths of Philip of Spain and Burghley
1599	Essex Lieutenant of Ireland
1601	Execution of Essex; reconciliation of the queen and Commons on Monopolies
1603	Death of Elizabeth

Chapter I

THE life of Elizabeth represents, in English history, the longest
and most spectacular period of a change in society. That change
began before her, and was not concluded until long after her.
It was the change from a society directed, at any rate in theory,
by a metaphysical idea, to a society directed, both in theory and
practice, by nothing but the continual pressure of events. It is
a change completed in our own day; beyond our present political
accommodation to events we cannot go. We are on the point of
discovering whether that accommodation is sufficient, or whether
we must return to a metaphysical idea—either that of the past
or some other.

This change in society was unintended, through Europe at
large as through England in particular. It took place because
the results of all human action are always different from anything intended or expected. No ruler and no statesman of the
Elizabethan period—except perhaps Maitland of Lethington—
wished to abolish metaphysical ideas from their place in society.
Elizabeth no more definitely desired it than did Philip of Spain.
Both she and he proposed that all events in their dominions should
be subordinated to themselves, and to the metaphysical schemes
which they respectively held. The nature of Philip held very
intensely to his metaphysical scheme; the nature of Elizabeth
much more lightly to hers. She was vividly and personally
aware of events; he, impersonally and abstractly. In the great
medieval society of Europe which preceded them there had been
many rulers who resembled one or the other; some had tended
to beliefs, some to events, but their natures, in every case, had
been modified by the nature of the whole society. Before the
rise of Elizabeth and Philip that society had received two violent
shocks, both of which compelled princes to take immediate
cognizance of beliefs other than their own. A belief other than
one's own is not, to oneself, a belief; it is an event.

The metaphysics of medieval Europe consisted of two cor-
related parts. The first part included the nature of God and the

*F   165

soul; the second, the temporal nourishment and instruction of the soul. The first dealt, largely, with the person and life of our Saviour; the second with the visible Church, the nature of the sacraments, and the ordering of morals. The first has throughout the history of Christendom remained practically untouched, except by a few scattered and suppressed teachers; it was the second part that received the shocks, first, of the Great Schism, and, second, of the Reformation.

The Great Schism of the West concerned the person—but not primarily the office—of the pope. It began when, in 1378, during the pontificate of Urban VI, certain cardinals, fleeing from Rome, elected one of their number to the papacy under the name of Clement VII. In theory, the organization of the Church remained unaffected by this action; one of the two, and later three, claimants was the true pope, and the true pope was the true pope, however many claimants there might be. In fact, however, that organization suffered throughout Europe all kinds of controversies and compromises. Not only were the religious nerves of Europe seriously shaken, but a considerable impetus was given to a movement already in progress—the Rise of the Nations. This rise, which had many causes, had many results, one of the most important of which was what may be called a deflection of mass. Medieval Europe had theoretically considered the mass of mankind as one, which was the Church, corresponding to the One Man which was Christ. There were heretics and infidels, but they were an outrage on the unity of mankind. Theoretically, mankind and Christendom were identical; anything else was disease. But however much the laws of belief still compelled attention to this supreme mass which was mankind, the laws of events during and after the schism compelled a much more immediate attention to those smaller masses which were the nations. The shadowy headship of the emperor, and the substantial headship of the pope, lost something of their prestige. National, or at least dynastic, glory obtruded itself upon universal glory. The close of the schism was followed by the continual rise of these secondary national glories, and by an accompanying weariness with metaphysics after the strain of the schism, which in turn assisted, even in the case of the popes themselves, the other glory of the Renascence.

This variation preceded the second metaphysical shock which Europe received; namely, the outbreak of the Reformation. This second shock, again, was not directed against the primal idea of Christianity—of redemption through the double nature and supernatural interposition of Christ. But it very seriously affected all ideas of the nature of the visible Church, of the sacraments, and of the official direction of morals. The question of the papacy itself was only one among a number of questions, and was not everywhere regarded as of the first importance. The Council of Trent had not yet met; nor had the Roman Church, as it now is, been adequately formulated. On that and other subjects, however, a new series of other people's beliefs—that is, of events—came into violent existence. The sovereigns of Europe had to deal with these events, and had to deal with them not as sporadic but as continuous. Heresy (whatever, in a short time, that came to mean in each state) was no longer a person, a sect, or even an idea; it had become an unbroken and militant series of persons, sects, and ideas. It was a permanent hostility outside each state and a permanent threat of revolt within, a threat acutely felt by the developed sense of royal and national glory which pervaded the kingdoms.

In England the serious dispute began not with metaphysics but with morals. The King of England, Henry VIII, had indeed written a book against Luther, a champion of the new metaphysics, and had been saluted as *Defender of the Faith* by the pope. His marriage had been arranged by a special action on the part of the pope. He had married his brother Arthur's widow, by dispensation from the papal authority, representing a moral law which normally forbade men to marry their brothers' widows. It was pontifically declared that Catherine of Aragon had not been Arthur's wife, and that Henry might justly marry her. The king very greatly desired a male heir. Unfortunately, in the next sixteen years Catherine bore five children—four stillborn, another dying just after birth. She had one child who lived, the daughter Mary. Presently she was beyond childbearing. It was clear that God had refused an heir to Henry by Catherine. The state of Henry's mind has received little sympathy, since nowadays few of us desire children, fewer marry their brothers' widows, and still fewer believe that there is a moral law forbidding such marriages. To understand his decision it is necessary to understand his dilemma: was God displeased at his marriage? His emotions said *yes*; the old metaphysics said *no*. It was an age in which natural events were held to be supernaturally significant, and, had circumstances been reversed, it is certain that Henry's five dead children would have been declared by the vocal champions of the Church to be very certain signs of God's displeasure.

Another series of events intensified the king's emotional crisis, and assisted its resolution: their name was Anne Boleyn. Henry fell violently in love with her; she demanded marriage. The king's fear, the king's hope, the king's desire, combined to urge him to discover a solution of his problem other than that maintained — but only just maintained — at Rome. Negotiations broke down. There was, of course, never any divorce between him and Catherine, but a decree of nullity was issued by English ecclesiastical authority without Roman assent. The breach between two metaphysics concerning the nature of the visible Church was immediately present. It was followed by an immediate and official intensification of an attack on the wealth and power of the clergy in England which had been for some time officially in motion. The monasteries were dissolved.

The decree of nullity was pronounced by Cranmer in May 1533. The king had been privately married to Anne in December 1532. The Princess Elizabeth was born in the following September. Three months afterwards she was given her own royal household at Hatfield, and her elder sister, the Lady Mary, now publicly declared illegitimate, was commanded to form part of the court that circled round the unconscious interloper. In another sense also Elizabeth was an interloper: the king had been hoping for a male heir. But he was gracious, and proceeded to take steps further to define the situation. In 1534 an Act and Oath of Succession was promulgated, by which the marriage with Catherine was declared 'against the laws of God,' and the marriage with Anne 'perfect ever.' A mass of detail concerning marriage and prohibited degrees was included in the Act and therefore in the Oath, as also was a renunciation of any contrary oath 'to any other within the realm, or foreign authority, prince, or potentate.' The Oath was almost universally received, by laity and clergy alike. John Fisher, Bishop of Rochester, refused; so, in spite of the Abbot of Westminster, and others, did Sir Thomas More. It may be allowed that they kept their integrity, but it is impossible to believe that all the rest of the hierarchy and the priesthood deliberately and consciously abandoned their own. A much more severe oath, expressly repudiating the jurisdiction of the Roman see 'and its laws, decrees, and canons, if any of them should be found contrary to the law of God and Holy Scripture,' was addressed to all orders of friars and monks; it was refused only in three places. Meanwhile the fleet of the King of France hovered in the seas ready to assist against Catherine's cousin, the emperor, if he should desire to interfere. Convocation, north and south, with five dissentients, resolved that by Holy Scripture the Bishop of Rome had no greater jurisdiction in England than any other bishop; the universities assented. In February 1535 all the bishops explicitly renounced the primacy of the see of Rome; a number of them wrote felicitating the king on his action. They provided for similar acts on the part of all their clergy. The same year saw the execution of More, Fisher, a small number of recalcitrant monks, and twice as many otherwise recalcitrant Anabaptists. Under such auspices the legitimacy of the child Elizabeth was declared and upheld; to this extent the events of the dead children and of Anne had shaken the pattern of metaphysical theory.

Nevertheless, in the very next year her legitimacy was, in a few days, utterly and royally denied. The life of the courts of the Renascence was as bloody and spectacular as its plays; its palaces were full of a perilous domesticity, and what actual life could not attain common report provided. Fact, rumour, and imagination mingled their melodrama. The peculiarity of Henry was his passionate desire to be moral, and even legal, in his marriages and murders. In that certainly he was less than strong; his spirit demanded popular support, and he took steps to ensure it. The weakness exposed him to something like blackmail; the lands of the clergy formed an unspoken union between the Catholic lords and their Catholic sovereign. But that bargain was separate from, though politically related to, the theological controversy; the unhappy figure of Cranmer unites them. He was concerned for the truth of doctrine, and he was involved in the falsehood of politics. He is a shy literary figure among those crimson Renascence splendours and terrors, and singularly out of place.

In January 1536 Anne Boleyn gave birth to a prince; the child, as if celestial anger renewed itself against the throne, was born dead. Again the superstition and the lust of the king grew together, but this time, Anne being his own subject, and he being more used to action, he struck more violently. On 2nd May, accused of great and heinous crimes, Anne was sent to the Tower; on 17th May, in the vaults of Lambeth, the marriage was declared by Cranmer, on the evidence laid before him, to be *nullum, invalidum, et inane*. On 19th May the wretched woman was executed. In June the Parliament also declared the marriage void, and the Princess Elizabeth illegitimate. In the eyes of Rome and half Europe she was already so; she was now to be so to all England. It became treason for any one to assert the legitimacy either of her or of her half-sister Mary, though, by a fantastic logic worthy of the theatre itself, the penalties against all those who had previously declared her illegitimate still remained in force. Meanwhile, Catherine and Anne both being dead, Henry achieved his first indubitably valid marriage—with Jane Seymour. Could events be certainly related to ideas, the result might be held to have justified all his doubts, all his denials, and all his destructions—a male heir was conceived, and born in July of 1537. So swift a celestial justification of his action must have hardened through his future life the king's belief in his own interpretation of doctrine and morals. The Lady Mary and the Lady Elizabeth were brought, from that joint household to which now they were both reduced, Elizabeth as the junior member, to be present at their legitimate brother's baptism. His mother, Jane, ensured the legal future of her son by dying soon after the ceremony.

The king had some virtue; he held no grudge against the children of his disasters. By 1544 he even established both his daughters in the right of succession to the throne. They remained formally illegitimate, but the bar sinister was to be merely ignored; *le Roi le veult*. The small Elizabeth grew; she had difficulty with her teeth; they came slowly—'causeth me,' wrote her governess, Lady Bryan, 'to suffer her Grace to have her will more than I would.' With her mental teeth she had no difficulty —'a toward child.' In the same year, 1544, when she was ten years old, she was translating French devotional poetry. Tutors were appointed—from the group of Cambridge humanists who represented more particularly the New Learning, and therefore the Reforming party. The intellectual influences brought to bear on her through the years of her education were those of 'true religion' as distinguished from the 'old faith.' To scholarship she grew easily—Greek and Latin; and modern languages— French and Italian and Spanish. 'Her mind,' wrote Ascham, 'has no womanly weakness.' Elizabeth would not have thanked him for the adjective. Whatever she admired in her masculine court of later years was not the mental capacity of its members; nor did she need.

In 1547 Henry died. Edward VI, at ten years old, began to reign, and his uncle, Edward Seymour, became Earl of Somerset and Protector of the Kingdom. The blackmail of the old reign ceased, and a simpler process of direct seizure was substituted. The Lady Elizabeth, then thirteen, was moved to the guardianship and house of Henry's widow, the Queen Catherine Parr.

She wrote letters, of dutiful affection and youthful piety, to her brother the king. The small king, also learned, also devotional, sent comfortable messages. Suddenly there fell upon her a personal crisis, and one in no sense theological.

It was two years since the king had died. He had been to the child a huge, terrifying, and thrilling wonder; all her life she recalled him, a fabulous and yet familiar splendour. He was her father, and he had put her mother to death; he had done so because, besides being her father, he was also the king, and her mother had sinned against the king in his kingdom. When she called herself 'Harry's daughter,' the very intimacy of the word increased the myth, and she made herself more ordinary and more extraordinary at once. The child's imagination of him, being through his death undefeated by any natural conflict or scorn, matured, but it did not change its characteristics. She loved thrills, and this was the great thrill of her childhood. At sixteen she was provided with another. Catherine Parr married again, this time the brother of the Lord Protector, Thomas, Lord Seymour of Sudely.

Lord Seymour was one of the less contented lords of the Council. He was irked by what seemed to him the unnecessary greatness of his brother, and he had at first proposed to himself to make an even more royal alliance than with his new wife; he thought of marrying Elizabeth herself. The protector and the Council stopped him, and he fell back, at first secretly, on Catherine. In the triple household Elizabeth, maturing, sensuous, intellectual, found herself introduced to a new freedom, and to unprecedented freedoms. The Lord Seymour had a broad taste in jollity, and the dowager queen little inclination, at first, to discourage him. There were jests and romps. Elizabeth's room was visited in the early morning; she was teased and tickled, mentally and corporally rolled and smacked. She was not alone in her experiences; the other young ladies of the household also enjoyed the Lord Seymour's attentions. He rollicked through his domestic world, as he attempted to rollick through his political. The gardens of the house received the laughter of the three great personages. The princess was held fast by the dowager while Lord Seymour cut up her skirt. Her education took a broad scope, and presently, even in that world, caused some scandal. Elizabeth was observed to blush when the talk veered round to Seymour; it was suspected that she was beginning to be acutely and unduly aware of him. The queen dowager grew difficult and the household strained. Elizabeth eventually withdrew, in

the spring of 1548, thus re-establishing friendship with Catherine.
In the autumn the dowager died.   Elizabeth's household were all
for Seymour; Elizabeth had by no means forgotten him.   Full
life had awakened in her.   He returned to his hope of marrying
her; meanwhile he had made himself intimate with the young
king.   His head grew full of visions of himself as Protector of
the King and husband of the princess.   He made vague general
preparations for something, and talked more vaguely.   He spoke
of his brother as intending to 'enslave England by mercenaries.'
In January 1549 the Council took action.   He was arrested.
Immediately upon the news there arrived from the Government
deputies to cross-examine the princess.   Members of her household found themselves under guard.   Had there been a plot?
What did she know of the plot?   Had she been in the plot?
Into the full stirring of amorous excitement, however watched and
warned it had been by her wary intelligence, there drove this
sudden close catechism of peril.   Her servants confessed all they
knew, and perhaps more than she knew.   Breathless, obstinate,
betrayed to suspicion, besieged by threats, persuasions, and
slanders, she denied 'any practice.'   She wept in private and
stormed in public.   She was agitated over Seymour's imprisonment, but she stood staunchly to herself.   Her exhausted
examiners said she needed two governesses rather than one:
'She hath a very good wit.'   Parry, her steward, testified that
he had asked her if she would be willing to marry Seymour.   She
had answered, as any one might, that 'she could not tell her mind
therein,' but in her it was prophetic of the long series of replies
in her future.   It is not conceivable that Seymour could have
roused in her any devotion of pure and superfluous self-sacrifice.
The whole episode terminated by accentuating the necessity of a
perpetual guard on her emotions and intelligence.   There may
have been also something of an angry contempt.   It was clear
that he had meant to use her.   She probably knew it before;
now she felt it, and felt that others knew it.

They executed him.   It was the second time the axe had swung
near her life.   Of her mother's death she knew only by reading
and report, and there the figure of her mighty and monstrous
father came between.   She was sixteen now, and was left to her
studies in Hatfield, peculiarly alone.   Her sister Mary had more
continuous difficulties, but Mary had the privilege, the peril, and
the protection of a cause and of a party, and of the attention of
half Europe.   Nothing except inconvenience hovered round
Elizabeth.   She retired into herself and her mind.

The lords continued intrigues. There were rebellions. The mercenaries marched—Hungarians against the Scotch, Germans and Italians against the men of Norwich and the men of the West Country. Certain of the Roman Catholic Italians afterwards sought absolution for having fought the battles of the heretic Protector; the Lutheran Germans were less troubled in conscience. Somerset, having crushed the revolting peasants, tried to crush the rising power of the Dudleys, and failed. He was put to death. Dudley succeeded; the king died; Lady Jane Grey, married to Guildford Dudley, was proclaimed queen. Dudley, now Duke of Northumberland, already at odds with Cranmer over Church doctrine and Church land, tried to raise the banner of the re-formed religion, and failed. Elizabeth, from wilfulness or wisdom, from principle or prudence, threw in her lot with her house and her sister. She came up to London with a great fol-lowing; on the last day of July 1553 she rode out to meet the triumphant Mary. She saluted and joined her. The daughter of events rode into London next after the daughter of meta-physic, two illegitimates. Into the city of the Reformation rode the crowned champion of the Counter-Reformation; after her short, thin figure, came the tall, handsome, and striking shape which was to be, in effect, both Counter-Reformation and Counter-Counter-Reformation. She was twenty, and she had learnt to keep her mouth shut on her heart.

Chapter 2

Elizabeth, the Queen, and the Roman Catholic Demand—Her Withdrawal from Court—The Wyatt Rebellion—The Princess in the Tower, and her Release—The Spanish Marriage, and the Reconciliation with Rome—Prospects of Elizabeth's Succession—Mary's Distrust of Her—Philip Accepts her Succession—Proposals for her Marriage—The Division between France and Spain, and the Schism in the Roman Catholic Front—Last Efforts of Mary—Loyalty to Elizabeth fashionable—Her Accession.

THE single danger to Elizabeth's person hitherto had been political; now an element in which, by nature, she had no keen interest, entered her life: the element of dogma. The change upon the throne had suddenly rendered herself and her household religiously suspect to the sovereign. Unless she could be con-verted she was bound to remain a precise threat of that permanent nature of heresy which was, in the period of the Reformation, its new and shattering characteristic. The two sisters, opposed in their theologies, were still more opposed in their temperaments. There was in Mary a strain of supernatural humility; she devoutly and sincerely adored God and obeyed a revelation from God. There was in Elizabeth a queer strain of natural humility—or of that common sense which is unsanctified humility. She thought it was always quite possible that she might be wrong, and even more strongly did she feel that everybody else might be wrong. When she was opposed or when she was angry, this natural humility was often lost in an equally natural obstinacy, but it existed. Mary exalted a hypothesis into faith—a superb and noble achievement. Elizabeth could hardly allow it to be even a hypothesis if she could not also feel that it was a fact. Elizabeth, expressing, after her own manner, her most sincere religious beliefs, would always have left Mary with a strong feeling that her sister was irreligious. Since, at present, from Mary's point of view, she was in matters of faith almost worse than irreligious, the hostility between them, bound at best to be subdued but permanent, grew to the worst and increased.

In a few months two things became clear. First, Mary's policy was to be actively and penally Roman; second, she proposed to marry the Prince of Spain. The first was unpopular among the stalwarts of the true religion; the second, almost everywhere. Spain was the great maritime commercial rival, the power threatening mastery. There was, if not a party, yet certainly a prejudice in favour of Elizabeth in two places—among the general populace of London and at the Court of France, both hostile to Spain. But Spain and papalism were two separate things, and Elizabeth's immediate difficulty was with the second. For a few weeks she held aloof from the spreading triumph of the old faith, but by the beginning of September she curtsied to a great monarch. *Cujus regio, ejus religio* was a phrase which then beat in the heart; nowadays it merely astonishes the brain. The princess contemplated the restored rites; she considered her sister's awful will, and it is to be remembered that the will of the sovereign meant a very great deal then. She considered her own position also; eventually she asked for instruction. She went to mass—not too often. The mistrustful Mary made inquiries of her; the princess protested the honesty of her devotion. The queen remained suspicious both of her sister's spectacular beauty and her sister's spectacular behaviour. But she knew she owed goodwill to Elizabeth as to all of God's creatures; she laboured to be intelligent and yet to pay her debt.

Her careful mind, a little taking after the legalism of her father Henry, proceeded to take steps to repeal the statute which declared her own illegitimacy; Elizabeth's, naturally, she left explicitly untouched. But she went farther. She thought Elizabeth, being a legal and canonical bastard, ought not to reign. The queen therefore desired to repeal that other statute, which set Anne Boleyn's daughter in the way of the succession. She was warned that it would prove impossible, and, thwarted in her logic, she grew less capacious in goodwill. The first political results of the new religious revival, of the faith which was pressed upon her, exhibited to Elizabeth a loss of her future right to the throne and a growing personal antagonism. She answered as well as she could. She did her best to hover interestingly at the gate of the Roman fold; at that personal cost she cóuld not want to enter, but she had no desire to be left to the dangers of the wilderness. It was not only her physical danger in, but her intellectual distaste for, the wilderness that revolted her. She did not much care for the fierce company of the extreme Reforming fanatics who wandered there. She did not want to go anywhere, yet it seemed she, first of all England, must make a public responsible decision to go somewhere—credally. She was the queen's sister and successor; it was impossible that she should not be a marked person. Cranmer and others were out of favour and soon to be in prison; Cecil and others were out of favour and living in retirement—Cecil himself discreetly going to mass after the old style. She fell from favour. In November the Lady Elizabeth asked permission to withdraw from the court. It was granted. On her way out of London, five hundred gentlemen in her train, she sent a message to the queen asking for a supply of vestments. It is by no means certain that she was not sincere, in her own way. She was not drawn to the Roman party by conscience, but neither was she conscientiously opposed. Nothing was more remote from her conscience than the whole ecclesiastical problem. Only she did not love yielding to threats, and to her of all people in the realm the doctrine came accompanied by implicit threats. She did not mind a pretence at a readiness to surrender. But a pretence of readiness to surrender is not quite a pretence of surrender—not quite the same to the actor and not quite the same to the spectator. It was this delicate distinction which caused uneasiness in her sister, her servants, and her enemies; it was this distinction which bewildered her contemporaries throughout her life.

At the beginning of January 1554 ambassadors came from the

emperor to settle the affairs of the queen's marriage; at the end, rebellion broke out in Kent and elsewhere. Sir Thomas Wyatt led a march on London. He was defeated by the measures and the ardour of the queen, and as soon as his defeat was accomplished orders were sent that Elizabeth should be brought back to London for examination. She was very unwilling to go; she said she was ill, which was at any rate partly true. She said she was innocent and ignorant, which is not so likely. A letter of hers had been found in the dispatches of the French ambassador. She and the ambassador both swore vehemently that it was not hers. There was evidence that letters had been written to her by Wyatt; she swore she had received none, and none from her to Wyatt could be found. The imperial ambassador was pressing for her execution. The anti-Spanish party in the council resisted him, and he wrote to his master complaining of their obstruction. The queen, who was not only religious but also moral, would do nothing unjustified by morals and law. The balance swung almost level.

Elizabeth came to London. In an open litter, very pale, very haughty, in extreme danger, she passed through the streets. Three weeks afterwards further orders against her were given; she was to be conveyed to the Tower. It was Palm Sunday, and a rainy day, when the barge received her—during the time of mass, when the streets would be least peopled. At Traitor's Gate, as she landed, she became, for the first recorded time, her public self. She stood still; she looked up to the dark skies; she cried: 'Lord, I never thought to come here as prisoner.' She turned from heaven to the people; she called out to the guards around her: 'I pray you all, good friends and fellows, bear me witness that I come in no traitor, but as true a woman to the Queen's Majesty as any now living, and thereon will I take my death.'

Nothing quite sufficient against her could be found to put in evidence, though the Lord Chancellor Gardiner was suspected of suppressing a packet of letters. Division in the Council, agitation in London, Wyatt's dying declaration that she was innocent, made it impossible for Mary to act, even if she wished. In spite of the imperial ambassador, Elizabeth was released in May, and dispatched to the honourable semi-captivity in which, now less and now more guarded, she was to remain. It was an experience not without an effect on her future years and acts; if she were so detained and watched, so might other royal persons properly be. She had inconvenient friends; so other royalties might have.

For the moment she breathed delight. She was sent, in the custody of Sir Henry Bedingfield, to Woodstock, making slow time, and turning the journey almost into a pastoral progress. Guns of salute were fired in London, bells rung in the country. Villagers cheered her, thronged round her, brought her presents. She came laughing through the country roads; she was not yet twenty-one. At Woodstock she remained for a year, watched, but left free to her personal tastes, even in religion. The Roman devotion of her earlier interest was for a while abandoned; she used—by permission—the English service. Her intellectual exploration had ceased, but the chance of things had thrown her with the New Learning and the Reforming party, and they with her. They had, both parties, nowhere else to look, though neither was quite at ease *tali auxilio*. She made herself as tiresome to the unfortunate Sir Henry Bedingfield as a young woman of a restless, provocative, cautious, witty, and intelligent temper could, but they remained good friends. She tried to sound— possibly she even tried to be—simple and honest to her sister, but Mary thoroughly distrusted her. With reason; Elizabeth was not by nature simple, and never succeeded in convincing anybody that she was. Honesty is another matter. She did not believe in a number of things, yet she was not quite clear that she disbelieved. In the intervals she attended to the small events about her. There was Sir Henry to provoke, young men to tease, and the fields and the people to enjoy. She let herself enjoy.

In London the preparations for the marriage with the Spaniard, and for the reconciliation with the Roman see, went on, not without difficulty between the two movements. The Prince Philip, created King of Naples by his father, landed in July; trains of Spanish gentlemen and soldiers paraded the capital. Philip, anxious to conform to English customs, drank ale. The formal marriage took place on 25th July. Mary became, then or later, by the grace of God, 'quene of Englande, Spaine, Fraunce, both Sicilles, Jerusalem, and Ireland. Archduchesse of Austria, Duchesse of Burgundy, Myllane, and Brabant. Countesse of Hapsburge, Flanders, and Tyroll.' In November the Lord Reginald Pole, Cardinal-Deacon of St Mary Cosmedin, came up the Thames in the royal barge, a silver cross shining at its prow; the fortunate tide swept him, an hour before his time, to Whitehall. The king and queen received him, Philip saying: 'We will place the queen between us'; the legate turned a sentence; the queen lamented the delay; the legate brought the salutations to a climax by saying that the Lord had delayed him till now he could say: '*Beatus fructus ventris tui.*' Five days later the House drew up a petition to the king and queen, imploring reconciliation with the Roman see; one member of the Commons spoke, and one more voted, in contradiction. On 30th November it was presented in the palace. The lord cardinal pronounced the absolution over the kneeling Houses. Within a few days they made more complete amends. They corrected legal heresy by reintroducing the old laws, and they created 'an Act repealing all statutes, articles, and provisions made against the See Apostolic of Rome since the twentieth year of King Henry the Eighth, and also for the establishment of all spiritual and ecclesiastical possessions and hereditaments conveyed to the laity.' In spite, however, of this last determination, which was unpalatable to the queen, to the legate, and to the apostolic see itself, the great new ordering of England had been achieved. The realm stood with Spain and those other scattered dominions of the royal title in the front of the Counter-Reformation. Not only Spain and England, but also France, rejoiced; thanksgivings were offered there in the churches. The champions of the Henrican formulation were converted—either honestly, like Gardiner, or dishonestly, like Cecil—or they were in prison or in danger of prison, like Cranmer. It seemed as if Europe were returning to its basis of philosophical unity. The great alliance awaited but one event to ratify it—the birth of an heir, which should make of no importance the unreliable religious mutations of the Lady Elizabeth.

She was not converted, like Gardiner; she was not in prison, like Cranmer; she was not quite conforming, like Cecil. She never would or she never could go quite far enough to be convincing. Interpretations of Elizabeth's character, especially at this time, turn always on how much there was in her of *would not* and how much of *could not*. That slender, swaying, unfixable division, in a Gallio-like mind sustaining a royal and sensuous body, the more avid of life that it was often liable to illness, is the mark upon which so much judgment has turned. But if her exact belief was, and is, uncertain, the implications of that belief were certain. Once she accepted, in her soul, the Roman obedience, that moment she would admit, to her soul and to the world, her canonical and legal illegitimacy. She would deny the validity of her mother's marriage; she would deny, publicly and profoundly, the justice of her claim to the crown. To hint at the denial of those things to others, in interviews or audiences, might be possible to her; it was not possible that she should deny them to herself. No woman ever possessed in a greater degree than Elizabeth that great feminine capacity for identifying her personal desires with righteousness and her personal needs with the justice of God.

She abandoned the English service for the Latin; she renewed her religious flirtation with the old order that was now the new. The pressure of events drove her more and more into a waiting on events. In 1555 she had another interview with the queen by night at Hampton Court. The queen, incredulously desiring justice, half-blamed, half-interrogated her sister. 'You stand stoutly on your truth; I pray God it may so fall out.' The princess answered with asseverations; if they were all true, it remained that her life and her temper of mind were, merely in themselves and without action, hostile to Mary's desire. The queen accused her of thinking and saying that she had been punished unjustly. The princess answered: 'No, if it please your Majesty, I have borne the burden and must bear it.' In a sense other than that of wardship and imprisonment she bore the burden —the fetters of illegitimacy, the phantasmal flicker of the crown.

For by now a change had taken place in the court, and, as time passed, and the course of nature produced no heir, that change became more marked. There was division, not only between orthodoxy and heresy, but in the whole front of papal orthodoxy itself. The chief division was between Spain and France. The king became aware that, if his wife had no child, and if Elizabeth did not succeed, then the throne would fall to the next heir, who was Mary of Scotland, the great-granddaughter of Henry VII. But Mary of Scotland was to be married to the Dauphin Francis of France, and then her accession would make one empire of France, Scotland, and England. It was a question in his mind whether the triumph of Catholicism were worth the triumph of France. He decided that it was not; perhaps to his orthodox eyes the union of the considerable heretical minority in France with the suppressed heretical minority in England seemed dangerous. The process of politics defeated his religious passion. He was compelled to compromise—in his statecraft, if not in his soul—and it was his misfortune that he had to compromise on Elizabeth, who by this time was rapidly becoming an incarnate variation of compromise. He did for his policy what she did for her life: he fell in with the situation. The Spanish influence at court was thrown on the side of Elizabeth's preservation and dignity. Better heresy and illegitimacy, which might be converted or subdued, than Catholicism and France, which would be secularly hostile.

It is part of the fantasy of politics that at the same time efforts were being made, with French help, to overthrow Mary and put Elizabeth on the throne. It seemed wiser to the French ambassador to establish her than to run the serious risk of the birth of a child or the uncertain attempt to impose Mary of Scotland. In the autumn of 1555 a plot was discovered by the Government; in Elizabeth's London house was found a mass of seditious books. Half a dozen of her servants were arrested, but she herself was not touched. The influence of Philip was decisive. The queen wrote kindly to her; she devotionally answered. The most that was done was to put her again under some sort of wardship. Her household was said 'to lead a licentious life, especially in matters of religion,' and Sir Thomas Pope was sent down to oversee it. In a combination of morals and metaphysics the loose behaviour of her subordinate court was to be trimmed by more rigorous discipline.

A more serious danger to her—a danger that could only be avoided by dexterity and obstinacy — was enforced marriage. It had once been proposed to marry her to a great English noble, William Courtenay; but Courtenay died in 1556. Philip was anxious to marry her to his ally, the Duke of Savoy, thus providing her with a Roman Catholic husband and himself with a secure England. She was urged; she refused. She was warned by her friends that it was proposed to marry her and carry her over to Flanders; she said she would die rather than go. The efforts to impose the discipline of marriage upon her failed as the efforts to impose the discipline of Roman doctrine had failed. The goodwill of France, the goodwill of Spain, the goodwill of the Reformers, all swayed on to her side. She did not conceive that she owed gratitude to any of them. In 1558 the queen desired once more to strike her from the succession, and was again defeated. Philip declined to agree. He claimed some credit afterwards, which Elizabeth only accorded when she wanted to placate him. In herself she gave the credit to her God and her own mind.

As if events hurried to help her, there came to England the news of the fall of Calais. The French war had been entered upon not entirely for the sake, but under the influence, of Philip. The shock of the capture of a city which had been English for centuries struck far. All discontent, religious and political, looked to Elizabeth. The year passed in fevers and famines, with labouring finances and amid the last executions. The executions under Mary, as those later under Elizabeth, were

nominally the business of the State for the preservation of the
State, as executions for heresy always had been. They were
not frequent or unusual enough to cause any violent increase of
popular anger, but at least they did not lessen popular discontent. In 1558 forty died; the last five at Canterbury on 10th
November, when the queen already lay dying. By then loyalty
to Elizabeth had become fashionable. She was no curmudgeon;
she proceeded to enjoy it. Sir William Cecil removed to Hatfield to be near her—the first arrival of the Cecils at Hatfield.
The court followed. Mary demanded, before she would sanction
the passage of the crown to her half-sister, a promise to maintain
Roman Catholic doctrine. Elizabeth was neither cruel nor
conscientious; what she had done for herself she did for Mary.
At that late hour it was unnecessary, for nothing could prevent
her accession. Her answer does not remain; it seems she gave
her promise. Mary sank into a semi-delirium. The attention
of all Europe was fixed on Hatfield. As if the order Mary had
established was also passing, thirteen bishops within a year
preceded or followed the queen in death. On 17th November,
in that almost oriental magnificence of priestly escort, Mary died.

The Lady Elizabeth received the news at Hatfield. She was
twenty-five years old. On the gold sovereigns that she was to
coin she retained the inscription set there by Mary: *a Domino
factum est, et est mirabile in oculis nostris*. *Mirabile* she remained;
factum est Domino is disputed.

Chapter 3

The Counter-Reformation—Cecil and Mary Queen of Scots—Elizabeth in
London—Her Coronation—Churches and Marriages—The Court of
Elizabeth—The Problem of her Legitimacy—Financial Reforms—The
first favourite, Robert Dudley—The Scandal of Amy Robsart—The
War in Scotland—Treaty of Edinburgh—The Return of Mary Stuart to
Scotland—Friendly Correspondence of the queens—The unsuccessful
War in France—Mary's proposed Marriage: the Offer of Dudley, the
Choice of Darnley.

AT the time of the queen's accession the division of Europe upon
the nature of the visible Church had been for some time accepted
as a temporary fact. It was a fact which neither side hoped or
feared or supposed could be permanent. It was expressed in
two definite events: the Diet and Confession of Augsburg (1555)
and the Council of Trent (1545–63). The one had determined

at least the right of the protesting Churches to supremacy in any
State where the sovereign was Protestant; the other, correcting
the decrees of the Council of Constance, was defining the reforms
in action and doctrine of the papal Church. At Constance the
council had decided between the conflicting claimants to Rome,
and had asserted its formal superiority to the see. At Trent
the legates of the pope controlled the council, and virtually
established the supernatural autocracy which later was to be
more exactly defined by the pope himself in the infallibility
decree of 1870. The conciliar movement within the bounds of
the papal Church was left to become the threat of the kings;
before the end of that century it had been perpended in France
and proposed in Spain, so uncertain yet was the pastorate of
Rome.

In 1560 the suspended council was resummoned. The expectation of the Churches and nations protesting against the
see of Rome was that its decisions would be followed by combined Catholic action to destroy all of them—or at least heresy
in all of them, which might mean the same thing. The pope
entertained a hope to the same effect; fire and sword were to
restore unity. He was willing, however, that they should first
express their views. Their divines could not, naturally, sit on
the council and vote, but they might address it and argue before
it. It was as far as he could possibly go—that may be conceded; but it must be conceded also that such a position would be
(except by such faith in a miracle as Christ seems to discourage)
impossible for Protestant divines. It was determined in England
that Anglican bishops should not attend.

It was not, however, the gathering at Trent which had defeated the progress of the Reformation so much as the new
spiritual energy which inspired Rome and her champions. Holy
and austere souls now shone round the Lateran on the Coelian
Hill; the Jesuits were founded in 1534 and approved in 1540 as
peculiar missionaries of the Church; the Inquisition, as the Holy
Office, was universally established as a means of purgation in
1541. The supreme utility of sanctity lay at the disposal of the
victorious papacy; names, now of world-wide invocation, had
then the meaning of men in streets and houses. Ignatius Loyola,
John D'Avila, Francis Xavier, Francis Borgia, Teresa, Philip
Neri, Charles Borromeo—these and others intensified the power
and lustre of the Roman cause. In 1558 it did not seem unlikely
that the whole of Christendom would be recovered by the Roman
see, in spite of the difficulties and disputes which continually

arose between that see and the kings of France and Spain, and between those kings themselves. Yet in fact something other than those bitter but domestic quarrels was to emerge—a spirit, a quality of mind, which may be called scepticism or realism or toleration or cynicism or wisdom according to the kind of mind which possesses it; perhaps, making allowance for her femininity, perversity, obstinacy, and fear, it might be called Elizabethan. It was the spirit which puts the supernatural in its place, a habit which, losing much, gains something, and without which religion is only tolerable in and by saints. At least that spirit, like her own, is flagrant in its egotism, and neither cares nor is able to conceal its own limited and earthly nature by borrowing glory from a vast universal religion; so far its honesty is manifest. A worldly hypocrite Elizabeth might be; she never succeeded in being a religious. Nor, at bottom, did she desire it; her refusal continually betrayed her hypocrisies to a perhaps not much less hypocritical world. It separated her from the minister who stood by her, who piously defended his pious frauds. Yet Cecil too had his sincerity; it was in his perfect realization of himself as an official and civil servant. If Mary had had an heir, Cecil might easily have remained Catholic—he had been one of the gentlemen sent by Mary to meet Philip of Spain in Flanders— and might still, though with more difficulty, become Treasurer. He could not keep away from business; he never failed in it; he never illumined it.

For forty years Elizabeth and he worked together; of old it was generally supposed for good, now it is as generally, and as fashionably, supposed for harm. They were intimate, and intimately dependent. Yet perhaps neither of them ever quite trusted the other, and each of them a little despised the other, working rather better for that element of comforting contempt. They both hid secrets. Cecil deliberately concealed facts; the queen, less deliberately, her heart. She chose him rather than he her, and for his capacity, especially a capacity which had ensured not only self-preservation but occupation both under Edward and Mary. It is more likely that she understood him than he her. The mind of a woman is mysterious; so, it is said, is the heart of a prince.

Cecil was her supporter; over the seas, in France, was one who wished to be her supplanter. As soon as Mary Tudor was dead, Mary Queen of Scots, wife of the Dauphin of France, quartered the royal arms of England on her own, and thus proclaimed to the world the illegitimacy and usurpation of the Queen of England,

According to Roman Catholic ecclesiastical order she was undoubtedly justified. The exact position of a sovereign who,
theologically incompetent of succession by birth, is yet legally
nominated to the succession by a previous occupant, was a
question for the legalists, whom it occupied. Except for Mary
Stuart, illegitimacy would have been mostly a term of abuse;
given Mary, it was a threat and a danger, for it meant Mary.
Yet at the moment, Mary, to England, was only a name.

In the dark closing days of November the young queen came
to London, and made processions—coming to Charterhouse on
23rd November, riding to the Tower five days later, going by
water to Somerset House a week after, and finally, on 23rd
December, moving to Whitehall. She played for the popularity
she loved, and won it. Now she was free to deal with men and
women under no suspicious eyes, and in no danger of hostile
reports. She had not been so free for eleven years, and before
that she had been but a child. The crowds roared round her,
and she smiled at them; they shouted at her, and she decorously
jested back. They brought her little bunches of flowers, and
she accepted them; they made Latin speeches to her, and she
understood them. Every spectacle was a harmony of joy; she
keyed it up to a higher and higher pitch by her own delight.
The Most High and Mighty Princess Elizabeth, by the grace of
God, etc., had come to her city—to the ostentation, the cheering,
the populace.

On Sunday, 15th January, 1559, she was crowned at Westminster, having had more processions and welcomes during the
preceding days. In Westminster Hall the bishops, coped and
mitred, received her. She came; she was censed; the Archbishop
of York and another bishop gave her holy water and the Pax.
They all sang *Salve, festa dies*, and the procession moved on,
along layers of purple cloth, to the abbey. She exhibited herself
to the people, and was acclaimed. Mass was said. She was
anointed, and crowned by the Bishop of Carlisle.

There had been at that coronation mass one small point of
alteration: the host had not been elevated after consecration.
What was more, the alteration had been at the Queen's own
instructions, for the same thing had occurred in the royal chapel
a few weeks before. There she had been disobeyed, and it was
reported that she had risen and left the chapel. Or, as some
said, she had ordered the celebrant not to elevate, and he had
answered that he must, and so she had left at the end of the
gospel. It was even reported that at the coronation there was

no consecration at all, which is nonsense. The certain thing is that neither in the chapel nor in the abbey was there elevation. It was a point immaterial; it did not directly concern doctrine but ritual. Nevertheless it was doubly significant. There were various hypotheses concerning the mode of the Presence in the sacrament. One—to speak roughly—held that a Presence of Christ existed at the moment of reception; one at the moment of consecration. The first had been held by Cranmer and others; the second was orthodox at Rome. There was also the hypothesis that the real Presence was in no sense intervolved with the bread and wine; that belonged to the more extreme Reforming bodies. It was arguable that the queen's action was insignificant; that it affected no doctrine. But if it affected any, it affected the Roman. It withdrew from the public declaration of the Roman hypothesis concerning the mode of the Presence; it did no more. It was the exact symbol of all Elizabeth's religious acts at the beginning. Even the Acts of Parliament that followed in 1559—only five years after the superb reconciliation—did not commit her to more than a kind of inconvenient silence towards Rome. The lands that Mary had restored to the Church were given back to the Crown, on the plea of necessity; the monasteries refounded by Mary were also made over to the Crown. The Queen's Majesty was declared the only Supreme Governor—she refused 'Supreme Head'—'as well in all ecclesiastical things or causes as temporal.' Foreign jurisdiction, princely or prelatic, was renounced. But no direct mention was made of the pope; indeed, in the last clause of one Bill a particular appeal to Rome on a marriage cause was allowed—on condition that Rome gave answer within sixty days. The queen withdrew, but that was expected; she withdrew only to a degree, and that at least was to the good. She became ambiguous, and that was merely perplexing. But the Spanish ambassador made allowances; she was but a girl, quick but imprudent.

There was dancing at Whitehall. The queen was twenty-five and free, and the mistress of a court of Renascence gentlemen, who all wrote poetry and made music and kissed hands and lips, and flaunted their colours and flashed their swords. Courtesies rose into compliments, compliments into flatteries, flatteries into the wildest flights of amorous verbal rapture. The queen enjoyed language, and the more dangerously passionate the language the more she enjoyed it. She delighted in cerebral adoration, and the stronger the hint of corporal madness the more she delighted in it. She had a supreme and unfair advantage; she was the

queen. She was entirely safe in her person, even from incivility,
except in a decent pretence of despair. Her servants' favours,
their fortunes, their freedom, their very lives, depended on her.
She could flash a look that struck the rashest courtier into terror,
and what any woman might attempt in arrogance of femininity
the power of England lay behind to encourage and protect. If
any authority existed to which she would bend, it must be an
authority as profound as the freedom and royalty in her which
had been the result of so many years' bitter awareness. She
danced and dined and rode and revelled, and all around her and
her few ladies circled euphuistic adoration.

The queen is by nature of a high spirit [wrote the Venetian ambassador in 1560], and has become more so owing to her good fortune,
and the many physical and mental endowments which she possesses,
so she has lofty designs, and promises herself success in all of them.

She had promised herself success. It was universally assumed
that she must have a husband to ensure it. It was also realized
that her husband—that is, her marriage—would, directly or indirectly, determine the particular scheme of metaphysics and
pattern of politics with which she would accord: Romanism and
France, or Romanism and Spain, or Protestantism and England,
or even (though less probably) Romanism and England. A
foreign marriage might not be popular, but it might be necessary;
only by such subordination to one of the Great Powers could the
small nation on their sea frontiers be preserved from conquest.
At the moment the small nation was at war with France—or,
rather, negotiating peace with France under the slightly detached
assistance of Spain. The chief desire of the English was the
recovery of Calais. Without the help of King Philip they were
hardly likely to get it.

Philip, a little slowly, and under the propulsion of his ambassador in England, came to a conclusion. The settlement of Europe
—that is, the establishment of Roman order and the diplomatic
defeat of the French monarchy—could be best served, he had
known for years, by the satisfactory settlement in marriage of the
Queen of England. The queen was coyly reluctant to accept any
of his nominees. He determined on a grand gesture; he offered
her himself. She must, of course, be converted; 'in this way it
will be evident I am serving the Lord by marrying her.' He did
not anticipate much difficulty. He felt, without perhaps admit-
ting it to his conscientious mind, that she would think her kingdom worth a mass. So she might have done apart from Philip
—if the old difficulty had not recurred: in order to gain a kingdom

that way, she must first acknowledge that she had no right to it in any way. The pope offered olive-branches: let her submit and all should be forgiven. Let her admit that she was a bastard and she should be treated as a queen. Let her admit that she was a bastard—and as an inevitable corollary that the other woman who in Paris magnificently flaunted the arms of England was justified, was rightful queen—let her admit that, and she might perhaps keep the crown as a papal or Spanish gift. Let her admit that she was a supplanter and she might be permitted to reign. Elizabeth was the last woman in the world to take refuge from another woman under the protection of a priest or of a husband. The King of Spain did not believe that she could maintain at once the show of right and the fact of rule. She believed that she could. Her emotional imagination maintained that she was that strange and superb thing, Harry's daughter, and Harry's daughter was Queen of England, and England was rapturous to have her. She had spent years defending her life and her freedom—such as it was—with all the resources of her intelligence. It did not seem to her much of a sin to use the same resources to maintain independently the crown she had independently achieved. She set herself to deal with events, unencouraged and unhampered by metaphysics, and (it must be admitted) by morals. It did not seem to her that her morals were less just, in their way, than those which marked the progress of her metaphysical and royal rivals. Her femininity assisted her; she hurled herself into her lack of pattern with as much ardour as other women—her sister Mary, for example—had hurled themselves into patterns, and her energy and her capacity in that motion were a principal element in the exclusion of philosophy from the councils of Europe.

Ambassadors and suits of marriage thronged her—from Scotland, from France, from Sweden, from the empire, from Spain. She showed willingness to them all, but Philip had been the first, and Philip's adventure was over before the others had well begun. His ambassador had written that he would 'pick to pieces one by one those whom she might marry here.' The ambassador talked; she responded, but she dallied. She said she was not inclined to marry. She said that to marry her sister's widower would be to insult the memory of her father, who had conscientiously put away his brother's widow. In fact, though the comment was not serious, the underlying fact was: to marry him would be once more to advertise her illegitimacy. She said she could not marry him, for she was a heretic. She did not seem to grasp that she need not go on being a heretic. She suggested that they might go on being friends. In April, Philip caused the proposal to be withdrawn. Elizabeth, between sighs and smiles, lamented to the ambassador that his master could not be much in love if he would not wait four months. It had not occurred to Philip or to the ambassador that he was, or was supposed to be. The queen went on dancing to the thrilling notes of the cerebralized passion of the court, and all the immediate marriage possibilities slid slowly by into the past. To the Commons, urging marriage, she had cerebralized virginity; she became almost lyrical over the marble sepulchre that should proclaim how a queen had lived and died a virgin. In fact the phrase objectifies what was by now an inevitable element in her nature—her vigil, her self-determination, her self-preservation. The marble stone with its epitaph symbolized them; so virgin, so buried, so gloriously famed as a beneficent sovereign to her people, she was indeed secure. Virginity in past times had been a vocation; she spoke of it so, but indeed in her speech it had changed its nature. Evitable or inevitable, it was already no more than an event.

Amid the thrilling and important concerns of love and religion was another, hardly less important, and, to Elizabeth's mind, hardly less thrilling—money. The finances of the country—that is to say, of the Crown, for in most matters all national expenses were the expenses of the Crown; subjects did not expect to have to pay—had been for years in a very improper state. Elizabeth and Cecil were in this at one. They set to work to re-establish credit, at home and abroad. The expenditure of the court was reduced. Tax returns were investigated, currency was improved—base coins called in, and a smaller proportion of good issued. The queen, unexpectedly, made a profit; trade was assisted. Money was sent abroad to pay off foreign debts. Her credit went up and up. All her life she worked at that reserve of strength. Her rhetoric was cut upon the stone of her economy, which was as hard to be moved as the imaginary lid of that other sepulchre which, in her rhetoric, she predestined for her grave. Money also she treated as a series of events, and no dogma could persuade her to loosen those events. There is in this a peculiar and satisfying likeness between her and that greater spirit, already close on birth, which was to be the chief glory of her reign; nor did the mind of Shakespeare, when it ceased from *Othello*, forget to use reasonable means to recover his proper dues from his debtor at Stratford. The English, a nation of shopkeepers, are a nation of poets, of whom a number of the best came literally out of shops. They, like the angel of the Apocalypse, set one foot on the known and one on the unknown; it is their balance, and Elizabeth and Shakespeare in their different ways are two of those who kept it.

Meanwhile, as those first months drew into years, the queen's more general appetite for enjoyment, without losing much of its general scope, distinguished a particular opportunity. The first favourite arose. Favourites were general through Europe in that age, and not only general but public. They were public figures as favourites; the very name was used without any sense of degradation. It was no more shameful to be the prince's favourite than to be a minister or secretary; often the favourite was used as a minister, and had to work as hard. He was, however, peculiarly the prince's intimate; his whole glory, his substantial being, under heaven, depended on the prince's personal liking. He was apt to be a difficulty to the normal diplomats. There arose, shining in her favour, at the Court of Elizabeth, the figure of Lord Robert Dudley, son of that Northumberland who had attempted to establish a dynasty. The queen and he had been friends in youth, and friends under Mary. On her accession he had been made Master of the Horse.

He appeared now, rising in the court and presently in the Council, portentous of the queen's personal delights and desires, distinguished by her femininity beyond all his fellows. It even began to seem as if that grand inscription on the marble sepulchre would never have a chance to get itself cut. Nobody had taken her protestations of a virginal future very seriously; at twenty-six, in the throb of a new life, women might talk so. It was but a spectacular event, that day when the young queen proclaimed that her life was to be dedicated to the motherhood of her people. Less spectacular incidents were reported in 1559; the queen was said to visit Lord Robert's lodgings by night. It was said that if his wife died—she was ill of cancer—Elizabeth would marry him. The ambassadors wrote of it, and the common people gossiped. The court grew busy with scandal and some anger. Dudley was of no such high birth or grand estate that he could be easily contemplated as a master. The queen made him all but master, yet if ever he presumed upon what she had given she struck him back. 'I will have here but one mistress, and no master,' she swore, and that one at least of her many oaths she kept.

The days ran on into 1560, to the autumn. There were many subjects of anxiety—the pope, Spain, Scotland, France. Even yet, as September came, the existence of the queen seemed strange; the lords of Europe momently expected something to happen—

G

conversion or rebellion, marriage or assassination. She was still a *lusus naturae*, a thing that could not last. Suddenly a new wave of an outrageous rumour swept over Europe. Lady Robert Dudley had been found dead in her country house. It was universally suspected that her husband had slain her—Cecil had hinted as much to the Spanish ambassador on the previous day— and that the queen had been passive accomplice. This, it was said in France, was the fruit of heresy; the English ambassador heard the taunt at the court where Mary Stuart dwelt, ignorant yet of Darnley and Bothwell and Kirk o' Field. The shocked ambassadors, writing frantically home, received small comfort from Cecil, who, while Dudley throve, stood in need of some comfort himself. Hearts almost stood still; would the queen take the last fatal step? Would she marry her—paramour?

For a while it looked as if she would. The coroner's jury declared a death by misadventure; another inquiry found no other conclusion. Dudley was officially innocent; the more, she. As opinion in England settled, she fell away from what in the one wild moment of crisis had seemed possible. The danger over, and nothing having happened—beyond Amy Robsart's death—she became irritable. In November, Dudley was on the point of being raised to the peerage. The patent was made out; they brought it her. She slashed it with a penknife, with a bitter reference to the treachery of the dead Dudleys. Then she became kind again. Cecil swung back into favour, and then again out, but, in favour or out, he stuck to his job, and she kept him at it. It was the one certain thing on which they were agreed. Through the growing winter of 1560 and longer the uncertainty lasted. In December a foreign event changed Europe: Francis, King of France, husband of Mary Stuart, died. Mary was deprived of a kingdom, and even of influence in it, for with the new king the influence of Catherine de' Medici became paramount. Mary's attention turned vividly to her own kingdom in the north.

During the years 1559 and 1560, while Elizabeth had been receding from Rome, manœuvring about marriage, reforming the finance, figuring in public scandal with Lord Robert, and, above all, manipulating the public spectacle of her own imagination of herself as Harry's daughter and Queen of England, she had been forced also, rather against her will, into activity in Scotland. There, as in the rest of Europe, metaphysical and political schisms ran varyingly criss-cross. The Calvinist and local Lords of the Congregation had attacked the Catholic and European regent in Leith, a Guise princess, widow of James V, and Mary's mother.

Elizabeth had no wish—she never had—to assist rebellion, especially Protestant rebellion, but she had no wish that the French armies of the regent and her daughter should control Scotland, 'the postern-gate' of England. In their hands the gate would be far too convenient an entry for Roman and Marian invasion; she herself would become more dependent than ever for her safety on the goodwill of the King of Spain. If she and the national mass which she thought to control and express were to swing free in their own orbit, she must keep it from the influence of both of the two great planets; that is, as far as possible, she must keep Scotland subordinate to her own influence. Since the Queen of Scotland in Paris was flaunting the English royal arms, Elizabeth felt herself the freer to interfere, without any flaunting of the interference, with the royal arms of Scotland. Neither to herself nor to the other members of the European guild of monarchs did she wish to admit that she was doing so. At no exact point could she be brought to admit that acts of war were being committed. She did not like war for many reasons: it was expensive; it was wasteful also of lives, and she was never one, unless greatly moved, to like spending lives any more than money; finally, it tended to be a decisive crisis, and all her involuntary training had brought her to dislike decisive crises. She had known too many and too dangerous. But when a crisis forced itself on her, she could act as if she had hastened to meet it. She did not hasten to this one. English money appeared in the camp of the Lords of the Congregation, English ships in the Firth of Forth. Their hovering neutrality flowered in hostile acts against the French. Protests to the queen produced only astonishment, incredulity, demands for more and more particulars, expositions of the impossibility of disciplinary action on the admiral without exacter knowledge. The Spanish ambassador secretly encouraged Cecil, who was much more pro-war than his mistress, being much more Protestant. Any damage to the French suited Philip's schemes of policy. He wanted neither heresy victorious nor Mary triumphant, and his compromising diplomacy lay tendentiously behind the young queen, who was certainly not Mary and might eventually not be heretical. At Rome his representatives exhorted the pope to patience.

Domestic troubles multiplied in France and Spain. The permissible moment for open war arrived. The queen allowed an English army to appear in the Lords' camp before Leith. Every one thought it very wrong, but no one was in an immediate position to interfere. The queen had a hand in the triumph of the Lords' party and gained a voice in the negotiation. In July 1560 the Treaty of Edinburgh was concluded, subject to ratification. By it, not only were the French to withdraw from Scotland, but Francis and Mary were to cease from bearing Elizabeth's blazon and claiming Elizabeth's throne. It was the first definite phenomenon of Elizabeth victorious, the first imposition of herself as an indubitable fact on dynastic and dogmatic Europe. The Lords of the Congregation rejoiced metaphysically, as if the treaty were a theological definition. To Elizabeth it was a personal event. She was urged by her ministers to spend money on the Lords; she consistently refused. She imposed her economy at home while imposing her reputation abroad—two sides of the spectacle which was Elizabeth.

At one point—and that the most important—she failed. She could not force the treaty on Mary Stuart, who merely refused to ratify it and continued to embroider her actual throne with the symbols of her potential. The scandal of Cumnor Hall in September encouraged her. The shocked horror of Elizabeth and Mary at each other's marital or non-marital adventures is not the least among the bitter-sweets of history. The refusal of ratification made of a political a personal quarrel; it fretted Elizabeth in the tender spot of her political relation to her father Henry, and combined with that a minor irritation on the question of orthodoxy. Elizabeth's religious emotions, by her nature perhaps but also by her early circumstances, were inextricably involved with her personal and patriotic, and they also together. Her character had been formed too early under the threat of violence; her unity lay in her idea of herself, and she suffered the disadvantage of that premature unity—she allowed too little to any law outside herself. Had it been possible for her to find in that blazing court of fervid and fantastic adoration any spirit of authority over her, could she have felt the mastery of power and greatness and, half against, half with her will, been subordinated to it, she might have found the thing she chiefly lacked and obscurely desired—lucid recognition of something mightier than herself. None could give it—neither Leicester nor Cecil, neither Hatton nor Walsingham, nor Essex at the end. The greatest spirits of her reign were separated from her—Shakespeare by degree and Bacon by age. She was left to wander in the dark night of existence, and only in her unfathomed heart to believe dimly in the motions of a mysterious God.

Meanwhile she continued to drive before the car of her spectacular majesty the else irreconcilable minds of her councillors. She enjoyed the small strain of their dislikes and inamities, knowing they dared not break into hostility, nor impose on her any but a temporary crisis. She maintained Leicester; she kept Cecil; her favours and her fierce irritations flew variably over them. Her intelligence, her pride, her royalty, derived nourishment from the subdued contentions. She sustained herself and the land was quiet.

But when the trumpets suddenly sounded the death of Francis, King of France, the prospect changed a little. Mary Stuart was about to return to Scotland. She applied (still refusing to ratify the treaty) to Elizabeth for a safe-conduct, to allow her, if she chose or was compelled by storm, to pass through England on her way to her native kingdom. No one was very anxious to have her there—not the Lords of the Congregation, nor Elizabeth of England, nor Philip of Spain. The new French Government was anxious to have her out of France. Elizabeth refused to send the safe-conduct unless Mary ratified the treaty. Mary preferred to remain Catholic and royal claimant, and in a superb Renascence style played her part of prospective victim. If she was compelled to land, she told Elizabeth's ambassador, 'the Queen your mistress will have me in her hands to do her will of me . . . she may do her pleasure and make sacrifice of me.' She embarked. Elizabeth sent a safe-conduct too late. It was generally expected, nevertheless, in France, in Spain, in Scotland, that Mary would be seized upon the way. She was left untouched; she landed.

It was clear with her coming that something had better be done between the two kingdoms, and embassies began to pass to determine exactly what. The queens, maintaining their technical division, began to express personal affection. Mary suggested that she should be recognized as heir presumptive; Elizabeth, that she herself should first be recognized as reigning queen. Elizabeth was uneasily aware that heirs presumptive, with or without their own consent, were thorns to sovereigns. 'Think you,' she said to Mary's ambassador, 'that I could love my winding sheet? . . . I have good experience of myself in my sister's time, how desirous men were that I should be in place, and earnest to set me up. And if I would have consented, I know what enterprises would have been attempted to bring it to pass.' Proposals for meeting were made; the queens, exchanging presents, applauded the idea. The Scottish ambassador, Maitland of

Lethington, was urgently in favour. He thought one of the two women would dominate, but that some arrangement would be made. He looked farther than any; he desired more. 'We shoot,' he wrote to Cecil, 'both at one scope—the union of this isle.' Cecil's almost permanent sense of disillusion with his mistress had reached one of its periodical pits of despair; he was talking of resignation and the illimitable ills that would fall on the country under his successors. The Council took alarm at the proposed meeting and made speeches. The queen, in full session, defied them. She, Mary, and Maitland pressed on the arrangements. It was fixed for the end of August or the beginning of September, somewhere in north England. It was prevented by another outbreak of war.

The Huguenots in France had been attacked by Mary's friends and relatives, the House of Guise. In France the national mass had swayed on to the Roman Catholic side, and the Counter-Reformation threatened to triumph. The civil war which followed on the first outbreak alarmed all Protestant feeling in England, and it was this alarm which had made the Council so strongly anti-Marian. The Huguenots appealed to the queen, and the queen consented to aid them. Besides the necessity of checking the Counter-Reformation, there was a minor theme in the decision—the hope of Calais. Elizabeth had failed to recover it by negotiation; she demanded it now as a compensation for armed help. The help was sent, and was of no use. The war petered out; Catherine de' Medici, who was not much more metaphysically minded than Elizabeth herself, managed a peace. The French unanimously agreed to dislike the English invaders, and the queen, having suffered military defeat and diplomatic disaster, was compelled to withdraw her troops.

The atmosphere was heavier than of old, with cloudy menace. In 1562 the queen fell ill of smallpox; she recovered, but there had been intense anxiety. The utterly unforeseen future emphasized itself. Mary Stuart was in Scotland and marriageable; the Guises were in touch with her and with Philip of Spain; Philip could contemplate an arrangement with her which did not add weight to France, and the militant Catholicism of the Guises chimed with his own. The marriage problems of both queens came to the front. Elizabeth, while always snubbing the Commons that spoke of hers, always encouraged foreign princes to do so. There was talk of her marrying Charles, King of France; there was talk of Mary marrying Don Carlos of Spain. There was renewed talk of the succession. Suggestions became schemes, and schemes more and more complex. In the summer of 1564 Elizabeth introduced a new pattern. She made one of those strange emotional moves which utterly defeat the mind of the later reader, a move which would be so wild an insult that it must be regarded as a serious altruism, so romantic that it must have been meant as intelligent. She proposed to Maitland that Mary should marry Lord Robert Dudley.

It was almost universally believed that he and the queen had been lovers; it had been a scandal everywhere. When she had thought herself dying she had declared that there had been nothing scandalous between them. In her strength, though she loved gossip, she was careless of scandal. She offered Dudley to Mary as the most intimate sign of her goodwill. It was a fantastic and unbelievable, but an actual and apparently a sincere gesture; yet the offer had in it an Elizabethan twist. She told Sir James Melville that she knew, if the marriage took place, Dudley would not allow any attempt to thrust her from the throne of England. The proposal defeated Maitland; it at first angered and then perplexed Mary. The same thought struck both of them: did this mean a promise of the succession? It apparently did not. Elizabeth conceived herself perhaps as offering Mary a gift of more value than many successions; it was not her own scheme of values, but she probably convinced herself emotionally that it ought to be Mary's. 'You think, madam,' Melville told her, 'that if you were married you would be but Queen of England, and now you are both king and queen. I know your spirit cannot endure a commander.'

There was, however, another man younger and better born than Dudley, great-grandson of Henry VII through the House of Lennox, and therefore not altogether out of touch with the succession. His name was Henry, Lord Darnley. Mary played with the idea, and, when the Don Carlos match fell through, played with it more ardently. The Lennoxes had fled to England in the reign of Henry VIII, and had been there since. If Mary could not by her marriage unite Roman Catholicism internationally, and put herself in the way of a great empire, by this at least she could draw herself even closer to the throne of two kingdoms, and draw nearer the Roman Catholic masses in England and Scotland. She could, in fact, make through the whole island a distinctively Marian and Roman party.

Elizabeth, since the Dudley plan looked like failing, and since she certainly did not wish Mary to contract a menacing foreign marriage, put no serious obstacles in the way. Against the

Council's wish she let Darnley go to Scotland. Mary passionately approved him—'the best-proportioned long man she had
seen.' Elizabeth kept Dudley with her in England; she made
him Earl of Leicester. There were intimacies of touch even at
the investiture. Mary became certain that Elizabeth was playing with her; she created Darnley Earl of Ross. Elizabeth
ordered him to return. He did nothing of the kind. Elizabeth
sent formal protests against the marriage, which was now definitely proposed. But as between a continental alliance and a
marriage with Dudley, perhaps, when it came to the point,
Darnley was the best compromise. She allowed it to happen;
in June 1565 it took place.

Its success was modified by the prompt rebellion of the Scottish Protestant lords. Mary made short work of them and
Elizabeth disowned them. She ranted at them in public. But at
least the work had been done by Mary's own troops; no French
or Spanish army had entered. There had been no promise of the
succession. The Queen of England had once more compromised
with events, and had emerged, as the next few years were to
show, in a position of increased strength. Darnley's character
was such that Mary, it was soon clear, had all the disadvantages
and none of the advantages of a political marriage, and all the
disadvantages and none of the advantages of a romantic. Elizabeth remained with none of the disadvantages of a romantic
marriage and as many of the advantages as her secret relation
with Leicester permitted, while being free, at the same time, to
contract a political, and (now Mary was maritally out of the way)
being again the best match in Europe. The beautiful hands, of
which was she so proud, could still be alluringly stretched out to
any suitor; and if the face, now past its early youth, pitted with
smallpox, and vitalized by fierce eyes, was not of the first beauty,
there lay still above the yellowish-red hair the gleam of the
crown.

It was 1565; she was thirty-one, and she had reigned for seven
years.

Chapter 4

The Archduke Charles and the Private Mass—Arrival of Mary Stuart in
England—Elizabeth's possible Courses—Mary's Claims—The Affair
of the Spanish Gold—The great Houses of the North—The Duke of
Norfolk—The Confederacy—Arrest of Norfolk—The Northern Rebellion—Its Destruction—The Queen's Anger—The Bull of Excommunication.

THE next few years accordingly were filled in the south by more
marriage negotiations, in the north by marriage infelicities. In
the north between 1565 and 1568 came the murder of Rizzio, the
rise of Bothwell, the murder of Darnley, the defeat and imprisonment of Mary, and at last her flight. In the south were long
discussions and controversies over a proposed match—this time
with the Archduke Charles. It came very near to success—so
near that it seemed as if only one thing in the end stood in the
way: might the archduke, if he consented, and if he consented
so far as even to accompany the queen to the English churches,
have his own private mass in his own private chapel? Even
Elizabeth's ministers, even Cecil, were ready to concede this.
Only, after long hesitation, the queen refused. She was certainly not more Protestant than Cecil, and she refused, partly
at any rate, because she was not. She would not tolerate the
existence, in the very centre of royalty, of an admitted distinction
between the two modes of faith. On the metaphysical side she
blurred the issue, which, in spite of all her efforts, was becoming
more, and more angrily, defined. On the side of events she was
clearer: she would not allow a rallying-point for disaffection.
The religious controversy in England was different from that in
the Netherlands, in France, in Scotland—almost in all Europe;
and its peculiar quality helped to leave Elizabeth undenounced
by Rome and to hold in a vague net all but the most determined
Protestants and Papalists. That quality was, simply, that the
controversy had not been between Churches, but about—even
within—a Church. There had been no violent schism between
the Marian and Elizabethan settlements. The buildings remained; most of their ministers remained; the celebrations remained. The chief events, as it were, of historic Christendom
went straight on in an unbroken succession, as did the succession
of bishops. They might or might not have lost their religious
value, but as exterior events they remained. As desirable events
Elizabeth was determined that not even the archduke's private
mass should be allowed secretly to contradict their sufficiency;

*G

as undesirable events the pope, soon now, was to contradict and denounce them and their governor.

From 1568 to 1570 or so came a rush of events. The first was Mary Stuart. She arrived, a fugitive sovereign, claiming help, reminding Elizabeth of old promises, demanding justice. She asked help from the princess whose legitimacy she denied and whose throne she claimed, in order that she might again occupy that throne from which, if she chose, she might the more easily attempt to seize this other. A Bayard might have lived up to such conditions; Elizabeth merely considered all the possibilities. She did not want Mary; she did not like having her; but she had her. There were a number of courses open: (a) to restore her by force of arms, which would be difficult and dangerous; (b) to send her on to France or Spain, which would present either country with an incarnate claim to England; (c) to hand her over to the Scottish lords, which would mean her death; (d) to keep her as a wronged princess at the Court of England, which looked like encouraging her own death or removal; (e) to keep her in England as more or less of a prisoner, more or less honourably; (f) to put her to death after a show of trial and sentence.

It seemed, in view of the feeling at home and in Scotland, that (a) was impossible. The queen's sense of her own self-preservation made her reluctant to do (b) or (d). Her guild-sense of Mary as a sovereign prince made her abhor (c) and (f). Remained (e). Elizabeth did not much want (e). She made spasmodic motions towards any and all of the others. She said things and wrote things which encouraged every one to fear or hope she was about to take an alternative course, but she never did—or not for seventeen years. On metaphysical grounds any course could be defended except this. Events alone pointed to this, and she took it. She did not—it is her disgrace and her glory—invent any kind of metaphysical theory to account for it. She did not pretend to like it. She merely said that if, since, and while she was Queen of England, it was impossible to do anything else. She added that it was all very sad and all very difficult.

In the intervals of claiming Elizabeth's help for her own restoration, Mary claimed the help of the Papalist sovereigns for the deposition of Elizabeth. She told both Elizabeth and the sovereigns that a very little help would do. When she was Queen of England she would restore Catholicism, and if (she cried out in anger) the Grand Turk would help her to her rights she would call in the Grand Turk. She demanded from Elizabeth the most

correct observance of the most exact duty, reserving to herself
the widest limits of possible convenience. If ever a position
could be called 'impossible,' it was the position of those two
women, yet it lasted for seventeen years. In those years many
wild and hysterical things were said by both queens, many foolish
and wicked things done. Through those years the will of
Elizabeth, forced by events yet contending with events, preserved Mary's life and forbade her freedom, in a combination of
courage and timidity, obstinacy and weakness, honour and falsehood. The one certain thing is that Elizabeth remained on the
throne, and Mary remained alive—in a world where, a little later,
even a high ecclesiastic and diplomat of the Papal Court declared
that the assassination of a heretic sovereign was an act well
pleasing to God.

Mary, like Elizabeth in her earlier days, took at one time to the
ritual of her custodian; she adopted the Book of Common Prayer.
But she also said quite frankly that it was no good her losing her
reputation among the Roman Catholic champions if she was uncertain of Elizabeth's friendship. On the whole, what with her
trust in God and her distrust of the Queen of England, she found
the old ways the best. It was as she settled to this determination
that there chanced three events which determined the formal
breach between Elizabeth and the Roman principles. They were
(i) the Spanish gold, (ii) the Northern Rebellion, (iii) the Excommunication. They determined that half of the queen's vision of
herself should dissolve into air.

(i) The affair of the Spanish gold took place in the year 1568.
The King of Spain had been dealing, through his lieutenant, the
Duke of Alva, with heretical and economic revolts in the Netherlands. They had been crushed, but the crushing had cost money.
Philip borrowed money; the Italian bankers agreed to let him
have a loan. It was agreed that it should be shipped under his
care to the Netherlands, and the actual loan should begin upon
its arrival there. It seems as if the Italians determined to make
the Spanish Government pay the cost of transport, and the
Government decided to cut down the cost; the ships carrying it
had practically no convoy. Near England, French and English
privateers got on the track; the unhappy Spanish merchantmen
fled into English ports. Under the moral pressure and warnings
of the English port governors, the Spanish captains unloaded their
chests of gold. Posts rode to London. The queen, stirred, as
always, by the idea of a great deal of gold, commanded the
treasure to be brought up also.

The Spanish ambassador asked for an audience to demand safe-conduct for the gold. Meanwhile he wrote to Alva desiring that all English goods and ships should be arrested. He meant it as a precautionary measure or a threat; Alva consented. The queen's advisers (including a French cardinal) urged Elizabeth to keep the gold; while she hesitated, it was discovered that it did not yet belong to Philip, but to the bankers. With immediate celerity the queen arranged to borrow it herself; the bankers, not being in a position to refuse, consented. But when she heard of the arrest of her ships and goods, so unwisely arranged before her decision was taken, she broke into rage. A similar arrest was immediately put on all Flemish and Spanish goods in England, and the result was heavily in favour of the English. The queen had the goods and the money too. The infinite patience of the King of Spain endured. But the already strained relations which had been established when, nine years before, in answer to his stupendous offer of himself, Elizabeth had promised to be a sister to him ('sister and perpetual confederate') received yet more exacerbation. Some years later, it is only just to add, the money was returned to him.

The effect on the Netherlands was disastrous. Alva was deprived of his money, and trade was damaged. To pay his troops, Alva put a tax on all sales, and damaged trade still more heavily. Prices soared; competition with other countries suffered. Shops were closed in protest. Orthodox Catholics regarded the Catholic Spanish army with new and hostile eyes. A revolt which had been mostly religious and sporadic became economic and universal. Catholic governors were expelled, fighting Calvinists welcomed. Philosophical toleration among the rebels became a necessity, and the Spanish army therefore found itself with a great deal to do.

(ii) Elizabeth had had, on the whole, a quiet country, but the northern half of it was only partly hers. There, between the mass of her subjects and the influence of the throne, lay the more immediate territorial power of the great northern lords, the Percys and the Dacres. There the Roman tradition was strongest, in spite of the operation of the bishops; and from the north the greatest possibility of revolt had threatened.

The arrival of Mary in England sent a thrill through all the quiescent opposition to the Government. Elizabeth was surrounded by the power of the families, but even among the families there were divisions. The older group—the families in being—leaned to territorialism and the Catholic tradition; the

newer—the families who were only becoming—to centralization
and the Protestant doctrine. The queen swayed equal in the
midst—knowing them all not as names and abstractions, but as
persons. In the end the Marian attraction was a misfortune for
the older group. Between sympathy for Mary and support for
Mary was not a wide margin; between support for Mary and
sedition to the queen, less; between sedition and full treason, even
less. Mary's fatal claim to the throne, potential always, if un-
mentioned, ensured that.

The families stirred, as it were, in their sleep. Dim hints,
vague menaces, began to pass. It was suggested that the Duke
of Norfolk, the queen's noblest and richest subject, would be a fit
match for Mary Stuart. He was a Protestant noble of thirty-
three (he had had Foxe of the *Book of Martyrs* as a tutor), but his
position was high, next to the blood, and he had shown feeling
for Mary, over the inquiry into whose statements, held in 1568,
he had presided. It was proposed to marry him to Mary, to
restore her to Scotland (on the condition of a general indemnity
to her enemies), to establish her in the succession, and to cause a
palace revolution in England, overthrowing Cecil. Leicester was
in the secret; so was Cecil, though that was in spite of the
confederates.

The marriage had first been proposed in the previous year;
then the queen had challenged Norfolk on it. In answer he had
protested that, since Mary pretended a title, 'your Majesty,' if
this were true, 'might justly charge me with seeking your own
crown from your head.' If this was how it struck Norfolk, it had
certainly struck Elizabeth in the same way. But she was willing
to restore Mary, and—on terms—she might have put up with the
marriage, watching to see what success the Protestant Howard
and the Roman Stuart made of it (Mary had been three times
married before this; so had the duke). She spoke lightly to him
once, after he had dined with her; she twitched his ear, and bade
him 'take heed of his pillow.' He remained obstinately silent;
she spoke of it on a later day, saying she wished to hear the truth
from himself. He admitted something; she commanded him to
go no farther in that matter.

But this was not so easy, and the final purposes of all the
confederates were not so limited as Norfolk's own. There was
to be a rising in the north; Alva in the Netherlands was to be
asked for support; the Spanish ambassador was consulted by
every one. Mary had written tender letters to the duke, but the
tenderness was tendentious—to the stuffed velvet of a double

crown. No harm was said to be intended to Elizabeth. But she was at the least to be told firmly what she must do. Cecil had faded away from the confederation; Leicester began to back out. The queen sent for Norfolk; he said he was ill and fled into the country, sending messages to beg the northern earls not to move. The ports were closed; the angry Mary was carried to another residence, the duke peremptorily ordered to return. He did not dare refuse; he feared too greatly the fierce temper of Elizabeth. First he again pleaded illness, then he came.

It was herself, and her energy, and Cecil, against a very heavy mass. She was intensely angry; her vision of herself as the loving mother of her people was outraged, and she was wild to restore it. She threw Norfolk into the Tower, and summoned the Earls of Northumberland and Westmorland to London. Their men rose even before they had decided, before they wanted, to lead them. The army marched; in Durham they tore up the English service books and heard the Latin mass. They hovered down, past York, and back again. They took Hartlepool, to give them a harbour for Alva's troops. Alva sent none. The queen's levies, from all the rest of the kingdom, came pressing north. There was no compensating outbreak anywhere else. Disheartened, the rebellion did not meet the queen's troops. They fled, and carnage followed them. Elizabeth struck at every village which favoured revolt. The earls had escaped, but the poor could not escape. It was—for Elizabeth and England— a dreadful vengeance, though perhaps, for that age and that Europe, it was not so out of the way. It was final; in the days of the Armada there was no rebellion. The queen had saved her State; it was certainly her State and not a complete England she had saved. It was above all a salvation dictated in her mind by no particular scheme of theology; what she avenged was not a doctrine but herself. She had no greater virtue and at that time no greater sin.

(iii) Doctrine, however, would not rest quiet; it is not in its nature. By 1569 the hopes of the Counter-Reformation that Elizabeth might be converted were failing, and even the hope that she might be vicariously converted by marriage to a husband in communion with Rome. To the devout and distant foreigner, unless he moved in the highest circles of Spanish or French diplomacy, she began to seem a curiously fabulous and archetypal heretic, and indeed they were right. From almost any doctrinal point of view, she was something of a heretic. 'I see many overbold with God Almighty, making too subtle scannings of

His blessed will,' she said once. She had been, in the shaping years of her youth, too much sworn sister to 'grim Necessity,' and her sisterhood was touched with irony. The mere language of the extreme doctrinalists offended her, and the habit of their minds. But to them in turn she began to grow gigantic, monstrous, and unnatural, putting forth many arms. She who was to have been nowhere began to be everywhere; she who might have been given the crown as a gift obtruded it as a right. Her power and her influence wandered subtly through the Christian world, nor had it yet pleased God to remove her. Mary Stuart was in her prison, and her feet were crimson with the blood of the faithful. In the centre of Roman Christendom the papacy roused itself to strike at the bastard heretic who had already sat for twelve years on her throne, the most ostentatious defiance of the recovery of Christendom. Paul IV and Pius IV had spared her, helped thereto by the continual expression of the wishes of Philip of Spain. Pius V spared her for five years. But the time for that forbearance which has been often, not unjustly, claimed as a quality of the Roman see, had gone by. There had been some kind of intention of smiting at her with the spiritual sword while the northern earls struck with the temporal; unfortunately for the alliance, the swords were drawn at different moments, and the temporal was already broken. But the spiritual was dangerous enough. In February 1570 the pope issued the bull *Regnans in Excelsis*. Elizabeth was declared illegitimate, excommunicate, diabolical, 'a servant of all iniquity.' Her subjects were freed from their allegiance; her laws were declared void; her person was terribly outcast from civilization and mankind in this world, and her soul from salvation and redeemed mankind in the next. In awful and perilous words she was 'severed from the body of Christ.' In May the bull was fixed by a devoted servant of the Roman see, a young student of Lincoln's Inn, by name John Felton, to the door of the Bishop of London's house in St Paul's Churchyard. Anathema was immediately answered by execution; the tortured body of Felton exhibited the defiance of the queen.

The bull exhorted the Catholic sovereigns to act. They left it to Felton. The emperor and the King of Spain wrote, almost rebuking their spiritual lord. Philip especially was very stiff with him. The King of France refused to allow the publication of the bull in his dominions, and, as it were, pretended it had not happened. This was not wholly altruism; it was not to the interest of sovereign orthodox states that doctrine should depose

kings, even heretical kings. Heresy was a chameleon-like word.
But in spite of their anger, the thing was done. The whole
population in England were officially commanded to be martyrs
or victors; any who refused were, *ipso facto*, sharers in the sin
and the doom. Elizabeth, who had been slowly living down her
illegitimacy, was confronted with a fervent declaration of it as
regnans in excelsis. She was placarded to Europe as in fact no
queen. She was thrown violently on to the side of Cecil and his
new assistant, the Puritan Francis Walsingham. From that
day she regarded—and rightly regarded—every missionary priest
who landed in England as an enemy to her person and her
throne, formally in doctrine, potentially in practice.

In 1570, therefore, in her own view she was at unspoken odds
with Spain; she had been outraged by her people, and outraged
by Rome. It was the decision of the permanent breach. She
was thirty-seven, and the perfection of her desire had been
dissipated.

Chapter 5

Money—The Captains and the Voyages—The Strained Relations with Spain
—Beginnings of Formal Persecution—The Ridolfi Plot—Execution of
Norfolk, after the Queen's five months' Delay—The Problem of Mary
Stuart—The Anjou and Alençon Courtships—The thirteen years'
Conversation on Marriage—Drake—The Queen at Fifty.

BEHIND all the shows, the pageants, of London, and the long
splendours of the progresses; behind the dances, the masques, the
dicing, and the hunting; behind the diplomacies, and the amours,
and the religions; behind the cultures—the Roman Catholic, the
Protestant, and that third style of mind which may be called
Shakespearian, because, though Shakespeare was yet only a boy
of six at Stratford, the matter which he was to vivify with his
genius was already in being, and a mode of consciousness was
being prepared for its education under his mature power, so that
the intellectual heart of England would never be the same again
—behind all these things, in some of which the queen took her
delight and of some of which she was as profoundly ignorant as
Cecil, there lay in her mind the steady matter of money. She
had come to a throne impoverished by blackmail, by robbery,
and by devotion; she set to work to restore it. Implicitly, and
without a full consciousness of the purpose of her labour, she
toiled to forestall the domination of the families. They throve

under her as under her predecessors; their estates grew. She
massed her treasury in their midst; it was for this that, with
them, she took so vivid an interest in the voyages to the ends of
the world. She took pleasure in the daring of her captains, and
rejoiced in their romanticism, but for her, as for all the capitalists
who encouraged them, it was gold and other precious commodities which were the great purpose. Among the commodities
were negro slaves. In the year 1564 the Earl of Pembroke, the
Lord Admiral, and the Lord Robert Dudley had shares, and Cecil
took a close interest, in a slaving voyage arranged by John
Hawkins, who gathered four hundred slaves on the coast of Africa
and disposed of them to the Spanish colonists of the West Indies
and South America, not without some threat of force. The queen
lent him a ship of the Royal Navy, the *Jesus of Lübeck*. The
Jesus, it is proper to note, was severely strained by the voyage.
Hawkins had to pay for its repair. The profit on the expedition
—on the goods brought back from the West rather than directly
on the slaves, but the slaves paid for the goods—was said by the
Spanish ambassador to be sixty per cent. The slave trade had
been discouraged by the Spanish Government, and one of the
officials who traded with Hawkins was punished. Cecil and
Leicester recommended the queen to grant Hawkins a coat of
arms, which she did: 'Sable, on a point wavy a lion passant or;
in chief three bezants; for a crest, a demi-Moor proper bound in
a cord.'

As for gold, in 1577 there was a voyage to Baffin Land, where it
was thought to have been discovered. The queen, Leicester,
Cecil, Walsingham, Philip Sidney, all had shares. It was unfortunate; the ore brought back yielded no gold, and the capitalists lost their money. Negro slaves were safer.

It may be said for Elizabeth that her gains, when they existed,
went into the necessities of government—to the upkeep of the
Navy, for example, for which she was expected to pay. Her
usual method was to lend ships and take a proportion of the whole
profits of the expedition.

It was not only by sea that the policies of the queen, especially
since the excommunication, distracted the action of Spain; they
crept also through the Flanders lands recovered from the sea,
amphibious Protestant beasts which the papal decree had now
defined, and denounced as of the tribe of hell. Hell is a game at
which two can play; unlike heaven, which is a game played
peculiarly by its single self. Antichrist was a name of many
applications; it could be used for the pope as easily as the queen,

and more and more the queen's servants applied it to him. The
queen, having failed to combine the two contending metaphysics
in the event of her remarkable person, was compelled to lean in
diplomacy towards one of them. She never identified herself
with it. Walsingham's godliness and Cecil's precisianism were
not for her. But she was compelled to support them in action,
though she might hate them in theory, and they had no doubts
of their duty. Away in the West, among 'evening isles fantasti-
cal,' the English pirates crept, small fortresses of hostility; narrow
rivulets of hostility—English money, English credit, English
volunteers, English secret commissions — flowed tortuously
through the Netherlands. On the other side, the heat of the fires
that burned or the rattle of the chains that bound an occasional
English sailor who had offended the dogmas of the papacy or the
dominion of Spain were blown across the seas. Both sides were
fretted; they were not maddened. Events dragged both Philip
and Elizabeth on; so far as they could, they dragged events back.

In 1571 the Parliament declared it to be high treason to call
the queen a heretic—the Act was an epigram of articulation, un-
sound in its terminology. 'England entered upon a course of
persecution'—formally. Its distinguishing mark was that it was
persecution not merely in defence of the State—that all persecution had always been; the Calvinists whom Mary Tudor or
Alva destroyed were destroyed as rebels as much as the Jesuits
who perished at Tyburn. It was persecution in defence of a State
which culminated in a princess who was the expression rather of a
series of events than a philosophical theory, who was in fact solely
a person. The Church she governed (in some views) was helped,
by the introduction into its history of this series of events, to
recover a quality—freedom, tolerance, comprehensiveness, whatever it is called—which made it not less after the mind of Christ
than any other. Certainly no theory which allows that the action
of kings may affect without invalidating the election of a pope
can deny, except by dogma, that the actions of a queen may have
similarly restored grace to the Church.

In 1571 the third of the blows which shaped the queen's habit
of mind for the remainder of her reign took place. The Northern
Rebellion had disturbed and alarmed her; the excommunication
had angered her; this other thing was more secret and, at its end,
felt as more intimate, than those public attacks. It is known
as the Ridolfi plot. Ridolfi was one of the more important
Italians in London, a Roman Catholic, a banker, a man of high
social standing and of easily hopeful temperament. He was in

contact with the Spanish ambassador, as every one always was, from Mary Stuart to Sir John Hawkins. He was also in contact with the Duke of Norfolk, who had been released from the Tower at Cecil's motion after making complete submission and promising fidelity. Ridolfi made himself the focus of a new plot. The idea of marrying Norfolk to Mary was renewed; aid was to be procured from Spain—arms, money, and men. The aims were as before—the restoration of Mary to her throne and of the Roman obedience throughout the island. Ridolfi left England (after an interview with the queen on the previous Sunday) and went to Alva. Alva refused to send aid until the insurrection was in being; if, he thought, the revolting English could defy the queen for about six weeks, then the enterprise would be worth supporting. Ridolfi passed on to Rome, secured support, and came at last to Madrid. Somewhere on the way the assassination of Elizabeth was added to the plan, as a final touch of polish. It was discussed by the King of Spain's council.

The spies maintained systematically by the English Government followed up the plot in the Low Countries and in England. By them, and by chance aiding them, the details came to Cecil (created in 1571 Lord Burghley). The exposure of the conspiracy led to a violent burst of public horror and excitement, and to a concentrated agitation against Mary. Elizabeth herself was shaken; a new thing had intimately entered her life—the possibility of sudden and secret death. Vaguely it might have been imagined earlier, but now it had come to words. In the high places of Europe her taking-off had, she heard, been a matter of open discussion. It was true that Norfolk and Mary were not concerned in this elaboration of detail. They were quite enough concerned. Norfolk was again sent to the Tower. The Spanish ambassador, after a scene with the Council, was ordered to leave the country, which, after lingering a little on the chance that Cecil might be shot by two men detached for the attempt, he did. The French ambassador, who spoke for Mary, was answered by the queen 'in a most furious rage.' She fell into a new mood against Mary, and seemed to have abandoned any possible intention of restoring her. On 16th January Norfolk was brought to trial and condemned. Then, suddenly, Elizabeth hesitated. Her nature revolted. He was her acquaintance and her kinsman. Twice she signed, twice she countermanded the warrant. She did not certainly feel it as a sin, as she certainly felt the later execution of Mary as a sin, but she did not wish to strike one so near herself and to renew the bloody decrees of old reigns. The

weeks slid by.   On 9th April she signed a third warrant; at two
in the morning of 11th April Cecil was awakened by a note saying
she could not do it:

> My Lord me thinkes that I am more beholdinge to the hindar part
> of my hed than wel dare trust the forwards side of the same, & there-
> fore sent to the Levetenant & the S., as you knowe best, the Ordar
> to defar this execution till the[y] here furdar.   And that this may
> be done I doubte nothing, without curiositie of my further warrant,
> for that ther rasche determination upon a very unfit day was counter-
> manded by your considerat admonition.   The causes that move me
> to this ar not now to be expressed, lest an irrevocable dede be in
> mene while committed.   If the[y] wyl nides a Warrant, let this
> suffice, all written with my none hand.

Your most lovinge Soveraine.

The whole of the court, all the vocal part of the country,
expected the duke's execution; abroad, it was thought more than
possible that Mary would also die.   For five months the queen
maintained an effort to spare her own subject.   It is not perhaps
unrelated to her failure that during those months she became
involved in an acrimonious correspondence with Mary, both
great ladies unsheathing their verbal claws.   They both had
claws enough, sharpened on facts.   Parliament, coming together
in May, in speech after speech railed against Mary, presenting
ways of dealing with her.   The queen, half yielding, half eluding,
at last concluded.   She gave way to the pressure; she consented
to Norfolk's execution; she consented to nothing more.   All
proposals against Mary she vetoed with 'La reyne s'avisera.'
On 2nd June he was put to death.   Elizabeth was unhappy.
The process of things was beginning to put an iron chain on her
will, nor could she free herself.

The English were becoming, if not exactly Protestant, then at
least non-Roman, except for those Romans who were, by their
devotion and their doom, to become even more Roman.   They
were becoming more patriotic.   They were also becoming more
vocal.   The national mass, deflected to follow her, became with
every year more national.   It was, so far, her success.   Her
feminine mind had imposed half of her natural will upon events;
the stamp of the rest was thwarted by supernatural belief.   She
was a personally popular figure, yet she might be assassinated at
any moment.   She enjoyed her people; she enjoyed the sensation
of their enjoyment of her.   Jests and speeches answered laughter
and cheers.   She belonged to that small group of princes who—
not only in theory but in appearance and behaviour—are at once
monarch and person.   In the court she was the centre of euphuis-

tic delights, and pleasures other than euphuistic; in the city she
was the patroness of extending trade and stabilized credit; in the
country she was a mistress, if not of curds and whey, at least of
cows and cowmen.   There were dark patches enough; the un-
employed, in spite of the justices, wandered through the country
and hung about the city.   In 1581 the queen's coach itself,
when she went to take the air, was surrounded at Islington by
'a number of rogues,' which provoked the Recorder of London
to a great clearance; he swept up something like two hundred
and fifty, of whom he remarked with pleasure that not more than
a dozen belonged to London, Middlesex, and Surrey.   It is likely
that the incident provoked one of those rages into which she so
often broke.   She threw her shoe at Walsingham; she boxed her
maids' ears; she cursed and swore in a deep contralto at her
ministers and her menials alike.   She could be rough with
preachers and bishops.   Yet also she was capable of tendernesses
and generosities.   She could throw a man into prison and then
write to his wife to ease her fears.   She was capable (on a famous
occasion) of raging at the Polish ambassador in a speech of
furious impromptu Latin.   She was capable of writing little
private notes of sympathy and good fellowship to her generals
and ambassadors, such as this postscript (of 1562) shows:

My deare Warwik if your honor & my desir could accord with the
los of the nidefuls fingar I kipe, God helpe me so in my most nide
as I wold gladly lis that one joint for your safe abode with me, but
sins I can not that I wold, I wil do that I may, & wil rather drinke
in an asin [ashen] cup than you or yours shude not be soccerd both
by sea & land yea & that with all spede possible, & let this my
scribling hand witness it to them all

                                          Yours as my own E. R.

Behind her the mass, deflected to nationality, moved.   By
1570, those who had been children at her accession were young
men and women; babies were children who knew of the queen,
and had in many cases seen the queen when she rode into a
provincial city or the train of coaches of her progress swung
slowly down the winding country roads.   She loved the mass, but
sometimes it oppressed her, in nothing more than in the unre-
solved matter of Mary Stuart.   The north was quiet; she had shed
blood enough to ensure that.   The south, and the gentlemen who
came to the Parliament, had all the rhetorical hostility and the
easy solutions of the irresponsible.   It was impossible that the
queen should not desire her rival's death; she laboured with the
wish and against it.   She could not and would not act, but she
could not prevent herself wishing that something might happen.

Similar emotions often ran riot in the courts of Paris and Madrid
and Rome concerning herself; indeed, the high historic ostentation
of royal drama has concealed from us its universality.   It is given
to few men and women to pass through the world without desiring
—even passionately—the death of another, could it be brought
about by some action other than their own.   We are all kindred
to the queen in that thing; she only had a chance of action.
Abroad, it was continually expected that she would act; the King
of France said he knew what he would do if he were in Elizabeth's
place, and had Mary Stuart a prisoner.   At home, it was lamented
that she did not act.   Once—in the shock of hearing of the St
Bartholomew—she was brought to offer to yield Mary to the
Scottish lords if they would certainly put her to death; they
refused, unless an English force assisted, and this Elizabeth in
turn refused.   She might have meant it; at the last moment it is
possible, but doubtful, if she would have carried out the plan.
Meanwhile the royal coach swayed on, and the high, pale face of
the queen smiled out on her fields, and the beautiful hands
gesticulated.   Or in the Presence the eyes flashed and the voice
screamed at some folly; or in the council chamber the inscrutable
gaze passed over the kneeling lords and delayed on Dudley with
still vivid affection, or lingered with a fantastic coyness on one of
the newer favourites, or returned again to measure meditative
looks with Cecil, while she listened and acknowledged and all but,
and hardly ever quite, acceded, and he, bowing, went away, and
she rose and went about her work, and changed from one of her
innumerable dresses to another, and adorned herself with jewels,
and grew older, and older, and longed to break the lonely secrecy
of her will, and again never quite would.   Under the domination
of that will her young and handsome servants rose one after the
other, and clung round her—parasitical brilliance, growing duller
with time.   Hatton rose—Captain of the Guard in 1572, and
Chancellor in 1587, after Raleigh had succeeded to his place as
Captain in 1586; 1587 also saw the more dangerous creature of
the queen, Essex, already Master of the Horse.   She watched
their quarrels as she watched the disputes of her ministers, and
with none of them her heart or her policy lay.   It is a tenable
belief that she was asked by God for one thing alone—surrender;
and that she refused.   If so, the thing was made as difficult as
possible for her—she was asked to thwart, to contradict, almost
to outrage, her whole nature, mental and physical.   She was
asked for heroic sanctity, and those who represented that demand
to her had been Mary her sister, with whom she was in such dis-

harmony, and the Lord Cardinal Pole, and the foreign face of
Spain, and the foreign voice of the pope. She refused; they may
blame her who will.

In foreign affairs the questionable centre lay in the Netherlands.
Elizabeth did not want Spanish armies there, as little did she
desire French. She did not much care for the Calvinistic dialect
of the Netherlands, either there or in her own Francis Walsingham
at home. She did not speak it, nor did the Church over whose
organization she presided; but, as the Duke of Alva once remarked, convenience must determine the keeping of treaties even
among Christian sovereigns. All the Governments of Europe
were engaged, somewhere, in the game of supporting foreign
minorities against the national Government; it was then as much
to their metaphysical honour as it would be considered to their
national dishonour now. Events had put the queen outside the
culture of Roman Catholic Europe, but they pressed her within
the urgent necessities of that culture, and, since assassination did
not touch her, talk of marriage revived. The most protracted
marriage negotiations in the history of England opened in 1570;
they lasted, on and off, till 1583. Elizabeth was thirty-seven
when they began, and almost fifty when they at last fell away—
and quite fifty when her wooer, or her wooed, died and she wept
for him. He was the brother of the King of France, first called
the Duke of Anjou, afterwards the Duke of Alençon.

In fact, the person of the proposed husband changed after the
first exchanges; but both the first and second were sons of Queen
Catherine, brothers to the King of France, and both, at different
times, bore the title of the Duke of Anjou. The twisted com-
plexity of this detail is an example of all; and in all the details
only two permanent facts exist—that Elizabeth continuously
talked of marriage, and that she did not marry. The single fact
that might help to illumine us—Elizabeth's capacity to bear
children—is still hidden, and historians of the highest eminence
hold opposite views on that single fact.[1] Deprived of that knowledge, one is left to observe the queen talking. It is certain that
she liked talking; it is equally certain that she liked talking about
her marriage, though she disliked being voted or petitioned into it
by the Houses. She liked it and she found it useful. Wooers—
even Roman Catholic wooers—who might be thinking of marriage

[1] 'Elizabeth knew that no heir could be born of her' (A. W. Pollard,
Political History of England, 1547–1603, p. 326). 'Gossip often tried to
explain [her failure to marry] by surmising that Elizabeth was incapable
of bearing children. . . . The tongue is an unruly member' (J. E. Neale,
Queen Elizabeth, p. 220).

with Mary Stuart found themselves unconsciously and newly magnetized towards another throne whence Elizabeth's beautiful regal hand waved to them.   In 1570 the hand was raised, ever so coyly, in the direction of the Duke of Anjou, brother of Charles of France.   Brothers of the King of France were often troublesome to the king, and both he and Catherine de' Medici urged the idea on his brother.   But Anjou was a Guise man; he demanded the private mass in his private chapel.   Even the Puritan Walsingham urged the queen to consent; she declined.   The French found themselves signing a treaty favourable to her, and the marriage faded, and reappeared presently with another face, that of the Duke of Alençon, Anjou's younger brother.

Between the two courtships came that political operation in the disguise of a theological quarrel which we call the Massacre of St Bartholomew.   The disguise was sufficiently realistic to enrage all the Protestants and delight many of the Catholics throughout Europe.   The provocation given by the Huguenots was forgotten or approved by their friends, and the majesty of England, whose hangmen had but recently returned from the executions in the north, put on mourning to receive the French ambassador.   It is a mark of the difference between things abroad and things at home.

> Only people like Us is We,
> And every one else is They.

But, just in proportion as Catherine seemed rashly to have given herself over to the Catholic cause, it became undesirable for Elizabeth by hostility to provoke her into any greater dependence on the Catholic Guises; and in the same proportion that the rashness seemed to have thrown Catherine on to the Spanish side, it became desirable for Catherine herself to recover ground.   The diplomatic manœuvres and conversations, interrupted by that dreadful midnight tocsin of Paris, began again.   A full account of a single month of their complications would fill too many books of this size.   In the first movements there was a closer connection between Elizabeth and Philip; then, as a weight in their scale, the French Government cast the person of the Duke of Alençon. He was eighteen when serious discussions began, without any such scruples as his brother had shown, not handsome, pockmarked, and eager to do something or other—especially, once the chance was his, to marry Elizabeth, even if she were (as she was) forty.   He was especially anxious to do something in the Low Countries, and Elizabeth was anxious that he should, so long as he did no more than she wanted, and did not seize them for France.

The whole affair divides into two parts; the first diplomatic, lasting till 1576, the second personal, beginning in 1578. Its interest here is chiefly in the fact that during the second period the queen was driven nearer than ever before to a pretence of doing what she had been pretending a readiness to do. Alençon took charge of the affair himself, and, poor creature that he might look, he took the right way with the queen. He supplied, at a moment when her very high intelligence told her that the adorations of her English minions were taking on yearly more of flattery and less of exactitude, a new, different, and ardent enthusiasm. The queen had never before had marriage urged upon her by quite so close a possibility, and never had any possibility urged it more thrillingly. At the beginning of 1579 came Alençon's servant, Jean de Simier, who began making love on his master's account with an enthusiasm which made it seem his own. He had perfectly the measure of Elizabeth's amorous technique; he played it with all skill. 'This discourse,' said the French ambassador, 'rejuvenates the queen.' Alençon himself came over in August, and took up the siege. The queen melted, reciprocated, flattered, sighed, flirted madly. The duke departed, but Simier lingered, and the queen lingered with Simier.

Agitation rose in the country and the city. The pulpit denounced; Elizabeth went angrily out in the middle of a sermon. A book was issued; Elizabeth had the right hands of author and publisher struck off. She was very angry; whether she could or would marry, no one but she knew, and perhaps not she. It was intolerable to her that she should be bullied. The Council met and argued. Cecil was strongly in favour; Leicester was against. They determined to ask her what her own wish was; then they would offer their opinion. At this she grew into worse anger. She told them furiously she had expected to have been desired to marry and have a child of her body. But no anger could persuade them to come to any conclusion except upon her instructions. It was what she did not want to give. To marry Alençon would be to lose herself and her kingdom in appendages, marital and political, of the probable future King of France. To refuse would be to throw away her last chance of marriage, and (what perhaps counted as much) of talking about it. It is no small loss when a vivid cerebralist comes to an age when his mental activity can no longer have any relation to actuality, and to be deprived of a fantasy is as painful as to be deprived of a fact. She clung,

diplomatically and personally, to the two terms in the phrase
'French marriage,' clung the more irritably that Simier had
revealed to her the year-old secret marriage of Leicester—
Leicester, who had been arguing against her own. Leicester
was flung from court; Walsingham was in retirement; Philip
Sidney, his son-in-law, who had written to her rhetorically against
the marriage, was in disgrace. But Simier also left for France
in November. Articles had been signed. She had insisted in
them on being given two months to reconcile her people.

The negotiations, the two months being up, floated on
Elizabeth talked about religion; Alençon talked about money.
Elizabeth and Catherine attempted to manipulate each other into
war with Spain, and, each defeating the other, remained still
ostensibly at peace. Ostensibly at peace meant continuous
ostentations of unofficial war. The Jesuit missionaries had landed
in England. They were strictly forbidden to have anything to
do with politics. But they were regarded as an order peculiarly
papal; and the bull of excommunication was also peculiarly
papal. The chief foreign Roman Catholic Government regarded
them with approval. 'Those who have recently come hither,'
wrote the Spanish ambassador to Philip, 'pray continually for
Your Majesty, recognizing that God has been pleased to make
you His principal instrument in this great work.' The English
Government felt precisely that Philip was extremely likely to be
the principal instrument in the work.

English Roman Catholics had been dispensed from rebellion
until there was some hope of success. The Government did not
propose to permit them any hope of success from within. But the
energy of those souls who gave themselves to the 'Enterprise of
England' was immediately rewarded. A cheerful devotion, a
readiness for loss and even martyrdom, awoke in the Papalist
remnant of England. The lapsed were won, new converts
made, faith and hope increased and nourished. All the signs of
a great revival went abroad.

In 1580 Philip of Spain put William of Orange under the ban,
declaring him 'out of law,' with a price on his head. The Queen
of England heard of it; she knew of the correspondence of Mary
of Scots; she did not know at what moment the dispensation of
quiescence given to her Roman subjects might be withdrawn,
nor what possibilities of murder hovered round her every day.
She consented to a thing against her temper and her will, but not
(in her view) sinful, any more than Norfolk's execution—the closer
execution of the penal laws. She limited them as far as possible;

ner ministers complained that she would not believe in the danger. But still she consented to the disunion of the English; and it had been the union of the English which, outside her passing excitements and her personal delights, she had chiefly in her heart desired. So far, she was defeated by Cecil and the pope. In effect, however, she had been defeated long before—at the moment of her birth. The conditions of her birth defeated her desires, and the mother by whom she had been born to the throne refused her the unbloody and wholly popular throne of her dreams. The sign of it was the execution, that year, of Edmund Campion.

It was in 1580, as if in compensation, that Drake returned from his voyage round the world, with much Spanish treasure seized in the West. Elizabeth went down to Deptford, taking the French ambassador with her, approved him, jested with him, and caused the ambassador to knight him. It was almost a demonstration of unity between the two countries. Creeds had receded very far into the background in international affairs, however catastrophic they might still be in national. The queen and the ambassador returned together to London.

The next year saw a sudden revival of the marriage idea, and Alençon once more in London. It was on this visit that the queen sent a private note to Cecil, telling him of the arrival, and adding: 'Let me know what you wish me to do.' It is impossible to believe that Cecil planned the lengths to which the queen was said to have gone; but it is unlikely that she wrote so in regard to a prince with whom she was passionately in love. Yet as the days ran by she encouraged and shared the love-making, as if in a kind of abandonment of herself. On 22nd November 1581 she went farther than she had ever gone in her personal commitment. The Spanish ambassador wrote to Philip:

I wrote . . . on the 20th, and on the following day Alençon and all his company displayed, not discontent alone, but entire disillusion as to the marriage taking place. On the 22nd, however, at eleven in the morning, the Queen and Alençon were walking together in a gallery, Leicester and Walsingham being present, when the French ambassador entered and said that he wished to write to his master, from whom he had received orders to hear from the Queen's own lips her intention with regard to marrying his brother. She replied, 'You may write this to the King: that the Duke of Alençon shall be my husband,' and at the same moment she turned to Alençon and kissed him on the mouth, drawing a ring from her own hand and giving it to him as a pledge. Alençon gave her a ring of his in return, and shortly afterwards the Queen summoned the ladies and gentlemen from the presence chamber in the gallery, repeating to them in a loud voice in Alençon's presence what she had previously said.

But a month later she told the Earl of Sussex that 'she hated the idea of marriage every day more,' and devoted herself energetically to getting rid of Alençon. She agreed to lend him sixty thousand pounds (he had already had thirty thousand); and on the last day of the year she paid him ten thousand.

Recourse was had to the most extreme measures; it is said his personal servants were bribed to persuade him to go. Elizabeth's demands on the King of France shot up. On 1st February 1582, he went, but before he finally embarked he asked for the other fifty thousand. He did not get it. The queen, who had accompanied him as far as Canterbury, returned to London and the indulgence of her safer emotions. She wept; she sighed for Alençon; she was angry with Leicester, who had been rude about him, and with Walsingham; and from a safe distance she went on talking about marriage. But it all came to nothing; Alençon's fiery shaft was quenched. Presently he died.

Chapter 6

Ignorance of Mary Stuart—Walsingham—The Babington Plot—Elizabeth's Dilemma—She Consents to Sin—Opinion in Europe—The Spanish 'Enterprise of England'—The Last of the Crusades—Defeat of the Armada—Death of Leicester.

THE events of the years 1569–70 had determined the queen's position; the events of 1580 had confirmed it. The events of 1585–8 determined her success in that position. Mary Stuart, a royal prisoner still, was ignorant of the slow change. The years betrayed her; she thought still that a little help might be found and would be sufficient. Time stood still with her; she thought that elsewhere things stood still in time. It was not so; to name only the greatest change—James VI sat on the Scottish throne, and, while she still plotted to gain the English kingdom, she had in effect lost her own. It seems now to be rather James than Elizabeth whose intangible influence kept her in custody; her great rival was half inclined to release her with certain formal conditions. Only the romanticism of Mary's story still went about, and her religion supported it. If her adherents could be gathered, encouraged, vivified, she might still have a chance in England; in Scotland, except from England, she had little more. When she had flung the blazon of the English royal arms abroad in Paris eighteen years before, Elizabeth had been in a desperate position; now the position was reversed. Mary had but one chance, and her enemies knew it even if she did not realize it. The game was no longer between claims and crowns but between lives; her single possibility was the death of the queen. If a dagger found Elizabeth's heart, a crown—two crowns—might still rest on Mary's head. If, that is, Philip of Spain did not prefer to take it for himself or his family; in the general clarification this was thought of; the king, it was remarked, was descended from the old House of Lancaster. There was some difference between the pope and Philip on who should dispose of the English egg. As it happened, the egg was never laid.

It was Mary's first misfortune that this narrowing of the issue was not apparent to her, and that she was still engaged in as many conspiracies as ever. Even the Bond of Association, created by Cecil and the Council in 1584, did not check her; though by it, in the event of an attempt on Elizabeth's life, all the signatories—and it was very widely signed—pledged themselves to pursue to the death the person for whose profit the deed was done. At the same time many of the signatories, in case the deed succeeded, privately made efforts to keep on good terms with Mary. Her second misfortune was the nature of the man who was now Secretary of State—Francis Walsingham. He was as much a child of Puritan ideas as she of Catholic, and he came more near in his heart to regarding her as a daughter of Satan than probably the pope to thinking Elizabeth a child of hell. He hated, as he saw it, the thing for which she stood, and he was as unscrupulous as she in fighting for his cause. Elizabeth no more liked him than Queen Victoria liked Mr Gladstone, though Victoria did not throw shoes. Walsingham insisted on regarding her as an ally in the service of God; the queen was not apt to think she certainly knew God's will; and she thought she was God enough for Walsingham. Mary's third and culminating misfortune was the fact that Elizabeth was capable of sin.

Walsingham was determined to kill Mary Stuart, if ever she gave him the chance. She did. In 1586 there arose, latest and last of all the Marian confederacies, the Babington plot. There had been once in Mary's service a page of the name of Anthony Babington; he was now a recusant gentleman of Derbyshire. He took up the captive sovereign's cause; others joined him. The Spanish ambassador wished the assassination of the queen to be extended to Cecil, Walsingham, and a few others. Philip was inclined to spare Cecil—'he is very old'—but otherwise he hoped for the best. 'Perhaps,' he wrote hopefully, with an allusion to God, 'the time has at last come when He will strike for His cause.' Walsingham, on his side, thought exactly the same; he also watched, and probably encouraged, the schemes. Hopes were equally high on both sides; and the death of a queen was a necessary element in both.

In a cask of beer the letters went to and from Mary; at the right moment the Secretary struck. The conspirators were seized. Fourteen were executed; the first seven with the full accompaniment of horror, the second seven on the next day being, by Elizabeth's personal command, allowed to hang till they were dead before the ritual of agony was carried out.

Mary remained. Elizabeth consented to her trial. While the Commission was sitting at Fotheringay, she sent a sudden message recalling its members to London. The queen was confronted with the worst crisis of her life. It is as certain as any mortal thing can be, not merely that she did not want to execute Mary, but that she thought she ought not to execute Mary. She was physically revolted by the idea, and more or less consciously she knew it was a contradiction of her life's basis. Mary was anointed and royal; she was not Elizabeth's subject, she was Elizabeth's equal, and as sacrosanct as the queen herself. In her blood and fibres Elizabeth felt it to be a sin to touch this other majesty—a dreadful, perhaps a mortal, sin. She was normally as casual of morals as of dogmas, but her scepticism had its limits, and all she had ever persuaded others, or herself believed, that she herself was, rose against the deed.

Her ministers, her Council, her Parliament, her bishops, her people—the preachers and the crowds—were united in pressing the deed on her. The two elements of her desire clashed. She was queen; she was Queen of England. The people of England were contradicting the principle of kingship. At Richmond the Parliament poured its petition before her. She answered that it was a miracle that she was still alive.[1] She added that she took no such pleasure in life that she much desired it, nor conceived such horror in death that she greatly feared it; 'Yet I say not, but if the stroke were coming, perchance flesh and blood would be moved with it, and seek to shun it. I have had good

---

[1] It was a common feeling. In 1584 William of Orange had been assassinated. In 1586 the French ambassador at Rome wrote to the King of France concerning Elizabeth: 'She cannot doubt that at every moment some attempt will be made on her life, and that she cannot again enjoy an hour of safety or of pleasure.' The pope himself said he had abhorrently rejected proposals for her assassination, which had been, on occasions, made to him.

experience and trial of this world.' It is one of her most universal moments.

From October to February she demurred and disputed with herself. She listened to the protests of ambassadors and snarled at the messengers of the Scottish king. At the very end she fell back on the possibility of private murder, and caused Walsingham to write to Paulet, Mary's jailer, suggesting that it might be within the bounds of his duty to take off his prisoner. It was not the justice of the sentence against Mary that troubled her, as certainly it troubled hardly any one else. That Mary was guilty of complicity every one knew. But that an anointed sovereign should put to death, by show of trial, another anointed sovereign—this was the crisis. In the position to which Elizabeth had come there were, for her, but two possibilities—a supreme determination after virtue or certain sin. She sinned. She signed the warrant. Walsingham was away; he was ill. She cried to his substitute to show him the warrant. 'The grief thereof will go near to kill him outright.'

The opinion of royal Europe supported her own; Mary should have been put to death privately. Elizabeth was not only heretical but barbarous; not only false to doctrine but false to her royal blood—a bastard of kingship. She was blamed for the manner, not for the fact, of the death. And, indeed, in that act, as in so many others, she had abandoned doctrine; this time against, as often with, her will. She had been the friend of events, and now events had betrayed her into offending against her own strong belief. There was to be but one other personal crisis in her life when another axe was to swing, and in that no doctrine was to have any place, and events were to run altogether wild. The daughter of things, she was to be finally hurt by things.

At the same time even bastards have their place. The King of France was not disposed to be unfriendly with the queen while the King of Spain still threatened. But with the King of Spain the time for friendship had gone by. At last he was moved to refuse to be a brother to Elizabeth any more. It was known he was making preparations, and now the death of Mary left him as the great Roman Catholic claimant—by descent perhaps, but anyhow by providential conquest. The King of France and the pope contemplated the prospect with some gloom, but the pope at least was compelled to lend his support—money and briefs. The 'Enterprise of England' took shape. Drake raided Cadiz, and delayed it; the chosen admiral died, and delayed it further; storms delayed it still more. But gradually it began to move.

The slow navies of the metaphysical world gathered in the harbours of Spain; the Duke of Medina Sidonia took command. The armies of metaphysics stood ready in Flanders; the Prince of Parma controlled them with military care. The last of the Crusades was about to begin. All the material resources of the champions of metaphysics were employed—the pope had promised a million gold ducats, Philip had taxed the food of his subjects: all their intellectual resources—the pope freed all Catholics from their temporary allegiance; Cardinal Allen yet once more described and denounced the queen in a printed *Admonition to the People of England*—'an incestuous bastard, begotten and born in sin of an infamous courtesan'; all spiritual aid was invoked—by processions, prayers, vigils, adorations. The double figure of sin had sat too long on the waters—thrice opprobrious: in her blood, in her belief, in her wickedness. Illegitimate, heretical, bloody, and debauched, sat she there like some horrible Scylla devouring the martyrs, and around her flew the ships of her vile company, Drake, Hawkins, Grenville. One voice only broke the chorus; in the centre of the Crusade, of all people, the Pope Sixtus V himself exclaimed in admiration, both of her and of Drake: 'What a woman!' 'Have you heard how Drake has offered battle? What courage!' 'If she were not a heretic she would be worth the whole world!' The queen is said to have courteously reciprocated, saying she knew but of one man worthy of her—and he was Sixtus V.

In spite of the papal admiration, the Spanish navy swept out. The king kept vigil before the Blessed Sacrament, and the mighty array passed north. No other metaphysic met them; for, though Cecil and Walsingham had done what they could, it was the ships of Howard and Hawkins and Drake that ran beside them, firing and wounding, and the unmetaphysical winds that drove them. They fled; they disappeared. 'God blew with His winds and they were scattered,' said the medal struck by Elizabeth. It seems unlikely that privately the queen more than half believed it. Once, in a later year, one of her present captains, Sir John Hawkins, coming back from a voyage with less gain than had been hoped, sent an explanation of his failure in some such terms: 'Paul might plant and Apollos might water, but only God gives the increase.' To which the queen said only: 'Fool! He went out a soldier and comes home a divine.' Less than most people by now did she think the universe likely to observe her desires. Her life's disillusion forbade it, yet perhaps her disillusion hardly went far enough. It did not lead her to the rock which is reality.

For Elizabeth, while she lived, that path was too strange, rather than too hard, a way. Events now had gone favourably; they might as well have gone unfavourably. Bitter and amused, fearful and courageous, she looked at them. They had involved her in much evil fate, and in something like dishonour. She was Elizabeth; she raged and endured.

In that heart-sickness of necessity she was still—it was her duty and her pleasure—a spectacle. In that certainly she was of her age. She determined to go to her Army and went. She was fifty-five, and old for that. She was bald, bony, rheumatic. But she was strongly active, and her centre of vitality was very firm. She came down to them; it was the ninth of August, and the Armada was already driven far away up the North Seas; but there was Parma yet in the Netherlands, and it was uncertain what he could or would do. She rode down, and, mounted on a white horse, reviewed the Army. There she delivered that famous speech, with its high Elizabethan combination of rhetoric and realism; she threw off her sin and made herself a hero. It was all wrong and yet all right at once, as the queen so often was. She sat on her horse, and (so they report) she said:

My loving people, we have been persuaded by some that are careful of our safety, to take heed how we commit ourselves to armed multitudes, for fear of treachery. But I assure you, I do not desire to live to distrust my faithful and loving people. Let tyrants fear. I have always so behaved myself that, under God, I have placed my chiefest strength and safeguard in the loyal hearts and goodwill of my subjects; and therefore I am come amongst you, as you see, at this time, not for my recreation and disport, but being resolved, in the midst and heat of the battle, to live or die amongst you all, to lay down for my God, and for my kingdom, and for my people, my honour and my blood, even in the dust. I know I have the body of a weak and feeble woman, but I have the heart and stomach of a king, and of a king of England too, and think foul scorn that Parma or Spain, or any prince of Europe should dare to invade the borders of my realm; to which, rather than any dishonour shall grow by me, I myself will take up arms, I myself will be your general, judge, and rewarder of every one of your virtues in the field. I know, already for your forwardness you have deserved rewards and crowns; and we do assure you, in the word of a prince, they shall be duly paid you.

On the fourth of September, in the same year, Leicester died.

H

Chapter 7

The Years after the Armada—Martin Marprelate—The Traders Abroad
and the Poets at Home—Gloriana—The New Ministers—The Life and
Death of the Earl of Essex.

THE defeat of the Armada and the death of Leicester seem to
close the period of the queen's purpose; the letter upon which
she wrote 'His last letter' is still extant. What remained was a
period of result—fourteen years and more, nearly a third of her
whole reign. Throughout that third, however, her position did
not much change. The defeat of the Armada opened a war with
Spain which dragged on through the years. Had Philip been
free to concentrate his attention and his power upon England,
the final decision might yet have gone the other way. He was
not; the affairs of Spanish diplomacy involved two worlds—or
indeed three, the Old and the New, and the next. In France,
assassination had its way; Henry III had the Duke of Guise and
the Cardinal of Guise killed, and was himself stabbed in 1589,
by a Dominican, as an enemy of the pope. The fortunes of the
kingdom went down and then rose; Philip laboured against the
succession of Henry of Navarre, and failed. Henry submitted
to Rome—'Paris vaut bien une messe'—and became Henry IV;
his conversion shook the old doctrinal order as much as his earlier
Protestantism. The English sent a military expedition against
Spain in 1589, which returned with heavy damage but high
prestige. The mere landing in Spain and the defeat of a Spanish
army were great things. In 1590 ten English merchantmen
defeated twelve Spanish galleys in the Strait of Gibraltar. In
1596 came the expedition against, and the capture of, Cadiz.
The war party in England was no longer desperate, religious, and
middle-aged; it was young, secular, and brilliant with victory and
victorious hopes. Expectation sat in the air.

Another struggle which had maintained itself through the reign
—less spectacular and less bloody, but hardly less bitter than that
with Spain and Rome—also ceased gradually to trouble the queen
—that with the Puritan champions. This, indeed, was not to
reach a climax of separating definition till the time of King James,
though in the very days of the Armada the most notorious demonstrations broke out in the Martin Marprelate pamphlets.
The 'Canterbury Caiaphas,' the 'froth and filth' of ecclesiastical
laws, 'the squealing of chanting choristers,' the 'idle loitering
lubbards' of cathedrals, the 'cursed uncircumcised murdering

generation' of the clergy, 'the horned monsters of the Conspiration House,' 'the pageant and stage-play' of the communion, were all 'run down with a saucy pertness.' No extreme of danger could reconcile the queen to those wilder extremes of Protestant doctrine. Not even Cecil's influence could win her to sympathy. It was impossible for her to believe that 'to ring more bells than one on the Lord's day was as great a sin as murder.' Metaphysically, it might be; practically, the queen felt it was not. By suppression and banishment, by discussion and exposition, this quarrel also was silenced. Numbers of Puritans fled abroad; numbers were mournfully still. Hooker and Andrewes began to be heard.

Beyond the European seas, the English name flew farther and farther. Virginia had been first founded in 1585 by Walter Raleigh. In the Old World the trade with Russia had been maintained all through the reign; in 1582 a permanent ambassador was established at Constantinople, in spite of French and Venetian opposition; in 1580 it had been suggested to captains in the Muscovy trade that 'opportunity may be had to sail over to Japan'—where the Jesuits had preceded them. Jesuit missionaries and English merchants rivalled each other in energy abroad, as at home; Jesuit ardour contended with national ardour; nor were the nationals and the merchants always without religious devotion, sometimes false, sometimes true, sometimes narrow and harsh, sometimes intelligent and lovely. The City of London laid hold on Java: the sentences of Hakluyt recount the tale of the distances:

. . . to speake a word of that just commendation which our nation doe indeede deserve: it can not be denied, but as in all former ages, they have bene men full of activity, stirrers abroad, and searchers of the remote parts of the world, so in this most famous and peerlesse governement of her most excellent Majesty, her subjects through the speciall assistance, and blessing of God, in searching the most opposite corners and quarters of the world, and to speake plainly, in compassing the vaste globe of the earth more then once, have excelled all the nations and people of the earth. For, which of the kings of this land before her Majesty, had theyr banners ever seene in the Caspian sea? which of them hath ever dealt with the Emperor of Persia, as her Majesty hath done, and obteined for her merchants large and loving privileges? who ever found English Consuls and Agents at Tripolis in Syria, at Aleppo, at Babylon, at Balsara, and which is more, who ever heard of Englishman at Goa before now? what English shippes did heertofore ever anker in the mighty river of Plate? passe and repasse the unpassable (in former opinion) straight of Magellan, range along the coast of Chili, Peru, and all the backside of Nova Hispania, further then any Christian ever passed, travers the mighty bredth of the South sea, land upon the Luzones in despight of the enemy, enter into alliance, amity, and traffike with the princes of the Moluccaes, and the Isle of Java, double the famous Cape of Bona Speranza, arive at the Isle of Santa Helena, and last of al returne home most richly laden with the commodities of China, as the subjects of this now flourishing monarchy have done?

At home, other conquests were being made. While the city trafficked with Java, the genius of the poets trafficked with experience. In 1590 *Tamburlaine* was presented 'on stages in the city'; in 1590 the first cantos of the *Faerie Queene* adored the Queen of faerie and of England; in 1594 appeared before the court at Greenwich 'William Kemp, William Shakespeare, and Richarde Burbage, servants to the Lord Chamberleyne.' The years became full of presentation and publication, and the name of the old queen became a synonym for one of the few supreme imaginative explorations of man. She was dead before the full achievement of it, but it is still, and justly, her name that presides. James Stuart had his own virtues, but they were not of her scope, nor was the royalty of his presence phenomenal like hers. 'The imperial votaress passed on'—aged, jewel-encrusted, perverse, egotistic, Gloriana. It was no smooth, placid simplicity they praised under that name, but rather a twisted, dangerous splendour, almost a monstrosity—violent, tender, intelligent, rapacious. The late Renascence blazed about her, interwoven with the deaths which accompanied it and waited for it. She went in their midst, and they sang: she was Gloriana.

She had always been lonely, but now her loneliness grew. Shakespeare acted before her; Francis Bacon was among her lawyers. But they were not her intimates. Leicester was dead; Walsingham was dead; her favourite Hatton was dead; her enemy and kinswoman Mary was dead; her enemy and ally Catherine de' Medici was dead. Cecil was very old; he had brought his second son Robert into his business, as it were, and almost into office. The queen named him 'my beagle,' one of that menagerie of small strange beasts it had been an amusement of her vivid mind to title. Alençon had been her frog; and Alençon's servant, Simier, her monkey; and James VI's servant, the Master of Gray, her hare. And there were other names: Hatton was her sheep; Walsingham her Moor; the elder Cecil had been her spirit; and the lost Leicester her eyes. So now the beagle came into the business, and set himself to the management, and to the management of the whims and the intellect of the chief shareholder. The work was not made easier by the existence of an opposite party. 'There was a party'—in all senses of the word. There were

intimate parties given in the queen's rooms; there was a political
party at the Council-board; and there was a 'party'—the old
vulgarity has a sense of the contempt and the hostility—whose
name was Essex.

He had come through Leicester; he was Leicester's legacy, and
might have been Leicester's rival, had Leicester lived, for he was
Leicester's stepson.   It was said that his stepfather had poisoned
his father.   He had been married to Walsingham's daughter, the
widow of Philip Sidney, who survived him.   He was twenty-one
in the year of the Armada, and in the years after the Armada he
became the first—and the last—of the queen's minions.

In 1593, the queen was sixty.   She did not easily abandon her
habits, and some of them had by now hardened into tyrannies
and even obsessions.   The question of the succession had always
angered her; now she would not allow it to be raised.   It had
meant talk and thought of Mary of Scots, and illegitimacy, and
possible death, and now she would have no more of it.   There
was no longer any close claimant to the throne.   Legitimate or
illegitimate, she and the chance of things had imposed her claim
upon things.   She was Queen of England; at least, there was no
one else.   She indulged herself, and forbade any talk of any one
else, to the serious inconvenience of her ministers and the serious
irritation of James of Scotland.   But while she indulged herself in discouraging talk of death, she indulged herself also in
encouraging talk of love.   Her culture had delighted in flattery,
and now the demand for flattery became an obsession.   Abuse
of culture, abuse of intimacy, tended to grow in her; yet she never
lost intelligence.   By such a mistress, greedy of adoration, greedy
of service, greedy of intelligence, the handsome young soldier
Essex was distinguished.   He accepted favour.

Had he had to do with some kinds of women, Essex might have
risen into godhead and retained it to the end.   As he rose, his
opinion of Elizabeth fell.   He mistook her ancient, uncomely
amorousness, not only for weakness, which it was, but for
thorough weakness, which it was not.   When he quarrelled with
her, which he did often, and violently, as none before him had
dared, he flung away and left her, and waited to be summoned
back, though he could be pretty enough in his worship when he
came.   He set up a foreign secret service of his own, shaped and
conducted by the skill of Anthony Bacon, elder brother of Francis.
Together Essex and Anthony played against Cecil, Essex at the
Council, Anthony in Essex House, conducting correspondence
with half Europe.   It was believed that Essex managed the

queen and that Anthony managed Essex, and it was to Anthony that great lords and ladies made application for favours desired. For a little it looked as if Anthony Bacon might defeat Robert Cecil and rule England through Essex and the queen. Francis Bacon was not much use to any one, and even Essex showed him magnificent gratitude rather because of his brother than of himself. But it was Francis who saw the danger to which things were coming. 'My lord,' he wrote afterwards, 'had a settled opinion that the queen could be brought to nothing but by a kind of necessity and authority.'

Necessity she had known, but never authority; she had never had any personal relation which imposed it on her, and there she had never even been false to it. It was her greater loneliness, and Essex could not bring any such authority to bear; how should he, who knew nothing of it himself? In September 1597, the older Cecil died. Essex was then sulking, after a scene in the Council chamber during which the queen had struck him and he had caught at his sword. More alone than ever before, she permitted herself to be reconciled, and let him go as he wished to Ireland. He went; he failed; he returned. For a moment she yielded and welcomed him fondly; then she remembered herself, and put him in custody. She was the queen.

Events had run wild; there was neither political nor religious cause of dissension. Elizabeth had, all her life, appealed to untheoretical life; from untheoretical life she received her reward. She had let the axe fall on Mary for the sake of her own person and rule; for the same cause she had to let the axe fall on Essex. The tragedy lingered for two years through its slow stages: custody, examination, freedom with banishment from court, rumours, gatherings. Essex House became full of discontented men. Essex—a mad comment upon the helplessness of events —appealed both to Puritans and Catholics. No more utter destruction of metaphysics could appear. He wrote an appealing, adoring letter to the queen, and tacked on to it—to such a woman!—a request for a renewal of his monopoly of sweet wines. Robert Cecil—more Cecilian and less theological than his great father—struck with more intelligence and with even more effect than his father had done of old.

In 1601 Essex, threatened again by the Council and kept separate from the queen, rode out of his house into the city, found no help there, and eventually surrendered. By craft or by accident a minor plot by an odd soldier against the queen's life was discovered immediately after. Essex was tried and condemned;

this time there was no delay. If Elizabeth woke by night, she sent no message; if she hesitated, she proposed no private destruction. She signed the warrant; three weeks after the outbreak, Essex, having first blamed everybody else, died.

The Council caused a statement of the earl's treasonable practices to be drawn up. The writer—it was Francis Bacon, who had played a perfectly consistent and loyal part throughout the drama, and been universally blamed as a result—used in phrases the style 'my lord of Essex.' She struck at her false lover once more: 'Write Essex.' It was so done.

Chapter 8

After Essex—Peace and War—Taxation and Monopolies—The Last Speech to the Commons—'These Fooleries'—Cecil Determines the Succession —Death of the Queen.

SHE was sixty-seven. The emotional crisis, or the loss of Essex, or the last necessary effort to maintain the quiet of the State, had all but exhausted her. She was still active in mind and body. In the December following the revolt she was at the Blackfriars Theatre, after having dined with the Lord Chamberlain. It is not known what play the company, in which now the greatest of her subjects held an important place, gave her. Shakespeare was only reaching the time of the tragedies. She had passed her own. She had—could she have known it?—given her own life to the cause to which she had given so much: the strange cause which was herself or her people or a kind of uncertain dream of freedom, or all compact, so that neither she nor they nor we can tell where sincerity ended and insincerity began. Like the line between belief and disbelief which had evaded the certain knowledge of her scrutineers in her young years, this other line has evaded all eyes ever since. The death of Essex lay on the sincere side; she suffered. Her pain grew into her. She remained, throughout it, in possession of her position and her people.

Yet her people, the very mass that her reign had deflected into a nation, with national prestige and national greed, were a little restless behind her. It was thirteen or fourteen years since the Armada, forty-four or forty-five since her accession. Generations that had not known the old fears or the old quarrels had arisen. On the religious side many desired honourable peace:

'What have wars, invasions, books, done these twenty years? You have heard; we to our sorrow have seen and endured,' wrote one priest to Rome. The queen was merciful; what might not the pope do, if only the Jesuits could be bridled! The Jesuits gained no more ground; they merely held their own. The Roman idea was becoming, as for long it unfortunately remained, the myth of a minority. Nothing was ever yet gained by mis-understanding a creed, nor does the Catholicity of the Church of England need to be maintained by ignorance. Rome must be decently known to be decently refused. The everlasting question of the succession caused dissension even here, and the Jesuit mission which supported a Spanish succession was opposed by the secular clergy, who leaned towards James of Scotland. Occasionally the quarrels between the two parties even resulted in appeals by the seculars to the queen herself. One of them had an audience, in which, speaking of the pope, she exclaimed justly: 'Your chief pastor pronounced sentence against me while I was yet in my mother's womb.'

The rest of the nation vibrated sometimes uneasily behind the antique figure. The death of Essex, least tolerable to Elizabeth of all the three grand executions, Norfolk's and Mary's and his, yet the most morally justified, was, ironically, the least popular. The queen's justice was defeated by the weapons she herself had used in her youth—spectacle and an appeal to the vulgar. Essex had been showy and handsome and liberal and brave; he had been for political war, and always for more war. The new stout-hearted generations backed him; it was their fathers whom the craft of the subtle young queen had wisely kept out of war, and their fathers were dying. 'Point de guerre,' Elizabeth had on occasion cried to her Council of old, but that was slow policy now. Essex was a hero, a dead Essex more certainly a hero than a living. In 1601, when the queen went to open Parliament, there was silence in the streets.

A more prolonged quarrel was opening—the financial. War was wanted, but not taxation. The queen all through her reign had kept herself as free as possible from dependence on subsidies; it was part of her superiority and her popularity. She asked for subsidies now. They were voted, but an attack was made on her methods, or on one of her methods—that of monopolies. Monopolies exist to-day, and money has been made out of them to-day, only all that is more hidden. The Elizabethan age was less ashamed of money than ours; it clamoured for it frankly and fought for it openly. The queen had granted monopolies—for rewards, for revenue, for protection of manufactures—but they were unpopular. The time had come when they could be attacked, and they were. In the Parliament of 1601 there was a great noise; the Government were abused. Robert Cecil was never a good man at managing the House; the attack dangerously approached the Prerogative. All her life Elizabeth had managed to 'put herself over'; she had baffled inquirers, perplexed ambassadors, maddened her ministers, and thrilled her people. The public Elizabeth, the queen who was Elizabeth rather than the Elizabeth who was queen, rose again. On 24th November 1601 the House had been in high confusion, and was gathering its courage to defy the Government, however Cecil might warn them of the danger of such a course. On 25th November he rose with a message from the throne: the queen consented to remedy their grievances. She consented—as a grace: she acted by proclamation—and kept the Prerogative intact. Five days later the Commons, on their knees in Whitehall, beheld for the last time above them the adorned figure of their high and mighty princess, and heard her speaking to them:

Mr Speaker, We perceive your coming is to present thanks to us. Know I accept them with no less joy than your loves can have desire to offer such a present, and do more esteem it than any treasure or riches; for those we know how to prize, but loyalty, love, and thanks, I account them invaluable. And though God hath raised me high, yet this I account the glory of my crown, that I have reigned with your loves. This makes me that I do not so much rejoice that God hath made me to be a Queen, as to be a Queen over so thankful a people, and to be the means under God to conserve you in safety and to preserve you from danger. . . . I never was any greedy, scraping grasper, nor a strict, fast-holding prince, nor yet a waster; my heart was never set upon any worldly goods, but only for my subjects' good.

With such a superb presentation of herself, her public life drew to a close. The Commons dispersed in gratitude and adoration; never before had she more greatly succeeded with an audience; and, if the actual truth was something lower than the graph of her rhetoric showed, it ran at least in a parallel curve. She believed utterly in herself as that kind of queen, and her belief was not only sincere, but largely justified. Few sovereigns have loved the common people better than Elizabeth; few have been more full of princely goodwill than she was to her servants. It is true they had to be utterly *her* servants.

It was 30th November 1601; by a twelvemonth later her constitution was breaking down. Through the year she still danced, rode, hunted, wrote letters in her own hand—'I end, scribbling

*H

in haste. Your loving sovereign'—gave audiences, thought of going on progresses. The cheers rose round her again. By the end of 1602, when she was drawing towards seventy, she began to know that things were at an end. Her godson, Sir John Harington, read her his verses; she listened with a smile and said: 'When thou dost feel creeping time at thy gate, these fooleries will please thee less. I am past my relish for such matters.' By the end of February 1603 it was remarked that she no longer took interest in serious political discussion; she 'delighteth to hear old Canterbury tales.' Robert Carey came to see her. She was sitting on her cushions on the floor—it was an old habit of hers; she took his hand, saying: 'No, Robin, I am not well,' and sighed continually in a heaviness of heart. Between the eleventh and twenty-third of March she grew worse. She lay silent, refusing medicine, refusing food, exclaiming sometimes when they pressed her. There are a score of tales, of uncertain value, of the closing days. The Council came to her, and for the last time the word 'succession' struck her dimming ears. It was the word that had been with her since she could first begin to understand the world; in the days of Harry her father, of Mary Tudor her sister, of Mary Stuart her cousin. One way or another it had dominated her life; it had kept her unmarried, and set the danger of death round her. No one lived more in the immediate present than Elizabeth, but that present had had always with it the spectral future, as a promise, as a right, as a danger, as a thing hated. Cecil and the Council had determined what they would do; they had determined for two years past to introduce that learned metaphysician—and he was —James of Scotland. They asked her if she consented. It is said she made an ambiguous movement, raising her hands to her head. It is said she did so in sign of assent; either that, or at the very last moment, did she still mazedly seek to protect her own crown? The Council went; the archbishop came. She kept him there, praying; at last even that dim awareness passed, and she lay unconscious. Two hours after midnight, at the nadir of the twenty-four hours, on Thursday, 24th March, she entered into death.

Chapter 9

Epilogue—The Intentions of the Queen and their Conclusions—Java
and the Lateran—'So Sweet a Bait.'

SHE had had no formal intention of multiplying dominion or
maintaining doctrine; she had, in effect, done both—had promulgated an empire and preserved a Church.   She had lent ships to
bring gold and they had sown government.   She had had personal preferences in religion, and they had so mingled with the
affairs of the time as to prevent both the papal and the extreme
Protestant influences.   No more than the revolution of Geneva
was the resolution of the Council of Trent allowed to define in
England the less settled medieval pattern.   She had drawn
India and Java into English trade, and excluded from English
religion the Lateran on the Cœlian hill.   All this she did without
intention, and because, though she loved herself in the common
egoistic way of men, she loved herself also as an objective fact.
She loved herself as a person, but also as a queen.   And though
there again her love was half selfish, though often when she looked
in the glass it was Elizabeth crowned she saw, it was often the
crowned Queen of England.   That, because she liked the English,
she loved, and the popular cheers of the English told her that
they loved it too.   She wrote once to Burghley in one of his fits
of gloom: 'Serve God, feare the Kinge, and be a Good fellow to
the rest'; it was her ideal of a man.   Even among the recusants
her popularity was not dead; and, unless she were maddened by
fear or anger, she had motions of mercy there; it is said she once
saved seventy priests and sent them over to the Continent.   This
again may have been calculated generosity; their living voice
might sound louder in papal Europe than the spiritual accusations of the dead.   Her calculations went very far, yet she was a
woman of the sixteenth century, and in the last analysis even
her calculations were rather intuitive than intellectual, however
the intellect subserved its twin.   Most women tend to be Calvinistic in their outlook upon this world, however this heresy
may be checked by their intelligence, and even Elizabeth's
sceptical nature beheld the world as composed of the elect, who
were her friends, and the reprobate, who were her enemies.   If
these last were in power or with desirable influence, she could
pretend to be ready to be friends; once only, in the incident of
Alençon, did she pretend to be friends.   In the phrase of John

Harington, quoting Hatton, 'The Queen did fish for men's souls, and had so sweet a bait that no one could escape her network.' They swam to that net; even if she cast them back into the waters, they came shooting towards her again, avid of capture. She enjoyed culture and jollity; she found physical or mental abandonment difficult; in that self-grasp, she could be cruel. She was lonely, for she was royal, and neither pious nor impious. One would like to know if ever she held philosophical talk with Maitland of Lethington, or if ever anything but formal talk, if that, passed between her and Shakespeare. Without his genius of exploration and expression, she had in her life a kind of kinship with the method of his genius. She is an active and debased caricature of the purity of his power, as egoistic as that was necessarily unegoistic. It is not absurd that, over an abyss, he should praise her. In a midsummer night's dream he saw her; her own midsummer's day was more fevered and more tortuous. Yet the general title of the plays, and of their method, might be *The Way Things Happen*. It is hers also. She happened, and she continued to happen. It was the sense of the unlikely chance of her that lingered, whether (as Cardinal Allen wrote) as an incestuous bastard begotten of an infamous courtesan or (as the French ambassador said) receiving 'blessings from the people as though she had been another Messiah.' Then and since, it has distinguished her. She was, then and since, unexpected, in her birth, in her succession, in her boast of singleness, in her bravery of success. Unassassinated and undeposed; untheological in an age of theologies; uncertain in a world of certainties, turning upon some hidden centre of her own, faithful to some dark belief of her own, and else as incalculable in her actions as unforeseen in her existence; brilliant and disingenuous, humble and sincere, a perverse portent, she sat on the English throne for forty years, and moved the English imagination for four centuries, an incarnate, memorable, and terrifying example of the way things happen. As common and as unusual as that, she was Elizabeth.

BIBLIOGRAPHY

It is difficult within the compass of this series to give any sort of general bibliography of Elizabeth that would be of real value to the reader. The latest life is *Queen Elizabeth* by Professor J. E. Neale (1934). Mr Milton Waldman's *Elizabeth* (1933) ends with the Armada. Dr Pollard's books on the period are always necessary. Mr Hilaire Belloc's drawing of her in his *History of England* ought to be observed; the other general histories supplement either him or Froude. Dr G. B. Harrison has recently edited the *Letters of Queen Elizabeth* (1935). *Shakespeare's England* (Clarendon Press, 1917) provides a background, as also do Dr Harrison's *Elizabethan Journals*. *The Reign of Elizabeth*, by J. B. Black, forms Vol. VIII in the Oxford History of England, and is authoritative.

BY GEOFFREY WEBB

Chronology

1632	Birth of Sir Christopher Wren
1634	The Reverend Christopher Wren becomes Dean of Windsor
1646	Christopher Wren leaves school; family removes to Bletchington
1649	Admitted gentleman commoner at Wadham College, Oxford
1653	Graduates M.A. Elected Fellow of All Souls College, Oxford. Wallis lectures on the 'Geometrical Flat Floor'
1657	Becomes Professor of Astronomy at Gresham College, London
1660	Royal Society founded
1661	Becomes Savilian Professor of Astronomy at Oxford. Consulted as to Old St Paul's
1663	Design of Sheldonian Theatre, Oxford. Pembroke College Chapel, Cambridge begun
1665	Visits Paris
1666	Scheme for repair of Old St Paul's. Fire of London. Appointed to Commission for the rebuilding of the city
1669	Appointed Royal Surveyor. Married to Faith Coghill. Begins design of new St Paul's
1670	Coal tax increased to 3s. Work on city churches begun
1672	Hooke's diary opens. St Stephen's, Walbrook, begun
1673	Knighted. First model design of St Paul's abandoned, and second great 'model' begun
1675	Royal warrant to proceed with St Paul's on design as shown. Work begun. Son Christopher born Lady Wren's death
1676	Library at Trinity College, Cambridge, begun
1677	Married to Jane Fitzwilliam
1679	Member of Council of Hudson's Bay Company. N. Hawksmoor joins his staff(?)
1680	Death of second Lady Wren
1681	President of the Royal Society. Tom Tower, Christ Church, Oxford, designed
1682	Chelsea Hospital begun
1685	Work at Whitehall for James II. Elected M.P. for Plympton
1689	Hampton Court and Kensington Palaces begun. Talman made Comptroller of the Works
1693	First schemes for Greenwich Hospital. Christ's Hospital additions
1697	Choir of St Paul's opened. Half salary for St Paul's suspended
1698	Fire at Whitehall Palace
1699	Greenwich Hospital begun. Vanbrugh designs Castle Howard
1702	Jane Wren (daughter) died. Vanbrugh made Comptroller of the Works
1704	St Paul's used for Thanksgiving Service after Blenheim
1707	Lead of dome undertaken at St Paul's
1711	St Paul's declared finished and salary paid up
1714–15	Partially retired from Office of Works
1718	Dismissal from Office of Works
1719	Scheme for north transept of Westminster Abbey approved
1723	Death of Sir Christopher Wren

Chapter I

Family—Wren Bishop—Dean Wren—The Holders—First Scientific Work
—Oxford after the Civil War—The Beginnings of the Royal Society—
Appointed Professor at Gresham College—Scientific Work of the Late
Fifties and Sixties—Recognition of the Royal Society—Savilian Pro-
fessor at Oxford.

SIR CHRISTOPHER WREN was born a gentleman. It would be
irrelevant to say this of Shakespeare or Sir Isaac Newton; and it
is perhaps something in the social preoccupation of architecture
that makes it of importance in the case of Wren. The members
of Sir Christopher Wren's family with whom he had most to do
were his father Christopher, his uncle Matthew, his sister Susan,
and her husband, William Holder. The brothers, Matthew, born
1585, and Christopher, born 1589, were sent by their father Francis
Wren, mercer and citizen of London, to Merchant Taylors'
School, and there had the good fortune to come under the notice
of Lancelot Andrewes, then Master of Pembroke College, Cambridge. Matthew was admitted there in 1601, Christopher going
not long after to St John's College, Oxford. The favour of
Lancelot Andrewes was a great thing for the Wren brothers, for
the master, now Dean of Westminster, was no less successful than
saintly; he was shortly (1605) made Bishop of Chichester, then,
four years later, Bishop of Ely, and in 1619 translated to Winchester. With him the Wrens rose also, especially Matthew, who
became a Fellow of his college, then Canon of Winchester, and
later was appointed one of the two chaplains who accompanied
Charles I, when Prince of Wales, on his visit to Madrid. By this
appointment Andrewes put his protégé in the way of further and
greater advancement in the new reign that began the year before
his death (1626). For personal acquaintance with and proximity
to the sovereign was in the seventeenth century the high road
to official promotion. The younger brother, Christopher, also
shared the bishop's favour, becoming his chaplain, and receiving
in succession the livings of Fonthill and East Knoyle in Wiltshire. And so the Wren family became attached to the High
Church Academic side of the court circle, and for the disciples of
Lancelot Andrewes it was a circle distinguished in other ways as
well as socially, for that great man had not only the gift of
divining merit in his followers, but of lending to his chosen some,
thing of his own extraordinary distinction of outlook. The expressions 'High Church,' 'court,' and 'Academic' may seem to

have a dry sound to modern ears; but it was men like Andrewes who themselves constituted the splendour of the Stuart court, the loveliness of the Church of England, and the greatness of her learned tradition; and Toryism for many generations to come was to find its justification in preserving intact the image of their work.

In the year that his patron died, Matthew Wren became Master of Peterhouse at Cambridge, where he applied himself to a thorough reorganization of the society, including its buildings. The crowning work was the building of the chapel, a curious and charming building, that seeks to combine the richness and fancy of the Flemish Renaissance fashion of the time with a conscious recollection of late Gothic, to enforce the continuity of English Church tradition. Wren finished the chapel *internally*, but left the outside brick and stone dressings. The later stone facings were the enterprise of his successor the famous Bishop Cosin. At the end of his life, Matthew Wren was to afford his nephew a first opportunity as an architect, in the building of another college chapel for Pembroke. In 1628, Matthew became Dean of Windsor and Registrar of the Order of the Garter, and, in 1634, Bishop of Hereford, an office he only held one year before his translation to Norwich. During that year, however, he had a most congenial task in drawing up a consecration ceremony for the renovated Abbey Dore, a twelfth-century abbey church which Lord Scudamore had restored for the parish use in the best taste of the day. The task was not only gratifying by reason of the occasion, but in itself, for we have Clarendon's evidence that Matthew Wren was 'particularly versed in the old liturgies of the Greek and Latin Churches.' He is also known to have composed services for the readmission to the Church of sailors who had been forced into apostasy by the Moslem pirates of Barbary. Mathew was succeeded at Windsor by his brother Christopher, who had himself been appointed a chaplain to the king in 1628.

Christopher Wren the elder married in September 1623, about the time that he obtained the living at East Knoyle. The young lady was just under twenty-one, he himself being thirteen years older. She was the only daughter and heiress of Richard Cox, the squire of Fonthill, the village where Christopher had held the living for the past three years. Knoyle is not far from Fonthill, in a charming countryside, the village lying on the lower slopes of steep down-like hills; and there the children were born, Mary in 1624, Katherine in 1626, Susan in 1627, Elizabeth (who died in infancy) in 1630, a son Christopher (born, baptized, and dead in the same hour), 1631, and Christopher, the subject of this book, Thursday, 20th October 1632. 'The bell rang eight (p.m.) as his mother fell in labour with him,' as Aubrey says on Sir Christopher's own authority. In spite of this parade of accuracy, *astrologiae ergo*, it is amusing to note that Aubrey made a muddle of it, and confused the two Christophers: this came of being too clever, and consulting the registers instead of taking Sir Christopher's own word for it. In a letter to Anthony Wood, the Oxford biographer, Aubrey says:

Dr Christopher Wren hath putt a trick on us, as it seems, for he hath made himself a yeare younger than indeed he is, though he needs not be ashamed of his age, he hath made such admirable use of his time. I mett t'other day accidentally with the parson of Knahill [Knoyle] who justifies the register, and not only so but proves it by his neighbour that was his nurse and her son that suckled with him —evidence notorious.

There is, however, no doubt; for Christopher Wren, the father, recorded the dates of family events on the flyleaf of a copy of Helwig's *Theatrum Historicum*, 1618, now in the National Library of Wales.

Mrs Wren had in all eleven children, of whom a second Elizabeth, born in 1633, died of consumption in 1644, and Anne, born in 1634, lived to marry a clergyman of the name of Brunsall and settle in Ely. She died in 1667. There were no surviving sons except Christopher, and the last child's birth is recorded in 1643; it is presumed that Mrs Wren died not long after. Of the other daughters, one, name unknown, married a certain John Hook, an Oxford don, and Katherine married Richard Fulbourne of Windsor. Of Susan's marriage to William Holder we shall have to speak later on. Two years after the birth of his son, Christopher Wren succeeded his brother as Dean of Windsor and Registrar of the Order of the Garter (1634), and the king further presented him to the living of Great Haseley in Oxfordshire. It would seem that Wren's youth must have been passed largely between those two places, though Aubrey records that the family were at Knoyle after the surrender of Bristol to Fairfax in the autumn of 1645. Moreover, Dean Wren got into trouble with the local Puritan committee in 1647, for adorning Knoyle church with stucco reliefs executed the year before.

Christopher, the father, who is variously described as a 'good general scholar and a good orator,' and as a mathematician, a good musician, and with some knowledge of drawing and architecture, has left some relics of his tenure of the rectory at Knoyle, which show him to have shared the taste of his time for ingeniously contrived inscriptions, and the kind of decoration which

the seventeenth century would have described as 'conceited.'
They consist of an inscription in the hall of the rectory giving the
date 28th July 1623, on which he moved into the new house; and
in the church, besides inscriptions on the columns, with an ingeniously illegible spacing of the letters (these have since disappeared), there are the elaborate plaster relief decorations of
scenes from Scripture adorned with flower borders and texts, to
which we have referred.   More practically, he restored the roof.

With the 1640's and the coming of the bad times of the Civil
War, incident comes thick and fast into the annals of the Wren
family.   The young Christopher had begun his education under
a tutor, the Rev. William Shepheard, of whom we know nothing
but the name, and from him is said to have passed on to Westminster School, where the great Dr Busby had not long assumed
the mastership.   His schooldays lasted till 1646.   But, in the
meanwhile, events had occurred both in the family and the outside world that completely changed the boy's home life.   In the
first place, his sister Susan had married William Holder, a young
don at Pembroke, Cambridge, Bishop Wren's old college, who had
been elected a Fellow in 1640 and received the living of Bletchington in Oxfordshire in 1642, the year before his marriage.   Holder's
is the first important personal influence on the young Christopher
Wren that we can trace at all clearly.

Aubrey, who knew both the Holders well, has left a very
attractive picture of this household where Wren passed so much
of his time in early life.   He specially mentions Holder's interest
in music and mathematics and adds: 'If one would go about to
describe a perfect good man one would drawe this Doctor's
character.'

The Wrens had need of all the comfort that the importation of
such a person into the family circle could bring, for not long
before the marriage, in October 1642, came to Windsor 'one
Captain Fogg pretending a warrant from the King and demanding
the Keys of the Treasury [of the Order of the Garter], threatening
if they were denied him by the Dean and Prebendaries, to pull
the chapel about their ears.'   If he did not quite do that, at any
rate he forced the doors with crowbars, and carried off the treasures with the exception of the smaller and more portable jewels,
such as the George and Garter of Gustavus Adolphus, which the
dean had prudently buried in anticipation of some such disaster
as this.   We also know that the Wrens' house was pillaged and
the dean's personal belongings carried off, for some six years later
he was able to get back a harpsichord, taken at this time, and also

three volumes of the records of the Order, though only at considerable trouble and expense. The altar plate and the buried jewels, which had been discovered at a later date, were never recovered. The dean and his family, including Holder, fled after this and, we hear from Aubrey, formed part of the garrison at Bristol throughout the period that the town was held for the king, from 1643 to 1645. After the surrender to Fairfax in the autumn of 1645 they returned to Knoyle. In that year also we hear that the deanery at Windsor was again pillaged, and the dean deprived of his living at Great Haseley, but it seems unlikely that the family had been in residence at either of these places for some time. How far the young Christopher shared in this exile, or whether he was all the time at school at Westminster, we do not know. But at any rate his natural homes, Windsor and Oxfordshire, were impossible, as being too close to the centre of warlike operations, for the district between London and Oxford was the no man's land of the Civil War. But these were not the only misfortunes of the Wren family. Bishop Matthew had been severe with Puritans, both inside and outside the Church of England, and especially so with the colonies of foreign Protestants who had been allowed to settle in his diocese. The memory of his administrative severity in the Norwich diocese outlasted the three years of his tenure of the quieter see of Ely and made him a marked man to the extreme Puritan party.

In 1640 he was already threatened in the proceedings against Laud; and in 1641, after officiating for the last time at Windsor, on the occasion of the marriage of Princess Mary to the Prince of Orange, he was committed to prison, where he was to remain for eighteen years, till March 1660, when he was released by order of General Monk, whom he had befriended in the early days of his captivity. In the summer of 1646, Dean Wren and his son-in-law moved to the latter's rectory at Bletchington, which was henceforward to be the dean's home. The war—or such of it as still continued, for the king was a prisoner in the hands of the Scotch—was far removed from those parts. At the same time young Christopher is said to have left school.

The removal to Bletchington marks a turning-point in the lives of both father and son. For the father it was to prove a place of peace and rest after the troubles of the last four years, the plunder of his intimate possessions, the insecurity, the alarms and excursions of his life at Bristol. Inevitably it was rather a melancholy peace, for his brother was in prison, and three years later the king his master—and it is hard for us to realize quite

what Charles meant to men of Dean Wren's way of feeling—was
to be put to death. In the ten years that the dean lived at
Bletchington he was to see the forces of evil go from triumph to
triumph, and when he died there in 1656 the usurping Government would seem settled in unassailable security. For young
Christopher the turning-point was of a very different and much
happier significance. To him the glories of Windsor can hardly
have meant much more than a vague but highly coloured background to the memories of his early childhood, and the disasters
of the past four years would sit fairly lightly on a schoolboy
of fourteen.

Schools in the seventeenth century were very different from
those of to-day; there was less team spirit, and presumably less
self-complacency. Moreover, Dr Busby's Westminster, in spite
of the fame of his beatings, and the supposed criticisms of Locke
the philosopher (we have good evidence that Locke was rather
difficult in his youth), seems to have owed its outstanding position
to the personal relationships established between the boys,
especially those who were going to the university, and the great
man himself. This personal factor in education has a value quite
other than that of tradition, which is often a propitiatory name
for herd feeling, and must have considerably softened the contrast between school and university for Wren and his contemporaries. There were other factors, too, tending in the same
way for Wren; all the evidence goes to show that he slipped into
university life by degrees, over a period of two or three years,
and had already established helpful connections in the academic
world before he came into residence. We have no details of his
schooldays. It has been suggested that he was a town boy, and
if that was so it would have almost certainly mitigated the
severity of his experience at Westminster. One or two Latin
exercises have survived. A Latin letter of a formal kind, written
to his father when he was ten years old, would be phenomenal
nowadays, but is not unprecedented in a seventeenth-century
child. Some Latin verses, written in 1645, are more remarkable,
not only for their skill and elegance, though these are sufficiently
striking for a boy of thirteen, but by reason of their subject-
matter—the presentation of an astronomical instrument, of his
own invention, to his father. The young man was about to
enter into the first of his kingdoms.

There is a confusion about the beginning of Wren's life at
Oxford. The *Parentalia*, a record of the Wren family compiled
by Sir Christopher's grandson, gives the date of his entry as a

gentleman commoner at Wadham College as 1646, the Wadham documents give 1649. He took his B.A. degree in March 1651. The date of the family removal to Bletchington, however, is certain, and it seems likely that his connection with Oxford, if not with Wadham itself, dates from this removal. Two other facts seem to point to an interval between school and regular attendance at the university. Aubrey in his Life of Holder says:

He was very helpful in the education of his brother-in-law, Mr Christopher Wren (now knighted), a youth of a prodigious inventive witt, and of whom he was as tender as if he had been his own child, whom he instructed first in geometrie and arithmetique, and when he was a young scholar at the University of Oxford, was a very necessary and kind friend. The parsonage house at Bletchington was Mr Christopher Wren's home and retiring place; here he contemplated and studied, and found out a great many curious things in mathematiques. About this house he made several curious dialls, with his own hands, which are still there to be seen.

The natural time for all this would be the first years at Bletchington, for it is difficult to see how Holder could have given young Christopher much instruction during the bad times while the boy was at Westminster and Holder himself at Bristol, but facts are so scarce that we cannot be sure.

Whenever Holder may have begun his teaching, it is certain that about this time (1646) Wren began his connection with Dr Charles Scarborough, an eminent scientist and physician, to whom the young man declares in one of his extant Latin letters that he owed his recovery from a serious illness if not his life itself. Scarborough's interests were not confined to the medical sciences, he was almost equally eminent in mathematics. In a Latin letter to his father dated 1647, young Christopher gives some details of his work with Scarborough. He refers to Scarborough's kindness to him, mentions a self-recording meteorological instrument, weather clock he calls it, that he has invented and Scarborough is having made, and, most important, tells how he is undertaking at Scarborough's instance the translation of Oughtred's treatise on Geometrical Dialling into Latin. There was no question of a mere academic exercise in one of the classic tongues in this, it was seriously intended to make the work available to foreign students. Scarborough and his friend Seth Ward were enthusiastic admirers of Oughtred, whose *Clavis Aurea* they had introduced as a mathematical text-book at Cambridge, and now the former passes on this new task to his young pupil. A letter from Wren to Oughtred on the subject of the translation is extant, and there are flattering references to the young scholar in the later editions of Oughtred's works. In the same year, 1647, Wren took out a patent for an instrument for writing with two pens, about which some difficulty later arose, others having claimed the invention for themselves. An undated letter is extant protesting at this, and saying that Wren's invention had been brought to the knowledge of Oliver Cromwell himself. We do not know the upshot of it all, but two facts emerge: first that at this time Wren's activities were not confined to Oxford and that he was a good deal in London, where Scarborough lived; and second, by inference, that he had already got in touch with those inner Cromwellian circles that we shall find him occasionally frequenting a few years later, in spite of his Royalist upbringing. It is most probable that such an invention as the 'diplographic pen' would be brought to the notice of Cromwell by Wilkins, the Warden of Wadham, who stood well in that quarter, and whose friendship for Wren probably dates from this time. It is almost certain that it is to this early association with Scarborough that Wren owed his interest in the medical sciences, the chief fruits of which were his work with Willis and Lower, especially the illustrations that he was to draw for Willis's *Cerebri Anatome*, and his own experiments on injections into the veins of animals and the transfusion of blood. But these were not to be Wren's chief scientific interests, which remained those of astronomy and the mathematical sciences.

There is a type of scientific worker whose gifts lie in the direction of mechanical aptitude for the devising and perfecting of experiments and apparatus, though it is impossible to excel in this without a profound understanding of the foundations of the subjects concerned, and it is no mere question of mechanical ingenuity or manual dexterity. It would seem that Wren as a man of science belonged by nature to this class, but this must be said with considerable reservations. Bishop Sprat, an Oxford friend and devoted admirer of Wren, has inserted in his history of the early years of the Royal Society a list of Wren's scientific discoveries and inventions, prompted to do so by the modesty of his idol 'who,' he says, 'is so far from usurping the fame of other men that he endeavours with all care to conceal his own.' The list includes many mechanical devices and improvements to existing instruments, such as a variety of self-registering meteorological instruments, and improvements to telescopes in the way of 'many sorts of rachis screws and other devises . . . for taking small distances and apparent diameters to seconds.' He also mentions Wren's improvements in the grinding of lenses. Be-

sides all this, there are the more lasting results of his experiments
to establish the 'Doctrine of Motion,' of the results of which
Sir Isaac Newton wrote:

From these laws [the laws of motion] Dr Christopher Wren,
Knight, John Wallis and Christian Huyghens, who are, beyond
comparison, the leading geometers of this age, arrived at the laws
of the collision and mutual rebound of two bodies; but their truth
was proved by Dr Wren by experiments on suspended balls in the
presence of the Royal Society.

One modern writer has claimed that Wren and his master, Wallis,
were the founders of modern mechanics, and another, who is
certainly not unmindful of the variety of Wren's scientific work,
has declared that his special gift was for geometrical demonstrations, citing his scheme for the graphical construction of solar
and lunar eclipses and the occultations of stars, and his 'beautiful
geometrical method for one of the steps in the graphical determination of a comet's path.'

The part of Wren's life when he was pre-eminently a man of
science covers twenty years, from 1645 to 1665; and, of that, for
the first five years he was hardly more than a precocious schoolboy, and in the last two he had already shown signs of that
interest in architecture which was eventually to become an almost
exclusive preoccupation.   It is a period in the history of science
in England between the great names of Harvey, the discoverer
of the circulation of the blood, and Sir Isaac Newton, when the
strength of the movement lay in the number of solid, able workers
rather than in the genius of one or two great men.   Moreover, it
was the time of the invention of methods and apparatus, Napier's
logarithms, Gunter's slide rule, the development of algebra under
Victor of Paris, Harriot and Wallis, Galileo's telescope at the
beginning, and later, in the middle of the century, the microscope
of which Wren himself was one of the earliest users.   The outstanding progress was of course in astronomy and anatomy, the
two sciences which had a real tradition of observed data behind
them and to which these last instruments were able to contribute,
but it is also the period when, from a general amalgam of scientific
knowledge, the separate sciences were beginning to emerge in
recognizable form.   The process was only in its infancy, as compared with the extreme specialization of our own day, and in
many ways Wren seems nearer to Leonardo da Vinci in the
multiplicity of his interests than to the modern man of science,
who confines himself so strictly to the cultivation of his own
garden.   An aspect of this variety of scientific interest is the
readiness to welcome all sorts of information, and to hazard

opinions on all sorts of subjects. We are constantly being
amazed at the credulity of Pepys for example, but credulity is
often the consciousness of an expanding world, and the men of the
seventeenth century were at once too eager to know, and too
conscious of the amount there was to be known, to be fastidious
about stories that later generations have learnt to despise. The
following titbits of information passed on to Aubrey by Wren
himself will serve to illustrate both the credulity and its limits:

> Strawberries have a most delicious taste, and are so innocent that
> a woman in childbed, or one in a feaver, may safely eat them: but I
> have heard Sir Christopher Wren affirm that if one that has a wound
> in his head eates them, they are mortall. Methinks 'tis very strange.

And on the subject of the mysterious drummings or knockings
at the house of Mr Mompesson at Tidworth, one of the most
famous seventeenth-century ghost stories:

> Another time Sir Christopher Wren lay there. He could see no
> strange things, but sometimes he should heare a drumming, as one
> may drum with ones hand upon wainscot; but he observed that this
> drumming was only when a certain maidservant was in the next
> room: the partitions of the rooms are by borden-brasse as we call it.
> But all these [includes other investigators] remarked that the Devil
> kept no very unreasonable houres: it seldome knock't after 12 at
> night, or before 6 in the morning.

Perhaps the outstanding quality of Wren's mind was its immense
fecundity and readiness of invention; it was his good fortune to
turn to science when those qualities were most needed, and to
turn to architecture in circumstances where those qualities more
than any others enabled him to excel.

The University of Oxford in the 1650's, when Wren was an
undergraduate and young don (1649–60), was in a very curious
state. The presence of the court and the headquarters of the
Royalist armies in the Civil War, the fortifications, the siege, the
surrender, the consequent parliamentary occupation, had all
borne hardly on the university, and Anthony Wood speaks of it
in 1646 as

> empty as to scholars, but pretty well replenish'd with parliamen-
> tarian soldiers. Many of the inhabitants had gained great store of
> wealth from the Court and Royalists that had for several years con-
> tinued among them; but as for the yong men of the city and university
> he found many of them to have been debauch'd by bearing armes and
> doing the duties belonging to soldiers, as watching, warding, and
> sitting in tipling houses for whole nights together.

During the following three years, things were straightening themselves out, and the Revolutionary leaders, in spite of much
denunciation of the universities by some of their left-wing sup-

porters, dealt honestly if ruthlessly by it. They were seriously determined to preserve it as a place of learning, and in many instances where they intruded new men in place of heads of colleges, dons, and university officials they chose them wisely. There were of course scenes that must have been distressing to many, when Lord Pembroke, the Chancellor, went from college to college, 'with a noisy rabble following behind,' turning out the former dignitaries and establishing the new ones. But by the time Wren came on the books of Wadham (1649) these things were a year old. The new men had settled into their offices, and the benefit that the university was to gain by the presence of such men as Owen (lately Cromwell's chaplain) and Conant as administrators and divines, and the even greater benefits from the introduction of such figures as Wilkins, the new Warden of Wadham, Seth Ward, and Wallis, were soon to become appreciable.

It was among these new intruded men that Wren was to make some of his most formative friendships. Wilkins, the warden of his college, was indeed Oxford born and bred, but Seth Ward and Wallis were both intruders. With these men he had probably established connections before he came into residence, perhaps through Scarborough, and possibly it was their presence there that determined his choice of a college. Wilkins, as warden of the college, had a spacious set of rooms along the front on the first floor, one of which, that over the gate with the oriel window, he gave over to Seth Ward and his young pupil, and it was known for long afterwards as the astronomy chamber. Wallis, who with Seth Ward is the next great influence on Wren after Scarborough, was not of his college, but must have been very much at home there in Wilkins's time, and if Ward was to pass on his astronomy professorship eventually to his young pupil, it was with Wallis, as we have already said, that Wren accomplished his most lasting scientific work. Through Wallis also there is a link between Wren's scientific and architectural careers, for in 1650 the new Professor of Geometry had a large-scale model made of his 'geometrical flat floor,' a demonstration of his solution of the problem of how to support a floor the area of which is wider than the length of the timbers available for joists. Wilkins had another model made for himself the following year, and, in 1652 and 1653, Wallis himself lectured upon it. Wren, in his first large building, the Sheldonian Theatre, Oxford, adapted Wallis's floor to use on a monumental scale.

Wren graduated B.A. in March 1651, and M.A. in 1653, in which year he was elected to a Fellowship at All Souls. Of this

part of his career we know only that he was working on his tract
on the planet Saturn, and possibly doing his first work with the
microscope.   Of his social activities at this time (or indeed any
other) we have very little evidence; we know that he took the
part of Neanias in a production of a translation of the *Plutus*
of Aristophanes, probably given before the Prince Palatine some
time about 1651, and that he joined with others in writing poems
prefixed to the account of how an Oxford servant girl, who had
been hanged for murdering her illegitimate child, was revived
by the medical students to whom the body had been sold for
dissection.   This is one of the few copies of verses by Wren that
we have, but a letter of Thomas Sprat refers to a verse translation
of Horace's epistle to Lollius in very laudatory terms; but then,
Sprat's partiality towards Wren is obvious in all their dealings,
and his recommendation is hardly fair testimony of quality.
For the rest of our picture of Wren's early life at Oxford we
must fill out from our knowledge of his friends and from Anthony
Wood as best we may.   In the first place, Wren was in rather a
special position as an undergraduate by reason of his close family
connections with academic life.   Moreover, he was a gentleman
commoner; that is to say he dined with the Fellows of the
college, not with the undergraduates (unless there were enough
gentlemen commoners to have a table to themselves), and enjoyed other special privileges.   All this must have kept him a
little apart from undergraduate society, and there were then no
organized games or undergraduate clubs to help the mixing
process.   The ordinary undergraduate relaxations seem to have
been picnics—Wood goes fishing and nutting in Shotover Wood
—and various kinds of rowdy frolics and ragging at degree ceremonies, and so on.   There was also a good deal of fighting,
sometimes as the result of informal football matches.   From
what we know of Wren's character, and especially bearing in
mind his extreme precocity, it seems unlikely that he indulged
much in the last of these amusements.

According to Wood, coffee-houses were first set up in Oxford
in 1650, but the fashion soon caught on and became an important
feature of university life, being in fact embryo clubs.   Among the
'wits' who frequented the coffee-house of Tillyard, 'apothecary
and great Royalist,' Wood mentions Christopher Wren and his
cousins Thomas and Matthew.

Thomas was a physician and fond of music, and Matthew,
whom we shall meet again in political employment, was interested
in political philosophy and wrote several works on it.

The most important of the social gatherings that Wren is
known to have attended were those held first at Dr Petty's
lodgings (over a chemist's), later at Dr Wilkins's at Wadham,
and later again, after Wilkins's departure to Cambridge, at
Robert Boyle's lodgings in the High Street, where he had established a laboratory. They had begun in 1649, being a continuation of earlier meetings in Dr Goddard's rooms in London as far
back as 1645. The meetings were held weekly, and among the
first mentioned as attending them are Wilkins, Seth Ward,
Ralph Bathurst, Dr Petty, Dr Willis, Lawrence Rooke, and, at
an early date after the removal to Oxford, Christopher Wren
and his cousin Matthew. This 'experimental philosophical
clubbe' was the beginning of the Royal Society, and may be
considered the most important thing that happened at Oxford
in the seventeenth century; certainly the most important factor
in Wren's life there. Of its early members many were to become
Wren's lifelong friends, and it was through these meetings that
he made the acquaintance of Robert Hooke who had come up to
Christ Church in 1653 and first came to the meetings about 1655.
Hooke, who was three years younger than Wren, had been at
Westminster, and before that apprenticed to Sir Peter Lely
with the idea of becoming a painter; not long after he came to
Oxford he became laboratory assistant to Dr Willis, helping him
in his chemical studies, and from him was passed on to Boyle,
with whom he worked on the celebrated air pump. Hooke was
destined to become the closest of all Wren's Oxford friends,
working with him, not only in science, but later in architecture.
It is almost certain that they were connected by marriage, for
Hooke later refers to 'cosin Wren-Hooke,' presumably that sister
of Christopher's who married John Hooke.

From the year 1654 we have two references to Wren in the
Diary of John Evelyn, who visited Oxford in the course of a
tour to the West Country. On 11th July he notes:

After dinner I visited that miracle of a youth, Mr Christopher
Wren, nephew of the Bishop of Ely; [and on the 13th of the same
month]: We all dined at that most obliging and universally curious
Dr Wilkins's at Wadham College . . . he had, about in his lodgings
and gallery, variety of shadows, dials, perspectives, and many other
artificial, mathematical, and magical curiosities, a way wiser (i.e. an
instrument for measuring distances travelled), a thermometer, a
monstrous magnet, conic and other sections, a balance on a demi-
circle; most of them of his own and that prodigious young scholar
Mr Christopher Wren: who presented me with a piece of white marble
stained with a lively red, very deep, as beautiful as if it had been
natural.

It is easy to deduce from this Wren's Oxford reputation. Evelyn in these passages initiates that chorus of superlatives in describing Wren which is interesting and important as coming from his contemporaries, but has exercised an unfortunate influence on his biographers.

An amusing anecdote appears in *Parentalia* which tells of a meeting of Wren and Oliver Cromwell at the house of Lady Claypole, the Protector's favourite daughter. Wren's presence there can be attributed to Wilkins, who had married into the Cromwell family, and to Claypole's known interest in mathematics. In the course of dinner the Protector addressed Wren as follows: 'Your uncle,' said he, 'has long been confined in the Tower.' 'He has so, sir, but bears his afflictions with great patience and resignation.' 'He may come out if he will.' 'Will Your Highness permit me to tell him this from your own mouth?' 'Yes, you may.' The young Wren hurried off as soon as he decently could to the Tower to tell his good news to his uncle, only to receive a snubbing for his pains, being informed that 'this was not the first time he [the bishop] had received the like intimation from that miscreant, but disdained the terms projected for his enlargement which were to be a mean acknowledgment of his favour, and an abject submission to his detestable tyranny.'

For the late 1650's and early 1660's we have a considerable mass of information about Wren's scientific work. To the year 1656 belong the experiments in the injection of fluids into the veins of dogs, and an exchange of mathematical pleasantries with the French men of science. About these there is a little mystery. Pascal challenged the English mathematicians to solve a certain problem: this Wren apparently did, or rather provided two geometrical solutions from which the answer could be derived, and returned the challenge by propounding a problem that had been proposed by Kepler. It is suggested that this was by way of irony as implying that the solution of the original challenge was implicit in Kepler and the French ought to have known it. In the next year (1657) Wren received his first important public appointment, as Professor of Astronomy at Gresham College, London, in succession to Lawrence Rooke who was translated to the chair of geometry in the same place. Gresham College was founded at the end of the sixteenth century and consisted of an endowment for professors of divinity, astronomy, geometry, music, law, physic, and rhetoric, and a building containing quarters for the professors, lecture-rooms, laboratories, and an observatory. It seems to have become about this time a close corporation of men of science, for, odd though it sounds, both the Professors of Music and Rhetoric, Dr Petty and Dr Crowne, were primarily physicians, though Dr Petty had so many other administrative interests, especially in Ireland, that he can have been little in London. Wren must have found himself among friends, for of the six other professors four are associated with him in the beginnings of the Royal Society. Gresham College was under the authority of the City of London, and Wren's inaugural lecture bears evidence of his desire to appeal to an audience in part composed of city fathers, in its references to astronomical explanations of scriptural difficulties, and to navigation and sea-borne trade and the greatness of the commercial city. Naviga-tion was a subject to which the astronomy professor had to pay particular attention by the terms of the foundation statutes of the college. It is a pity these formal compliments to the authori-ties should have survived, and not his Wednesday lectures on the astronomy of Kepler, delivered in Latin in the morning, and in English in the afternoon. There are two passages from the inaugural lecture that deserve quotation. One because, as a modern astronomer has said, it is so strangely before its time that we are left wondering what was in Wren's mind:

[Future ages] may find the Galaxy [of stars] to be myriads of them, and every nebulous star appearing as if it were the Firmament of some other World—hang'd in the vast abyss of intermundious vaccuum.

The other as an admirable summing up of the scientific point of view of his time:

Mathematical Demonstrations being built upon the impregnable foundations of Geometry and Arithmetick, are the only Truths, that can sink into the Mind of Man, void of all Uncertainty; and all other Discourses participate more of less of Truth, according as Their Subjects are more or less capable of Mathematical Demonstration.

It would seem from Sprat that Wren's appointment to Gresham College had an effect upon the meetings of the 'experimentall philosophicall Clubbe,' for he says:

About 1658 . . . being call'd away to several parts of the nation, and the greatest number of them coming to London, they usually met at Gresham College, at the Wednesdays and Thursdays lectures of Dr Wren and Mr Rooke, where there joyn'd with them several eminent persons of their common acquaintance, the Lord Viscount Brouncker, the now Lord Brereton, Sir Paul Neile, Mr John Evelyn, Mr Henshaw, Mr Slingsby, Dr Timothy Clark, Dr Ent, Mr Ball, Mr Hill, Dr Crone, and divers other Gentlemen whose inclinations lay the same way. This custom was observ'd once, if not twice a week

in term time till they were scattered by the miserable distractions
of that fatal year; till the continuance of their meetings there might
have made them run the hasard of the fate of Archimedes, for then
the place of their meetings was made a quarter for soldiers.

Two letters from his friend Sprat and his cousin Matthew show
that this was in the confusion following the death of Oliver
Cromwell, and give a lively picture of the desolation of the college
under military occupation.

In the year of his appointment to Gresham College Wren had
been experimenting with his barometer, and in the year following
(1658) he communicated his tracts on the cycloid to Wallis,
who did not publish them till later. In 1659 we find him again
at Oxford attending the classes in chemistry held by Peter
Sthael at the suggestion of Boyle. Wood describes Sthael as
'the noted chemist and Rosicrucian, Peter Sthael of Strasburgh
in royal Prussia, a Lutheran, a great hater of women, and a
very useful man.' Wood himself attended the classes a few
years later, but enumerates the original class, amongst whom,
besides Wren, were Wallis, Millington, Bathurst, Lower, and
John Locke (the philosopher); the last-named, says Wood, 'a
man of turbulent spirit, clamourous and never contented. The
club wrote and took notes from the Mouth of their Master, who
sat at the upper end of a Table; but the said J. Locke scorned to
do it: so that while every man besides at the club were writing,
he would be prating and troublesome.' Some time in 1659,
however, Gresham College must have renewed its sessions, as
we have a note that Wren lectured there on light and refraction.

The Restoration of Charles II in May of 1660 was at first a
relief after the alarms and excursions of the last two years,
though it shortly became a full-blooded reaction. For the Wren
family it was, of course, a great stroke of fortune. The bishop
was released and returned in triumph to Ely, and Cousin Matthew
became secretary to the new Lord Chancellor, Hyde, now Lord
Clarendon. As for Christopher, he duly returned to the new
Dean of Windsor the records of the Order of the Garter, that had
been in his keeping since his father's death at Bletchington in
1656, and continued his work at Gresham College. Moreover:

November 28th of that year [1660] there being then present at his
lecture, William Lord Brouncker, Mr Boyle, Mr Bruce, Sir Robert
Moray, Sir Paul Neile, Dr Wilkins, Dr Goddard, Dr Petty, Mr William
Balle, Mr Rooke, Mr Wren, and Mr Hill, they withdrew afterwards
to Mr Rooke's apartment where they agreed to form themselves into
a Society, and to continue their weekly meetings on Wednesdays at
three o'clock, at Mr Rooke's chambers in the Terms and at other
times at Mr Balles in the Temple.

After Wren's next lecture, on 5th December, Sir Robert Moray, one of the foremost of Charles's advisers on Scotch affairs, brought the news of the king's personal interest in the new society, and on 6th March 1661, it became the Royal Society by charter. *Parentalia* contains a draft preamble for the charter composed by Christopher Wren, who from the first had been most active in working for it. By this time, however, he himself had received academic promotion. On the retirement of Seth Ward he was elected to succeed him as Savilian Professor of Astronomy at Oxford, taking up his duties in May 1661. Later in the year he became D.C.L. at Oxford and a similar degree was conferred on him at Cambridge.

During these early years of the Restoration we have ample evidence of Wren's scientific activities. In 1660 he was ordered by the society to prepare, against the next meeting, for an experiment with the pendulum, the first work of the new body, and to this year belongs the geometrical demonstration of solar eclipses already mentioned. In 1661 he was busy on the eclipses of Jupiter's satellites, and a committee on the production of lenses, and he suggested the use of blacklead as a lubricant for watches; but more important than these, by royal command conveyed by Sir Robert Moray, he was required to make a series of microscopic drawings of insects for the royal collection and also a large-scale globe of the moon, 'representing not only the spots and various degrees of whiteness upon the surface, but the hills, eminences and cavities moulded in solid work. The globe thus fashioned into a true model of the moon, as you turn it to the light, represents all the Monthly phases, with the variety of appearances that happen from the shadows of the mountains and valleys.' The globe was duly constructed, and set up on a fine turned stand of lignum vitae with a scale and a complimentary inscription.

During the latter part of 1661, the whole of 1662, and the first half of 1663, we must suppose Wren as resident in Oxford but making occasional visits to London for meetings of the Royal Society. The list of his works in the Lansdowne MSS. gives 1662 as the date of his Oxford lectures on spheres, on Pascal, and on navigation. The globe of the moon was occupying some of his time, and we know of other scientific work of this period. Willis's *Cerebri Anatome* was published in 1664, for which he had drawn the illustrations, though at what date we do not know. In June of 1663 we have a picture of him at Oxford in Monconys's *Voyage d'Angleterre*, published in 1666. Monconys says:

Besides the College [i.e. All Souls], which I went to see, as I did all

I

the others out of curiosity, I went there even more to see M. Renes
[*sic*] the great Mathematician, though a slight little man, but at the
same time one of the most civil and frank that I have met in England:
for though he was unwilling that his ideas should be made publicke
he did not hesitate to tell me most freely of his weather-clock,

etc., and there follows a descriptive list of apparatus of Wren's
devising, most of which is familiar from other sources.

Chapter 2

The Sheldonian Theatre—The Profession of Architecture in the Seventeenth
    Century—The Visit to Paris—The First St Paul's Scheme—The Fire
    of London and the Rebuilding of the City—Contemporary Architects—
    Appointment as Royal Surveyor—The Office of Works—Sir John
    Denham—Hugh May—Wren's First Marriage.

IN these first years of the Restoration, while Wren was resident
in Oxford, Archbishop Sheldon decided to present to the university a new building in which the university ceremonies might
be conducted, especially the 'Act,' as it was called, when the
M.A. degree was conferred with much ceremony including
speeches. Formerly, the ceremonies, with all their attendant
undergraduate levity, had been held in the University Church.
Wren was asked to make a design. This was in 1662, for a model
was finished and shown by him to the Royal Society by April
1663. About the same time Bishop Wren presented a new chapel
to Pembroke College, Cambridge, the foundation stone of which
was laid in May 1663. We have no documentary evidence that
Wren designed it, though the association of the Wren family with
the building, and certain detail resemblances to the Sheldonian
Theatre, make it more than probable. There is, however, one
point worth mentioning: *Parentalia* omits this chapel from the list
of his works at Cambridge and only refers to it in connection with
Bishop Wren. It is indeed a relatively small and unambitious
though delightful building, and, though it is almost certainly
Wren's first executed work, it has not for a student the importance of the Oxford work. This was a grand affair and
appealed to the imagination of Wren's time in quite a remarkable
degree. To understand this appeal it should be borne in mind
that it is a building of considerable size, measuring internally
eighty feet by seventy feet, and is with Inigo Jones's Banqueting
Hall, Whitehall, and his church of St Paul's, Covent Garden, one
of the largest buildings of the class that includes churches and

public halls—all buildings, that is, where a single internal space
is the chief element of the design, as contrasted with multiple-
space buildings (e.g. houses, palaces, offices, etc., with many
rooms or spaces)—that had been erected since the introduction
of fully developed Italian architecture fifty years before.   More
than this, the design appealed most happily to both the ruling
intellectual fashions of the day, the interest in and admiration for
Roman antiquity, and, even more important, the enthusiasm for
all things scientific and intellectually ingenious.   The design was
based on Sebastian Serlio's account of the antique theatre of
Marcellus at Rome.   Serlio, an Italian architect of the mid-
sixteenth century, was the most important architectural writer
available to Wren in an English translation.   The plan of the
theatre of Marcellus, as of all Roman theatres, was a D with the
seats for the audience ranged round the inside of the curve, the
actors ranged along the straight side facing them.   The whole,
in Roman examples, was unroofed and covered with a flat awning
of canvas.   Wren, wishing to get the same internal effect in a
roofed building, devised an ingenious timber truss which enabled
him to span the great space with a flat ceiling, without any
columns or piers to support it between the outside walls.   This
truss was Wren's variant solution of the problem of Wallis's
geometrical flat floor that had been engaging the attention of his
teachers when he first came to Oxford, and it was this that excited
the admiration of the men of science and is the reason why the
model of the building was exhibited to the Royal Society.   The
reference to the awning over a Roman theatre was enforced by
the painting on the ceiling which represented the cordage and
canvas of an awning drawn aside to admit of a view of allegorical
figures, executed with all that display of perspective and fore-
shortening, the mathematical aspect of painting, that the age
delighted in.   There were also original ingenuities in the construction of the attic windows and the semi-circular ventilators
of the main storey, which are noted with admiration by contemporaries.

The Sheldonian Theatre has not received from modern writers
on Wren the attention it deserves; we are blasé about spans of
seventy feet now made easy by modern materials; the external
proportions of the buildings are not altogether happy and, moreover, have not been improved by the nineteenth-century restoration.   But the seventeenth-century critics regarded it as one of
the most important of his buildings, and in the eighteenth-
century *Parentalia* it occupies a foremost place in the list of his

works. The defects of the exterior are not confined to those of
the major proportions: there is a very natural clumsiness in the
handling of the classic *motifs* of the façade as well as in the treatment of the rounded sides. Wren's was one of the greatest minds
that ever turned to architecture, but even he could not master
the technique of Baroque composition at one stroke, and in detail
he succeeded far better with the simpler design problems of the
Pembroke Chapel façade. There is an entry in Evelyn's *Diary*,
which gives a description of the opening of the Sheldonian when
Evelyn was extremely shocked by the jokes of the semi-official
university buffoon. It was partly the activity of this func-
tionary that had prompted Sheldon to provide new quarters for
the 'Act.'

Though Pembroke Chapel and the Sheldonian are Wren's first
executed buildings, it seems probable that the authorities had
consulted him on questions of constructional engineering as early
as 1661. *Parentalia* refers to the offer of an appointment to
'Survey and direct the works of the Mole, Harbour and Fortifications of the Citadel and Town of Tangier,' which had come into
English possession as part of the dowry of Queen Catherine of
Braganza. The offer was made through Cousin Matthew, the
Lord Chancellor's secretary, and suggested that, in addition to
an ample salary, Wren would be granted special leave from the
university and, further, offered the reversion of the office of
Surveyor-General of the Royal Works; that is, the promise that
on the death of Sir John Denham, the then surveyor, Wren should
succeed him. The offer was declined, in the words of *Parentalia*,
'[being not then consistent with his health] but [he] humbly
prayed his Majesty to allow of his excuse and to command his
duty in England.' We are not certain of the date of this offer,
but a letter by Sprat from Oxford, telling how Dr Bayly, the
Vice-Chancellor, had complained of Wren's absence from his pro-
fessorial duties, refers to Tangier and to the repairing of St Paul's
as occupying Wren's time and keeping him in London, and must
date from 1661, the last year in which Dr Bayly was Vice-
Chancellor. September 1661 is also the date of the fitting out of
the naval expedition to take over Tangier. It is probable that
these employments are the foundation of the persistent tradition
that Wren was appointed deputy surveyor for Sir John Denham
as early as 1661, for which there is otherwise no evidence at all.

Both the Tangier appointment and St Paul's, being specially
matters of constructional engineering, make it easier to understand how Wren slipped into architecture from pure science in a

way that seems curious to our modern ideas of what an architect should be. Wren, with his skill as a draughtsman—witness his anatomical drawings for Willis's book—his mathematical attainments, and mechanical ingenuity, would appear to the seventeenth century as peculiarly adapted to the profession of architecture, given a reasonable business administrative ability and an interest in the art. That Wren should have cared to interest himself in architecture may seem remarkable to a generation that tends to regard a man of science as of a superior order of creation to such a thing as an architect, but to the seventeenth century, and indeed to the sixteenth, and even the fifteenth century in Italy, architecture was a learned pursuit and, moreover, one not unallied to science. The Italian type of architecture that Inigo Jones had introduced into England was distinguished from the rule of thumb building tradition by the system of design—the very word is used first in English in Jones's time—worked out in rules and principles which seemed to the men of those times to be the reduction of a visual art to order and natural laws. It seemed to promise that art also, which we associate with the ideas of romance, inspiration, and arbitrary taste, could be brought completely within the power of reason. Even the, to us, dreary mathematical game of linear perspective seemed to them another instalment of the conquest of art by mathematical reason. These considerations gave to architecture a very different intellectual standing from that which it enjoys to-day.

In 1665, Wren got his next job as an architect to design a block of students' rooms for Trinity College, Oxford. Some drawings of this building are extant, though the block itself has been altered and added to out of all recognition. The drawings show a pleasant, fairly simple, well-planned block with well-spaced windows and good general proportions, but is chiefly remarkable for the form of its roof, a French double sloped roof or mansard, which is the more interesting in view of the persistent French influence on Wren's work throughout his career. In this instance it must have come through picture-books; but in a letter about this building written to Dr Bathurst, the president of the college, we get a reference to a visit to France, the only occasion, as far as we know, that Wren left England.

From the letter it appears that some work was to go forward in Wren's absence, in which case a good deal of reliance must have been placed in Minchin, the builder, though this would be quite in accordance with the customs of the time. It is interesting to note that Minchin came from Bletchington. This is not the first

reference we have to the French visit, for in a letter of Evelyn's
to Wren, asking him to recommend a man to be a tutor for his
son, and written in April 1665, he mentions that Sir John Denham, the Royal Surveyor, had told him of Wren's intended
journey. The letter to Bathurst mentions Mansard and Bernini,
and the absence of any reference to the French men of science he
might hope to meet may perhaps be taken as a sign of Wren's
changing interests. Bernini was the greatest name in architecture and sculpture of his age; he had ten years before completed the great piazza before St Peter's in Rome, and François
Mansard's work at Maisons and his Parisian churches are perhaps
the finest Renaissance buildings in France. For an architect it
was just the right moment to visit Paris where the whole artistic
world was humming with architectural activity and gossip.
Louis XIV had decided to embark on the completion of the Palace
of the Louvre; he had obtained designs from Rainaldi and Cor-
tona, Bernini's most important contemporaries in Rome, all the
French architects were producing schemes, and Bernini himself
had arrived in Paris by special invitation at the end of May.
Besides all this, great works were already in progress, mainly by
Le Vau, an architect only inferior to Mansard in distinction and
certainly more successful in retaining court favour.

The French visit is described in a letter from Wren to his
friend, Dr Bateman, probably the Fellow of Merton College of
that name, which is given in extracts in the *Parentalia*. In it
Wren describes the intense activity in all departments of art in
the Paris of the time, especially remarking the personal supervision of the great Colbert who 'comes to the works of the
Louvre every Wednesday and, if business hinders not, Thursday.'
And the regularity of the workmen's pay-day, a sore point in
Wren's later career. He passes not altogether favourable comments on Le Vau's Collège des Quatre Nations and the earlier
building at Versailles, and gives a list of the buildings he visited,
adding also: 'Mons. Abbé Charles introduced me to the acquaintance of Bernini who showed me his designs of the Louvre
and of the King's statue.' Adding again later in the letter:

I shall bring you almost all *France* in Paper, which I found by some
or other ready design'd to my Hand, in which I have spent both
Labour and some Money. *Bernini's* Design of the *Louvre* I would
have given my Skin for, but the old reserv'd *Italian* gave me but a
few Minutes View; it was five little Designs in Paper, for which he
hath receiv'd as many thousand Pistoles; I had only Time to copy
it in my Fancy and Memory; I shall be able by Discourse, and a
Crayon, to give you a tolerable Account of it. I have purchas'd a

great deal of *Tailledouce*, that I might give our *Country-men* Examples
of Ornaments and Grotesks, in which the *Italians* themselves confess
the *French* to excel. I hope I shall give you a very good Account
of all the best Artists of *France*; my Business now is to pry into Trades
and Arts, I put myself into all Shapes to humour them; 'tis a Comedy
to me, and tho' sometimes expenceful, I am loth yet to leave it.

There are various curious points about this letter, but perhaps
the most striking is that all the buildings mentioned in it are, with
one exception, palaces, châteaux, or great garden schemes. Presumably before the Fire of London the chances of doing much in
the way of church architecture would seem remote to Wren, but
still his interest was already, to some degree, engaged at St Paul's,
and the omission is surprising. He does not confine himself to
very recent buildings, and some of those mentioned, as Écouen
and Chantilly, date back to the end of the sixteenth century and
the first introduction of developed Renaissance architecture into
France. That he saw and studied the great domed churches of
the early and middle seventeenth century is certain from the
evidence of his own work. They were in fact the only domed
buildings that Wren can ever have seen except his own. But
the things that interested him most seem to have been the
Louvre works, and of those he seems to have been as much impressed by the organization and the technical engineering problems of moving great stones as by the actual designs or his
interview with Bernini. This is apparent from his references in
his later report on St Paul's. Of the personalities mentioned in
the letter, the most interesting, Abbé Charles, who introduced
Wren to Bernini, defies identification.

Parentalia says that in the early part of the letter the recipient
is thanked for an introduction to Lord St Albans, famous as the
devoted friend of Queen Henrietta-Maria and perhaps the most
important go-between of the English and French courts. A
better introduction could hardly have been desired. Lord St
Albans had himself a considerable interest in architecture and
was the chief promoter of the development of St James's Square
and the adjacent areas, in which Jermyn Street preserves his
name. From Boyle we learn that Wren got back to London
towards the end of February.

After his return from Paris, Wren busied himself with a report
on the renovation of St Paul's, which he presented to the king,
together with drawings illustrating his proposals, on 1st May.
The report and some of the drawings, rather elaborate finished
affairs as befitted drawings prepared for his Majesty, are still
extant. Briefly, the scheme was to complete the restoration of

the nave and transepts, begun by Inigo Jones who had refaced
them externally and added the great portico at the west.   Wren
now proposed to reface the interior, using a great order of Corinthian pilasters embracing both the arcade and triforium arches,
and to replace the medieval vault with a new brick one consisting
of a series of shallow saucer domes above a series of rather small
clerestory windows.   The vault scheme was not unlike the one
eventually carried out in the new church.   But the most revolutionary proposal in the report was the substitution of a dome at
the crossing of nave, choir, and transepts for the celebrated great
central tower.   This dome was much taller in proportion to its
internal width than the one we know, and would presumably
have produced on a spectator at floor level rather the effect of
being at the bottom of a well.   It was to consist of an inner
dome and lantern of stone or brick, and an outer one of timber
springing from about one-third way up the curve of the inner.
By this means Wren was able to get a total external height of
some 360 feet.   The whole scheme of the dome seems to be based
on the dome of the Church of the Sorbonne in Paris, begun by
Lemercier in 1635, but Wren had also derived some features
from the pictures of Bramante's design for the dome of St Peter's
as published in Serlio's book.   The great external height of the
dome and lantern was no doubt occasioned by the celebrity of the
old central tower as a landmark to Londoners: indeed, in his
report, Wren suggests that the new dome should be built round
and outside the old tower, 'partly because the expectations of
persons are to be kept up; for many unbelievers would bewail
the loss of old Paul's steeple, and despond if they did not see a
hopeful successor rise in its stead,' but chiefly as a means of
economizing scaffolding in the new operations.   And Evelyn
gives an account of how a committee visited the church in
August and supported Wren against the majority of expert
opinion as to the necessity of replacing the central tower.

Within a week of this meeting the Fire of London broke out,
and on the second day of the fire 'the stones of Pauls flew like
grenadoes, the melting lead running down the streets in a stream,'
and on the 7th September, Evelyn notes:

At my return I was infinitely concerned to find that goodly Church,
St Paul's, now a sad ruin, and that beautiful portico (for structure
comparable to any in Europe, as not long before repaired by the late
King) now rent in pieces, flakes of vast stone split asunder, and
nothing remaining entire but the inscription in the architrave, showing by whom it was built, which had not one letter of it defaced.   It
was astonishing to see what immense stones the heat had in a manner

calcined, so that all the ornaments, columns, friezes, capitals, and projectures of massy Portland stone, flew off, even to the very roof, where a sheet of lead covering a great space (no less than six acres by measure) was totally melted. The ruins of the vaulted roof falling, broke into St Faith's [i.e. the crypt], which being filled with the magazines of books belonging to the Stationers, and carried thither for safety, they were all consumed, burning for a week following.

Within a few days of the disaster, Wren presented to the king a scheme for laying out a new city. His was the first of several such, his friends Evelyn and Hooke producing them among others. The practical importance of these plans can easily be exaggerated. They are all rather in the nature of ideal cities. The urgency of the situation, the need of rehousing the tens of thousands of homeless people, and of doing something at once to mitigate the dislocation of all business, made it impossible to contemplate the delays entailed in laying out a complete new system of streets regardless of the existing foundations, water conduits and drains, as well as the legal complications of the adjustment of the new site values to existing property rights. An absolute monarch might have overcome some of these difficulties, but the City of London was the least amenable of all Charles's domains to arbitrary treatment by the central government. All these schemes are interesting as expressions of the town-planning ideals of the time, and Wren's plan, which is by far the most ingenious and imaginative, is a *tour de force*, considering that it was produced in about four days, but its practical possibilities in the circumstances of the moment were negligible. Even the quay or embankment from London Bridge to Black-friars Bridge, the idea of which was common to both Wren and Evelyn, though it was made part of the London Buildings Acts and pressed by the Crown and seems to have got some way to accomplishment, failed to materialize completely. One result, however, may perhaps be attributed to Wren's promptitude in presenting his plan to the king; he was appointed with Roger Pratt and Hugh May as one of the representatives of the Government to treat with the city authorities with regard to the re-building. It would seem probable that it is to these men that we owe the framing of the Building Acts and other regulations which not only governed the rebuilding of the city, but served as a standard to builders and clients all over the country. In the Pratt MSS. is an account of the first work of these Commissioners:

His Majesty King Charles the 2nd was pleased out of his owne meere motion to appoint his Surveyour for ye present Mr Hugh May, Doctor Renne, and myselfe to be his Commissioners to treat with such as the Citty should think fit to nominate about the more quick

* I

and orderly reedification of the Citty, who sente to us Mr Milles their Surveyour and Mr Hooke Professor of ye Mathematics in Gresham Colledge, and Mr Germain an experienced man in buildings.

This committee began work at the beginning of October, and at our third meeting October the 11, upon the motion of some of the Lords of ye Council, who resolved to sitt to heare the progresse of our affaires every Tuesday in the afternoon, wee resolved the breadth of the several future streetes.

Wren must have been a busy man in those next few months, for we have evidence of his works for the Royal Society and we know him to have been a good deal in Oxford, presumably attending to the duties of his professorship. How arduous the duties of the Commissioners may have been after the first rush of work it is hard to tell, but Hugh May is allowed to have a deputy at the Office of Works by reason of his 'extraordinary business' in March 1667, and Pratt was knighted in July 1668, one may suppose in recognition of his services. It is possible that Pratt and May were at first the most active members of the Commission. Wren's eventual emergence as by far the most important of the three has obscured the whole matter. Undoubtedly at this time both the other men had more experience of actual building practice than he, and works to their credit of a size and in quality of design, if not in constructional ingenuity, at least the equal if not the superior of his. Moreover, May was an official of the Office of Works of some years' standing. The whole question of Wren's architectural rivals was to become acute in the course of the next three years, and we shall have to return to it when the time comes of Wren's appointment as Surveyor-General of the Works. By that time, however, Pratt was out of the running, for that fortunate man inherited an estate in Norfolk in 1667, married a rich wife in 1668, and in 1669, the year of Wren's appointment, began on his own property his last architectural work, a house for himself. It is possible that the fall of Clarendon, Pratt's patron, in August 1667 had some effect on his retirement from architectural practice, more especially as the great house he had built for the minister had played an unfortunate part in the political attacks that caused his ruin. In any case, Pratt's retirement removed an important rival from out of Wren's way, and one whom we know to have been interested in that branch of architecture which Wren was to make especially his own—church building. We know from a letter in the Pratt MSS. that hopes were entertained in certain quarters, about 1666, that he might be architect to St Paul's, and with Clarendon's influence in all church affairs to back him he might indeed have had a good chance of the job. Amongst his papers there are notes on church design in relation to St Paul's, and criticisms of some of Wren's schemes, dating from the early seventies, that show he still retained his interest in the problem after his retirement.

Of Wren's known architectural activities between the Fire and his appointment to the Office of Works in March 1669, the most important is Emmanuel College Chapel at Cambridge. The design dates from the end of 1666 or early the next year, to judge from the extant letters, and the work was put in hand early in 1668. Wren's buildings include, besides the actual chapel, wings flanking the chapel façade and forming an arcaded side to the court. The character of the design is still rather immature and has very definite signs of French influence in the management of the roofs of the wings. Another building of this time given in the most authoritative list of his works is the new Customs House in London. The list gives it under the date 1668, and there is mention of Wren's name in connection with it in the Treasury Papers of that year. It would seem that Wren was acting with the Office of Works in this matter, for Denham and May are the names which appear most often, and this may account for the persistent legend that Wren was an official of the works before March 1669. The building was burnt early in the eighteenth century; but we know that it was admired for the convenience of its planning, though, to judge from an engraving, the external effect, which was Dutch rather than French, shows an inability to handle the Renaissance apparatus of design that is quite consistent with Wren's authorship, bearing in mind the clumsiness of his other designs for large buildings in this early period.

Two other works of this time must be mentioned, Wren's report on Salisbury Cathedral (1668), drawn up for his friend, Seth Ward, now bishop there, and his report on St Paul's after the Fire. This last has a certain importance. It is clear from it that the effects of the Fire had made the old scheme quite impossible. The Gothic choir, where the vaults had fallen and crashed through into the crypt, was now in a worse state than the nave that had so concerned the commissioners before the disaster. It is equally clear that the financial outlook did not warrant any very ambitious schemes for the present. Parliament had imposed a tax of one shilling per chaldron on coal coming into London in 1666, but the proceeds of this had to cover such a number of pressing jobs that there can have been little hope of St Paul's getting much for a long time. The same applies to the

rebuilding of the parish churches of the city, for the eventual
rebuilding of which Wren seems to have been appointed architect
as early as 1666. Most of the money allotted to the cathedral
and the parish churches out of the tax must have been required
for the clearing of the ruins and the provision of temporary
accommodation pending better times. Wren's report on St Paul's
is indeed mainly concerned with these two points, especially the
question of the position of the temporary building within the
ruins. His advice was apparently followed. In 1668 we have
two letters to Wren at Oxford from Sancroft, the Dean of St
Paul's, a close friend to whose good offices he seems to have owed
his employment at Emmanuel College. The first is mainly concerned with the state of the ruins and the difficulties they were
having in patching up a temporary building. This is in April.
The second letter, dated 2nd July, suggests that some attempt at
beginning a new church should be made, part to be built as immediately necessary and to encourage contributions that might make
possible the completion of the whole. On 29th July the king
issued an order to the commissioners to take down the eastern
parts of the church and the tower, and to clear the way for a new
choir, though the order enjoins that special care should be taken
of the western parts of the church with a view to re-using the
material in the new building. Both Sancroft's letters are urgent
in their demand that Wren should return to London. One other
curious little document survives from these years, quite unrelated
to Wren's other activities. It is an engraved view, by Wen-
ceslaus Hollar, of Windsor Castle from the north, dated 1667. It
is an interesting and charming example of Wren as a landscape
draughtsman and, as far as is known, the only one.

On 5th March 1669 the Surveyor-General of the Works, Sir
John Denham, addressed a letter to Lord Arlington, the Secretary
of State, as follows:

> You will find that I have power to make my deputie during my
> life. And accordingly by the King's desire intimated to me by my
> Ld Duke of Buckingham I have deputed this bearer Dr Christopher
> Wren my sole deputie with a revocation of any verbal deputations
> (though I know of none) if Mr May or any else pretend, it was without
> my knowledge or consent in the time of my sicknesse or absence.

The grant was made next day, and makes mention of Sir John's
ill health. On 19th March he died, and Wren succeeded to his
office. This was great promotion, for to be Surveyor-General was
the greatest official position to which an architect could aspire.

The Office of Works, of which Wren now became the head, had

been re-established at the Restoration as consisting of the surveyor and the comptroller, the two great officers, the patent
artisans, as the king's master mason, the king's master carpenter,
the sergeant plumber, etc., the paymaster, the clerk engrosser,
who was required to have some knowledge of architecture, the
purveyor and four clerks of the works of which that of Whitehall
was the most important. The business of the office was first of
all the care of the royal residences, and this included what may
be compared to the duties of a borough surveyor in all those parts
of London round about Westminster and St James's that were
royal property. The office was also called upon for innumerable
jobs of varying importance, as the altering and fitting up of
rooms, offices, and lodgings in the government buildings which
were all nominally part of the royal residences. These jobs varied
from looking after detail repairs of offices to contriving and carrying out the adaptation of state rooms as theatres for court entertainments, and designing the mounting and *décor* of the operas
and plays performed there. It also included the fitting up of
places for great state functions, as Westminster Hall for a state
trial or the Abbey for a coronation or royal funeral. Besides all
this, any royal building undertakings on a grand scale were
usually designed by the surveyor or comptroller and carried out
by the office. The whole organization, the internal working of
which is rather obscure, had been overhauled in 1662–3, when the
salaries of the officers had been increased to reduce the temptation
to perquisites and other unofficial sources of remuneration.

In Sir John Denham's time the chief officers had been an
obscure Francis Weathered the comptroller and Hugh May the
paymaster. May had succeeded to the comptroller's position in
July 1668. The situation had been complicated by the ill health
of the surveyor who suffered from an attack of temporary insanity
in 1666, and by the pretensions of John Webb. These were well
founded, for Webb, who had been trained under Inigo Jones, was
certainly the best educated architect of the time in the modern
sense, and especially an expert in matters theatrical, in which his
training under Jones, a great theatre designer, gave him a great
prestige. Webb enjoyed considerable court patronage after the
Restoration, being employed to design the new palace at Greenwich and to stage the grand production of *Mustapha* in a new
theatre of his own contriving at Whitehall in 1666. Denham
himself has suffered in reputation from his position coming
between Inigo Jones and Wren. He was, however, a considerable
poet, and there is every reason to believe that he was a perfectly

competent official. The one work of architecture known to be
by him, Old Burlington House, is a not particularly distinguished
but perfectly creditable building typical of its time. His work
was in the main administrative, and there was some evidence of
his interest in town planning and street improvement.

Not unnaturally this elevation of Wren over the heads of
Webb and May did not pass without protest. Among the State
Papers is a most interesting document, unfortunately without a
date, in which Webb recounts his services to the Crown since the
Restoration, tells how Sir John Denham obstructed the grant of
his reversion of the surveyorship, and protests that he 'cannot
now act under Mr Wren, who is by far his inferior, but if joined
in the patent with him, will instruct him in the course of the
Office of Works, of which he professes ignorance.' This sounds
odd in view of the astonishing achievements of Wren's career
at the Office of Works, but at the time it was written was a perfectly reasonable plea. To a man like Webb, brought up strictly
as an architect under Inigo Jones, Wren's extant works in 1669
must have seemed very barbarous and uninstructed. As far as
we know, nothing was done to compensate Webb for this disappointment. Presumably the Greenwich commission was considered enough. With Hugh May, things were rather different.
On 21st March 1669, Pepys notes:

> Met with Mr May, who tells me the story of his being put by Sr
> John Denham's place, of Surveyor of the King's Works, who, it seems
> is lately dead, by the unkindness of the Duke of Buckingham, who
> hath brought in Dr Wren: though, he tells me, he hath been his
> servant for twenty years together, in all his wants and dangers,
> saving him from want of bread by his care and management, and
> with a promise of having his help in his advancement, and an engage-
> ment under his hand for £1,000, not yet paid, and yet the Duke of
> Buckingham is so ungrateful as to put him by: which is an ill thing,
> though Dr Wren is a worthy man. But he tells me the King is kind
> to him, and hath promised him a pension of £300 a year out of the
> Works; which will be of more content to him than the place, which
> under their present wants of money is a place that disobliges most
> people, being not able to do what they desire to their lodgings.

And three days later is the document in the State Papers con-
firming the extra £300 a year 'as a mark of the King's gracious
acceptance of his services.' As May had been promoted comptroller in the July before, he was ultimately very well placed; but
as if this were not enough, in the following year (1670) he was given
two more jobs, one of which, the Inspectorship of French and
English Gardeners at Whitehall, St James's, and Hampton Court,
carried a salary of £200. The comedy of Hugh May's compensa-

tions does not end here, for on 29th November 1673, just eighteen days after the issue of letters patent authorizing the commissioners to proceed with a scheme of a new St Paul's and nominating Wren as the architect, May was appointed architect for the large works of reconstruction at Windsor Castle. It would seem that someone had a very bad conscience about the appointment of Christopher Wren.

On 7th December 1669, Wren was married in the Temple Church to Faith Coghill, daughter of Sir Thomas Coghill of Bletchington. His wife was thirty-three when they married and it is to be supposed that they had known each other since childhood. Sir Thomas Coghill was the squire of Bletchington, and his house had been garrisoned during the Civil War and captured by Cromwell in 1645. We have one letter, dated 14th June, but no year, written by Wren to his future wife, one of the few intimate personal documents of his that have survived.

MADAM,—The artificer having never before mett with a drowned Watch, like an ignorant physician has been soe long about the cure that he hath made me very unquiet that your commands should be soe long deferred; however, I have sent the watch at last and envie the felicity of it, that it should be soe neer your side, and soe often enjoy your eye, and be consulted by you how your Time shall passe while you employ your hand in your excellent workes. But have a care of it, for I put such a spell into it that every Beating of the Ballance will tell you 'tis the pulse of my Heart which labours as much to serve you and more Trewly than the watch; for the watch I believe will sometimes lie, and sometimes be idle and unwilling to goe, having received so much injury by being drenched in that briny bath, that I despair it should ever be a Trew servant to you more. But as for me (unless you drown me too in my teares) you may be confident I shall never cease to be

Your most affectionate, humble servant,

CHR. WREN.

Wren had a house in Scotland Yard where the Office of Works was accommodated, and to which Denham had made additions, and there presumably Wren and his wife took up their residence.

No special mention has so far been made of Wren's scientific work during the years 1664–9. These years would seem to have been among his most active in that field, but the chronology of his communications to the Royal Society and his experiments is rather confused. It seems that Wren is often producing the results of long past work that he has set on one side, so that it is very hard to arrive at any orderly sequence in his scientific interests. Moreover, the publication of the *Philosophical Transactions* by the society, which begins in 1664, encouraged

such resurrections, and from a biographer's point of view almost
adds to the confusion. Certain work mentioned in the MS.
list under 1669 may really be the publication of the results of
work done as much as ten years earlier. Some points, however,
stand out. There is extant a discourse to the society, which
would seem to date from 1664, outlining a programme of work
and strongly advocating the use of the society's organization for
the systematic collection of data, especially meteorological. The
following year the society set up committees for different sciences,
Wren being nominated a member of three of them, mechanics,
astronomy, and the general committee, which seems to have
covered the fields suggested in his discourse. About this time,
i.e. just before his visit to Paris, he and Robert Hooke were
working together on the determination of the paths of comets.
Eventually Hooke published the results of their work with due
acknowledgments to his friend. Another astronomical problem
which was occupying him about 1667 was the measuring of the
diameters of planets. In 1668–9 we have news of further work
on the cycloid and on the laws of motion, when Wren was in
touch with Huygens through the society, and this latter work
seems to have been his main preoccupation in the months
immediately preceding his appointment as Surveyor-General of
the Works.

Besides these major scientific interests, Wren, who had been
elected to the Council of the Society in 1666, seems to have concerned himself with a number of minor problems of very various
importance. The remarks of the editors of Robert Hooke's
Diary on the nature of Hooke's work for the society apply in a
considerable degree to Wren also:

His occupation almost forbade a systematic investigation of any
one problem. He had to serve a group of men of widely varying
interests, many of whom were merely dilettantes seeking amusement,
all of whom had an insatiable curiosity in almost any and every
aspect of natural phenomena. The early records of the Society's
activities present a weird agglomeration of trivialities and discoveries
which the attrition of subsequent investigation has shown to be of
basic importance.

Among these minor activities are his communication of the details
of a new kind of lamp, of a level for taking the horizon of a circle,
and one, in the form of a letter from Oxford, on the strangely
diseased bones in a boy's head there. To these may be added a
second edition of the lunar globe he had made for the king, and
a communication on the form of grain elevators used at Danzig.
Also, just after the Fire, when the society had perforce left

Gresham College, which had been taken over by the city authorities as temporary offices, he and Hooke were both concerned in the design of a proposed building for the society on a site that was offered them by a rich and generous member. Nothing, however, seems to have come of this scheme, presumably for lack of money.

Chapter 3

Periods of Wren's Architectural Career—Hooke's Diary—The City Churches —Secular Buildings of the Seventies—Trinity College Library, Cambridge—Charles's Mausoleum Design—St Paul's first model—St Paul's Second Model—St Paul's Warrant Design—Wren and Hooke— Death of Lady Wren—Wren's Second Marriage—Births of his Children.

WITH his appointment as surveyor-general, and, what is perhaps more important, the increase of the coal tax to 3s. per chaldron in 1670, Wren's architectural career develops so largely that it overshadows all his other activities; and in 1673 he resigned his position as Savilian Professor at Oxford. It is possible to divide Wren's buildings into four periods; the first, early one, before 1670, which has already been discussed. Then the second period, from 1670 to 1687; the third, from 1687 to 1700; and the last, after 1700. The justification for the break at 1687 is shown in the figures of the distribution of money derived from the coal tax. From 1670 to 1687, £88,468 14s. 3d. went to St Paul's and £264,206 2s. 9d. to the city churches; from 1687 to 1700 St Paul's received £147,674 17s. 4d. and the city churches only £53,300. To the second period, then, belongs the bulk of the city church work, and after 1675 the beginnings at St Paul's and the series of non-ecclesiastical buildings, as Trinity College Library, Cambridge (1676), Chelsea Hospital (1682), the palace at Winchester (1683), and the work at Whitehall for James II (1685). The third period includes the main work at St Paul's and much that is most important in the design, also Hampton Court and the beginnings at Greenwich Hospital. After 1700 the finishing of St Paul's and the continuation of Greenwich are the main concerns.

The second period is the most interesting and important, for in its early years Wren was developing very rapidly from the inexperienced, rather amateurish designer of the first buildings to the great master of the mature designs. It would be difficult to exaggerate the part played by the city churches in this development. Wren is distinguished among architects, not only by his natural gifts and early distinction as a man of science, but also by the timing of his opportunities. It was a stroke of extra-ordinary good fortune that gave him the city churches to design just when he had finally devoted himself to architecture, and an even greater that the carrying out of the St Paul's design was delayed until the experience on the city churches had been di-gested. For it was his work on the city churches that helped to develop that superb gift for space composition that distinguishes the completed St Paul's, to mention only one of the many benefits he derived from it.

During a large part of this second period we have more direct knowledge of Wren's personal life than at any other time, from the Diary of Robert Hooke, which runs from 1672 to 1680. Hooke was acting throughout this time as Wren's assistant, and receiving a salary from him, as he himself puts it, 'on ye City Churches account.' In addition to this he was a close personal friend, dining with him frequently, going to coffee-houses with him even more frequently—Stukeley remarks that Wren and Hooke were notorious for the amount of coffee they drank— walking with him in the park and discussing all manner of scientific and general matters. It is a little difficult to be certain what Hooke's duties were in regard to the city churches. The statement in *Parentalia* that he was employed to survey the sites is almost certainly untrue as a description of his work, for there were other less distinguished men who were paid for that job at fixed rates. In the Diary, Hooke frequently mentions visits to the churches in course of construction, sometimes with Wren or the other assistant, Woodruffe, sometimes by himself. He certainly had a great deal to do with the contracts and agree-ments with the craftsmen, and sometimes, as at St Stephen's, Walbrook, he passes the accounts instead of Wren, though more often he and Wren go through them together. During the period of the Diary, Hooke has also his work as city surveyor and his own practice as an architect; building Bedlam Hospital (one of the largest undertakings of the time), Montagu House (on the site now occupied by the British Museum), a new building for the College of Physicians (including the celebrated demonstrating theatre), and several country and town houses. This is not an exhaustive list. With Wren, in a degree of collaboration it is difficult to determine, he designed the Monument in 1673. Be-sides Hooke, Wren had other assistants, as Woodruffe and Oliver, whose names appear from time to time in the accounts.

The work on the city churches began with a rush. Seventeen

were started in 1670 and within six years there were twenty-eight in hand. Considering his other duties, as surveyor-general for example, it is not surprising that Wren required assistants, or that the work is less finished and of a lower standard on the whole than we find in his later buildings, especially St Paul's. But another point must be made: it is not clear how far Wren was responsible for the interior finish and the fittings of the churches; certainly the vestries had a very considerable say in the matter, though equally certainly Wren was often consulted and could keep a general control over the appearance of his work. The churches vary very much in importance and ambition. Three stand out from among the first undertaken as especially note-worthy—St Lawrence, Jewry; St Mary-le-Bow; and St Stephen's, Walbrook. All three were more costly and ambitious than the average, and the last two may well be considered the first works in which Wren showed the quality of his genius. Both these buildings are distinguished for the arrangement of their interior spaces. St Stephen's is an extraordinarily subtle and ingenious combination of the dome with a rectangular plan, so that not only is a real effect of breadth of space given by the dome, but the interior is given a definite axis east to west. With St Paul's it is the work of Wren that has had the greatest reputation with foreign critics. St Mary-le-Bow is chiefly celebrated for its tower and spire design, but the body of the church is also interesting. Hawksmoor, Wren's chief assistant in later life, says that the internal arrangement is derived from the Temple of Peace, a Roman building published by Serlio among others, on which Wren also based the relation of the order and arches at St Paul's. At Bow Church the same system is employed for the order and arches, but the resemblances to the Temple of Peace go much further, for the arches open into three large barrel-vaulted bays linked to each other by small connecting arches, and it is in this essential quality of the main arrangement of internal spaces that it derives from the Temple of Peace as well as in the treatment of the order. The tower, lantern, and spire of St Mary-le-Bow are too complicated an arrangement of forms to be described here. The tower and steeple stand largely detached from the main body of the church facing on to the neighbouring main street, and on the ground level form part of an entrance vestibule to the church. In them the richness of Wren's invention displays itself to the greatest advantage. In succeeding years Wren produced an extraordinary number of fine tower and lantern or steeple designs; his fecundity in this vein is one of the most striking qualities of

his work as a whole; but, though many of the later examples are
more accomplished than this, it would be hard to say that any is
more successful. St Mary-le-Bow was begun in 1670, the tower
a year later, and St Stephen's, Walbrook, in 1672.

The reference to Bow steeple raises the whole question of
Wren's towers and spires. In general these are later than the
churches and some of the finest belong to the latter part of our
third period and even to the fourth. Such are the lovely steeple
of St Vedast (1697) and the lantern of St Magnus (1705), two of
the finest things he ever achieved and belonging in time rather
with the western towers of St Paul's than with St Mary-le-Bow.
Other striking examples are St Edmund the King, Christ Church,
Newgate Street, and St Bride's, for all of which we have evidence
of a stage in their history or designs when the towers were not
determined or were much inferior to those actually built. St
Edmund is the most remarkable example, for there the lead
lantern is more than thirty years later than the body of the church
and tower, and certainly by its addition raises the whole quality
of the building.

It is usual to discuss the city churches mainly from the point
of view of the variety of their planning, and certainly that is their
most striking quality apart from the tower and spire designs.
It is, moreover, in the fecundity of invention that Wren was able
to display in internal space-arrangements that a large part of
their importance for his architectural development consists.
Indeed, the variety is amazing; there are plain rectangular plans
with vaulted ceilings, there is every variety of single- and double-
aisled plan, and there are such interesting variations as the east
end of St Clement Danes. Perhaps most fascinating of all are
the domed churches, domes on square plans, as at St Anne and
St Agnes, and St Mildred, Bread Street, domes on polygons as in
the two lost churches of St Antholin and St Benet Fink or the
surviving St Swithin's, Cannon Street, and the supreme example
of St Stephen's, Walbrook. The detail treatment of the ex-
teriors, however, is also interesting from the point of view of
Wren's development. Broadly, the growing certitude that came
with experience can be observed in these features too, and,
whereas the earliest churches show an extraordinary catholicity
of taste in the sources on which Wren has drawn, some churches
clearly deriving in detail *motifs* from French and even Dutch
sources, while others of approximately the same dates have a
strictly orthodox Italian derivation—in the later examples there
is more discrimination in the borrowings. As might be expected,

the main sources are Serlio and the French buildings that Wren had seen or knew from engravings.

Not all the churches were built from the proceeds of the coal tax, and three very important examples were paid for by subscription or by private enterprise: St Andrew's, Holborn; St Clement Danes; and St James's, Piccadilly—the last being due to that Lord St Albans whom Wren met in Paris, who built it as part of his development schemes in the West End. All these three are comparatively late churches, built in the eighties, and all are aisled churches with galleries. Some time towards the end of Queen Anne's reign, when Wren wrote a memorandum on parish church requirements in form of a letter to one of the Commissioners under the new Act of Parliament for building fifty additional churches, he singled out St James's, Piccadilly, for special mention as a design both economical and capacious.

I can hardly think it practicable to make a single Room, so capacious, with Pews and Galleries, as to hold above 2,000 Persons, and all to hear the Service, and both to hear distinctly and see the Preacher. I endeavoured to effect this, in building the Parish church of St James, Westminster, which, I presume, is the most capacious, with these qualifications, that hath yet been built; and yet at a solemn Time, when the Church was much crowded, I could not discern from a Gallery that 2,000 were present. In this Church I mention, though very broad, and the Middle Nave arched up, yet there are no Walls of a second Order, nor Lanterns, nor Buttresses, but the whole Roof rests upon the Pillars, as do the Galleries; I think it may be found beautiful and convenient, and as such, the cheapest of any Form I could invent.

The whole letter is interesting, though too long for further quotation here, but this is the only reference to his own work that it contains.

Of the buildings of the early seventies, other than churches, the first one of importance is Temple Bar, now standing as an entrance gate to Theobald's Park. In its design Wren abandoned the scheme deriving from a Roman triumphal arch, that Inigo Jones had adopted for the earlier building on the site, and used a scheme rather like the upper part of a French church façade resting on a broad, flat-arched bridge. The triumphal arch *motif*, of which there were plenty of examples in Serlio, was abandoned, in spite of the prestige of Jones's name, probably for reasons of traffic. The building has the same rather gauche charm as the Emmanuel College Chapel façade. The Wren drawings at All Souls also include a section of a theatre which is believed to be Drury Lane, said to have been rebuilt by Wren for Killigrew in 1672, but this is not certain.

At Wren's appointment to the surveyorship in 1669 the Crown was engaged in building at Greenwich under Webb, and at Newmarket, where a residence for Charles was begun in 1668 by an architect called Samuel who is known also as the author of the seventeenth-century Eaton Hall, Cheshire, both buildings having since disappeared. These works at Greenwich and Newmarket were carried out under their respective architects, and after 1673 the rebuilding of Windsor by Hugh May was put in hand. Wren himself did not get the chance of a first-rate building for the Crown until the Winchester Palace scheme of 1683. Of the two royal works that he did undertake, the first is Greenwich Observatory, which was built by the Ordnance Department, not the Office of Works, in the words of the order, 'to such plat and design as shall be given you by Sir Christopher Wren.' This was in June 1675, and on 22nd June the entry appears in Hooke's Diary: 'At Sir Chr. Wren order . . . to direct Observatory in Greenwich park for Sir J. More. He promised money.' This is Sir Jonas Moore, a member of the Royal Society and Surveyor of the Ordnance. The Greenwich Observatory is a curious building, and a few years later Wren made this amusing comment on it in a letter to Dr Fell, who was anxious to put an observatory on the top of the gate of Christ Church, Oxford, now Tom Tower:

Wee built indeed an Observatory at Greenwich, not unlike what your Tower will prove, it was for the Observatory habitation and a little for Pompe; It is the instruments in the Court after the manner I have described which are used, the room keeps the clocks and the instruments that are layed by.

The other work was a more ambitious matter, a great mausoleum to be built at Windsor for Charles I. Elaborate drawings for this, including two for sculptural groups by Grinling Gibbons, are in the collection at All Souls, together with a detailed estimate working out at £43,663. Parliament voted the money on 30th January 1678, but nothing was done. In relation to the date of the designs it is curious to note that as early as October 1677, Wren and Hooke had several discussions on mausolea as described by the ancient authorities. The designs are extremely fine, a circular, rusticated building on a plinth surrounded by an order of Corinthian half-columns surmounted by a dome and lantern standing on a drum. These last bear a strong resemblance to the drum and lantern of the warrant design for St Paul's and derive from Michael Angelo's model for St Peter's. There are several other related designs by Wren, of later date than this, intended for a detached baptistery to stand before the west end

of St Paul's, and it is curious to note that Nicholas Hawksmoor,
who is said to have come to Wren as a pupil in 1679, seems to
have recurred to these designs in the last building he ever did,
the mausoleum at Castle Howard (1726–36).

In the course of Wren's work as surveyor we find him in these
years with a great variety of special duties.   He had to report on
Samuel's work at Newmarket and to deal with difficulties that
arose there with the builders.   In the state papers there are also
reports by him on rebuilding schemes at the Savoy and at Mile
End, and we find him taking a stand about an incipient slum that
was growing up in Soho.   A less pleasant duty is mentioned in a
news-letter of 1670: 'On Saturday 13th [June 1670] according to
an order of the Council Board, Dr Wren, the King's Surveyor,
disfurnished four or five places erected by Nonconformists of
several persuasions in and about the city.'   Sometimes he had
to make ready the court theatre for performances, but it is worth
remarking that Streeter, the painter who had decorated the
Sheldonian, seems to be employed to design the scenery and
costumes, a job that in Inigo Jones's time was always done by
the surveyor himself.

There are some private commissions of these years that deserve
attention, of which the first was Bishop's Hostel, Trinity College,
Cambridge, begun in 1669.   We have no documents connecting
Wren's name with this building, but a very strong probability
that his advice was taken at any rate; for the building contractor
was that Minchin who appears in the letter of 1665 to Bathurst,
and, moreover, Minchin was a Bletchington man.   Wren's authorship of the second building is suggested by the State Papers for
1671, which contain some letters to Williamson, Lord Arlington's
secretary, from Dr Fell, the Dean of Christ Church, Oxford.   In
the first letter Dr Fell refers to some small work that Wren was
doing at Oxford, but leaves its identity uncertain, but in the
second he says: 'Mr Surveyor will assist you in the particulars of
your contract besides the measuring of the whole building with
reference to strength and ornament.'   This refers to the building
begun the following year at Queen's College, Oxford, at Williamson's expense.   It still exists in an altered condition, but our best
knowledge of it is from Loggan's print of the college issued three
years later.   In 1673 the State Papers record that Packer, the
Paymaster of the Works, visited Oxford to inspect the building.
These two buildings may be taken as typical of works with which
Wren was certainly connected, though exactly how much he did
about them is not known.   Probably he gave a scheme and

advised about the contracts, though in some cases he seems to
have revised schemes which were originated by the local builders.
An instance occurs in 1682 about some work at Easton Neston
House, Northamptonshire, where a letter from Wren to the
owner implies that he had never seen the place, and only advised
the builder who had been sent to London to consult him.   The
much debated case of Trinity College Chapel, Oxford, is another
instance where the degree of Wren's responsibility is uncertain;
though, of course, with these Oxford buildings, Wren certainly
knew the local circumstances perfectly, and he was presumably
often there even after he had resigned his official position in 1673.
There are no doubt degrees of responsibility varying with different
buildings.

Some time in 1674 or 1675, Wren seems to have been called in
again at Cambridge, probably through Dr Barrow, Master of
Trinity College, an old friend and a great admirer of his mathematical abilities.   The university was contemplating the building
of a library and senate house.   *Parentalia* mentions a design for
this, and gives the date 1678, but in the Hooke Diary there is a
reference to the Cambridge 'theatre' as early as March 1675.
The design exists among the Wren drawings at All Souls.   It is
an interesting and ingenious scheme, and seems to show that Wren
was affected by Palladio about this time, an impression that is
confirmed by the first design for the library of Trinity College,
which must date from 1675 or earlier, for work began on the final
scheme in the following year.   The first design seems to be based
on Palladio's Villa Rotonda, a square building with a portico on
every side, and a dome.   There are also signs of a study of
Palladio in some of the early parish church designs.   The Senate
House scheme came to nothing, and the actual building that was
begun at Trinity College in 1676 is finer than the building suggested by the domed design.   Again, in working for a learned body,
Wren has set out to recapture the sober splendour and dignity
of the antique.   The design is one of his finest, and one in which
he was least interfered with, and which has suffered least from the
alterations of succeeding generations.   The building is very fully
documented, with several drawings and a letter to the clients sent
with them.   The letter is too long to quote in full, but the following extract refers to the most celebrated point of the design, the
level of the library floor in relation to the arches of the cloister:

I have given the appearance of arches as the order required fair
and lofty; but I have laid the floor of the library upon the impostes,
which answer to the pillars in the cloister, and the levels of the old

floors, and have filled the arches with relieves of stone, of which I have seen the effect abroad in good buildings, and I assure you where porches are low with flat ceilings is infinitely more grateful than flat ceilings would be, and is much more open and pleasant; nor need the mason feare the performance, because the arch discharges the weight and I shall direct him in a firm manner of executing the design.   By this contrivance the windowes of the Library rise high and give place for desks against the walls and being high may be afforded to be large. . . .

The reference to the building abroad is an interesting one, an instance of what Wren means is the arcade treatment of the Hôtel Beauvais which he almost certainly had seen, but there are other examples.   The interior of the library was not finished with all its fittings and the carvings by Grinling Gibbons till the nineties, but the drawings at All Souls show how closely Wren supervised all the details even down to the reading-tables and stools.

The name of Grinling Gibbons is frequently associated with the early work of Wren at the city churches; this, however, is without foundation.   The vestries employed their own favourite carvers, and Gibbons, who was a court rather than a city man, remains outside that circle.   Indeed, the only parish church on which he worked is St James's, Piccadilly, about 1685.   This must be the earliest surviving work that he did for Wren, though he had been brought to his notice as early as 1671, when Wren and Pepys dined with Evelyn, and were taken to see the work of the new carver that Evelyn had just discovered, and in 1678 they had certainly collaborated on the design for Charles I's mausoleum. The story of Evelyn's discovery of the young carver and his presentation to Charles and the queen is well known; but it is interesting to note that it was the introduction to Hugh May that brought immediate employment.   Wren had no occasion to employ Gibbons, except on the mausoleum design, until the work for Charles at Whitehall in the early eighties, as far as we know.

As the quoted figures of the coal tax show, the years following the increase of the tax in 1670 did not provide sufficient funds to warrant a very go-ahead policy in regard to St Paul's.   These years are, however, a time of quite extraordinary interest in relation to the design.   The actual work that was going on was mainly the clearing away of the ruins of the old building, but at the same time Wren was continually working on the design for the new building, though it was not until 1675 that he was finally authorized to proceed with the work.   The works of demolition are described in *Parentalia*, and the accounts supplement this. It was no small task, and we hear of scaffolding being erected for

the taking down of the great rose window at the east end, familiar
to us from engravings. *Parentalia* mentions battering-rams as
being employed to knock down walls. Any seventeenth-century
architect, and especially Wren with his mechanical turn of mind,
must have rejoiced in such an opportunity to put into practice
the instructions of Vitruvius and his Italian followers, for such
antique military engines occupy a large part of their books.
Wren went even further and used gunpowder, but unfortunately
a large piece of stone flew and struck the balcony of a neighbouring house. After this the blasting operations seem to have been
abandoned, and the services of the gunner from the Tower were
no more required. The demolitions went on after 1675 parallel
with the rebuilding, and it was not till the nineties that the convocation house which had long served as an office for the works
was pulled down, though most of the old building seems to have
gone by 1687.

The stages through which the St Paul's design passed from
1669 to 1673 are obscure. A model was made and finished in
1672, which Hooke saw in the November of that year, and says
had been approved by the king. This was no doubt the first of
the two models described in *Parentalia*, and the one seen and
criticized by Sir Roger Pratt in the summer of 1673. Recently a
much damaged model has come to light at St Paul's which is
certainly the remains of this. By comparing the two accounts
of it with the remaining fragment a very curious building results.
It consists of a rectangular main body without aisles on the ground
level, but with long external arcaded loggias above which were
galleries looking into the church. The loggias were returned
round the east end where they had some sort of portico above.
At the west end was an 'ante-chapel,' with three state entrances,
and surmounted by a lofty dome, in this respect anticipating the
design of the chapel of Greenwich Hospital. Internally the main
body of the church would have resembled a larger version of
St James's, Piccadilly, or St Andrew's, Holborn, if the aisles
beneath the galleries of those churches were cut off by walls from
the central part of the nave. The effect produced was one in
which the main volume of the interior was at gallery level as it
still is in these parish churches. It is possible that the external
loggias were intended as covered walks for the citizens, a compensation for their exclusion from the inside of the church except
for purposes of worship, and that they are a survival of the idea
that St Paul's was a place of public resort for business and
conversation as well as a church, as we know it to have been

considered in the earlier seventeenth century. The whole building was on a considerably smaller scale than any of the later schemes. It is possible that the state vestibule or 'ante-chapel' survived as a feature of the second model, which was begun in October 1673, and is mentioned in the royal letters patent of November:

> We have caused several designs to that Purpose, to be prepared by Dr Christopher Wren, Surveyor-General of All our Works and Buildings, which we have seen and one of which we do more especially approve and have commanded a model thereof to be made."

This is the great model that still exists entire, a splendid piece of work some eighteen feet in length and big enough to show the effect inside as well as out. It took very near a year to complete, for it was not till September 1674 that Hooke saw it complete with the little statues in place. These have now disappeared, but are shown in a picture in Longman's *Three Churches dedicated to St Paul*. The great model is a church the main body of which is a large dome at the intersection of an equal-armed cross, set in an octagon, the oblique sides of which are concave. It is preceded at the west end by a domed vestibule with three entrances. This last is the feature that seems to be a survival from the earlier model, though in its present form it appears to derive from Sangallo's design for St Peter's. There are drawings of a version of the great model design lacking this domed vestibule. Foundations were marked out during the summer of 1674, and even some preliminary work done for starting on this design.

Some time in the latter part of 1674 the St Paul's design underwent a revolution. *Parentalia* says the chapter and clergy thought the great model not cathedral-like enough, especially as regards the form of the choir, which was circular. A more cogent objection may well have been that it was difficult to build it gradually in parts, for this point is especially mentioned in the eventual warrant for starting work in 1675. *Parentalia* also says that the great model was the favourite scheme of Wren himself. In beginning again, Wren went back to something more closely related to his pre-Fire of London combination of Inigo Jones's restoration with a dome at the crossing. His work on the great model and its related drawings seems to have confirmed in his mind the desire to get breadth of spatial effect out of his dome, the very point in which the pre-Fire scheme was weakest. There are numerous drawings which seem to be leading up to the warrant design of May 1675, which are all alike in this search after a broad internal effect for the dome space. There is, however, an

essential difficulty about a broad, low dome at the intersection
of the arms of a big, cross-planned church. The length of the
nave, transepts, and choir are liable to obscure the dome from the
four main viewpoints. It was one of the merits of the great
model scheme that with its octagonal form and concave sides it
avoided this difficulty in the main. Moreover, as Wren emphasized in his pre-Fire report, people expected St Paul's to have
a high central feature. In the final scheme on which the royal
warrant to proceed was issued, he endeavoured to get a compromise by placing a very large lantern, itself a considerable
dome on a tall drum, on top of his main, broad, low dome, and
surmounting the whole with a spire rather in the manner of that
later built at St Bride's. The effect of all this in true elevation
—it would probably have looked better in actual fact as seen
from ground level—is rather uncouth and bizarre, and has led to
much extraordinary speculation as to how it came about. Apart
from the dome, lantern, and spire, the external treatment of the
warrant design is clearly derived from Inigo Jones's restoration.
There is a similar projecting portico at the west, and even the
window treatment is reminiscent of his. In plan, however, the
design is of the very greatest importance and is certainly the
basis of the existing plan. The treatment of the west end and
of the transept porches has been changed, but the choir plan of
the warrant design is the one on which work was immediately
begun, and is that of the present St Paul's. The ground plan of
the dome space is also very nearly as at present. In *Parentalia*
it is said that the king allowed Wren the liberty to make changes
in the design. However that may have been, changes were
certainly made in the external effect of the choir quite soon, for
by 1681, when the work had reached the springing of the arches
of the windows, the external treatment in two arches with
coupled pilasters must have been settled. The bay design of the
upper order, with its pillared and pedimented niches between
pilasters, seems to derive from Serlio's illustrations of the treatment of the interior of the Pantheon, just as the relation of the
interior order to the arcade is based on the Temple of Peace in
the same book, another change that must have been decided
within the first few years of the undertaking.

Important as the years 1670 to 1680 are for Wren's career as
an architect, they are equally eventful in his personal life, and
thanks to Hooke's Diary we are well informed about them, for
the Diary is quite as illuminating about this aspect of Wren as
about his architecture or the scientific interests that Hooke

shared with him. The Diary is, moreover, apart from Evelyn and the very few personal letters that have survived, the only real evidence we have on the subject. The two men were very intimate and met either on business or convivially (sometimes both) almost daily. At times they would dine together as often as twice a week. Their fondness for coffee-houses has been mentioned, and, indeed, it is quite surprising how much of their time seems to have been spent there. Wren's favourite coffee-houses seem to have been Garraway's in Cornhill and Child's in St Paul's Churchyard, though Man's in Chancery Lane runs them close. The editors of the Hooke Diary quoted a good description of a coffee-house of this time from an Italian traveller who came here in 1667. He says that other drinks were sold besides coffee: 'tea, chocolate, sorbets, cider, etc., according to season. These houses have rooms or alcoves for the reading of the news, where one may hear what has happened or what is rumoured,' whether it be true or false. In winter, to sit at a great fire and smoke for two hours costs but two pence and one pays for one's drinks besides.' It is in such surroundings as these that one must picture them both in February 1678, when Hooke records: 'With Sir Christopher at coffee-house. Spoke of his Theory of Respiration, Muscular motion, etc. delivered to Mr Boyle. Shewed me his draught of Mausoleum' (for Charles I at Windsor). Perhaps the most amusing reference to a tavern occurs on 20th October 1676, being a Friday: 'Post prandium at Sir J. Hoskins. With him and Aubrey to Sir Chr. Wren at Palsgraves Head. Sir Chr. Wren's birthday. He paid all. . . . Good discourse.' And next day comes the entry: 'Sent Sir Chr. Wren's son a hobby horse, 14*sh* paid.' The son was young Christopher, born in February 1675. Wren's eldest child, Gilbert, had been born in October 1672, when Hooke curiously records: 'Dr Bradford assured Dr Wren that his next child would be a boy, this being born in the increase of the moon.' Gilbert apparently was delicate—we hear of convulsions—and died in March 1674. On 4th September 1675, Lady Wren died of smallpox, after an illness of eleven days, leaving Sir Christopher with the young baby of only seven months old.

In the Diary, Hooke seems to become closer friends with Wren as the years go on. This is perhaps noticeable after Lady Wren's death, when he and Aubrey and Sir J. Hoskins seem to stand out as Wren's especial friends. These and some others formed a sort of informal club and met together frequently. With our knowledge of Wren and Hooke, and especially of Aubrey, it is not surprising to find that the conversation touched on an immense range of topics: 'Discoursed about petrifactions of bodys, about plaister, about forming of glasse, form of arches, light gold statues, staining marble (an old topic this), Filigreen, sodering with bran, about printing stuffs and guilding stuffs, about Dr Moor's notions, about ghosts and spirits.' On that occasion Dr Holder was present, and it is pleasant to find him often with Wren at this time. He still retained his interest in musical theory, it seems, and had long discussions on the subject with Hooke. One friend who must have been sadly missed was cousin Matthew who had died in the summer of 1672.

Wren did not remain long a widower. On 24th February 1677, he married Jane Fitzwilliam, sister of Lord Fitzwilliam of Lifford, who was eventually to become Earl Fitzwilliam in the early years of the eighteenth century. Apparently it was a rather sudden match, for Hooke, who was seeing Wren regularly in the days just before the marriage, could not remember the lady's name in his entry of 24th February. He does not mention meeting her till April. In the next few years, however, he and Lady Wren became good friends and the marriage does not seem to have interfered in any way with the intimacy of the two men. In 1679, for example, we find Hooke making Wren a present of a grand watch made by Tompion and costing £8. On 9th November 1677 Wren's daughter Jane was born; said to be the favourite of his children. Another child, William, was born to them in June 1679, who seems to have been delicate, for we hear on occasion of his ill health, and in his will Sir Christopher left him to the charge of his elder brother. Wren's second marriage lasted even less time than his first, for by October 1680 the second Lady Wren was dead. It would seem that she had been ill for some little time, for Hooke remarks on 18th September that she was recovered.

The miscellaneous information about Wren scattered up and down among the telegraphic entries of the Diary is surprising. Hooke and he used to smoke together, though this does not appear in the earlier part of the Diary. Occasionally they went to entertainments: once to a performance of *The Tempest*; another time 'with Sir. Chr. Wren to Boyle, and near coffee-house at Bartholomew Fair, saw Elephant wave colours, shoot a gun, bend and kneel, carry a castle and a man, etc.' Three days after the visit to Boyle and the elephant we find: 'Walk'd with Sir Chr. Wren in the Park, told him of double vaulting Pauls with cramps between.' The date of Wren's knighthood appears

amusingly as '(1673) Friday November 14th Dr Wren knighted
and gone to Oxford.' Wren's health is the occasion of remarks
every now and again. He takes physic or has a sore throat or
the trouble with the stone in March 1675; but on the whole he
seems to have fairly good health, and Hooke was very obser-
vant on that point. Sometimes his temper is noted, as 'At Sir
Chr. Wren's, Mrs Marshall angry. Sir Chr. not kind'; and there
are other occasions. Where Wren lived, Hooke never bothers to
say. Sometimes he mentions Scotland Yard; but there was
obviously another house as well, for in March 1676, 'Sir Christopher let his house for £32 per annum for one year.' Wren is
said to have had a house in Bloomsbury, and perhaps this was it.
He certainly lived in some state and kept a coach and a footman,
for Hooke often gets lifts and occasionally tips the coachman
and footman. One of the most interesting features of the Diary
to the student of Wren is the references to architectural books
and pictures that Hooke acquired. They give some idea of the
sources of precedent available to architects at that time. There
is a very high percentage of French books, such as Marot, Le
Muet, Félibien, and a vast quantity of loose engravings by Perelle
and Israël Sylvestre, and including a quantity of engraved
designs for furniture, ornament, and so forth; but Italian prints
are not lacking. Hooke had St Peter's, Sta Maria della Pace,
the Gesù, the Piazzo del Popolo, Bernini's Piazza San Pietro, as
well as Sandrart's book, Rubens's Palazzi di Genova, and Vasari
and Palladio. Only one Dutch architectural book is mentioned,
Philip Vingboom's.

Chapter 4

Chelsea Hospital and Winchester—Alterations at Whitehall for James II
    and Mary II—Work at the Temple—Christ Church, Oxford, and
    Wren's Gothic—The Royal Society—Parliament—Wren as a Man of
    Affairs—Progress of St Paul's—Wren's Craftsmen—Hampton Court
    and Kensington Palaces—Wren's later Colleagues—Greenwich Hos-
    pital and the Designs for Whitehall.

THE greatest surviving building by Sir Christopher Wren from
the sixteen-eighties is Chelsea Hospital. It is also the only building of the first magnitude, other than St Paul's, that he ever
completed, for Hampton Court and Greenwich Hospital are but
fragments of larger schemes. Moreover, Chelsea is alone among
his greater buildings in not being in some degree conditioned

by pre-existing buildings. It is a work of his early maturity carried out in one effort from 1682 to 1691, and the building was completely roofed by 1684. And though there was time enough in these nine years for a certain amount of detail revision of the design of the interior fittings and finishings, there was no question of that long, slow, matured consideration of the principal features that distinguishes St Paul's among his works. All these circumstances combine to give it a special importance.

The scheme of the building is a great three-sided court facing south; the central range of the three consists of the hall and chapel, and the east and west wings are of three stories and attics. On the outer sides of these wings large subordinate courts are formed by smaller and lower pavilions standing at right angles to the great wings. This arrangement provides for the maximum of light and air for the soldiers' wards in the great wings. The building is carried out in brick with stone and painted wooden dressings. It has a hipped roof with a bold wooden eaves cornice, dormer windows, and bold chimneys, all in the typical late seventeenth-century manner as introduced by Jones and Pratt in the middle years of the century. Each long front of the main building, including the sides of the great wings towards the main court, has central features with colossal columns or pilasters and pediments. Of these features those which form climaxes at the ends of deep courts stand very boldly forward from the brick buildings. Across the end of the main court is a covered cloister supported on coupled columns, interrupted in the middle by the bold portico of colossal columns which forms the centre feature on that side and above which rises the lantern tower over the entrance passage to the hall and chapel. An especially interesting and daring feature of the design is the chimneys of the small low pavilions, which form the sides of the subordinate east and west courts. They are proportioned to their position in relation to the great wings which form the ends of the courts, and in consequence have been made of enormous size, having regard to the building on which they stand. Chelsea is justly admired as an example of Wren's handling of brick building. He had, of course, used this material often before, and one of his most delightful brick designs is St Benet's, Thames Street, begun in 1677. Wren was extremely fortunate in that he came to architecture when brick-work in England was at a very high level. The movement initiated under Inigo Jones to encourage brick buildings in London, and the work of successive authorities, including Pratt and Wren himself, had encouraged and promoted the use of brick and its technical improvement and led to the establishment of a fine tradition.

Another feature of the Chelsea Hospital design is the use of a colossal order with a smaller one in close juxtaposition. This seems to link it with the design for Charles II's palace at Winchester, a work almost exactly coinciding with it in dates. Evelyn says that the intention to build at Winchester was much strengthened by the burning of the king's house at Newmarket in June 1683, but it certainly dates back to more than a year before. The Winchester palace was never completed, and there are not many drawings. The plan seems to have resembled that of Versailles as altered by Le Vau before the enlargements by Mansard began in the eighties. As at Chelsea, one of the main features was a deep three-sided court, the climax of which seems to have been a portico of colossal columns associated with smaller ones. The materials were brick and Portland stone. The window-dressings were of rather a Palladian type, and, instead of the normal late seventeenth-century domestic roof with dormer windows and heavy eaves cornice that we find at Chelsea, there was to be a parapet pierced at intervals with balustrading. This was no doubt considered more monumental and fitting for a royal palace. After Charles's death, in February 1685, work seems to have been suspended. In May of that year, James II started his important alterations to Whitehall, which were pressed on with all possible speed and were in fact complete by November of the following year.

These Whitehall buildings for James II consisted in the main of a range of large buildings running from near the western end of the Banqueting Hall nearly to the river. They included a grand staircase, a long gallery, new apartments for the queen, a new royal chapel with accommodation for the priests, and a council chamber. We know a certain amount about them from the accounts, and a few drawings have survived which show them to have been of brick with stone and rubbed brick dressings. They had the high-pitched roof, dormers, and eaves cornice of the time as at Chelsea, but naturally the work was carried out more solidly and expensively and stone was employed where wood sufficed at Chelsea. The great point of the design was the interior arrangements and decorations, and from the accounts we can get some idea of these sumptuous baroqueries, the marble chimney-pieces, the painted ceilings and the great staircase of Portland stone and marble with a wrought iron balustrade, the first feature of the kind Wren had the chance to carry out.

K

Above all, the royal chapel attracted public attention as much
because it scandalized Protestant feeling and reminded folk that
their new king was a devoted Catholic, as by the splendour of
its interior. All that remains of its provocative grandeur are
some fragments of Quellin's sculptured altar-piece in a country
church in Somerset, and the organ which Queen Mary II gave to
St James's, Piccadilly, after the dismantling of the chapel at the
Revolution of 1688. It is interesting to note that Wren had done
a certain amount of grand interior decoration at Whitehall in
the king's new apartments for Charles II in 1682, to which reference is made in the estimate for the larger building. At the
very end of his reign, James II began a further extension of the
queen's apartments at Whitehall in the form of a fine block by
Wren facing the river. Drawings of this exist, and it is shown in
the bird's-eye view of Whitehall drawn between 1695–8. In
this it appears as it was completed by the formation of an embankment terrace projecting into the river and laid out as a formal
garden. This sounds an extravagant if delightful idea, but
almost certainly was intended to serve the very practical purpose
of substituting a garden terrace for the unsavoury tidal mud that
extended all along the river side of the palace at low water. The
embankment garden stretched along the wide front of the queen's
new block and the king's apartments as done up in 1682. The
new block was in building in 1688 and 1689, and the embankment
garden followed in 1691–3.

Another group of brick and stone domestic buildings of this
time are those executed to Wren's design for the Temple. Of
these the Middle Temple gate is the most important, but Wren
also did a scheme for the cloisters between the Inner and Middle
Temple, where the exploitation of the site had been handed over
to Dr Barbon, a well-known building speculator of the time.
Barbon's scheme seems to have been superseded in favour of
Wren's. The Middle Temple gateway is not a design of the first
importance, but it is a very fine and admirable example of ingenious handling of brick and stone. The facing bricks between
the stone pilasters are all 'rubbers'—that is, soft bricks that can
be rubbed down so as to make a very fine join. They had been
introduced in the first half of the century, and were used in
Wren's time, sometimes with extraordinary virtuosity in carved
brick effects. At the Middle Temple they are used quite simply
but very originally to give a specially rich surface texture to the
walls. These works at the Temple date from 1680 for the cloisters
and 1683 for the gate. It is interesting to note that the societies

presented Wren with twelve silver trencher plates to the value
of some £48 on the completion of the building.   Presents of this
kind seem to have been customary when he worked for learned
bodies, for the grandest of them was that of Archbishop Sheldon,
who gave Wren gold plate to the value of £200 on the completion
of the Sheldonian Theatre.

Two other interesting brick buildings of the early eighties have
been attributed to Wren—the south range at Christ's Hospital
(1682), and Kilmainham Hospital, Dublin (1679).   The work at
Christ's Hospital was a charming composition in brick, and Wren
was certainly closely connected with the government of the
school, and equally certainly designed some further additions to
it at a later date; but we cannot verify this particular design from
documents, and there were other architects, including Hooke,
also connected with the institution.   Kilmainham Hospital was
a scheme similar to Chelsea, dating from a few years earlier.   The
ascription to Wren rests on an account of the institution published
in 1711, in which it is said that 'orders were issued to H.M.
Surveyor of Buildings (whom they thought most proper to advise
in that behalf) requiring that he do with all convenient speed view
the lands of Kilmainham near Dublin.'   But there was an official
of the Government of Ireland with that title (which was not
Wren's), by name, William Robinson, who was certainly concerned with the building of Kilmainham, and it seems almost
certain that it is to him we should give the credit of this delightful
little work.

There is one design by Wren of 1681 that deserves special
attention, though it is not on the largest scale—the completion of
Tom Tower gateway, at Christ Church, Oxford.   It is interesting
partly because we have a series of letters from Wren to the Bishop
of Oxford about it which well illustrate his methods and the
difficulty he had in carrying out work at a distance from London.
He had peculiar difficulties in getting an accurate survey of the
building to which he was adding.   But the main interest of Tom
Tower consists in the fact that it is a Gothic design.   It is not
actually the first building Wren did in this manner, for St Mary,
Aldermanbury, was finished in 1682, the same year as Tom Tower,
but had presumably been begun earlier.   Wren's other Gothic
designs—the towers of St Dunstan's in the East; St Alban's,
Wood Street; St Michael, Cornhill; and the work at Westminster
Abbey—mainly belong to the last phase of his career.   It seems
probable that the use of Gothic at St Mary, Aldermanbury, was
imposed on Wren by the desire of the benefactor who paid for it,

and that this interested him and accustomed him to the manner. He had, of course, undertaken to advise and report about structural problems at Salisbury Cathedral as early as 1668. Wren's Gothic, and even more that of his pupil Hawksmoor, at All Souls and Westminster, has come in for much abuse and misunderstanding, which is the survival of the general neglect of any attempt to understand the point of view of the Baroque architects on the part of the nineteenth-century critics. To Wren and his followers, especially Hawksmoor, medieval architecture was largely interesting as affording suggestions for bold compositional effects, striking silhouettes, effects of strong vertical shadows, and so forth. When they executed these with classically derived detail, as in some of Wren's most admired city church towers or in Hawksmoor's fine hall of All Souls, and some of his church towers, the admirable effect is more easily appreciated than when they actually imitate Gothic details, which are harder for us to stomach. One of the most interesting documents bearing on this picturesque Baroque view of Gothic is a drawing in the Wren collection at All Souls, showing Warwick Church in perspective with the detail hardly shown, but all the shadows and the effects of vertical masses clearly indicated. Tom Tower, though the earliest of the Gothic towers, is one of the most successful. Wren had to do some very skilful adaptation of the lower sixteenth-century part of the structure, which was presumably intended to carry a rectangular gatehouse tower with angle turrets, to enable him to build his octagonal lantern with its ogee dome. All this is explained very clearly in one of the letters, but the description is too complex to quote here.

During this long period of architectural activity from 1670–90, Wren remained an active member of the Royal Society, becoming vice-president in 1674 and president for two years from 1681–3, when he was succeeded by his friend, Sir John Hoskyns. Wren attended most of the meetings and took part in the discussions, often having to take the chair. He also served on various special sub-committees of the society to investigate the work submitted to them, such as Hooke's new quadrant in 1674, and in the same year he was appointed to a special commission, with Hooke and Seth Ward and others, to try to discover some satisfactory method of finding longitude at sea. This was an urgent practical problem, and Wren occupied himself with it on and off all his life. It was not solved in a practical way until after his death. It is quite clear from the Royal Society's records and from the Hooke Diary, that Wren's interest in scientific matters was as keen as

ever during this period, but inevitably had become an interest
on the part of a busy man of affairs rather than a part of his
real work. It was in his term of office as president that the
society sold the land on which he built Chelsea Hospital. Undoubtedly the whole conception of that scheme as an institution
and organization as well as a building is very largely due to him,
and when the building was finished he remained for many years
one of the most important of the commissioners who governed it.
Wren as a man of affairs, as well as an architect and man of
science, appears increasingly in the late 1670's and 1680's, for, in
addition to his work for the Royal Society and in promoting the
Chelsea scheme, he served from 1679 to 1683 as one of the council
of the Hudson's Bay Company, and from 1685 to 1687 as member
of Parliament for Plympton in Devon. It is difficult to find out
much about his parliamentary career. He was presumably first
of all a 'place man'—that is, one of the solid body of members
who held paid offices under the Crown, and on whom the Government of the day relied to support their policy in the House. We
can also suppose, I think, that he was a Tory, i.e. one of the High
Church monarchical party. Family tradition would suggest it,
and it is borne out by the fact that he stood for the University
of Oxford in 1673, when, however, he was unsuccessful. Possibly
he was not Tory enough. The fact that his election to the Con-
vention Parliament of 1688 for Windsor, where he still had
considerable family connections, was declared void would seem,
however, to suggest that he belonged to the Tory party, for these
things were always decided by the House on party lines, except
that the Tory Parliament of 1690 again disallowed his election.
Almost certainly he was not seriously a party man. He was to
get into Parliament again for a few months from December 1701
to July 1702 as member for Weymouth. We have only one
record of Wren's work actually in Parliament, when in June 1685
he was one of the members selected to bring in a Bill for financing
Chelsea Hospital out of the proceeds of a tax on hackney coaches.

From 1688 there is a document surviving which shows Wren
in partnership with a certain Roger Jackson, buying land at the
Barbican in the city to the value of £4,400. This was a very
considerable amount in those days, and was possibly a land, or
more probably a building, speculation. Quite apart from the
results of the Great Fire, the late seventeenth century was a time
of considerable activity on the part of building speculators, for
London was growing very fast. Wren had much to do with this
in his capacity as Surveyor-General, regulating and controlling it.

In 1684 he had to take drastic action in a very troublesome matter involving Dr Barton, the most famous of these speculators. It is curious from a present-day point of view to find Wren apparently involved in such transactions himself, but to the seventeenth century such conduct would not seem to be even an indiscretion. This speculation with Jackson also raises the question of Wren's financial position. Clearly, from the evidence of his way of life, and his subsequent purchase of a country estate for his son, he made a very comfortable fortune. His official positions were comfortably but not extremely highly paid. It is said that his fees for the city churches amounted to a very large sum, but it is difficult to be certain. For some works he got a special fee, as £1,000 for Chelsea Hospital, but he certainly gave his services in some instances free or for a purely nominal reward. During the 1680's Wren received an increase of official salary, but it was not a large one. Hugh May died in February 1684, and in the same year Wren succeeded to his position at Windsor. Work on the new building was, however, finished by then, and the appointment did not mean very much.

In the warrant of 1675 the design of St Paul's had been approved, partly on the grounds that it could be completed by instalments. This intention was followed in some degree, for the choir was certainly finished and fitted up first, and was complete by the autumn of 1697, when Evelyn notes that '5 December was the first Sunday it had had a service performed in it since it was begun in 1666.' The official opening had taken place three days before the celebration of the Peace of Ryswick. The work was not, however, undertaken as strictly by parts as a modern enterprise of the kind—for example, Liverpool Cathedral—and by the time the choir was open the western parts of the church and the great lower works of the dome were in quite an advanced state. The western parts were taken seriously in hand after 1687, but the transepts and dome supports had been well advanced in 1685. Of the great changes from the warrant scheme, we have mentioned the bay design both internally and externally, and the raising of the outer walls to the full height of the church to screen the aisle roofs and the buttresses of the main high vaults as early changes. The curved porticos at the transept ends must also have been decided on fairly early. The two greatest modifications of the warrant design, the form of the western part of the church with its porticos and chapels to the east of the towers, and the form of the dome and drum were made much in that order, the first about 1687 and the second

nearly ten years later. The extant drawings show various
suggestions for these features. The colossal single-order portico,
having the authority of Inigo Jones behind it, remained for a
long time an *idée fixe*, but even after that had been abandoned
the dome remained undetermined. A fine drawing exists
showing the building very much as built, except that the dome
and drum are an obvious derivation from Michael Angelo's St
Peter's design, though the dome of the Invalides, published in
1684, is a possible half-way house. The actual dome and drum
seem to be a combination of ideas from the two great St Peter's
schemes—Bramante's, with the peristyle round the drum, and
Michael Angelo's, with the strong projecting buttresses; and undoubtedly, of all the St Paul's dome schemes that have survived
to us, the executed design is the finest.

Of the changes to the west end, the double portico has been
very adversely criticized, and the outside columns in the lower
storey are said to support nothing adequate to their importance;
but undoubtedly by the addition of the western chapels and the
corresponding enlargement of the western bay of the nave with
its large saucer dome, Wren has obtained one of the finest of the
interior effects of his church. It is curious to reflect that this
seems to be a creeping back into the design of that domed western
vestibule that survived from the first to the second model, and
disappeared in the warrant scheme. This part of the church,
with the western towers, including the fine geometrical stair of
the south-west tower, and the lantern of the dome and the
finial, are almost the greatest of Wren's achievements in design.
The exterior features, and with them must be taken the towers of
Greenwich Hospital and some of the late city church spires, such
as St Vedast, Foster Lane, and St Magnus, London Bridge, are
among the finest Baroque designs in Europe. An early triumph
such as St Mary-le-Bow has an almost unsophisticated charm
compared with these infinitely accomplished compositions, but
with all their accomplishment they have lost nothing of spon-
taneity. There are signs in them of a knowledge of seventeenth-
century Italian architecture, especially of the towers of
Borromini's St Agnese, which was derived, no doubt, through
engravings such as Falda's book though there are other features in
the early designs for Greenwich, and some late schemes for
Windsor, that show Wren still keeping in close touch with
contemporary French mannerisms.

In the internal finishing of the choir at St Paul's, Wren had
the inestimable advantage of the co-operation of Jean Tijou, the

smith, and Grinling Gibbons. Tijou seems to have come over
about the time of the Revolution, but little is known of his early
work. He appears here at St Paul's, and at Hampton Court and
Kensington, all buildings of the 1690's, but how long he stayed is
obscure. The work that he did is in the most advanced manner
of the late seventeenth-century French smiths, who were very
good at publishing their designs in engraving, and it is probably
as much, if not more, to these engravings that the English school
of ironwork of the first quarter of the eighteenth century owes
its rise, as to the example of Tijou's own work. Grinling Gibbons, however, is a much better known figure, and his work at
St Paul's is perhaps the greatest of his achievements. It is
fairly clear from the accounts and extant drawings how it was
carried out. Drawings were made in Wren's office, showing the
architectural lines of the choir stalls and organ screen, the
mouldings being carefully indicated and a certain amount of
sculptural enrichment suggested. It is to be supposed that
these were made in consultation with Gibbons, and that the
architect indicated which members were to be enriched. These
designs were often carried out by the joiners and afterwards *in
situ* by Gibbons. It should be borne in mind that the St Paul's
stalls and screens were structurally much larger and more complicated things than panelling, cornices, and chimney-pieces, in
which Wren and Gibbons collaborated elsewhere, and in which
Gibbons may well have been left a freer hand. In any case, the
close collaboration with Wren at St Paul's is certain. Very
important things depended on it, especially in regard to the great
organ, for as originally placed over the screen the silhouette of
this formed a sort of climax to the view up the nave and across
the dome space, enhancing the effect of the extension of that
space into the choir itself. The present arrangement whereby
the organ is tucked away into the arches of the choir has almost
certainly vitiated Wren's intentions in a very serious way. The
drawings for a small organ in such a position, which were used by
the restorers to bolster up their desire for a vista, do not affect
the question. Gibbons's woodwork at St Paul's is confined to the
choir; the finely designed screens to the Morning Chapel, and
that of St Michael and St George opposite, are the work of
Jonathan Maine. The joiners, such as Hopson, who with others
built the walls for Gibbons to enrich, played a very important
part in the work of designing the cathedral by making wooden
models of particular details, capitals, cornices, etc., as well as
the great models of the whole building in the early stages of its

design which have already been discussed. Sometimes the detail models were executed by Doogood or Grove, the plasterers, and it is evident that Wren relied very largely on such models for ensuring the effects he desired. St Paul's was an exceptional task in Wren's eyes, and it is not to be supposed that such elaborate pains were taken with all his works.

The ingenuity of the construction of St Paul's, especially the dome, is celebrated. The two major examples of this are all that can be mentioned here. The device of the screen walls, which hide the aisle roofs and the clerestories with their flying buttresses, also serves to buttress the re-entrant bastions at the angles of the dome space, just where the great arches on which the dome in part rests discharge their maximum thrusts. These are perhaps the supreme example. This subtlety must have been worked out early, though it is not suggested in the warrant design. But it is to be supposed that the idea of the most celebrated structural feature of the church, the great brick cone which rises above the inner dome to support the lantern and the timber framing of the outer leaden dome, did not reach its final form until comparatively late. There are many dome studies in various collections of Wren's drawings, some of which seem to show gradual evolution of this device. And it is in the final solution to the problem of the St Paul's dome that Wren's scientific and architectural gifts find their joint consummation.

It would be unfair, perhaps, to suggest that Wren's structural ingenuity led him to feats of indiscreet daring in two of his other buildings of the 1690's, Hampton Court and Kensington Palace. In both cases the strongest pressure had been brought to bear on him—by the king and queen themselves—to hasten the work, and, to comply with this, 'Wren,' to quote the editor of the Wren Society, 'took great risks, for he had adopted the method of running up the outer walls in brickwork while forming the interior with crossed timber partitions on which he balanced the chimney breasts and heavy brick stacks.' In both buildings the results were disastrous and collapses occurred entailing loss of life. It is also possible that the contractors managed to evade supervision to some degree in the rush of work executed at some little distance from the architect's headquarters, and indeed a letter of Queen Mary's says something of the kind. It is possible that the special constructional methods employed in these two buildings had been tried with success at Whitehall, where the buildings of James II had been executed with extraordinary speed.

Both Hampton Court and Kensington were begun in 1689.

* K

Of the two, Hampton Court was by far the more ambitious and important work. The two great garden fronts and the Fountain Court are among the finest of Wren's designs. The interiors were left in the main unfinished, and even in 1699, when a new effort was made, only a few of them were fitted up. The quality of the work internally was extremely high, and some of these rooms are among the finest of their kind. The nature of the collaboration between Gibbons and his architect is more doubtful here than at St Paul's. There are a number of drawings extant which seem to be of Hampton Court, some of them by Gibbons and some, apparently, by Daniel Marot, a French engraver and decorator employed by William III in Holland. In those which seem to be by Gibbons, only the barest outlines have been given and the rest left to him. These outlines are far less limiting than some of the St Paul's drawings, presumably because the structural part of the woodwork was less complicated. Moreover, in an estimate in the Record Office we find Wren merely concurring in a detailed statement drawn up by Talman, the Comptroller of the Works. The design of the great garden fronts and the court can be traced through several stages. The supposedly earliest designs show a very rich decorative treatment, reminding one a little of the kind of thing Wren had seen on his visits to Versailles in 1665, when a large part of the earliest building there was still visible before Le Vau masked it. There are two other schemes very much more severe in manner, the last employing two orders, and then a series of drawings leading up to the design as built. It is interesting to note that the earliest and richest design has a very picturesque sky-line with domes and lantern cupolas on towers. Something of this survives into the first plainer version, but has quite disappeared from the two-order scheme; and although the final scheme goes back to the freedom of enrichment of the earliest one in some degree, the sky-line remains uneventful.

The building as it stands, with its reliance on the contrast of brick and Portland stone and a great variety of sculptural enrichment, is a scheme that could only have been undertaken if Wren had complete reliance on the master carvers at his command. At Hampton Court they were Emmett, Gibbons, and Caius Gabriel Cibber. As in the St Paul's choir scheme, Wren is undoubtedly responsible for the placing and degree of enrichment on each decorative feature, but it was only with a sculptor whose feeling for the exact height and relief was absolutely trustworthy that he could rely on getting his wishes carried out. The Fountain Court with its splendid range of round windows carved by

Emmett is cloistered. There is a story in *Parentalia* that, in the treatment of the arches of the cloisters, Wren was overruled by King William, who afterwards acknowledged his mistake, and it has been suggested that Wren originally intended a filled-in tympanum like the one that he used at Trinity College, Cambridge. These Hampton Court elevations are the one example of his work in brick and stone that can compare with St Paul's in the richness of the design or the quality of the collaboration that he could command. Kensington Palace is a very much smaller affair in every way. Here Wren was merely enlarging the country house of a nobleman, and though he produced the fine south front in brick, the whole conception is quieter and less ambitious than Hampton Court. Internally there are some delightful rooms, in the decoration of which Gibbons played his part, and a fine staircase with wrought-iron balustrade of the kind to be found at Hampton Court, and known from the accounts to have been made at Whitehall for James II.

In this late period of Wren's career the personality of his colleagues and assistants takes on a new importance, for among them are to be found the only architects who can reasonably be described as forming a school deriving from him. Of his earlier colleagues, May was too well established a designer and too remote from Wren in his training as a painter to be influenced by him. If anything, the influence might be expected to flow the other way, and Hooke, whom from his close personal friendship with Wren and similar scientific bent one would expect to be most influenced by him, was carrying out his most important buildings, such as Bedlam, the Physicians' College, and Montagu House, at a time when Wren's style was only just maturing. It is the men who worked with Wren in his grand final period who felt the full effect of the great architect's personality. To this, William Talman is to be considered an exception, for there is nothing in either Chatsworth or Dyrham, his best two authenticated buildings, or any extant drawings of his, that especially suggest Wren. Where his interiors do show a superficial likeness to Wren's it is probably due to the employment of the same carvers.

Talman became Comptroller of the Works in 1689, and almost at once difficulties arose between him and Wren. The Kensington Palace accident had occurred on 7th November, and early in December the more serious collapse at Hampton Court took place. There are several interesting entries in the Treasury Minutes referring to this. At the first meeting, Wren and Talman are pressed for reports on the state of things at Hampton Court. It

would seem that they both put in reports containing evidence of
craftsmen described by Wren as 'able men, not interested, brick-
layers, carpenters, masons that have left off their aprons and are
without suspicion of being influenced.' These reports when submitted were at variance, and the minutes record the following
scene:

January 13th at Whitehall. King not present. Sir Christopher
Wren the Surveyor General of the Works and Mr Talman Comptroller
of the same are called in and their reports are read. The Surveyor
objects against Mr Latham (in the Comptroller's certificate) for a
madman and says the work on the new buildings of their Majesties'
Palace at Hampton Court has stood a new tryall in a hurrycane. Mr
Tallman says My Lord Chamberlains lodgings kept the winds absolutely from this building and that Latham is not mad. Mr Banks
says there are 24 piers next the garden and but 4 stones crackt, and
the cracks no bigger than a hairs breadth; that the building every day
it stands is stronger and grows lighter. Mr Talman says every pier
is cracked that one may put his finger in. Mr Oliver says none of the
masons Mr Talman brought understood so good work as this is.
Mr Talman says Pierce, Tompson and another (in his certificates)
are three masons that Sir Christopher employs, that the piers are all
hollow and crampt with iron to keep them together. Sir C. Wren:
'What was done for greater caution ought not to be maliciously
interpreted.' Talman: 'Pray let 6 be chosen by me and 6 by you
to judge in this matter.'
My Lords think they'l never agree, one part will say one thing,
th' other another.
Wren: 'Put it on this—a man cannot putt his finger in the cracks.'
Mr Talman says they are stopped.

We have no knowledge of the upshot of all this unpleasantness,
but Wren and Talman continued to work together for another
eleven years, so we must suppose the matter was smoothed over.

Nicholas Hawksmoor is a much more significant figure in
relation to Wren than Talman. He is supposed to have come to
Wren in some such capacity as personal pupil and assistant in
1679 at the age of eighteen, and, though his name does not appear
in the Hooke Diaries, in the works of the eighties and early
nineties he crops up in the accounts, often in company with
William Scarborough, mainly doing measuring work, but sometimes as a draughtsman, and at Kensington he became clerk of
the works in 1689. In 1698, in succession to Symonds, who
himself had succeeded Scarborough (both had died), he became
clerk of the works at Greenwich, a job of the utmost importance
for his career and his development as an architect. A year before
that, he had been acting as Wren's clerk, and had received a
special extra fee for preparing all the drawings for the hospital.
Some time in the nineties—how early is not certain—Wren began

to recommend Hawksmoor to private clients who had approached him for designs or advice. The earliest documented instance of this is at St John's College, Cambridge, where Wren was consulted about a bridge in 1696, but shortly after handed over the matter to Hawksmoor. Both Wren's and Hawksmoor's drawings and letters are still extant in the college. The same thing was to happen in the case of King's College many years later. Another instance of uncertain date, but in the nineties, is Easton Neston House, Northamptonshire, about which Wren had been consulted as early as 1682. A model, showing extraordinary ingenuity in planning and elevations which seem to derive from some of Wren's early drawings for Hampton Court, was made by Hawksmoor, and the house, the shell of which was finished in 1702, is certainly based on this model, but with several significant changes in the elevations. There is a strong tradition that, earlier again than these examples, Hawksmoor acted for Wren, if not perhaps independently of him, in the rebuilding of Queen's College Library at Oxford, begun in 1692. Hawksmoor certainly worked at Queen's College at a later date, and it might well be that the college's first experience of him was over the library. He would be thirty-one years of age when it was begun, and with the recommendation of some ten or more years under Wren.

For the early development of the school of Wren the most important documents are Greenwich Hospital and the designs for Whitehall, prepared after the fire of January 1698. The idea of a hospital at Greenwich seems first to have been put forward as early as January 1693, when Luttrell records that Wren went down there with the Lords of the Admiralty to inspect Webb's palace with a view to converting it to the use of a hospital. No doubt the just completed Chelsea had suggested the scheme. There do not seem to be any indications as to whether Wren tried to draw out a scheme for this, for the drawings referring to Webb's building in the Wren collections are all for palaces. The scheme then passed through the phase in which it was proposed to pull down Webb's building and start further to the east, thus leaving the view to Inigo Jones's Queen's House unimpeded, a point Queen Mary is said to have insisted on, and which forbade the completion of Webb's building on the lines he had planned. The next schemes seem to date from about 1696, in which year work was authorized to begin on the existing Webb building and a second subordinate range to the west of it, known as the Base Wing of King Charles. At this time it was undecided whether to cut off the Queen's House from the river with a central domed feature or to allow a vista through. All that seems to have been common to both schemes was the duplication of the King Charles block and its base or subordinate wing on the opposite side of the vista.

These Greenwich designs presented Wren with a new kind of architectural problem, the design of a monumental building in a series of related blocks—a group design, in short. Chelsea had been something of this kind, and the block plan for a complete rebuilding of Hampton Court was another example, but we know nothing either of its appearance or its date. The entrance court at Winchester had also been a problem of a similar kind, but all these lacked the quality of monumental scale given to the Greenwich design by the intention to retain the Webb block with its colossal order and large attic. All Wren's designs for Greenwich are distinguished by a striving after picturesque effects of grouping, whichever of the two alternative schemes he was favouring at the moment. The documents relating to Greenwich Hospital indicate that after 1702, when Vanbrugh's name first appears among the building committee, he had an increasingly important share in the design. It is even possible that he may have influenced the work before he became officially connected with it. But it is hardly possible to doubt that the dominating features of the great group of buildings, the long colonnades and the hall, with its splendid domed tower, are Wren's. They were already in hand before Vanbrugh joined the committee, and with the western towers of St Paul's the Greenwich towers derive in part from Borromini's St Agnese.

The Whitehall drawings at All Souls show the same preoccupation with effects of picturesque grouping by systems of related blocks, and in that case also the problem was complicated by the retention of Inigo Jones's Banqueting Hall, which alone of the early palaces had survived the fire. The drawings are elaborately treated with washes and are vast in size, some of them as much as six feet in length, and altogether rather smack of projects by some assistant such as Hawksmoor, rather than firsthand works of Wren himself. All that is known of the intention to rebuild is contained in two notes of Luttrell, who says, first, that Wren was ordered in January 1698 to survey Whitehall, which it was intended to rebuild in four years, and then, in March, that temporary lodgings for the king, and a council chamber, were to be put up at the Westminster end of the Banqueting Hall, the rest to be left till Parliament should decide. None of the drawings seem to take note of this decision of March. The real interest of these Whitehall drawings, especially the first group, seems to be in relation, not to the body of Wren's work either before or after that date, but to that of John Vanbrugh, who appears first as an architect in 1699. In that year he designed a house for Lord Carlisle, and in 1701 it was begun, with Hawksmoor acting as his assistant, and it is interesting to notice that Hawksmoor's own building at Easton Neston, designed and executed shortly before 1702, shows Vanbrugh's influence very strongly. In 1702 Vanbrugh succeeded Talman as Comptroller of the Works.

Of the curious odd jobs that Wren's position as Surveyor of the Works entailed, the most interesting during the nineties is perhaps that noted by Luttrell in February 1690: 'Sir Xtopher Wren hath completed the itinerant house for His Majesty to carry into Ireland for him to lye in in the field; it is to be taken to pieces and carried on two waggons that may be quickly fixt up.' It is a pity no picture of this contraption is surviving, for it must have given scope to all Wren's constructional ingenuity. Otherwise the records are a chronicle of small beer from the architectural point of view, with the exception of the preparations for Queen Mary's funeral. An engraving of the cenotaph design for the occasion is extant. Even more important is the statement in 1692, that appears in Luttrell and one or two news-letters, that Wren had designed a new House of Commons, to which the newsletters add that materials are at the site and work is to go forward. Whether this referred only to the minor works mentioned in Wren's report of 1691 on the conditioning of the building, or to some large scheme such as that suggested in the Whitehall plans, it is impossible to decide. Two buildings of the nineties attributed to Wren by long-standing tradition should also be mentioned—the chapel at Trinity College, Oxford, and Morden College, Blackheath. Letters of Wren to his old friend Bathurst about the chapel survive, but these seem to suggest that Wren merely revised and improved a scheme submitted to him, rather in the way that he did at Easton Neston in 1682. The building is a charming one, and fitted up by the best craftsmen of the time, including Gibbons, but does not seem to stand in any direct relation to the main current of Wren's work. Morden College is a more obscure matter; it is not far from Greenwich, and its founder sat with Wren on the Greenwich Commission, so that there is a possibility, even a likelihood, that Wren had a hand in it, but almost certainly in some such advisory fashion as we have often found elsewhere. A minor building of the nineties that was

certainly designed by Wren, but has since been pulled down, was
the addition to Christ's Hospital made in 1693–4, and consisting
of a large single schoolroom raised on an arcade. Some drawings
exist of an alternative design to that executed. The most
striking event affecting Wren in the routine of the Office of Works
in these years was the fire at Whitehall, which has been mentioned as destroying one of his most important buildings and
giving occasion to the schemes for building a new palace. The
fire which destroyed the palace in 1698 had been preceded by
another fairly serious one in 1691, when the windows of the
queen's new lodgings that Wren had just built were damaged by
explosions occasioned by fire. The last fire began on the 4th
January 1698, about four o'clock in the afternoon, in the corner
of the buildings on the river side towards Westminster, and burnt
all night. By seven the following morning it was mastered, but
the greater part of the main buildings of the palace had been
destroyed, including all Wren's work of the eighties. There is an
interesting sidelight on Wren and this event contained in the
petition of a bricklayer, by name John Evans, who gives an
account of some of the events of that night in making an application some years later for the post of king's master bricklayer.
He says:

> And when the Fire happened in the Royal Palace at Whitehall, I
> immediately went to Sir Christopher's House, where I found him and
> offered my assistance, who directed me to stay there and take care
> of some books and other things in his closet, and then went out of
> his house, but forthwith returned from viewing that conflagration,
> and in great consternation cry'd out in this manner (viz) Wee are all
> undone, for the fire hath seized the Banqueting House, For God's
> sake lett all things alone here and try to save that Fabrick, or to that
> very effect. Whereupon by God's assistance of my indefatigable
> endeavours with great expence of money and eminent hazard of my
> life, I did preserve it from being destroyed, though not by the means
> Sir Christopher is pleased to alledge in his report, nor had I the least
> directions from him by what means in particular to perform it, But
> only in general terms to try to save that Fabrick. And from the
> time I received that direction from Sir Christopher and left him at
> his own house, I never saw him at or near the place where the Fire
> happened until two days afterward.

In Wren's comment on his application he casts doubt on the
claims for reward, but admits: 'I set him in a very dangerous part
in the high window of the Banqueting House,' and agrees that
it was largely due to Evans that the building was saved.

Chapter 5

Wren and his Builders—The Office of Works under Queen Anne—Last
works at St Paul's and the Difficulties with the Commissioners—
Wren's Family—Partial Retirement from the Office of Works—Dismissal—The Last Works at Westminster—Architectural writings.

THE first ten years of the eighteenth century are for Wren above
all the time of the finishing touches to St Paul's, and the building
of the tall dome of Greenwich. He was still very active at the
Office of Works all these years, but the Minutes of the Greenwich
Committee seem to show the increasing importance of Vanbrugh
in that work. The greatest architectural work undertaken by
the State during these years was Blenheim Palace, given as a
token of the nation's gratitude to the Duke of Marlborough, and
for this Vanbrugh was responsible, with Hawksmoor as his colla-
borator, though on occasion we find that Wren was consulted and
gave advice. Another important work, though much smaller,
was the Kensington orangery, and here again Vanbrugh and
Hawksmoor seem to have had as much to do with it as Wren.
The association of the three men seems to have been of the
happiest, to judge by the way in which both the juniors referred
to Wren in their later letters, always with affection as well as
respect; and even Vanbrugh's letter of protest to the Lord
Treasurer, Godolphin, about the management of the affairs at the
orangery is careful to repudiate any personal charge against Wren.
This is a most interesting document, of which the following is an
extract:

Before I acquainted yr L'dship this Summer with that shamefull
abuse in the Board of Works; of those very officers doing the Work
themselves, who rec'd Sallarys from the Queen to prevent her being
imposed on by Others; I made severall attempts upon Sir Chr Wren
to perswade him to redress it himself without troubling yr Lordship;
putting him in mind that besides its being utterly against common
Sense, it was contrary to an Express Direction to the Board upon
the Establishment after the Restoration.
He always own'd what I urg'd him to was right and often promis'd
to join with me in Overruling so bad a practice; but when I press'd
him to the Execution, he still evaded it, and that so many times, that
at last I saw he never intended it, and so I gave your L'dship the
trouble of a Complaint.
Your Lordship was pleas'd upon it to send us a Letter, in as express
Terms as it could be penn'd, that, no such thing for the future should
be Suffer'd directly or indirectly.
Upon this Order I desired Sir Chr there might immediately be

another mason got to work at Kensington upon the New Greenhouse; but wou'd recommend none to him, leaving that entirely to himself. He at last nam'd One Hill, and gave me leave to send for him and give him Directions; which I presently did, and he promis'd me to go to Work. But a few days after finding he had not begun, and enquiring into the reason; I found he had been frighten'd with some hints of what should befall him if he durst meddle with the Master Masons business. And this had been so put home to him that he sent to me desire I would excuse him. I went to Sir Chr Wren and tould him what had passed. He said the Man was a Whimsical Man, and a piece of an Astrologer, and would Venture upon nothing till he had consulted the Starrs, which probably he had not found favourably enclin'd upon this Occasion and therefore had refus'd the Work. I desir'd he would employ somebody that was less superstitious which he said he wou'd and next day I went out of Town for the North; but when I return'd I found Mr Jackson's man at Work. I ask'd one of his foremen who they work'd for: but he tould me One Palmer whom his Master had made his Deputy. I was very much surpris'd at this, and went to Sir Chr Wren, but was much more so when he confessed to me that he had allow'd Jackson to go on, only oblig'd him to enter his Bills in Palmer's Name. I ask'd him if he had forgot your Lordship's Letter and all that had past on this Subject. He said no; but Jackson would not be quiet without he let him do the Work. This Story is so very improbable I'm afraid y'r L'dship will scarce give me credit for it; yet it is a plain and literal truth in every Article. As for Sir Chr Wren I dont believe he has any Interest in his part of it; but y'r L'dship will see by this Decisive proof the power those Fellows have over him wch they never made so effectual a use of as when they prevail'd with him (against your L'dships Directions) to let 'em have a Clerk of the Works of White-hall, whom he himself own'd but a Week before he could put no trust in: one who by nature is a very poor Wretch; and by a many years regular Course of morning Drunkennesses, has made himself a dos'd sott.

It is, of course, impossible to judge how far Vanbrugh's complaint in this letter may have been justified. It may have been simply a case of the new broom, and, as the editor of the Wren Society has suggested, that Vanbrugh did not understand the shifts to which the Office of Works was put to get work done, in those days of long-deferred payments when the Government departments were not in a position to be too haughty with men to whom they owed so much money. As against this, Vanbrugh had been over two years at the Office of Works when he wrote the letter, and in view of the difficulties with Talman, and the questions that were later to arise at St Paul's, it is at least a question whether Wren's handling of his contractors was not sometimes too easy-going. Wren was a man who had his first administrative experience in good King Charles's golden days, when other things besides loyalty meant no harm. Things were somewhat better in Queen Anne's reign, but not so much. Moreover, Wren was getting an old man, and it seems certain that there were irregularities at St Paul's.

It seems that age as much as press of work was causing Wren, from 1702 onwards, to delegate more and more work to his juniors. Hawksmoor at King's College, Cambridge, has already been instanced, but a more remarkable example would be Marlborough House in 1709, if it could certainly be determined whether the architect was Sir Christopher or his son. The confusion that comes of their both having the same Christian name is probably impenetrable, but young Christopher was at this time certainly turning towards architecture, and Campbell, who knew them both, gives Marlborough House to the son. The greatest delegation of work comes in 1708, on the passing of the Act for building fifty new churches, which was to give Hawksmoor his greatest opportunity outside Oxford and to be the occasion of the public employment of such men as James Gibbs, the most famous, and Archer, the most neglected, architect of the times. The recent discovery of some drawings apparently by Gibbs among the Wren collections seems to suggest that they were working together on other jobs than the churches at about this time. Another assistant of Wren who has come to light of recent years is Dickinson. He seems to have been very closely associated with him in his later years, especially at Westminster Abbey, but, dying in 1724, had hardly opportunity to practise as an independent architect. It is possible that the designs for the Westminster dormitory are by him. They were, however, superseded in favour of those by Lord Burlington. Hawksmoor's name has also been suggested in connection with some of those Westminster designs, and he certainly was employed at the Abbey after Wren's and Dickinson's death. These Westminster drawings belong to the very last years of Wren's life, some of them being of 1718–19 and perhaps even later.

Wren had certainly two moments of glory in Queen Anne's reign, of which the most famous is the laying of the last stone upon the lantern over the dome of St Paul's. This is said to have taken place in 1710 in the presence of his son Christopher and young Strong, the mason, though the accounts seem to indicate that it must have happened fully two years earlier. From that height the old architect (he was seventy-six at the earliest dating, and had probably been drawn up in a basket as the Duchess of Marlborough describes) could look down at the evidence of an achievement that compares with anything that the great men of the past could show in quality, and in quantity almost rivals the

modern successful practitioner. But perhaps an even greater
moment was that described by Evelyn, when the queen, 'full of
jewels,' and beside her the Duchess of Marlborough, 'in a very
plain gown,' went in state to the new cathedral, the interior of
which was then just finished, to celebrate the greatest military
victory of English history on 7th September 1704. It is pleasant
to recall that his old friend Evelyn, who had known the church's
beginnings, survived to see it on that day of days, and to record
it as one of the last important entries in his Diary. He died in
February two years later. Another old friend that Wren lost
about this time was Robert Hooke, who died in 1703, but for the
last few years of his life Hooke had been a complete invalid, and
Wren can have seen very little of him.

In some respects the winding up of that splendid work was
accompanied by meanness and petty quarrelling that are not so
much tragic as indecent considering the occasion. Towards the
end of 1710 and in the early months of 1711, Wren began to
agitate for the payment of the accumulated half of his salary, as
surveyor to St Paul's, that had been withheld since 1696. The
reason for this suspension of salary was said to be to encourage
the architect to press on with the completion of the building, and
it may well be that Wren, in his desire to secure that the whole
of his design should be carried out, had neglected to build the
church in instalments in the way suggested in the original warrant.
It is clear that Wren had not been on good terms with the later
commissioners, and things came to a minor crisis over the question
of the iron railings to be placed round the outside of the building.
Wren had wanted a wrought-iron railing, the commissioners had
forced upon him a cast-iron one, to be executed by a Mr Jones, a
founder often employed by the Ordnance Department. The
situation was further complicated by the action of the commissioners in discharging Jennings (the master carpenter, and one
of the most important contractors to the church), and endeavour-
ing to get the Crown to prosecute him for fraudulent practice.
The upshot of it all was that Wren, after petitioning the Archbishop of Canterbury, the Crown, and the House of Commons,
was eventually given his money, the Attorney-General, Northey,
declaring that Wren's case was 'very hard.' The sum in question
was £1,375 at Christmas, 1710, and was ordered to be paid him
by December 1711. A document in the Portland Papers sums
up the evidence and concludes with this opinion of the Attorney-
General: 'On the whole matter from the opinion I have of workmen in general I cannot doubt but that there have been great

frauds committed by them in the great work of rebuilding the Cathedral of St Paul's, but have little expectation of advantage from a prosecution of Jennings on such general charges'—and there, as far as the law was concerned, the matter ended. It is perhaps significant that, in the new commission that was appointed not long after this, some of the most active members of the former one were omitted. Matters did not rest there, however, for a pamphlet appeared entitled *Frauds and Abuses at St Paul's*, to which Wren published a reply. The whole miserable affair was conducted with the utmost bitterness, and there is a paper among the Portland MSS., apparently by Wren, for it is annotated in his hand, which shows a very human lack of dignity in some of the charges of trickery, corruption, and incontinence levelled against the commissioners.

Wren had, however, some consolation in these times: for example, his own was not the only reply to *Frauds and Abuses*. A more solid comfort to the old man and his work was the presence, since 1694, of his son Christopher as clerk engrosser at the Office of Works, and, when Vanbrugh was dismissed from the comptroller's place in April 1713 for political reasons, there was even some little talk of young Christopher's succeeding him, though it came to nothing.

Two letters of Wren to his son Christopher have survived. In the first, which seems to date from the nineties, he is writing to the young man then on a visit to Paris in company with Strong, a son of the contractor. Sir Christopher is discouraging about a scheme for visiting Italy, partly on financial grounds.

I sent you to France at a time of businesse and when you might make your observations and find acquaintance who might hereafter be usefull to you in the future concernes of your life: if this be your ayme I willingly let you proceed, provided you will soon returne, for these reasons, the little I have to leave you is unfortunately involved in trouble, and your presence would be a comfort to me, to assist me, not only for my sake, but your own that you might understand your affaires, before it shall please God to take me from you, which if suddenly will leave you in perplexity and losse.

The whole letter is a little melancholy, and concludes with a post-script referring to the bad health of the second son, William. The second letter is dated 1705 and is written to Holland. It is mainly concerned with public and family news, and contains the sentence: 'I am very well satisfied you have layd aside your designe for the army which I think had not been safe or pertinent.' It was the year after Blenheim.

Between the writing of these letters, Jane Wren, his daughter, died in 1703, and was buried in St Paul's, with an elaborate sculptured monument by Bird, one of the chief sculptors employed on the building. It shows her sitting at an organ, and the inscription particularly refers to her skill in music. The delicate son, William, survived to 1738. The young Christopher, in the year following his Dutch visit, married the daughter of Philip Musard, jeweller to Queen Anne. It is perhaps significant of a community of interests with his father-in-law that the young man published in 1708 a work on antique coins, of which he was a collector. The son Christopher was returned to Parliament for Windsor in 1712 and again in 1714, and in the following year married his second wife, the widow of Sir Roger Burgoyne, a Warwickshire gentleman, from whose family his father bought for him the estate of Wroxall Abbey, where he settled down in due course as a country squire. There are some evidences that the Wrens had Warwickshire connections, which may have inclined Sir Christopher to this purchase.

On the accession of George I great changes were made in the Office of Works. Vanbrugh was reinstated as comptroller and made a knight. The whole constitution of the Office of Works was revised, the most important change being the formation of a board or commission to exercise the office of surveyor. Wren was a member of this body with Vanbrugh, Dubois the paymaster, and others specially appointed, as an example of whom one may take Brigadier-General Watkins with the office of Keeper of His Majesty's Private Roads and Guide in the Royal Progresses, a man who appears very pleasantly in Vanbrugh's later letters. Wren retained the title of surveyor, but had no casting vote or special authority other than personal. This arrangement was made, Wren himself tells us, mainly on account of his age, and he adds that he attended as often as his infirmities would permit. Some such scheme had been formulated as early as March 1713 in anticipation of Wren's death or resignation, and contained the suggestion that young Christopher should be one of the commissioners in remembrance of his father. In the event, no such occasion arose, and young Christopher remained at the Office of Works in his capacity as clerk engrosser.

At about this time (August 1716) Wren resigned his surveyorship at Greenwich Hospital to Vanbrugh. Wren had been attending the Greenwich Committees less and less for some years past, and on this occasion definitely mentions his age as the reason of his withdrawal. It is curious to note that, though Vanbrugh had been dismissed from the Office of Works, he still retained his place on the Greenwich committee throughout the years he was out of office. The new arrangement seems to be both reasonable and generous and the best possible considering Wren's great age, eighty-four, his immense service to the State, and experience. The old gentleman was in effect retired with full honours, and yet was in a position to keep in touch with the office with which he had been so long associated. It is possible that the credit of this arrangement may be due to Vanbrugh, who certainly advised as to the reconstruction of the office at that time, and who may be referring to this occasion in his letter to Tonson in 1719, in which he says, speaking of some later changes at the office: 'I have likewise had a very hard disappointment in not being made Surveyor of the Works: which I believe you remember I might have had formerly but refus'd it out of tenderness to Sir Christopher Wren'; but this amiable and reasonable scheme of things was not destined to endure.

On 26th April 1718 Wren was deprived of his position as Surveyor-General of the Royal Works, and was succeeded by William Benson. There can be no doubt that this was the result of one of the meanest jobs ever put through. Ker of Kersland in his *Memoirs* wrote: 'It is very well known that Mr Benson was a favourite of the Germans,' by which he meant the personal entourage of George I. This is confirmed by a letter of Vanbrugh's, written the December before the blow fell, from which it is clear that the conduct of the Board of Works was already called in question, and that Vanbrugh well knew what quarters were interesting themselves in the matter, for he says in a letter to the Duke of Newcastle: 'My Ld Sunderland has told me, when your Grace and Ld Stanhope have spoke, he'll then talk effectually wth the Dutchess of Munster.' This lady was the most politically important of King George's mistresses, and perhaps it is to her that Wren referred in his letter of the October before his dismissal, protesting against the addition of a balustrade round the upper part of St Paul's, in which he says 'ladies think nothing well without an edgeing.' William Benson is hardly known as an architect, except for his own house at Wilbery in Wiltshire and some fountains at Herrenhausen, the king's palace in Hanover; otherwise he was a Whig pamphleteer. Of the two architectural works, the fountains confirm the Hanoverian connection; the house, a rather charming though not very ambitious piece of work, is illustrated in Colin Campbell's *Vitruvius Britannicus*, published in 1715. Campbell was evidently a friend of

Benson, for when on his appointment the new surveyor made a
clean sweep of the junior part of the office, dismissing Hawksmoor
and some of the clerks, Colin Campbell and Benson's young
nephew were given places there. It is sad to find Campbell's
name in such company, for architectural historians owe him
much for his books and he was a not inconsiderable architect.

The plea on which this revolution was made was that of
economy, and the new regime was not long in being before, in
Vanbrugh's words of January 1719:

> I have a wild strange acct. of the rout my friend and Superior
> Officer, Benson, makes at the Treasury. I find poor Dartiquenave
> (the Paymaster) scar'd out of his Witts about a Memorial given in
> by Campbell and Benson the Young to decry the Managements of
> former Boards and exalt this precious New One.

Vanbrugh himself had weathered the storm by the strength of
his political friendships. He adds significantly: 'Let me but be
protected from any dark stroaks in the Kings closet and I have
nothing to fear.' This memorial, which is extant among the
Treasury Papers, eventually brought forth one of Wren's most
remarkable letters, dated from his house at Hampton Court,
21st April 1719.

MAY IT PLEASE YR LDSHIPS,

My Surprize is equal to my concern to find, that after having
serv'd the Crown and the Publick above fifty years, and at this great
Age, I should be under a necessity of taking a part in answering a
memorial Presented by Mr Benson to yr Ldships chargeing some
Mismanagement on the late Commissioners of the Board of Works.

It was his Majesties Pleasure, on his happy accession to the Throne
to continue me in the Office of Surveyor of the Works; but soon after,
in regard of my great age, He was Pleas'd of his Royal clemency to
Ease me of the burden of the Business of that office, by appointing
other Worthy Gentlemen with me in commission, which was under
such Regulations and Restrictions, as that altho' I had the honour
to be first nam'd with the old title of Surveyor, yet in acting I had no
power to over-rule, or give a casting Vote:—I did however as often
as my Infirmities would permit, attend the Board, and endeavour'd
to doe his Majesty all the Service I was able, with the same integrity
and zeal wch I had ever practised.

I doubt not but the Gentlemen concern'd in the late Commission
will lay before yr Ldships such particular answers to the Memorial
of Complaint, as will be satisfactory; I crave leave to Refer thereto;
and may presume to say, that notwithstanding the Pretensions of
the Present Surveyor's Management to be better than that of the
late Commissioners, or theirs to be better then what Preceeded, yet
I am perswaded upon an impartial view of matters, & fairly distinguishing all particulars, with due consideration had to long protracted payment of artificers, there will be no just grounds for the
Censuring former Managements; and as I am Dismiss'd, having worn

out (by God's Mercy) a long Life in the Royal Service, and having
made some Figure in the World, I hope it will be allowed me to Die
in Peace.

> I am, May it Please yr Ldships
> With most sincere Respect
> Yr Ldships most Obedient Humble
> Servant
>
> CHR. WREN.

The letter is not in Wren's own hand, though he signed it, and the
signature is very shaky. It is satisfactory to record that, in the
course of the summer following, Benson displayed such egregious
incompetence in the matter of some repairs to the House of Lords
that he was dismissed with ignominy and the whole of his following with him. He himself still had sufficient purchase at court
to get himself compensatory pickings, and Campbell, whose architectural views were in fairly close accord with those of the
Palladianists who reacted against Wren and his Baroque successors, crept back in due course into the State employment.

After his supersession at the Office of Works, Wren, according
to *Parentalia*, retired to the house at Hampton Court that for
some years past he had leased from the Crown. Five years of life
remained to him, of which we know little. He applied himself
once again to the problem of longitude, and left a curious memorandum upon it in cipher. As to architecture, he still retained
the surveyorship of Westminster Abbey, and is said to have come
up from time to time to a house in St James's Street in order to
keep his eye on that business. Wren had been appointed to this
position in 1698, and during Anne's reign had been gradually
getting the fabric into decent repair, paying special attention to
the vaulting. In 1719 his scheme for the great north transept front
was approved and his last executed work put in hand. The
faithful Dickinson, who had been associated with him at Westminster from the first, was still with him there, and must be
mainly responsible for the extant drawings of this and other
projected works, of which the most remarkable is a curious domical
central lantern. The Wren work on the north transept front has
been restored out of existence, and the most important relic of
his surveyorship is the long report on the building drawn up for
Bishop Atterbury in 1713. This is a most interesting document
and, like the early Salisbury Cathedral report, bears witness to
the enlightened character of Wren's attitude towards Gothic
architecture, though inevitably much of the historical matter of
the report is far beside the mark.

There has been little mention of Wren's architectural writings

in this book.   There are not very many of them, and, except for
these reports and memoranda on particular problems, none are
complete.   They are collected together for the most part in
Parentalia, and consist of short discussions of celebrated ancient
buildings, as the Mausoleum of Halicarnassus or the Temple of
Diana at Ephesus, as these were known to him from the descriptions of Pliny.   The former, no doubt, dates from the time of his
discussion of the subject with Hooke, and the designing of the
mausoleum for Charles I.   The two most interesting are a tract
largely concerned with the geometry of vaults and domes, and
another fragment which is hardly more than a jotting of
aphorisms, some of which have a great interest, as for instance:

> There are two causes of Beauty, natural and customary.   Natural
> is from Geometry, consisting in Uniformity (that is Equality) and
> Proportion.   Customary Beauty is begotten by the use of our senses
> to those objects which are usually pleasing to us from other causes,
> as Familiarity or particular Inclination breeds a Love to Things not
> in themselves lovely.   Here lies the great Occasion of Errors; here
> is tried the architects Judgement: but always the true test is natural
> or geometrical Beauty.

And again:

> The architect ought, above all things to be well skilled in Per-
> spective; for everything that appears well in the Orthography, may
> not be good in the model, especially where there are many Angles
> and Projections; and everything that is good in Model, may not be
> so when built.

An interesting point in relation to his extensive use of models at
St Paul's.   Rather similar to these are the marginal notes on
Wotton's *Elements of Architecture*, published by the late Sir
Lawrence Weaver from a copy that belonged to Wren which is
now at Sherburn Castle; for example, of an overlighted building,
as against Wotton, Wren says: 'Christchurch Newgate St was
practically nothing but window and fitter for a stage than a
church, although for the kind of building it is a thorough piece of
work.'   This is one of the very few comments of Wren's on a
building of his own.

The last series of architectural designs for Westminster, those
for the school dormitory, have been mentioned already.   In 1722
all the schemes emanating from his office, whether by himself,
Dickinson, or Hawksmoor, were superseded by the design of
Lord Burlington, the young Palladianist architect who, with his
wealth and social and political position to reinforce him, was to
establish himself in the next few years as an arbiter of architectural taste.   Burlington's importance in the history of English

architecture is as the leader, with his friend William Kent, of the
Palladianist reaction to the free Baroque of Wren, Vanbrugh, and
Hawksmoor. It is curiously fitting that his first public achievement should be at Westminster, the scene of Wren's last employment as an architect. Within a year the great man was dead.
By tradition he had made a trip to London and had visited
St Paul's, on returning from which to St James's Street he had
caught a chill. On 25th February 1723 his servant is said to have
found him dead in his chair on coming in to waken him from his
after-dinner nap.

Wren's school, as we have called it, did not long survive him.
Dickinson died the year following, and Vanbrugh in 1726.
Hawksmoor lived on to complete the towers of Westminster
Abbey, All Souls and Queen's Colleges at Oxford, and to build
at Castle Howard the great mausoleum that seems in some degree
to be based on Wren's studies for the St Paul's Baptistery. He
died in 1736, leaving the Palladianists to finish it. But, though
Hawksmoor and Vanbrugh were personally close to Wren and
learnt much if not everything from him, their curious 'Heroic'
Baroque is a different thing, more declamatory, more coarse-
grained than the architecture of their master, which kept to the
end of his days something of the spirit of the lyric poets of his
youth.

Appendix

NOTE ON THE PORTRAITS OF SIR CHRISTOPHER WREN

Based on notes kindly supplied by C. K. Adams, Esq., of the National Portrait Gallery

THE earliest of the portraits which indisputably represents Sir Christopher Wren and is known to be executed in his lifetime is the marble bust in the Ashmolean Museum at Oxford. This was executed about 1673 by Edward Pierce, a carver who worked much for Wren. It was presented to the university by the architect's son in 1737.

The portrait in the possession of the Royal Society was presented by Stephen Wren, grandson of Sir Christopher. An engraving made from this portrait by Elisha Kirkall (*d.* 1742) is inscribed ' I. Closterman ad vivum pinx.' The costume and Wren's age suggest that it was painted about the year 1695.

The portrait in the Sheldonian Theatre at Oxford is described as being begun by Verrio and finished by Thornhill and Kneller, and presumably represents Wren a little before Verrio's death in 1707.

The portrait in the National Portrait Gallery is inscribed ' Sir Godfrey Kneller' and dated 1711. It was engraved by John Smith in 1713, and Kneller's name and the date of painting appear on the engraving.

Besides these authentic portraits there is the death-mask bequeathed in 1851 to All Souls College, Oxford, by a Miss Wren. It is possible that the Rysbrack bust at Queen's College, Oxford, dated 1726/7, is based on this, and that the portrait of Sir Christopher in *Parentalia*, inscribed ' Engraved from a bust,' is founded on this bust.

The boxwood plaque at the Royal Institute of British Architects, which belonged to James Wyatt, P.R.A., is ascribed to Grinling Gibbons, and may well be a contemporary portrait of Wren, whom it certainly represents.

Of other portraits called Wren, that at Welbeck, formerly at Strawberry Hill, appears to be of the time of Charles II, but the coat of arms represented in the picture is not Wren's, and the subject may be one of Wren's wealthier contractors. Sir Edwyn Hoskyns's portrait, inherited from a lineal descendant of Wren's, appears to represent a man not over forty years of age about A.D. 1700. It is possibly Christopher Wren, junior; the pair of dividers that he holds agrees well with the known architectural ambition of Sir Christopher's son.

BIBLIOGRAPHY

SEVERAL short lives of Sir Christopher Wren are extant, among which those by Miss Phillimore, Dean Milman, and Sir Lawrence Weaver may be mentioned. These are in the main based on the *Memoirs of Sir Christopher Wren* by Elmes (1823), and *Parentalia*, a compilation of family records published by Sir Christopher's grandson in 1750. They do not, however, take the critical consideration of the material much further than the compilers of these source books. Of recent years the Wren Society volumes have been steadily adding to our documentary knowledge and publishing the drawings of Wren and his contemporaries.

Stephen Wren, *Parentalia*. Elmes, *Memoirs of Sir Christopher Wren*. Aubrey, *Brief Lives*. Sprat, *History of the Royal Society*. Ward, *Lives of the Gresham Professors*. Wren Society, volumes to date. Royal Institute of British Architects, Sir Christopher Wren Memorial Volume. Oxford Historical Society, *Life and Times of Anthony Wood*. Gunther, *Early Science in Oxford*. Gunther, *Notebooks of Sir Roger Pratt*. Tipping, *English Homes*, Period IV, vol. i; Period V, vol. ii. Tipping, *Grinling Gibbons*. Birch, *City Churches*. Belcher and Macartney, *Later Renaissance Architecture in England*. Knoop and Jones, *London Masons of the Seventeenth Century*. Royal Commission on Historical Monuments, vols.: London East, West, and City. Willis and Clark, *Architectural History of the University of Cambridge*. London County Council, Survey of London. Domestic State Papers. Treasury Papers. Robert Hooke, *Diary*. Pepys, *Diary*. Evelyn, *Diary*. Vanbrugh, *Letters*. Inner Temple Records. Middle Temple Records. Caroë, *Tom Tower*. Brett-James, *The Growth of Stuart London*. Perks, 'London Town Planning Schemes in 1666,' *R.I.B.A. Journal*, 1919.